Payroll Accounting

7th Edition

A Practical, Real-World Approach

Eric A. Weinstein, CPA

Suffolk County Community College

LABYRINTH
LEARNING™

Payroll Accounting: A Practical, Real-World Approach, 7th Edition
by Eric A. Weinstein, CPA

Copyright © 2020 by Labyrinth Learning

Labyrinth Learning
PO Box 2669
Danville, CA 94526
800.522.9746
On the web at: lablearning.com

President:
Brian Favro

Product Manager:
Jason Favro

Development Manager:
Laura Popelka

Senior Editor:
Alexandra Mummery

Editor:
Alexandria Henderson

Production Manager:
Debra Grose

Indexer:
Joanne Sprott

Interior Design:
Mark Ong, Side-by-Side Studio

Cover Design:
Sam Anderson Design

Editorial Team:
Carol Rogers, Pam Hillman,
and Sharon O'Reilly

eBOOK ITEM: 1-64061-202-5
ISBN-13: 978-1-64061-202-0

PRINT ITEM: 1-64061-200-9
ISBN-13: 978-1-64061-200-6

Manufactured in the United States of America

GPP 10 9 8 7 6 5 4 3 2 1

Contents in Brief

Table of Contents

Preface

This seventh edition of *Payroll Accounting: A Practical, Real-World Approach* affords an exciting opportunity to address a widespread need among instructors for an applied textbook that is accessible, clear, and resolutely practical for modern payroll courses.

Grounded in solid pedagogy and the extensive experience of our author, this text focuses on the hands-on tools students and instructors need for building fundamental learning, without overwhelming students with unnecessary theory far removed from practical applications.

The clear, logical, step-by-step approach—highlighting basics such as how to perform calculations and complete forms—guides students through exercises that build understanding and skills.

Supported by an online Learning Resource Center and a robust instructor support package, the text is designed to teach the complete payroll accounting cycle to students with little or no prior accounting knowledge.

Key features include:

- Useful chapter organizational items that help guide readers, such as start-of-chapter Learning Objectives, Case Studies, and engaging in-chapter features that break up content and focus attention.
- Excel templates, PDFs of payroll forms, and myriad resources to provide students with support and direction.
- QuickBooks trial software that enables students to complete the One-Month and Three-Month Comprehensive Projects using computerized payroll software.
- eLab Homework Grader that allows students to work through the Practice Set exercises online with automatic grading and feedback.
- Progressive exercises that build simply and reinforce key concepts, including:
  - Case in Point case studies
  - Self-Assessment quizzes
  - Practice Set A and B reviews
  - Continuing Payroll Problems
  - Critical Thinking exercises
  - Comprehensive Projects
  - Fresh, engaging, and easily understood design and graphics

Visual Conventions

In addition to the core features already noted, the text employs a variety of functional, engaging visual graphics to help students incorporate key content and find useful information.

Accounting Terms included in the glossary are set in boldface. If you are using an ebook, note that the terms are linked to the associated Glossary definitions.

TIP! Tip! graphics identify helpful shortcuts, advice, or suggestions.

NOTE! Note! graphics call attention to key points, unusual exceptions, or other key information that may not be included in the main text.

WARNING! Warning! graphics highlight important points for students to be aware of and on the lookout for.

On the Web On the Web sections provide URLs that lead students to documents or web pages with the most current government forms.

Acknowledgments

Many individuals contribute to the development and completion of a textbook. We deeply appreciate the careful attention and informed contributions of Carol Rogers, Accounting Faculty at Central New Mexico Community College; Rick Street, Accounting and Entrepreneurship Instructor at Spokane Community College; and Christine Galli, Executive Director of Technology In A Box, LLC.

Labyrinth would also like to express our appreciation for the important contributions of the following advisory group members in the development of this text:

Bruce Welnetz, *Lakeshore Technical College*

Erik Richter, *Colorado Community College System*

Linda Rains, *Pikes Peak Community College*

Margaret Pond, *Front Range Community College*

Lindy Byrd, *Augusta Technical College*

Regina Young, *Wiregrass Georgia Technical College*

Rosemary Hall, *Bellevue College*

Tomeika Williams, *Georgia Piedmont Technical College*

Rick Street, *Spokane Community College*

Carol Rogers, *Central New Mexico Community College*

We are also deeply grateful to the instructors and professionals who reviewed the text and suggested improvements for this edition. This book has benefited significantly from the feedback and suggestions of the following reviewers:

Kim Anderson, *Elgin Community College*

Myra Bruegger, *Southeastern Community College*

Charles Bunn, *Wake Technical Community College*

Meg Costello Lambert, *Oakland Community College—Auburn Hills Campus*

Curtis Crocker, *Southern Crescent Technical College*

Chris Crosby, *York Technical College*

Harry DeWolf, *Mt. Hood Community College*

Kristine Duke, *Arizona Western College*

Pamela Fack, *Santa Barbara City College*

Michael Fann, *Central Carolina Community College*

Corey Frad, *Eastern Iowa Community College District*

Ken Gaines, *East-West University*

Diann Hammon, *J.F. Drake State Community and Technical College*

Kathy Hewitt, *Klamath Community College*

Merrily Hoffman, *San Jacinto College Central*

Carol Hughes, *Asheville-Buncombe Technical Community College*

Kim Hurt, *Central Community College*

Shirley M. Jack, *Southwest Tennessee Community College*

Katherine Johnson, *Jefferson College*

Valissa Lowery, *Robeson Community College*

Molly McFadden-May, *Tulsa Community College, Metro Campus*

Yvonne Morton, *Northern Virginia Community College*

William Ostrander, *Stark State College*

D. Paulen, *Tarrant County College*

Roxanne Phillips, *Colorado Community Colleges Online*

Ida Ponder, *Columbia College*

Matthew Probst, *Ivy Tech Community College*

Judith Slisz, *Naugatuck Valley Community College*

Greg Swango, *NorthWest Arkansas Community College*

Robin Turner, *Rowan-Cabarrus Community College*

Tilda Woody, *Navajo Technical University*

Peter Young, *San Jose State University*

About the Author

Eric A. Weinstein (MBA, CPA) is a Professor of Business Administration at Suffolk County Community College on Long Island, NY. Eric graduated summa cum laude from Georgetown University in 1999, where he earned a BS in Business Administration and majored in Accounting. In 2004 he earned an MBA from the Fuqua School of Business at Duke University. Eric has received many awards in his career, including the State University of New York Chancellor's Award for Excellence in Teaching. Eric has also been a practicing Certified Public Accountant in New York for more than 10 years, where he provides accounting services for small businesses and individuals. Eric and his beautiful wife, Cara, are the proud parents of sons Tyler, Lucas, and Noah. The family lives in Dix Hills, NY, where they enjoy being bossed around by their mini-dachshund, Molly.

Processing a New Employee

LEARNING OBJECTIVES

- Define the Fair Labor Standards Act

- Utilize Circular E

- Complete various forms for new employees

- Convey the importance of workers' compensation insurance

- Create an employee earnings record

Accurately determining payroll can be a complex and confusing process. A careful examination of the step-by-step procedures involved is necessary. In this chapter, you'll begin by reviewing the regulations and forms related to hiring a new employee. You'll also examine a number of basic payroll records, including a paystub and an employee earnings record. Lastly, you'll learn the ways in which many companies employ a payroll service to handle payroll-related matters.

 Videos available! Check out the Video Launch Pad in your student exercise file download to access videos associated with this chapter. One video presents a chapter overview, and the other provides more detail on a key chapter topic.

CASE STUDY

Hiring a New Employee for Lucky Ties Apparel

Lucky Ties Apparel is a clothing store in Rochester, NY. It has been in business for over 15 years and is a favorite location for local college students. You've worked at the store for three years and have recently taken over all payroll responsibilities. You feel confident that you can complete all the payroll tasks but intend to review the entire payroll process in preparation for this new role.

The store's sales increase during school months, and Lucky Ties Apparel typically hires new employees for these months. You've just interviewed and hired a new employee in anticipation of the upcoming term and are eager to review all related payroll tasks.

The Employer's Tax Guide (Circular E) provides excellent guidance for payroll-related matters.

Department of the Treasury
Internal Revenue Service

Publication 15
Cat. No. 10000W

(Circular E), Employer's Tax Guide

For use in **2019**

Get forms and other information faster and easier at:
- *IRS.gov* (English)
- *IRS.gov/Spanish* (Español)
- *IRS.gov/Chinese* (中文)
- *IRS.gov/Korean* (한국어)
- *IRS.gov/Russian* (Русский)
- *IRS.gov/Vietnamese* (TiếngViệt)

Contents

Future Developments

For the latest information about developments related to Pub. 15, such as legislation enacted after it was published, go to *IRS.gov/Pub15*.

What's New

Social security and Medicare tax for 2019. The social security tax rate is 6.2% each for the employee and employer, unchanged from 2018. The social security wage base limit is $132,900.

The Medicare tax rate is 1.45% each for the employee and employer, unchanged from 2018. There is no wage base limit for Medicare tax.

The Employee Paystub

If you have ever received a **paycheck**, you know that the attached **paystub** lists a variety of amounts that are not included in your check. Although you've earned these amounts, they are withheld from your check, each for a different reason. In addition to the withholdings, other pertinent payroll information is also found on the paystub.

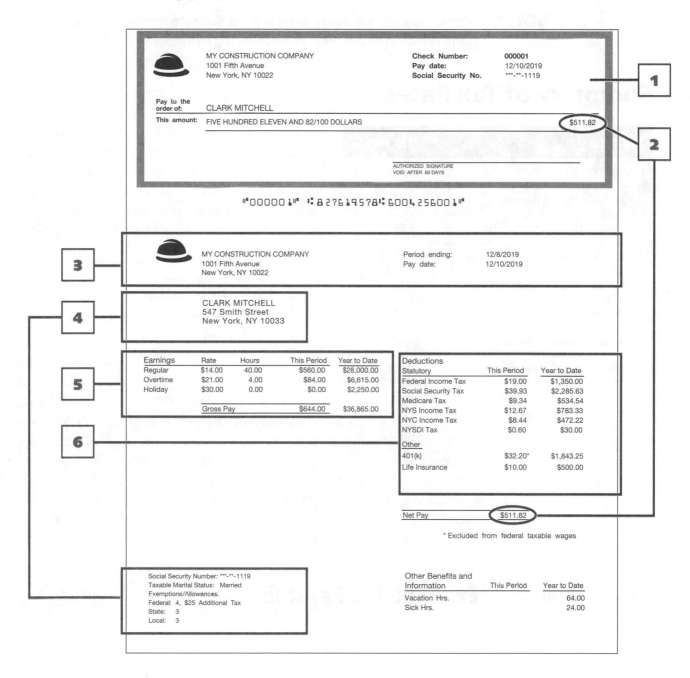

1. Paycheck
2. Net Pay (Paycheck Amount)
3. Company and Pay Period Information
4. Employee Information
5. Current and Year-to-Date Earnings (Chapter 2)
6. Amounts Withheld (Deducted) from Employee Pay (Chapter 3 and Chapter 4)

Aside from standard employee information such as name and address, the paystub also indicates the employee's marital status and the number of exemptions claimed. This information is used to determine the amount of state and federal income tax withholding that is subtracted from **gross pay** (total amount earned by the employee). Once these and other deductions are subtracted from gross pay, the result is **net pay** (amount actually paid to the employee). Notice in the previous figure that the calculated net pay on the paystub equals the amount of the employee's check.

NOTE!   Don't worry if you are unsure about some of these elements at this stage. You will examine each in further detail in the upcoming chapters.

Summary of Tax Rates

Tax Type	Tax Rate
State income tax withholding	5%
Social Security (OASDI) tax	6.2%
Social Security wage base (threshold)	$132,900
Medicare (HI) tax	1.45%
FUTA (federal unemployment) tax	0.6%
FUTA wage base (threshold)	$7,000
SUTA (state unemployment) tax	3.4%
SUTA wage base (threshold)	$8,500

Before moving forward with our examination of the various elements of the paystub, it's necessary to identify certain assumptions made within each chapter. Throughout this book you will employ consistent tax rates. While you learn how to utilize each of these rates, you can return to the summary table (at left) whenever necessary.

The state income tax withholding amount varies for each employee based on his/her state, marital status, and number of exemptions. An examination of each of these rates is beyond the scope of this book, so we will employ one consistent rate of 5%.

The Social Security and Medicare tax rates listed, along with the Social Security wage base (over which Social Security tax is not levied) of $132,900, are consistent with rates in effect for 2019. The **federal unemployment tax (FUTA)** rate for 2019 is 6%; however, it may be reduced by a maximum of 5.4%, which employers are permitted to deduct for paying state unemployment taxes. Therefore, in most instances we will utilize 0.6% (6% − 5.4%) as the FUTA tax rate, along with a FUTA wage base of $7,000. The **state unemployment tax (SUTA)** rate, which varies from state to state, is assumed to be 3.4%, while the SUTA wage base (which also varies) is assumed to be $8,500.

Case in Point 1-1	**Examine the Paystub**

In these examples, we further examine a number of paystub elements.

1. What is the difference between the *Period Ending Date* and the *Pay Date*?

   The Period Ending date represents the final day for which the employee is being paid in the current paycheck. The Pay Date is the date on which the actual check is written.

2. Why are more allowances claimed for federal taxes (four) than for state and local (three)?

This can be due to a number of reasons, but the most likely is that an employee can claim a federal allowance for him/herself, but cannot do so in New York State (where this individual is employed) for state and local taxes. We will examine allowances further in the W-4 Form section later in this chapter.

3. Why are there three different earnings categories on the paystub?

Employers offer different pay rates for different types of hours worked. For example, employees typically earn 1.5 times more pay for overtime hours than for regular hours. Therefore, hours worked are broken down by type, so that the correct pay rate may be applied to each.

4. Is every displayed deduction withheld from all employee paychecks?

No. Certain deductions, such as federal income tax and Medicare tax, are *mandatory deductions* (i.e., they must be withheld from all paychecks), while others such as 401(k) and life insurance are *voluntary deductions* (the employee can elect to have them withheld). We will examine these deductions in detail in Chapter 3.

The Fair Labor Standards Act

Before the paystub elements are calculated and the paycheck is distributed, an employer must ensure compliance with the **Fair Labor Standards Act (FLSA)**. The FLSA dictates a variety of regulations that the majority of employers must follow. The act, originally passed into law in 1938, has been amended many times. Among its most influential provisions are the establishment of a **federal minimum wage**, the mandating of 1.5 times regular pay (time and a half) for overtime hours, and the restriction of child labor.

The Federal Minimum Wage

Historical Federal Minimum Wage Rates

Effective Date	Minimum Wage Rate
July 24, 2009	$7.25
July 24, 2008	$6.55
July 24, 2007	$5.85
September 1, 1997	$5.15
October 1, 1996	$4.75
April 1, 1991	$4.25
April 1, 1990	$3.80

To comply with the FLSA, employers must be aware of the federal minimum wage. As of July 24, 2009, the United States Congress increased the federal minimum wage rate to $7.25. Individual states have also passed their own minimum wage laws. When these state-enacted rates conflict with the federal rate of $7.25, the higher wage rate takes precedence. Recent historical federal wage rates are as shown at left.

Exceptions to the Federal Minimum Wage

There are several exceptions to the current federal minimum wage rate. One is for *workers with disabilities*, who may be paid a lower minimum wage. This wage is a percentage of the current prevailing wage rate for a comparable position and is based on the productivity level of the employee with the disability.

Full-time students working for specific employers (colleges and universities, agriculture, and retail or service stores) may be paid 85% of the current minimum wage rate, and are limited to a maximum of 8 hours/day, 20 hours/week while school is in session.

Young workers (under 20 years old) may be paid $4.25/hour for the first 90 days of employment, as long as they do not replace another employee. The pay reverts to the federal minimum after 90 days or after the employee turns 20, whichever comes first.

Tipped employees may be paid $2.13/hour, as long as their tips, when added to this amount, equal or exceed the federal minimum wage. These employees must retain all their tips and regularly receive at least $30 in tips per month. Any deficit (below the federal minimum wage rate) must be made up by the employer. Certain states provide greater benefits to tipped employees.

Student learners enrolled in a vocational school may be paid 75% of the federal minimum wage, as long as they remain in the educational program while employed. Employers must obtain an authorizing certificate from the U.S. Department of Labor to pay these reduced wages.

Who Must Pay the Federal Minimum Wage?

The federal minimum wage applies to employees of all of the following:

- Businesses with gross revenues of at least $500,000
- Federal, state, or local government agencies
- Hospitals
- Schools

Domestic workers, and a wide range of employees working for businesses engaged in interstate commerce, are also covered by the federal minimum wage.

TIP! The federal government allows a wide range of exemptions to the federal minimum wage and other provisions of the FLSA. The most notable exemptions are for executive, administrative, and professional employees.

Calculating Overtime Wages

Per the FLSA, employees must be paid 1.5 times regular wages (time and a half) for all hours worked beyond the first 40 in any given workweek. Similar to the federal minimum wage, certain employees are exempted from this overtime-wage provision, including executive, administrative, and professional employees.

WARNING! The term *overtime* is often used to refer to a wide variety of working hours (such as hours worked on holidays, weekends, or evenings). It is important to recognize that the definition of overtime hours within the FLSA, and therefore the guideline that employers are legally required to follow, is narrowly defined as those hours worked beyond the first 40 during a single workweek.

To calculate overtime wages, a **workweek** is defined as any seven-day period designated by the employer. It must begin and end consistently each week, but it does not need to coincide with the standard calendar and can vary for different groups of employees.

Child Labor Restrictions

The FLSA dictates the type of work that may be performed by children of various ages. Children younger than 14 years of age may perform only specific activities, such as performing arts, newspaper delivery, and working for their parents' sole proprietorships (certain business types are prohibited).

Children aged 14 and 15 may work in a variety of jobs outside of manufacturing and mining, but they are subject to extensive hour limitations. They may work for only three hours on a school day, 18 hours in a school week, eight hours on a nonschool day, and 40 hours in a nonschool week. They may work only between 7:00 a.m. and 7:00 p.m. (or 9:00 p.m. between June 1 and Labor Day). Certain children may take advantage of other special programs with more relaxed requirements.

Children aged 16 and 17 may work an unlimited number of hours.

WARNING! Under no circumstances may a child 17 years of age or younger work in a job classified as hazardous, including coal mining, explosives manufacturing, and roofing.

Children employed in agricultural jobs are subject to less stringent requirements, and children employed by their parents on a farm may perform any nonhazardous job duties.

Case in Point 1-2	**Interpret the Fair Labor Standards Act**

In this example, we'll review four independent employment circumstances and determine whether each employer complies with the Fair Labor Standards Act.

1. Robert is a tax advisor for a regional accounting firm in Macon, GA. During one long evening at the office, he uses his annual salary to calculate how much he earns on an hourly basis. He discovers that he is earning $6.85/hour during the current year. Is Robert's employer violating the FLSA?

   No, Robert's employer is not in violation of the FLSA. White-collar workers (executive, administrative, and professional employees) are exempted from the federal minimum wage requirements. Therefore, regardless of the number of hours Robert works, he is entitled only to his agreed-upon annual salary.

2. Maria is 15 years old, and she works each weekend during the school year as a roofer. She works seven hours each Saturday and five hours each Sunday. During nonschool weeks Maria works an additional eight hours per day, Monday through Wednesday. Is Maria's employer violating the FLSA?

   Yes. Although Maria is working fewer than the maximum number of permissible hours, children aged 17 and younger may not work in a variety of hazardous professions, including roofing. Maria's employer is in violation of the FLSA.

3. Kenneth works for a local diner. On a recent Wednesday he worked six hours, was paid $2.13/hour by his employer, and earned $29.46 in tips throughout the day (which he fully retained). In Kenneth's state, the federal and state minimum wages are identical. Is Kenneth's employer violating the FLSA?

   Yes, Kenneth's employer is in violation of the FLSA. When employers use the tip credit provision to pay tipped employees $2.13/hour, they're responsible for demonstrating that the combination of wages and tips exceeds the hourly federal minimum wage of $7.25. Kenneth earned $29.46 in tips, which when divided by the six hours he worked, yields $4.91/hour. The sum of hourly wages ($2.13) plus tips ($4.91) is $7.04, which is below the minimum wage of $7.25. It is the employer's responsibility to pay Kenneth the difference of $0.21/hour.

4. Tina is a full-time college student who works in her university's bookstore. She works six hours/day on Tuesday, Friday, and Saturday each week and is paid $6.20/hour. Is Tina's employer violating the FLSA?

   No, Tina's employer is not in violation of the FLSA. Full-time college students working for certain employers (including universities) may be paid 85% of the federal minimum wage. Tina's $6.20/hour wage is higher than this 85% threshold.

Circular E and Form SS-4

On the Web

irs.gov/pub/irs-pdf
/p15.pdf

Circular E is an Employer's Tax Guide written and distributed free of cost by the U.S. Internal Revenue Service (IRS). Also referred to as *Publication 15*, Circular E provides employers with an excellent starting point when hiring employees. Becoming familiar with Circular E helps ensure that employers comply with all elements of the FLSA.

Among the benefits provided in Circular E are a list of due dates for payroll-related forms, tables used to calculate federal income tax withholding, and a summary of new payroll regulations.

TIP! You'll benefit from keeping a copy of Circular E as a reference guide, so be certain to obtain one as soon as possible.

If an employer has questions not addressed in the publication, the final pages of Circular E provide contact information.

How To Get Tax Help

If you have questions about a tax issue, need help preparing your tax return, or want to download free publications, forms, or instructions, go to IRS.gov and find resources that can help you right away.

Tax reform. Major tax reform legislation impacting individuals, businesses, and tax-exempt entities was enacted in the Tax Cuts and Jobs Act on December 22, 2017. Go to *IRS.gov/TaxReform* for information and updates on how this legislation affects your taxes.

Preparing and filing your tax return. Go to *IRS.gov/EmploymentEfile* for more information on filing your employment tax returns electronically.

 Getting answers to your tax questions. On IRS.gov, get answers to your tax questions anytime, anywhere.

- Go to *IRS.gov/Help* for a variety of tools that will help you get answers to some of the most common tax questions.

- You may also be able to access tax law information in your electronic filing software.

Getting tax forms and publications. Go to *IRS.gov/Forms* to view, download, or print most of the forms and publications you may need. You can also download and view popular tax publications and instructions (including Pub. 15) on mobile devices as an eBook at no charge. Or you can go to *IRS.gov/OrderForms* to place an order and have forms mailed to you within 10 business days.

Getting a transcript or copy of a return. You can get a copy of your tax transcript or a copy of your return by calling 800-829-4933 or by mailing Form 4506-T (transcript request) or Form 4506 (copy of return) to the IRS.

Resolving tax-related identity theft issues.

- The IRS doesn't initiate contact with taxpayers by email or telephone to request personal or financial information. This includes any type of electronic communication, such as text messages and social media channels.

- Go to *IRS.gov/IDProtection* for information.

- If your EIN has been lost or stolen or you suspect you're a victim of tax-related identity theft, visit *IRS.gov/IdentityTheft* to learn what steps you should take.

Making a tax payment. The IRS uses the latest encryption technology to ensure your electronic payments are safe and secure. You can make electronic payments online, by phone, and from a mobile device using the IRS2Go app. Paying electronically is quick, easy, and faster than mailing in a check or money order. Go to

IRS.gov/Payments to make a payment using any of the following options.

- **Debit or credit card:** Choose an approved payment processor to pay online, by phone, and by mobile device.

- **Electronic Funds Withdrawal:** Offered only when filing your federal taxes using tax return preparation software or through a tax professional.

- **Electronic Federal Tax Payment System:** Best option for businesses. Enrollment is required.

- **Check or money order:** Mail your payment to the address listed on the notice or instructions.

- **Cash:** You may be able to pay your taxes with cash at a participating retail store.

What if I can't pay now? Go to *IRS.gov/Payments* for more information about your options.

- Apply for an *online payment agreement* (*IRS.gov/OPA*) to meet your tax obligation in monthly installments if you can't pay your taxes in full today. Once you complete the online process, you will receive immediate notification of whether your agreement has been approved.

- Use the *Offer in Compromise Pre-Qualifier* (*IRS.gov/OIC*) to see if you can settle your tax debt for less than the full amount you owe.

Understanding an IRS notice or letter. Go to *IRS.gov/Notices* to find additional information about responding to an IRS notice or letter.

Contacting your local IRS office. Keep in mind, many questions can be answered on IRS.gov without visiting an IRS Tax Assistance Center (TAC). Go to *IRS.gov/LetUsHelp* for the topics people ask about most. If you still need help, IRS TACs provide tax help when a tax issue can't be handled online or by phone. All TACs now provide service by appointment so you'll know in advance that you can get the service you need without long wait times. Before you visit, go to *IRS.gov/TACLocator* to find the nearest TAC, check hours, available services, and appointment options. Or, on the IRS2Go app, under the Stay Connected tab, choose the Contact Us option and click on "Local Offices."

Watching IRS videos. The IRS Video portal (*IRSVideos.gov*) contains video and audio presentations for individuals, small businesses, and tax professionals.

Getting tax information in other languages. For taxpayers whose native language isn't English, we have the following resources available. Taxpayers can find information on IRS.gov in the following languages.

- *Spanish* (*IRS.gov/Spanish*).

- *Chinese* (*IRS.gov/Chinese*).

- *Vietnamese* (*IRS.gov/Vietnamese*).

- *Korean* (*IRS.gov/Korean*).

Page 68   **Publication 15 (2019)**

Employer Identification Number

On the Web

irs.gov/pub/irs-pdf/fss4.pdf

To report employment taxes or provide employees with tax statements, which are both required if a company hires employees, a company must first obtain an **Employer Identification Number (EIN)**, also known as a Federal Tax Identification Number, by completing Form SS-4 (Application for Employer Identification Number). If a company intends to pay any employees, obtaining an EIN should be one of the first actions taken after it is formed.

TIP! An employer may also apply for an EIN via the Internet or telephone if a faster response is desired.

Examine the Form: SS-4

Completion of Form SS-4 is necessary prior to remitting employee payroll.

Form **SS-4** (Rev. December 2017) Department of the Treasury Internal Revenue Service	**Application for Employer Identification Number** (For use by employers, corporations, partnerships, trusts, estates, churches, government agencies, Indian tribal entities, certain individuals, and others.) ► Go to *www.irs.gov/FormSS4* for instructions and the latest information. ► See separate instructions for each line. ► Keep a copy for your records.	OMB No. 1545-0003 EIN

Type or print clearly.

1 Legal name of entity (or individual) for whom the EIN is being requested

2 Trade name of business (if different from name on line 1)	**3** Executor, administrator, trustee, "care of" name

4a Mailing address (room, apt., suite no. and street, or P.O. box)	**5a** Street address (if different) (Do not enter a P.O. box.)
4b City, state, and ZIP code (if foreign, see instructions)	**5b** City, state, and ZIP code (if foreign, see instructions)

6 County and state where principal business is located

7a Name of responsible party	**7b** SSN, ITIN, or EIN

8a Is this application for a limited liability company (LLC) (or a foreign equivalent)? ☐ Yes ☐ No	**8b** If 8a is "Yes," enter the number of LLC members ►

8c If 8a is "Yes," was the LLC organized in the United States? ☐ Yes ☐ No

9a **Type of entity** (check only one box). **Caution.** If 8a is "Yes," see the instructions for the correct box to check.

☐ Sole proprietor (SSN) _____
☐ Partnership
☐ Corporation (enter form number to be filed) ► _____
☐ Personal service corporation
☐ Church or church-controlled organization
☐ Other nonprofit organization (specify) ► _____
☐ Other (specify) ►

☐ Estate (SSN of decedent) _____
☐ Plan administrator (TIN) _____
☐ Trust (TIN of grantor) _____
☐ Military/National Guard   ☐ State/local government
☐ Farmers' cooperative   ☐ Federal government
☐ REMIC   ☐ Indian tribal governments/enterprises
Group Exemption Number (GEN) if any ►

9b If a corporation, name the state or foreign country (if applicable) where incorporated	State	Foreign country

10 **Reason for applying** (check only one box)
☐ Started new business (specify type) ► _____
☐ Hired employees (Check the box and see line 13.)
☐ Compliance with IRS withholding regulations
☐ Other (specify) ►

☐ Banking purpose (specify purpose) ► _____
☐ Changed type of organization (specify new type) ► _____
☐ Purchased going business
☐ Created a trust (specify type) ► _____
☐ Created a pension plan (specify type) ► _____

11 Date business started or acquired (month, day, year). See instructions.	**12** Closing month of accounting year
13 Highest number of employees expected in the next 12 months (enter -0- if none). If no employees expected, skip line 14.	**14** If you expect your employment tax liability to be $1,000 or less in a full calendar year **and** want to file Form 944 annually instead of Forms 941 quarterly, check here. (Your employment tax liability generally will be $1,000 or less if you expect to pay $4,000 or less in total wages.) If you do not check this box, you must file Form 941 for every quarter. ☐

Agricultural	Household	Other

15 First date wages or annuities were paid (month, day, year). **Note:** If applicant is a withholding agent, enter date income will first be paid to nonresident alien (month, day, year) ►

16 Check **one** box that best describes the principal activity of your business.
☐ Construction ☐ Rental & leasing ☐ Transportation & warehousing
☐ Real estate ☐ Manufacturing ☐ Finance & insurance
☐ Health care & social assistance ☐ Wholesale-agent/broker
☐ Accommodation & food service ☐ Wholesale-other ☐ Retail
☐ Other (specify) ►

17 Indicate principal line of merchandise sold, specific construction work done, products produced, or services provided.

18 Has the applicant entity shown on line 1 ever applied for and received an EIN? ☐ Yes ☐ No
If "Yes," write previous EIN here ►

Third Party Designee	Complete this section **only** if you want to authorize the named individual to receive the entity's EIN and answer questions about the completion of this form.	
	Designee's name	Designee's telephone number (include area code)
	Address and ZIP code	Designee's fax number (include area code)

Under penalties of perjury, I declare that I have examined this application, and to the best of my knowledge and belief, it is true, correct, and complete.

Name and title (type or print clearly) ►
	Applicant's telephone number (include area code)
Signature ►   Date ►
	Applicant's fax number (include area code)

For Privacy Act and Paperwork Reduction Act Notice, see separate instructions.   Cat. No. 16055N   Form **SS-4** (Rev. 12-2017)

Line 1: Enter the full name of the individual requesting an EIN or the legal name of the business making the request.

Line 2: Complete this line if the request is being made by a business operating under a different name (a *Doing Business As,* or *DBA,* name) than is declared on line 1. Note that all sole proprietorships enter the business name here.

Line 3: This line is primarily used by estates and trusts, and may be left blank when the form is being completed for the purposes of remitting payroll.

Lines 4a and 4b: Enter the company's mailing address.

Lines 5a and 5b: Enter the company's physical address if different from line 4.

Line 6: Enter the county and state of the business's physical location.

Lines 7a and 7b: Enter the name and Social Security number (SSN) of the responsible person (individual who exerts control over the business).

Lines 8a–8c: Complete these lines only if the business was formed as a limited liability company (LLC).

Line 9a: Check the box that correlates with the type of business making the request.

Line 9b: Complete this section only if you selected one of the corporation options on line 9a.

Line 10: For payroll purposes, you will typically check either *Started new business* or *Hired employees*, depending on the circumstance.

Line 11: Enter the starting date or date the business was acquired. If the corporate form was changed, enter the effective date of the new ownership form.

Line 12: Enter the final month of the company's fiscal year. While this is commonly December, a company may end its fiscal year during any month.

Line 13: Enter an estimate of the number of each type of listed employee.

Line 14: For all businesses except those with the smallest annual payroll, do not check this box. When unchecked, a quarterly Form 941 will be required.

Line 15: For a new business, or for an existing business that has now hired employees, enter the first date on which wages are paid.

Line 16: Check the box that most closely represents the company's line of business. If checking *Other*, include a brief description.

Line 17: Provide a one- or two-sentence synopsis of the business.

Line 18: Check the appropriate box, and if a previous EIN was issued, include it here.

Third Party Designee: Complete this section only if you want an outside party (such as an outside accountant) to answer questions regarding the form on the company's behalf.

Signature Line: Fully complete all components within this section.

TIP! For a more thorough examination of the elements of Form SS-4 (or any other federal form), refer to the instructions provided by the IRS. A simple online search can quickly locate any desired IRS instructions.

Case in Point 1-3	# Complete Form SS-4

In this example, we'll complete Form SS-4 for a newly formed company named Wood Furniture Builders, Inc., which creates custom wood furniture. It was started on August 26, 2019, as a sole proprietorship by its president, Samuel Williams (SSN 555-55-5555). His phone number is 516-555-5555, and his fax number is 516-555-5556. The company is located at 748 Negra Arroyo Lane, Massapequa, NY 11758 (in Nassau County), where it receives all mail. The company uses the calendar year as its fiscal year and expects to employ five individuals (earning an average of $36,500/year) in the first 24 months of operations. Payroll is to be paid biweekly on Fridays, with the first pay date scheduled for September 6, 2019.

1. Complete lines 1 through 7 with basic information. Leave line 3 blank, as it is not applicable for a new business. Leave lines 5a and 5b blank, as the mailing address and physical address are identical.

2. Complete lines 8 through 10 using information provided about the business entity. Select "No" on line 8a, as this company is a sole proprietorship and not a limited liability company. As a result of this selection, lines 8b and 8c are left blank. Select "Sole Proprietor" on line 9a, and enter the company president's Social Security number beside this box. Leave line 9b blank, as this company is not a corporation. Select "Started new business" on line 10, and include the basic business description.

3. Lines 11 through 15 relate to the company's start date, fiscal year, and payroll. Enter the business start date of 8/26/2019 on line 11 and "December" on line 12, as the company follows a calendar year (operations are reported annually from January through December). The company's five employees don't qualify as agricultural or household employees; therefore enter "5" in the "Other" category on line 13. Employees are projected to earn an average of $36,500 each per year, and therefore the company must file Form 941 quarterly. As a result, do not check the box on line 14. Enter the first pay date of 9/6/2019 on line 15.

4. Lines 16 through 18 provide information about the company's current and prior operations. Check "Manufacturing" on line 16. Line 17 contains a more extensive description of the business than was written on line 10. As this is a new business, and therefore has not previously applied for an EIN, check "No" on this line.

5. No third-party designee is referenced, so leave this section blank. Finally, Samuel Williams completed all information in the final section and has signed the form.

Form **SS-4** (Rev. December 2017) Department of the Treasury Internal Revenue Service	**Application for Employer Identification Number** (For use by employers, corporations, partnerships, trusts, estates, churches, government agencies, Indian tribal entities, certain individuals, and others.) ► Go to *www.irs.gov/FormSS4* for instructions and the latest information. ► See separate instructions for each line. ► Keep a copy for your records.	OMB No. 1545-0003 **EIN**

Type or print clearly.

1	Legal name of entity (or individual) for whom the EIN is being requested
	Samuel Williams

2	Trade name of business (if different from name on line 1)	3	Executor, administrator, trustee, "care of" name
	Wood Furniture Builders		

4a	Mailing address (room, apt., suite no. and street, or P.O. box)	5a	Street address (if different) (Do not enter a P.O. box.)
	748 Negra Arroyo Lane		
4b	City, state, and ZIP code (if foreign, see instructions)	5b	City, state, and ZIP code (if foreign, see instructions)
	Massapequa, NY 11758		

6	County and state where principal business is located
	Nassau County, NY

7a	Name of responsible party	7b	SSN, ITIN, or EIN
	Samuel Williams		**555-55-5555**

8a	Is this application for a limited liability company (LLC) (or a foreign equivalent)? . . . . ☐ Yes ☑ No	8b	If 8a is "Yes," enter the number of LLC members . . . . . . ►

8c	If 8a is "Yes," was the LLC organized in the United States? . . . . ☐ Yes ☐ No

9a Type of entity (check only one box). **Caution.** If 8a is "Yes," see the instructions for the correct box to check.

- ☑ Sole proprietor (SSN)   **555-55-5555**
- ☐ Partnership
- ☐ Corporation (enter form number to be filed) ► _____
- ☐ Personal service corporation
- ☐ Church or church-controlled organization
- ☐ Other nonprofit organization (specify) ► _____
- ☐ Other (specify) ►

- ☐ Estate (SSN of decedent) _____
- ☐ Plan administrator (TIN) _____
- ☐ Trust (TIN of grantor) _____
- ☐ Military/National Guard   ☐ State/local government
- ☐ Farmers' cooperative   ☐ Federal government
- ☐ REMIC   ☐ Indian tribal governments/enterprises

Group Exemption Number (GEN) if any ►

9b	If a corporation, name the state or foreign country (if applicable) where incorporated	State	Foreign country

10 Reason for applying (check only one box)
- ☑ Started new business (specify type) ► _____
  Furniture Builders
- ☐ Hired employees (Check the box and see line 13.)
- ☐ Compliance with IRS withholding regulations
- ☐ Other (specify) ►

- ☐ Banking purpose (specify purpose) ► _____
- ☐ Changed type of organization (specify new type) ► _____
- ☐ Purchased going business
- ☐ Created a trust (specify type) ► _____
- ☐ Created a pension plan (specify type) ► _____

11	Date business started or acquired (month, day, year). See instructions. **08/26/2019**	12	Closing month of accounting year **December**
13	Highest number of employees expected in the next 12 months (enter -0- if none). If no employees expected, skip line 14.	14	If you expect your employment tax liability to be $1,000 or less in a full calendar year **and** want to file Form 944 annually instead of Forms 941 quarterly, check here. (Your employment tax liability generally will be $1,000 or less if you expect to pay $4,000 or less in total wages.) If you do not check this box, you must file Form 941 for every quarter. ☐

Agricultural	Household	Other
0	0	5

15	First date wages or annuities were paid (month, day, year). **Note**: If applicant is a withholding agent, enter date income will first be paid to nonresident alien (month, day, year) . . . . ► **09/06/2019**

16 Check **one** box that best describes the principal activity of your business.
- ☐ Construction   ☐ Rental & leasing   ☐ Transportation & warehousing
- ☐ Real estate   ☑ Manufacturing   ☐ Finance & insurance
- ☐ Health care & social assistance   ☐ Wholesale-agent/broker
- ☐ Accommodation & food service   ☐ Wholesale-other   ☐ Retail
- ☐ Other (specify) ►

17	Indicate principal line of merchandise sold, specific construction work done, products produced, or services provided. **Sale of custom-built furniture based on client-provided specifications**

18	Has the applicant entity shown on line 1 ever applied for and received an EIN? ☐ Yes ☑ No If "Yes," write previous EIN here ►

Third Party Designee

Complete this section **only** if you want to authorize the named individual to receive the entity's EIN and answer questions about the completion of this form.	
Designee's name	Designee's telephone number (include area code)
Address and ZIP code	Designee's fax number (include area code)

Under penalties of perjury, I declare that I have examined this application, and to the best of my knowledge and belief, it is true, correct, and complete.

Name and title (type or print clearly) ► **Samuel Williams, President**

Signature ► *Samuel Williams*   Date ► 8/26/19

Applicant's telephone number (include area code) **516-555-5555**
Applicant's fax number (include area code) **516-555-5556**

For Privacy Act and Paperwork Reduction Act Notice, see separate instructions.   Cat. No. 16055N   Form **SS-4** (Rev. 12-2017)

Hiring an Employee

When a new employee is hired, a number of considerations must be made by both the employee and the employer. These considerations not only provide employers with information required to properly process payroll, but also enable them to comply with applicable federal and state laws.

The Personal Responsibility and Work Opportunity Reconciliation Act of 1996

The **Personal Responsibility and Work Opportunity Reconciliation Act of 1996 (PRWORA)** significantly strengthened child support throughout the United States. This was achieved in various ways, including through the mandatory reporting of new employees within 20 days of hire, enabling better enforcement of child-support laws. Employers can satisfy the provisions of this act by submitting the newly hired employee's W-4 Form to the state. We'll examine the W-4 Form in more detail further ahead in this chapter.

WARNING! Some states have more stringent requirements than those required in the federal provisions for PRWORA.

Form SS-5

On the Web

socialsecurity.gov/online/ss-5.pdf

The W-4 Form requires the employee's Social Security number. Employees who don't have a Social Security card can obtain one by completing and submitting Form SS-5 to their local Social Security office.

TIP! Form SS-5 is also used to obtain a replacement Social Security card or to correct information in the Social Security record.

Examine the Form: SS-5

Form SS-5 is completed by any employee who does not have a Social Security number.

SOCIAL SECURITY ADMINISTRATION
Application for a Social Security Card

Form Approved
OMB No. 0960-0066

1

NAME TO BE SHOWN ON CARD	First	Full Middle Name	Last
FULL NAME AT BIRTH IF OTHER THAN ABOVE	First	Full Middle Name	Last
OTHER NAMES USED			

2 Social Security number previously assigned to the person listed in item 1 ☐☐☐ – ☐☐ – ☐☐☐☐

3 PLACE OF BIRTH _____
(Do Not Abbreviate)   City   State or Foreign Country   Office Use Only   FCI

4 DATE OF BIRTH _____ MM/DD/YYYY

5 CITIZENSHIP (Check One)
☐ U.S. Citizen
☐ Legal Alien Allowed To Work
☐ Legal Alien **Not** Allowed To Work(See Instructions On Page 3)
☐ Other (See Instructions On Page 3)

6 ETHNICITY
Are You Hispanic or Latino?
(Your Response is Voluntary)
☐ Yes   ☐ No

7 RACE
Select One or More
(Your Response is Voluntary)
☐ Native Hawaiian   ☐ American Indian   ☐ Other Pacific Islander
☐ Alaska Native   ☐ Black/African American   ☐ White
☐ Asian

8 SEX   ☐ Male   ☐ Female

9

A. PARENT/ MOTHER'S NAME AT HER BIRTH	First	Full Middle Name	Last

B. PARENT/ MOTHER'S SOCIAL SECURITY NUMBER (See instructions for 9 B on Page 3) ☐☐☐ – ☐☐ – ☐☐☐☐   ☐ Unknown

10

A. PARENT/ FATHER'S NAME	First	Full Middle Name	Last

B. PARENT/ FATHER'S SOCIAL SECURITY NUMBER (See instructions for 10B on Page 3) ☐☐☐ – ☐☐ – ☐☐☐☐   ☐ Unknown

11 Has the person listed in item 1 or anyone acting on his/her behalf ever filed for or received a Social Security number card before?
☐ Yes (If "yes" answer questions 12-13)   ☐ No   ☐ Don't Know (If "don't know," skip to question 14.)

12

Name shown on the most recent Social Security card issued for the person listed in item 1	First	Full Middle Name	Last

13 Enter any different date of birth if used on an earlier application for a card _____ MM/DD/YYYY

14 TODAY'S DATE _____ MM/DD/YYYY

15 DAYTIME PHONE NUMBER _____ _____
Area Code   Number

16 MAILING ADDRESS (Do Not Abbreviate)
Street Address, Apt. No., PO Box, Rural Route No.
City   State/Foreign Country   ZIP Code

I declare under penalty of perjury that I have examined all the information on this form, and on any accompanying statements or forms, and it is true and correct to the best of my knowledge.

17 YOUR SIGNATURE

18 YOUR RELATIONSHIP TO THE PERSON IN ITEM 1 IS:
☐ Self   ☐ Natural Or Adoptive Parent   ☐ Legal Guardian   ☐ Other Specify _____

DO NOT WRITE BELOW THIS LINE (FOR SSA USE ONLY)

NPN			DOC	NTI	CAN			ITV
PBC	EVI	EVA	EVC	PRA	NWR	DNR	UNIT	
EVIDENCE SUBMITTED					SIGNATURE AND TITLE OF EMPLOYEE(S) REVIEWING EVIDENCE AND/OR CONDUCTING INTERVIEW			
							DATE	
					DCL		DATE	

Form **SS-5** (08-2011) ef (08-2011)   Destroy Prior Editions   Page 5

Examine the Form: SS-5 (continued)

Most lines within Form SS-5 are self-explanatory. Those lines that warrant specific mention are as follows:

Line 2: Leave this blank if requesting a Social Security card for the first time.

Lines 6 and 7: These lines are optional and may be left blank.

Lines 9b and 10b: Complete these lines only when the application is for a child under the age of 18.

Line 17: If the application is for a child under the age of 18, the child's parent or legal guardian may sign on behalf of the child.

When submitting Form SS-5, additional documentation is required to corroborate information about the applicant, such as the applicant's age, identity, and U.S. citizenship (or immigration status). While the combination of a U.S. birth certificate and U.S. driver's license suffices, other documents such as a final adoption decree, U.S. passport, or a current document from the Department of Homeland Security indicating immigration status can corroborate some details.

Form W-4

On the Web

irs.gov/pub/irs-pdf /fw4.pdf

Every employee must complete a W-4 Form (Employee's Withholding Allowance Certificate), which provides the employer with information necessary to calculate both federal income tax withholding and applicable state income tax withholding. Completing the W-4 Form should be one of the first steps taken by a newly hired employee.

The employer retains the W-4 Form in its files. If his/her circumstances change, the employee may submit a new W-4 Form.

Line 5 of the W-4 Form requires the employee to indicate the number of tax allowances being claimed. The IRS provides a worksheet (attached to the top of the W-4 Form) that helps determine the appropriate number of allowances. This worksheet is retained by the employee.

The Personal Allowances Worksheet provides guidance on the tax allowances an employee may claim.

	Personal Allowances Worksheet (Keep for your records.)	
A	Enter "1" for yourself	A ___
B	Enter "1" if you will file as married filing jointly	B ___
C	Enter "1" if you will file as head of household	C ___
D	Enter "1" if: { • You're single, or married filing separately, and have only one job; or • You're married filing jointly, have only one job, and your spouse doesn't work; or • Your wages from a second job or your spouse's wages (or the total of both) are $1,500 or less. }	D ___
E	**Child tax credit.** See Pub. 972, Child Tax Credit, for more information. • If your total income will be less than $71,201 ($103,351 if married filing jointly), enter "4" for each eligible child. • If your total income will be from $71,201 to $179,050 ($103,351 to $345,850 if married filing jointly), enter "2" for each eligible child. • If your total income will be from $179,051 to $200,000 ($345,851 to $400,000 if married filing jointly), enter "1" for each eligible child. • If your total income will be higher than $200,000 ($400,000 if married filing jointly), enter "-0-"	E ___
F	**Credit for other dependents.** See Pub. 972, Child Tax Credit, for more information. • If your total income will be less than $71,201 ($103,351 if married filing jointly), enter "1" for each eligible dependent. • If your total income will be from $71,201 to $179,050 ($103,351 to $345,850 if married filing jointly), enter "1" for every two dependents (for example, "-0-" for one dependent, "1" if you have two or three dependents, and "2" if you have four dependents). • If your total income will be higher than $179,050 ($345,850 if married filing jointly), enter "-0-"	F ___
G	**Other credits.** If you have other credits, see Worksheet 1-6 of Pub. 505 and enter the amount from that worksheet here. If you use Worksheet 1-6, enter "-0-" on lines E and F	G ___
H	Add lines A through G and enter the total here	▶ H ___

Examine the Form: W-4

Form W-4 is completed by all employees upon their hiring.

W-4 Form Department of the Treasury Internal Revenue Service	**Employee's Withholding Allowance Certificate** ▶ Whether you're entitled to claim a certain number of allowances or exemption from withholding is subject to review by the IRS. Your employer may be required to send a copy of this form to the IRS.	OMB No. 1545-0074 20**19**

1 Your first name and middle initial	Last name	2 Your social security number

Home address (number and street or rural route)	3 ☐ Single ☐ Married ☐ Married, but withhold at higher Single rate. **Note:** If married filing separately, check "Married, but withhold at higher Single rate."
City or town, state, and ZIP code	4 **If your last name differs from that shown on your social security card, check here. You must call 800-772-1213 for a replacement card.** ▶ ☐

5 Total number of allowances you're claiming (from the applicable worksheet on the following pages) **5**

6 Additional amount, if any, you want withheld from each paycheck . . . . **6** $

7 I claim exemption from withholding for 2019, and I certify that I meet **both** of the following conditions for exemption.
 • Last year I had a right to a refund of **all** federal income tax withheld because I had **no** tax liability, **and**
 • This year I expect a refund of **all** federal income tax withheld because I expect to have **no** tax liability.
 If you meet both conditions, write "Exempt" here . . . . ▶ **7**

Under penalties of perjury, I declare that I have examined this certificate and, to the best of my knowledge and belief, it is true, correct, and complete.

Employee's signature
(This form is not valid unless you sign it.) ▶ _____ Date ▶

8 Employer's name and address (**Employer:** Complete boxes 8 and 10 if sending to IRS and complete boxes 8, 9, and 10 if sending to State Directory of New Hires.)	9 First date of employment	10 Employer identification number (EIN)

For Privacy Act and Paperwork Reduction Act Notice, see page 4. Cat. No. 10220Q Form **W-4** (2019)

The lines an employee enters on the W-4 Form are as follows:

Line 1: Enter their name and home address.

Line 2: Enter their Social Security number.

Line 3: Typically, check either "Single" or "Married." A married employee may obtain some tax advantages by checking "Married, but withhold at higher Single rate." A tax professional can provide advice as to when this is appropriate.

Line 4: This is commonly checked when an employee is recently married or divorced and has not yet changed his/her Social Security card to match the name reported on line 1.

Line 5: Complete the Personal Allowances Worksheet to determine the correct number of allowances. The final instructions indicate that, in some circumstances, employees should complete one of two additional worksheets that provide guidance for employees who intend to itemize deductions on their personal tax return, and for those who work a second job or whose spouse also works. Note that, as more allowances are reported, fewer taxes are withheld from the employee's pay.

TIP! The number of allowances claimed does not necessarily equal the number of exemptions reported on the employee's personal tax return.

Line 6: Employees may elect to withhold more from each paycheck by listing an additional amount. Although this is not usually necessary, it further reduces the employee's tax burden (and may lead to a refund) when the personal tax return is submitted.

Examine the Form: W-4 (continued)

if something is in Line 5 - Do not write exempt

Line 7: The employee can enter "Exempt" here only when both listed conditions are met. For those who qualify, this entry prevents taxes from being withheld for federal withholding, thereby simplifying the personal tax return. In this instance, the employee must complete only lines 1–4 and 7.

Signature Line: The employee must sign and date the completed form before it is submitted to the employer.

Lines 8–10: These lines are completed by the employer only if the W-4 Form is submitted to the IRS. This is necessary when the IRS requests a specific W-4 Form to review an employee's indicated allowances or exempt status.

Case in Point 1-4   # Complete Form W-4

In this example, we'll complete Form W-4 for Ryan Jackson (SSN 333-33-3332), a newly hired employee of Apex Textiles. Ryan is single; lives at 37 McDonald Lane, Nashville, TN 37204; does not want any additional withholding amounts; and is not exempt from federal income tax withholding. Ryan has no children and does not hold any other jobs. He claims his elderly father as an exemption on his personal tax return, and he therefore files as head of household. He also expects to have total income of $65,000, and the only credit he will claim is a dependent care credit.

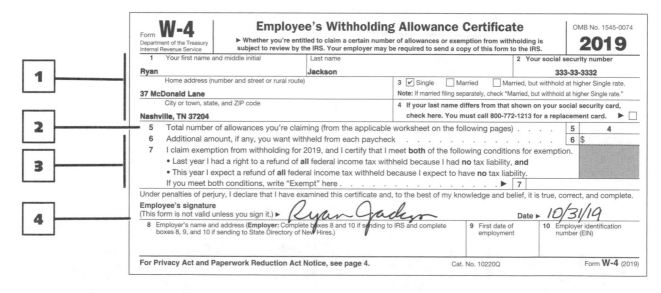

1. Complete lines 1 through 4 with Ryan's name, address, Social Security number, and single status. No provided information indicates that Ryan's name is different from that on his Social Security card, so leave line 4 blank.

2. To complete line 5, use the Personal Allowances Worksheet to arrive at the proper number of allowances. Note that in the following worksheet, lines C and F display "1," since Ryan files as head of household and expects to earn less than $71,201 while claiming one eligible dependent. Because the allowances on the worksheet total 4, this figure is entered on line 5 of Form W-4.

Personal Allowances Worksheet (Keep for your records.)

A	Enter "1" for yourself	A	1
B	Enter "1" if you will file as married filing jointly	B	0
C	Enter "1" if you will file as head of household	C	1
D	Enter "1" if: { • You're single, or married filing separately, and have only one job; or • You're married filing jointly, have only one job, and your spouse doesn't work; or • Your wages from a second job or your spouse's wages (or the total of both) are $1,500 or less. }	D	1
E	**Child tax credit.** See Pub. 972, Child Tax Credit, for more information. • If your total income will be less than $71,201 ($103,351 if married filing jointly), enter "4" for each eligible child. • If your total income will be from $71,201 to $179,050 ($103,351 to $345,850 if married filing jointly), enter "2" for each eligible child. • If your total income will be from $179,051 to $200,000 ($345,851 to $400,000 if married filing jointly), enter "1" for each eligible child. • If your total income will be higher than $200,000 ($400,000 if married filing jointly), enter "-0-"	E	0
F	**Credit for other dependents.** See Pub. 972, Child Tax Credit, for more information. • If your total income will be less than $71,201 ($103,351 if married filing jointly), enter "1" for each eligible dependent. • If your total income will be from $71,201 to $179,050 ($103,351 to $345,850 if married filing jointly), enter "1" for every two dependents (for example, "-0-" for one dependent, "1" if you have two or three dependents, and "2" if you have four dependents). • If your total income will be higher than $179,050 ($345,850 if married filing jointly), enter "-0-"	F	1
G	**Other credits.** If you have other credits, see Worksheet 1-6 of Pub. 505 and enter the amount from that worksheet here. If you use Worksheet 1-6, enter "-0-" on lines E and F	G	0
H	Add lines A through G and enter the total here . . . . ▶	H	4

For accuracy, complete all worksheets that apply. {
• If you plan to **itemize** or **claim adjustments to income** and want to reduce your withholding, or if you have a large amount of nonwage income not subject to withholding and want to increase your withholding, see the **Deductions, Adjustments, and Additional Income Worksheet** below.

• If you **have more than one job at a time** or are **married filing jointly and you and your spouse both work,** and the combined earnings from all jobs exceed $53,000 ($24,450 if married filing jointly), see the **Two-Earners/Multiple Jobs Worksheet** on page 4 to avoid having too little tax withheld.

• If **neither** of the above situations applies, **stop here** and enter the number from line H on line 5 of Form W-4 above.
}

3. Leave lines 6 and 7 (see page 18) blank, as Ryan doesn't want additional monies withheld from his paycheck and is not exempt from federal income tax withholding.

4. Sign and date the form below line 7.

Additional Hiring Considerations

Before an individual can become an employee of any company, the employer must confirm that the prospective employee is permitted to work in the United States. The Immigration Reform and Control Act of 1986 (IRCA) outlines these regulations. All employees must complete Form I-9 (Employment Eligibility Verification) as part of the verification process.

The Immigration Reform and Control Act of 1986

The **Immigration Reform and Control Act of 1986 (IRCA)**, which was passed on November 6, 1986, strengthened immigration law in the United States. As part of this legislation, employers became responsible for maintaining I-9 Forms for all employees. To complete these forms, employers must verify both the employee's identity and employment authorization. Completion of Form I-9 by all employers is intended to reduce the illegal employment of foreign workers in the United States.

Form I-9

On the Web

uscis.gov/system
/files_force/files/form
/i-9-paper-version.pdf

Form I-9 (Employment Eligibility Verification) contains three sections. The first section is completed by the employee, while the employer completes either the second or third section, depending on the circumstances. The employee must complete Section 1 of Form I-9 no later than the first day of employment, but the employer has three business days from the first day of employment to complete Section 2 for new hires. Section 3, which is completed by the employer, is used only when an employee is rehired or when reverification of an employee's eligibility is required (such as when a previously examined employee document has expired).

Attached to Form I-9 is a list of acceptable documents that an employee may furnish for the purpose of verification. Depending on the document(s) provided, an employer may need to review one or more of these and record information about them in Section 2. An employer may not specify which of the listed documents the employee must furnish, as all are acceptable. Additionally, an employer may not request that the employee complete Form I-9 prior to the acceptance of a job offer.

Employees may provide either one document from List A, or one from both List B and List C.

LISTS OF ACCEPTABLE DOCUMENTS
All documents must be UNEXPIRED

Employees may present one selection from List A
or a combination of one selection from List B and one selection from List C.

LIST A	LIST B	LIST C
Documents that Establish Both Identity and Employment Authorization OR	**Documents that Establish Identity** AND	**Documents that Establish Employment Authorization**
1. U.S. Passport or U.S. Passport Card	1. Driver's license or ID card issued by a State or outlying possession of the United States provided it contains a photograph or information such as name, date of birth, gender, height, eye color, and address	1. A Social Security Account Number card, unless the card includes one of the following restrictions:
2. Permanent Resident Card or Alien Registration Receipt Card (Form I-551)		(1) NOT VALID FOR EMPLOYMENT
3. Foreign passport that contains a temporary I-551 stamp or temporary I-551 printed notation on a machine-readable immigrant visa		(2) VALID FOR WORK ONLY WITH INS AUTHORIZATION
	2. ID card issued by federal, state or local government agencies or entities, provided it contains a photograph or information such as name, date of birth, gender, height, eye color, and address	(3) VALID FOR WORK ONLY WITH DHS AUTHORIZATION
4. Employment Authorization Document that contains a photograph (Form I-766)		2. Certification of report of birth issued by the Department of State (Forms DS-1350, FS-545, FS-240)
5. For a nonimmigrant alien authorized to work for a specific employer because of his or her status:	3. School ID card with a photograph	3. Original or certified copy of birth certificate issued by a State, county, municipal authority, or territory of the United States bearing an official seal
a. Foreign passport; and	4. Voter's registration card	
b. Form I-94 or Form I-94A that has the following:	5. U.S. Military card or draft record	
	6. Military dependent's ID card	4. Native American tribal document
(1) The same name as the passport; and	7. U.S. Coast Guard Merchant Mariner Card	5. U.S. Citizen ID Card (Form I-197)
(2) An endorsement of the alien's nonimmigrant status as long as that period of endorsement has not yet expired and the proposed employment is not in conflict with any restrictions or limitations identified on the form.	8. Native American tribal document	6. Identification Card for Use of Resident Citizen in the United States (Form I-179)
	9. Driver's license issued by a Canadian government authority	
	For persons under age 18 who are unable to present a document listed above:	7. Employment authorization document issued by the Department of Homeland Security
6. Passport from the Federated States of Micronesia (FSM) or the Republic of the Marshall Islands (RMI) with Form I-94 or Form I-94A indicating nonimmigrant admission under the Compact of Free Association Between the United States and the FSM or RMI	10. School record or report card	
	11. Clinic, doctor, or hospital record	
	12. Day-care or nursery school record	

Examples of many of these documents appear in Part 13 of the Handbook for Employers (M-274).

Refer to the instructions for more information about acceptable receipts.

Examine the Form: I-9

The employee completes Section 1 of Form I-9.

Employment Eligibility Verification
Department of Homeland Security
U.S. Citizenship and Immigration Services

USCIS
Form I-9
OMB No. 1615-0047
Expires 08/31/2019

▶START HERE: Read instructions carefully before completing this form. The instructions must be available, either in paper or electronically, during completion of this form. Employers are liable for errors in the completion of this form.

ANTI-DISCRIMINATION NOTICE: It is illegal to discriminate against work-authorized individuals. Employers **CANNOT** specify which document(s) an employee may present to establish employment authorization and identity. The refusal to hire or continue to employ an individual because the documentation presented has a future expiration date may also constitute illegal discrimination.

Section 1. Employee Information and Attestation *(Employees must complete and sign Section 1 of Form I-9 no later than the **first day of employment**, but not before accepting a job offer.)*

Last Name *(Family Name)*	First Name *(Given Name)*	Middle Initial	Other Last Names Used *(if any)*

Address *(Street Number and Name)*	Apt. Number	City or Town	State	ZIP Code

Date of Birth *(mm/dd/yyyy)*	U.S. Social Security Number	Employee's E-mail Address	Employee's Telephone Number
	☐☐☐ - ☐☐ - ☐☐☐☐		

I am aware that federal law provides for imprisonment and/or fines for false statements or use of false documents in connection with the completion of this form.

I attest, under penalty of perjury, that I am (check one of the following boxes):

☐ 1. A citizen of the United States

☐ 2. A noncitizen national of the United States *(See instructions)*

☐ 3. A lawful permanent resident   (Alien Registration Number/USCIS Number): _____

☐ 4. An alien authorized to work   until (expiration date, if applicable, mm/dd/yyyy): _____
    Some aliens may write "N/A" in the expiration date field. *(See instructions)*

Aliens authorized to work must provide only one of the following document numbers to complete Form I-9:
An Alien Registration Number/USCIS Number OR Form I-94 Admission Number OR Foreign Passport Number.

1. Alien Registration Number/USCIS Number: _____
            OR
2. Form I-94 Admission Number: _____
            OR
3. Foreign Passport Number: _____
    Country of Issuance: _____

QR Code - Section 1
Do Not Write In This Space

Signature of Employee	Today's Date *(mm/dd/yyyy)*

Preparer and/or Translator Certification (check one):
☐ I did not use a preparer or translator.   ☐ A preparer(s) and/or translator(s) assisted the employee in completing Section 1.
(Fields below must be completed and signed when preparers and/or translators assist an employee in completing Section 1.)

I attest, under penalty of perjury, that I have assisted in the completion of Section 1 of this form and that to the best of my knowledge the information is true and correct.

Signature of Preparer or Translator	Today's Date *(mm/dd/yyyy)*

Last Name *(Family Name)*	First Name *(Given Name)*

Address *(Street Number and Name)*	City or Town	State	ZIP Code

 Employer Completes Next Page

Form I-9 07/17/17 N

Page 1 of 3

Examine the Form: I-9 (continued)

While completing *Section 1*, the employee should be mindful of the following:

- Other Names Used: Include any previously used maiden name.

- Address: Unless the employee commutes to work from a Canadian or Mexican location close to the border, this must be a United States address.

- Social Security number, email address, and telephone number are optional unless the employer utilizes E-Verify (an online federal government system that verifies employee eligibility), in which case a Social Security number is required. Write "N/A" if omitting the email address and telephone number.

- Remaining Checkboxes: Check the appropriate box related to citizenship/immigration status. Complete all requested information.

- Signature Line: Sign and date Form I-9.

- Preparer and/or Translator Certification: Completed by the preparer or translator only if the employee required assistance.

Upon receiving verifying documents from the employee, the employer completes Section 2 of Form I-9.

	Employment Eligibility Verification	USCIS
	Department of Homeland Security U.S. Citizenship and Immigration Services	Form I-9 OMB No. 1615-0047 Expires 08/31/2019

Section 2. Employer or Authorized Representative Review and Verification
(Employers or their authorized representative must complete and sign Section 2 within 3 business days of the employee's first day of employment. You must physically examine one document from List A OR a combination of one document from List B and one document from List C as listed on the "Lists of Acceptable Documents.")

Employee Info from Section 1	Last Name (Family Name)	First Name (Given Name)	M.I.	Citizenship/Immigration Status

List A Identity and Employment Authorization	OR	List B Identity	AND	List C Employment Authorization
Document Title		Document Title		Document Title
Issuing Authority		Issuing Authority		Issuing Authority
Document Number		Document Number		Document Number
Expiration Date (if any)(mm/dd/yyyy)		Expiration Date (if any)(mm/dd/yyyy)		Expiration Date (if any)(mm/dd/yyyy)
Document Title				
Issuing Authority		Additional Information		QR Code - Sections 2 & 3 Do Not Write In This Space
Document Number				
Expiration Date (if any)(mm/dd/yyyy)				
Document Title				
Issuing Authority				
Document Number				
Expiration Date (if any)(mm/dd/yyyy)				

Certification: I attest, under penalty of perjury, that (1) I have examined the document(s) presented by the above-named employee, (2) the above-listed document(s) appear to be genuine and to relate to the employee named, and (3) to the best of my knowledge the employee is authorized to work in the United States.

The employee's first day of employment *(mm/dd/yyyy)*: _____ *(See instructions for exemptions)*

Signature of Employer or Authorized Representative	Today's Date (mm/dd/yyyy)	Title of Employer or Authorized Representative	
Last Name of Employer or Authorized Representative	First Name of Employer or Authorized Representative	Employer's Business or Organization Name	
Employer's Business or Organization Address (Street Number and Name)	City or Town	State	ZIP Code

While completing *Section 2*, the employer should be mindful of the following:

- Complete the List A column or the List B and C columns only, based on employee-submitted documents. Although you may photocopy documents (in which case, you must do so for all employees), you must complete this section.

- Some acceptable documents for List A are combination documents (such as a foreign passport and Form I-94), which necessitates recording the information for each document.

- Certification section: The individual reviewing documents on behalf of the employer must complete and sign the certification.

- The IRS provides multiple versions of Form I-9. Depending on the version you use, some items within this section may be populated by "N/A" by default. If so, these entries are replaced when data is entered.

Section 3 of Form I-9 is completed by the employer only in certain circumstances.

Section 3. Reverification and Rehires *(To be completed and signed by employer or authorized representative.)*			
A. New Name *(if applicable)*			**B.** Date of Rehire *(if applicable)*
Last Name *(Family Name)*	First Name *(Given Name)*	Middle Initial	Date *(mm/dd/yyyy)*
C. If the employee's previous grant of employment authorization has expired, provide the information for the document or receipt that establishes continuing employment authorization in the space provided below.			
Document Title		Document Number	Expiration Date *(if any) (mm/dd/yyyy)*
I attest, under penalty of perjury, that to the best of my knowledge, this employee is authorized to work in the United States, and if the employee presented document(s), the document(s) I have examined appear to be genuine and to relate to the individual.			
Signature of Employer or Authorized Representative	Today's Date *(mm/dd/yyyy)*	Name of Employer or Authorized Representative	

Form I-9 07/17/17 N   Page 2 of 3

If *Section 3* must be completed, the employer should be mindful of the following:

- New Name and Date of Rehire: Leave these sections blank if not applicable.

- Date of Rehire: This section is applicable only if the employee is rehired within three years of completing the original I-9 and if the information on the original form remains valid.

- Document Section: List B documents never require reverification. Complete this section based on the employee's List A or List C document if either reverification is necessary (previously submitted document has expired) or the employee is rehired within three years of completing the original I-9 and a previously submitted document has expired.

- Signature Line: If Section 3 is completed, it must be signed and dated by the individual completing the section on behalf of the employer.

TIP! The "Handbook for Employers," which may be found at uscis.gov/i-9-central/handbook -employers-m-274, provides further guidance on the completion of Form I-9.

E-Verify

Most employers are not required to use the online E-Verify system, which enables employers to verify employment eligibility quickly, securely, and accurately. However, using this free system offered by the federal government can provide reassurance that employees are eligible to work in the United States.

The system operates by comparing information provided by the employee with information contained in records from both the Social Security Administration and the United States Department of Homeland Security. While matching information typically results in an "Employment Authorized" response, any discrepancies result in a "Tentative Nonconfirmation (TNC)." When a TNC response is received, the employee is given an opportunity to resolve the discrepancy.

WARNING! Receiving a Tentative Nonconfirmation does not necessarily mean that an employee is unauthorized to work. A variety of reasons (such as accidentally including incorrect information on Form I-9) can result in a TNC for an eligible employee. The employee has eight workdays to take action to correct the TNC.

| Case in Point 1-5 | Complete Form I-9 |

In this example, we will complete Sections 1 and 2 of Form I-9 based on the information provided below:

1. Warren Franklin (SSN 901-23-4444) has requested assistance in completing the employee portion of Form I-9. Warren was born on April 2, 1981, is a United States citizen, and (although you are providing him with assistance) completes the employee section of Form I-9 himself on his first day of employment (7/15/2019). He lives at 212 Steeple Place, Madison, WI 53704.

Employment Eligibility Verification
Department of Homeland Security
U.S. Citizenship and Immigration Services

USCIS
Form I-9
OMB No. 1615-0047
Expires 08/31/2019

▶**START HERE:** Read instructions carefully before completing this form. The instructions must be available, either in paper or electronically, during completion of this form. Employers are liable for errors in the completion of this form.

ANTI-DISCRIMINATION NOTICE: It is illegal to discriminate against work-authorized individuals. Employers **CANNOT** specify which document(s) an employee may present to establish employment authorization and identity. The refusal to hire or continue to employ an individual because the documentation presented has a future expiration date may also constitute illegal discrimination.

Section 1. Employee Information and Attestation *(Employees must complete and sign Section 1 of Form I-9 no later than the **first day of employment**, but not before accepting a job offer.)*

Last Name *(Family Name)*	First Name *(Given Name)*	Middle Initial	Other Last Names Used *(if any)*		
Franklin	Warren				

Address *(Street Number and Name)*	Apt. Number	City or Town	State	ZIP Code
212 Steeple Place		Madison	WI	53704

Date of Birth *(mm/dd/yyyy)*	U.S. Social Security Number	Employee's E-mail Address	Employee's Telephone Number
04/02/1981	9 0 1 - 2 3 - 4 4 4 4	N/A	N/A

I am aware that federal law provides for imprisonment and/or fines for false statements or use of false documents in connection with the completion of this form.

I attest, under penalty of perjury, that I am (check one of the following boxes):

☒ 1. A citizen of the United States

☐ 2. A noncitizen national of the United States *(See instructions)*

☐ 3. A lawful permanent resident   (Alien Registration Number/USCIS Number): N/A

☐ 4. An alien authorized to work   until (expiration date, if applicable, mm/dd/yyyy): N/A
     Some aliens may write "N/A" in the expiration date field. *(See instructions)*

Aliens authorized to work must provide only one of the following document numbers to complete Form I-9:
An Alien Registration Number/USCIS Number OR Form I-94 Admission Number OR Foreign Passport Number.

1. Alien Registration Number/USCIS Number: N/A

OR

2. Form I-94 Admission Number: N/A

OR

3. Foreign Passport Number: N/A

   Country of Issuance: N/A

QR Code - Section 1
Do Not Write In This Space

Signature of Employee	Today's Date *(mm/dd/yyyy)*
Warren Franklin	07/15/2019

Preparer and/or Translator Certification (check one):

☒ I did not use a preparer or translator.   ☐ A preparer(s) and/or translator(s) assisted the employee in completing Section 1.
(Fields below must be completed and signed when preparers and/or translators assist an employee in completing Section 1.)

I attest, under penalty of perjury, that I have assisted in the completion of Section 1 of this form and that to the best of my knowledge the information is true and correct.

Signature of Preparer or Translator	Today's Date *(mm/dd/yyyy)*

Last Name *(Family Name)*	First Name *(Given Name)*		

Address *(Street Number and Name)*	City or Town	State	ZIP Code

🛑 *Employer Completes Next Page* 🛑

Form I-9 07/17/17 N   Page 1 of 3

2. Warren's employer (Chapman Industries; 91784 Buttress Court, Madison, WI 53704) uses the E-Verify system to determine employment eligibility. Warren provides his U.S. passport (issued by the U.S. Department of State, #000022222, expires 03/13/2023) to his employer (Dexter Hall, President), who completes the form on Warren's first day of employment.

		USCIS
Employment Eligibility Verification		**Form I-9**
Department of Homeland Security		OMB No. 1615-0047
U.S. Citizenship and Immigration Services		Expires 08/31/2019

Section 2. Employer or Authorized Representative Review and Verification

(Employers or their authorized representative must complete and sign Section 2 within 3 business days of the employee's first day of employment. You must physically examine one document from List A OR a combination of one document from List B and one document from List C as listed on the "Lists of Acceptable Documents.")

Employee Info from Section 1	Last Name *(Family Name)*	First Name *(Given Name)*	M.I.	Citizenship/Immigration Status
	Franklin	Warren		1

List A OR	List B AND	List C
Identity and Employment Authorization	**Identity**	**Employment Authorization**

List A	List B	List C
Document Title U.S. Passport	Document Title N/A	Document Title N/A
Issuing Authority U.S. Department of State	Issuing Authority N/A	Issuing Authority N/A
Document Number 000022222	Document Number N/A	Document Number N/A
Expiration Date *(if any)(mm/dd/yyyy)* 03/13/2023	Expiration Date *(if any)(mm/dd/yyyy)* N/A	Expiration Date *(if any)(mm/dd/yyyy)* N/A
Document Title N/A		
Issuing Authority N/A	Additional Information	QR Code - Sections 2 & 3 Do Not Write In This Space
Document Number N/A		
Expiration Date *(if any)(mm/dd/yyyy)* N/A		
Document Title N/A		
Issuing Authority N/A		
Document Number N/A		
Expiration Date *(if any)(mm/dd/yyyy)* N/A		

Certification: I attest, under penalty of perjury, that (1) I have examined the document(s) presented by the above-named employee, (2) the above-listed document(s) appear to be genuine and to relate to the employee named, and (3) to the best of my knowledge the employee is authorized to work in the United States.

The employee's first day of employment *(mm/dd/yyyy):* 07/15/2019 *(See instructions for exemptions)*

Signature of Employer or Authorized Representative *Dexter Hall*	Today's Date *(mm/dd/yyyy)* 07/15/2019	Title of Employer or Authorized Representative President
Last Name of Employer or Authorized Representative Hall	First Name of Employer or Authorized Representative Dexter	Employer's Business or Organization Name Chapman Industries

Employer's Business or Organization Address (Street Number and Name) 91784 Buttress Court	City or Town Madison	State WI	ZIP Code 53704

Section 3. Reverification and Rehires *(To be completed and signed by employer or authorized representative.)*

A. New Name *(if applicable)*			B. Date of Rehire *(if applicable)*
Last Name *(Family Name)*	First Name *(Given Name)*	Middle Initial	Date *(mm/dd/yyyy)*

C. If the employee's previous grant of employment authorization has expired, provide the information for the document or receipt that establishes continuing employment authorization in the space provided below.

Document Title	Document Number	Expiration Date *(if any) (mm/dd/yyyy)*

I attest, under penalty of perjury, that to the best of my knowledge, this employee is authorized to work in the United States, and if the employee presented document(s), the document(s) I have examined appear to be genuine and to relate to the individual.

Signature of Employer or Authorized Representative	Today's Date *(mm/dd/yyyy)*	Name of Employer or Authorized Representative

Form I-9 07/17/17 N

General Payroll Topics

Additional considerations must be made prior to, or concurrent with, the hiring of employees. Among these are the acquisition of workers' compensation insurance and the establishment of an employee earnings record for each employee. Other payroll topics that warrant consideration include the decision to use a payroll services provider, or whether a payroll professional should pursue a specialized payroll certification.

Workers' Compensation Insurance

On the Web

dol.gov/owcp/dfec/regs
/compliance/wc.htm

Most businesses are required by their state to obtain **workers' compensation** insurance, which provides financial assistance to employees injured during the course of their employment. In most instances, employers may satisfy this requirement either by purchasing it from a state-operated fund or private insurance carrier, or by becoming authorized by the state to be self-insured.

Insurance premiums paid by employers are based on the relative risk associated with different job types. For example, the premium required for an employee working in an office setting is far less than that required for an employee who chops down trees. Depending on the state, benefits that employees receive are used to pay medical bills, make up for lost wages, compensate for permanent injury, and/or provide an employee's beneficiaries with a death benefit.

Payroll Certifications

For those who pursue a career in payroll, obtaining a professional certification can lead to enhanced job opportunities as well as to promotions. The American Payroll Association offers payroll professionals the opportunity to earn two different professional certifications:

- The Fundamental Payroll Certification (FPC) establishes that an individual has a baseline level of payroll competency. This is the lower-level certification offered by the American Payroll Association.

- The Certified Payroll Professional (CPP) designates a higher level of payroll mastery, and the examination can be taken only upon the satisfaction of specific criteria. These criteria involve both the length of time worked in the payroll profession and the payroll courses completed.

Utilizing a Payroll Service

As you'll discover throughout this textbook, payroll can be a complicated topic. While it's possible for a business to handle all of its payroll-related tasks, many instead choose to hire a **payroll service**. These services (some of the most prominent include Paychex and Intuit) can calculate employee net pay; generate employee paychecks; complete and file all monthly, quarterly, and annual payroll tax forms; and provide many additional services. Given the potential penalties associated with mishandling payroll (which can be levied at both the federal and state levels), and the amount of time spent on payroll tasks, many companies decide that a payroll service is worth the added expense.

Employee Earnings Record

An **employee earnings record** should be established upon the hiring of each employee. This record contains both key employee information (name, Social Security number, marital status, etc.) and payroll information for a given year. By providing a summary of annual payroll figures for a single employee, the employee earnings record facilitates completion of a variety of payroll tax forms.

Most businesses use computerized payroll systems, which automatically generate these records. However, understanding the components of the employee earnings record, and the manner in which it is generated, is vital. Therefore, we'll work with manual versions of the employee earnings record throughout multiple chapters.

An employee earnings record displays a summary of payroll information for a single employee.

Employee Earnings Record

Name	_____	Marital Status	_____
Address	_____	Fed. Withholding Allow.	_____
	_____	State Withholding Allow.	_____
SS#	_____		

	Earnings							Deductions									
Pay Period Ending	Regular Hours Worked	Regular Pay Rate	Regular Wages	Overtime Hours Worked	Overtime Pay Rate	Overtime Wages	Gross Pay	Federal Withholding Tax	State Withholding Tax	Social Security Tax	Medicare Tax	Retirement Contribution	Life Insurance	Charitable Contribution	Additional Withholding	Check Number	Net Pay

Case in Point 1-6   # Create an Employee Earnings Record

In this example, we will establish an employee earnings record for Stacey Rodriguez, a newly hired employee of Acme Safe Co. Stacey (SSN 333-44-5555) is single; lives at 1986 Series Drive, Reno, NV 89509; and claims one allowance for both her federal and state taxes. She has agreed to a regular wage rate of $9.25/hour and an overtime wage rate of $13.88, both of which will initially be applied to her first week of employment, ending on 7/19/2019.

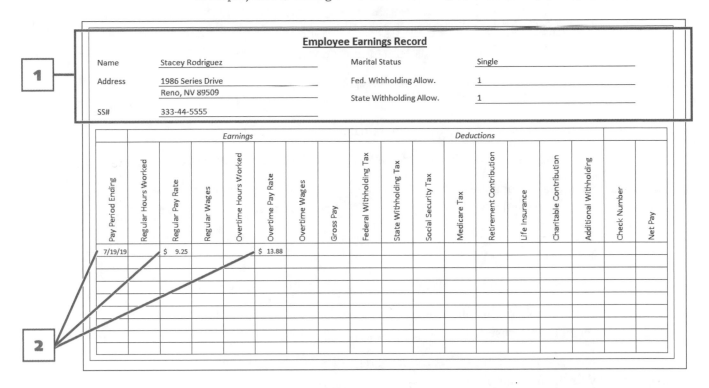

1. Complete the top portion of the employee earnings record. This section is unlikely to change frequently and therefore does not need to be listed for every pay period.

2. Fill in those items for the first pay period that have already been determined. The majority of columns, such as Regular Hours Worked and Social Security Tax, are left blank. These items cannot be determined until after the first pay period has ended (i.e., after 7/19/2019).

Self-Assessment

Complete the Self-Assessment as directed by your instructor, whether that is in the book or your eLab course, if applicable.

True/False Questions

1. An employee's paycheck displays the gross pay amount.   *True   False*

2. Certain employees are not subject to the federal minimum wage of $7.25.   *True   False*

3. The federal minimum wage rate takes precedence, regardless of whether it is the same as the applicable state minimum wage rate.   *True   False*

4. The Internal Revenue Service charges users a nominal fee for Circular E.   *True   False*

5. Form SS-4 is used by an employer to apply for an Employer Identification Number.   *True   False*

6. The provisions of the Personal Responsibility and Work Opportunity Reconciliation Act can be satisfied through the submission of the W-4 Form to the state.   *True   False*

7. Form SS-5 (Application for a Social Security Card) should be submitted to the employee's local Social Security office.   *True   False*

8. Form I-9 (Employment Eligibility Verification) is completed entirely by the employer.   *True   False*

9. E-Verify is an online system that allows employers to verify a prospective employee's employment eligibility status.   *True   False*

10. Workers' compensation insurance costs the same regardless of the type of work performed by the insured employees.   *True   False*

Multiple Choice Questions

11. Which of the following cannot be found on a standard paystub?
    A. Employee address
    B. Prior year's gross wages
    C. Overtime hours worked (if any)
    D. Pay date

12. Which of the following groups may not be paid less than the federal minimum wage?
    A. Tipped employees
    B. Full-time students
    C. State government workers
    D. Executive employees

13. The Fair Labor Standards Act requires that, for non-exempt employees, the overtime hourly pay rate be at least what percentage of the regular hourly pay rate?
    A. 75%
    B. 100%
    C. 150%
    D. 200%

14. Which of the following jobs may be held by an individual younger than 18 years of age?
    A. Roofer
    B. Explosives manufacturer
    C. Coal miner
    D. Landscaper (bagging leaves)

15. The Personal Responsibility and Work Opportunity Reconciliation Act (PRWORA) was designed to strengthen what?
    A. Child support programs
    B. Workers' compensation coverage
    C. Federal minimum wage rates
    D. Immigration law

16. Which of the following is not requested on Form SS-5?
    A. Father's Social Security number
    B. Ethnicity
    C. Number of allowances
    D. Place of birth

17. The Immigration Reform and Control Act (IRCA) was signed into law in what year?
    A. 1960
    B. 1974
    C. 1986
    D. 1990

18. Which of the following is insufficient for the purposes of verifying employment eligibility on Form I-9?
    A. Driver's license and Native American tribal document
    B. Voter's registration card and U.S. Coast Guard Merchant Mariner card
    C. Military dependent's ID card and an unrestricted Social Security card
    D. United States passport

19. The workers' compensation insurance requirement may typically be satisfied through all of the following methods except:
    A. Submitting applicable state forms verifying that all full-time employees have approved an uninsured status.
    B. Becoming authorized by the applicable state to be self-insured.
    C. Purchasing workers' compensation insurance from a state-operated fund.
    D. Purchasing workers' compensation insurance from a private insurance carrier.

20. An employee earnings record typically displays each of the following except?
    A. State withholding allowances
    B. Employee signature
    C. Overtime pay rate
    D. Marital status

Practice Set A

The IRS forms and Excel templates needed for these assignments are included in the Student Exercise Files download for this course. If directed to do so, complete these assignments in Homework Grader.

PSa 1-1 Define Paystub Elements

Define the following items found within a typical paystub:

1. Paycheck
2. Gross pay
3. Deductions
4. Net pay

PSa 1-2 Identify Compliance with the Fair Labor Standards Act

Examine the following independent circumstances and identify whether each complies with the Fair Labor Standards Act:

1. A hospital employee is paid $6.95/hour.

2. A full-time student who works for a local college earns $7.20/hour for working four hours/day, four days/week, during the school year.

3. An administrative (office) employee earns an annual salary which, when divided by total hours worked during the year, is the equivalent of $6.68/hour.

4. An employee at a local bakery begins working on June 1. He turns 20 on October 14 and earns $4.25/hour during his first six months of employment.

5. A student learner in a qualified vocational program earns $5.50/hour. The employer has not yet applied for an authorizing certificate.

6. A federal government employee earns $7.48/hour.

PSa 1-3 Use the Internet to Explore Circular E

Examine Circular E to answer a series of questions. (Recall that Circular E is found at: irs.gov/pub/irs-pdf /p15.pdf.)

1. How long should an employer retain records of employment taxes?

2. What form should be both furnished to employees and filed with the IRS by January 31 each year?

3. Define the term *payroll period*.

4. Must income tax withholding be handled differently for part-time workers than for full-time workers?

5. If payday falls on a Friday for a semiweekly depositor of Social Security, Medicare, and withheld income taxes, by what day of the following week must taxes be deposited?

PSa 1-4 Complete Form SS-4

Complete Form SS-4 for a newly formed company.

1. Adam's Diner is a new eatery that was formed as a sole proprietorship by its owner, Adam Spruce (SSN 777-77-7777), on January 21, 2019, and serves only locally sourced foods. As a result of having started a new business, the company files Form SS-4 so that it may begin distributing payroll checks as of January 25, 2019. The diner is located at 95 Main Street, Atlanta, GA 30311 (it is in Fulton County and is the only address associated with the business), and both its telephone and fax number are 478-555-8129. The company uses the calendar year as its fiscal year and expects to employ four people (earning an average of $19,900/year) throughout the first 12 months of operations. Payroll is to be paid weekly on Fridays, with the first pay date scheduled for Friday, January 25, 2019. Form SS-4 is completed on the date of formation of the company. The company does not assign a third-party designee.

PSa 1-5 Complete Form W-4

Assist a friend in completing Form W-4. As part of this process, you will also assist him in completing the Personal Allowances Worksheet.

1. David Valentine (SSN 888-88-8888) is single; lives at 752 Amusement Court, St. Louis, MO 63108; does not want any additional withholding amounts; and is not exempt from federal income tax withholding. David has no children or dependents, does not hold any other jobs, does not take advantage of any credits on his tax return, and files as single on his tax return. Note that this Form W-4 is not being sent to the IRS.

PSa 1-6 Complete Form I-9

Complete both Sections 1 and 2 of Form I-9.

1. Thomas Quinn (SSN 999-99-9999) has requested assistance in completing the employee portion of Form I-9. Thomas was born on November 13, 1972, is a United States citizen, and (although you are providing him with assistance) completes the employee section of Form I-9 himself on his first day of employment (7/15/2019). He lives at 950 Harvard Place, Newport, RI 02840.

2. Thomas's employer (Carpet Warehouse; 8114 Princeton Avenue, Newport, RI 02840) utilizes the E-Verify system to determine employment eligibility. Thomas provides his U.S. passport (issued by U.S. Department of State, #000055555, expires 8/11/2025) to his employer (Barry Coleman, HR Manager), who completes the form on Thomas's first day of employment.

PSa 1-7 Create an Employee Earnings Record

Create an employee earnings record for a new employee.

1. Patrick Workman (SSN 123-45-6789) begins working for Fishing Experts Co. on Monday, 6/17/2019. He lives at 817 Remote Lane, Bentonville, AR 72712; is single; and claims two federal and two state withholding allowances. He earns $9.00/hour in regular wages and $13.50/hour in overtime wages, and payroll is paid every Monday for the weekly pay period ending the previous Friday.

Practice Set B

The IRS forms and Excel templates needed for these assignments are included in the Student Exercise Files download for this course. If directed to do so, complete these assignments in Homework Grader.

PSb 1-1 Identify the Appropriate Paystub Section

Identify the standard paystub section (Company and Pay Period Information, Employee Information, Current and Year-to-Date Earnings, Amounts Withheld [Deducted] from Employee Pay, Paycheck, or Net Pay) that corresponds to each item below. Note that a paystub section may contain more than one of the items listed.

1. Overtime hours worked

2. Period ending date

3. Marital status

4. Gross pay

5. Social Security tax amount

6. Check number

7. Federal income tax amount

PSb 1-2 Determine Compliance with Child Labor Restrictions

Determine the youngest age (if any) at which an employee may perform each of the job duties below:

1. Milking cows on a parent's farm.

2. Taking measurements for roof construction.

3. Working as a teller at a grocery store on Monday, Tuesday, and Wednesday from 4:00 p.m. to 7:00 p.m.

4. Performing as lead actor in a local play.

5. Stocking shelves at a convenience store during the school year on Saturday and Sunday from 6:00 a.m. to 3:00 p.m.

PSb 1-3 Use the Internet to Explore Circular E

Examine Circular E to answer the following questions. (Recall that Circular E is found at: irs.gov/pub/irs-pdf/p15.pdf.)

1. What phone number may an individual with disabilities call in order to ask a federal tax question?

2. If a husband and wife jointly run a business, is it treated as a sole proprietorship, partnership, or corporation for tax purposes?

3. If wages are not paid in money (cash or check), is an employer obligated to remit federal income tax withholding, Social Security, Medicare, and FUTA taxes based on these wages?

4. Identify three examples of fringe benefits provided to employees that are not taxable.

5. May an employer substitute their own version of Form W-4 for the IRS-published version? If so, are there any restrictions on this policy?

PSb 1-4 Complete Form SS-4

Complete Form SS-4 for an insurance agency.

1. Local Insurance Corp. is an agency that was formed as a corporation by its founder, Jane Detworth (SSN 111-11-1111), on May 1, 2019, and operates under the name JD Insurance. The company specializes in homeowner's insurance, and as a result of having started the new business, it files Form SS-4 so that it may begin distributing payroll checks as of May 31, 2019. It is located at 2 State Avenue, Tuscaloosa, AL 35405 (it is in Tuscaloosa County and is the only address associated with the business). It was incorporated in the state of Alabama. The company will file Form 1120S each year. Its telephone number is 205-555-9991, and its fax is 205-555-8000. The fiscal year runs from May through April, and it expects to employ three people (each earning an average of $30,000/year) throughout the first 12 months of operations. Payroll is to be paid semimonthly on the 15th and on the final day of the month, with the first pay date scheduled for Friday, May 31, 2019. Form SS-4 is completed on the date of formation of the company. The company does not assign a third-party designee.

PSb 1-5 Complete Form W-4

Assist a friend in completing Form W-4. As part of this process, you will also assist him in completing the Personal Allowances Worksheet.

1. Billy Darling (SSN 343-43-4343) is single; lives at 40 Tabasco Lane, Minneapolis, MN 55423; and is not exempt from federal income tax withholding. Billy files as single on his tax return, does not take advantage of any credits on his tax return, has one job, and has no children or dependents. Note that this Form W-4 is not being sent to the IRS.

PSb 1-6 Complete Form I-9

Complete both Section 1 and Section 2 of Form I-9.

1. Alan Strawberry (SSN 111-11-1111) has requested assistance in completing the employee portion of Form I-9. Alan was born on January 4, 1965, is a Lawful Permanent Resident (USCIS #555-555-555), and (although you are providing him with assistance) completes the employee section of Form I-9 himself on his first day of employment (8/26/2019). He lives at 214 Indian Lane, Billings, MT 59107.

2. Alan's employer (Uniform Specialists; 12 Pent Drive, Billings, MT 59107) utilizes the E-Verify system to determine employment eligibility. Alan provides his Permanent Resident Card (issued by U.S. Citizenship and Immigration Services, expires 11/28/2021) to his employer (Joel Weiner, Director of Personnel), who completes the form on Alan's first day of employment. The document number displayed on the Permanent Resident Card is #xyz5555544444.

PSb 1-7 Complete an Employee Earnings Record

Create an employee earnings record for a new employee.

1. Brian Price (SSN 252-52-5252) begins working for Costume Creativity on 12/11/2019. He lives at 8888 Searcher Boulevard, Wheeling, WV 26003; is married; and claims three federal withholding allowances and two state withholding allowances. He earns $12.50/hour in regular wages and $18.75/hour in overtime wages, and payroll is paid twice/month, on the 15th day and final day of the month for the pay period ending that day.

Continuing Payroll Problem

The IRS forms and Excel templates needed for these assignments are included in the Student Exercise Files download for this course. If directed to do so, complete these assignments in Homework Grader.

CPP 1-1 Start a New Business and Assist a New Employee

Complete Form SS-4 for TCLH Industries, a manufacturer of cleaning products. You will then work with Zachary Fox, a new employee, to ensure that all necessary payroll forms are completed.

1. Complete Form SS-4 for TCLH Industries. The company was formed on January 1, 2019, as a corporation (which files Form 1120S and was incorporated in North Carolina) by Michael Sierra (CEO; SSN 232-32-3232) and David Alexander (President; SSN 454-54-5454). Day-to-day operations, such as the filing and signing of federal and state forms, are handled by the CEO, whose phone number and fax number are 919-555-7485 and 919-555-2000, respectively. The company is located at 202 Whitmore Avenue, Durham, NC 27701 (in Durham County), where it receives all mail. The company uses the calendar year as its fiscal year, and expects to employ four individuals (earning an expected average of $90,000/year) throughout the first 18 months of operations. Payroll is to be paid weekly on Thursdays, with the first pay date scheduled for Thursday, January 10, 2019 (for the one-week period ending the prior Sunday). The company does not assign a third-party designee.

2. Complete the W-4 Form for Zachary Fox, a new employee who is hired on December 9, 2019. Zachary (SSN 121-21-2121) is married (and files as married filing jointly); lives at 1483 Independence Road, Durham, NC 27701; does not want any additional withholding amounts; and is not exempt from federal income tax withholding. Zachary (who expects to earn approximately $67,000 this year) has one child, does not hold any other jobs, and his spouse earns $68,200/year. He does not file as head of household and does not have other dependents or other credits. Note that this Form W-4 is not being sent to the IRS and that to accurately complete Form W-4, you should first fill out the Personal Allowances Worksheet.

3. Complete the I-9 Form for Zachary Fox (SSN 121-21-2121), a new employee who lives at 1483 Independence Road, Durham, NC 27701. He requests assistance in completing the employee portion of the form. Zachary was born on February 27, 1977, is a United States citizen, and (although you are providing him with assistance) completes the employee section of Form I-9 himself on his date of hire. TCLH Industries, which is located at 202 Whitmore Avenue, Durham, NC 27701, utilizes the E-Verify system to confirm employment eligibility. Zachary provides his driver's license number (NYS, 888 888 888, expires 2/27/2023) and Social Security card (issued by the Social Security Administration) to his employer, who completes the form on Zachary's date of hire (December 9, 2019). All forms are signed by the CEO of the company, Michael Sierra.

4. Establish an employee earnings record for Zachary Fox (SSN 121-21-2121), beginning with the first pay period after his date of hire (12/9/2019). Zachary, who lives at 1483 Independence Road, Durham, NC 27701, claims the same number of federal and state withholding allowances, earns regular wages of $28/hour, and earns overtime wages of $42/hour. Each weekly pay period of TCLH Industries runs from Monday through Sunday.

Critical Thinking

CT 1-1 Examine the E-Verify System

The E-Verify system, although not mandatory for most employers, is an important tool that should be utilized regularly. For this system to yield beneficial results, the employer must fully understand how it functions. In this exercise, you will study and report on the functionality of the E-Verify system.

Open a new Microsoft Word document (or use a comparable document program) and save the file as **PA01-CT1 -[Your Last Name]-E-Verify**. Use the Internet to research the E-Verify process (hint: The E-Verify system is on the United States Citizenship and Immigration Services website). Write at least three paragraphs in which you discuss the E-Verify enrollment process, the E-Verify verification process, and the steps an employee should take in the event of a Tentative Nonconfirmation.

Submit your final file based on the guidelines provided by your instructor.

CT 1-2 Research Major Payroll Services

Understanding the differences between available payroll services can allow an organization to select the service that is most suitable for its needs. In this exercise, you will research four major payroll services and list two benefits of utilizing each.

Open a new Microsoft Word document (or use a comparable document program) and save the file as **PA01-CT2 -[Your Last Name]-PayrollService**. Use the Internet to identify major payroll services, and select four of the most prominent. Research the services provided by each, and write at least one paragraph for each in which you identify two ways that the payroll service distinguishes itself from its competitors. Lastly, write one paragraph in which, based on these characteristics, you select your preferred payroll service and discuss why you made this selection.

Submit your final file based on the guidelines provided by your instructor.

Calculating Employee Pay

When calculating employee pay, a number of considerations must be taken into account. Primarily, the job duties determine the most appropriate method for calculating employee pay. In this chapter, you will first examine the distinction between salaries and wages. You will also consider a number of additional types of pay, as well as methods for determining each. Lastly, you will practice entering employee pay data within both the employee earnings record and the payroll register.

 Videos available! Check out the Video Launch Pad in your student exercise file download to access videos associated with this chapter. One video presents a chapter overview, and the other provides more detail on a key chapter topic.

CASE STUDY

Calculating Employee Pay for Lucky Ties Apparel

Lucky Ties Apparel employs a number of people who occupy different positions, and thus uses a variety of compensation methods. Some employees are paid on an hourly basis, while others have agreed to annual pay. The company is considering allowing employees who work on the sales floor the opportunity to earn commissions in addition to their hourly pay, in which case a few managers would be eligible for bonuses based on the store's overall performance.

Having recently taken over all payroll responsibilities, you want to be certain that you fully comprehend not only how to calculate the various types of compensation, but also the regulations relating to each. You decide to review the process underlying all of the store's payroll calculations and to examine the store's payroll-recording process.

A variety of components are used to calculate an employee's gross pay.

MY CONSTRUCTION COMPANY
1001 Fifth Avenue
New York, NY 10022

Check Number:	000001
Pay date:	12/10/2019
Social Security No.	***-**-1119

Pay to the order of: CLARK MITCHELL

This amount: FIVE HUNDRED ELEVEN AND 82/100 DOLLARS $511.82

AUTHORIZED SIGNATURE
VOID AFTER 60 DAYS

⑆000001⑆ ⑈827619578⑈ 6004256001⑈

MY CONSTRUCTION COMPANY
1001 Fifth Avenue
New York, NY 10022

Period ending: 12/8/2019
Pay date: 12/10/2019

CLARK MITCHELL
547 Smith Street
New York, NY 10033

Earnings	Rate	Hours	This Period	Year to Date
Regular	$14.00	40.00	$560.00	$28,000.00
Overtime	$21.00	4.00	$84.00	$6,615.00
Holiday	$30.00	0.00	$0.00	$2,250.00
Gross Pay			$644.00	$36,865.00

Deductions		
Statutory	This Period	Year to Date
Federal Income Tax	$19.00	$1,350.00
Social Security Tax	$39.93	$2,285.63
Medicare Tax	$9.34	$534.54
NYS Income Tax	$12.67	$783.33
NYC Income Tax	$8.44	$472.22
NYSDI Tax	$0.60	$30.00
Other		
401(k)	$32.20*	$1,843.25
Life Insurance	$10.00	$500.00
Net Pay	$511.82	

* Excluded from federal taxable wages

Social Security Number: ***-**-1119
Taxable Marital Status: Married
Exemptions/Allowances:
Federal: 4, $25 Additional Tax
State: 3
Local: 3

Other Benefits and Information	This Period	Year to Date
Vacation Hrs.		64.00
Sick Hrs.		24.00

Pay Periods and Workweeks

Employees are paid periodically throughout the year. The necessary payroll calculations are based on consistent definitions of the **pay period** and workweek for each employee. Understanding these terms enables an employee to verify the accuracy of a paycheck.

Pay Period Options

Employers can choose to pay employees on any of a number of different schedules. The most common options are weekly, biweekly, semimonthly, and monthly.

Pay Period Definitions

Pay Period Type	Frequency of Pay Dates
Weekly	Pay dates occur once per week, on the same day of the week
Biweekly	Pay dates occur once every other week, on the same day of the week
Semimonthly	Pay dates occur twice per month, typically at the midpoint and on the final day of each month
Monthly	Pay dates occur once per month, typically on the same date each month

This weekly pay period runs from Monday through Sunday.

July 2019						
Sun.	Mon.	Tues.	Wed.	Thurs.	Fri.	Sat.
	1	2	3	4	5	6
7	8	9	10	11	12	13
14	15	16	17	18	19	20
21	22	23	24	25	26	27
28	29	30	31			

This biweekly pay period covers the equivalent of two consecutive weekly periods.

July 2019						
Sun.	Mon.	Tues.	Wed.	Thurs.	Fri.	Sat.
	1	2	3	4	5	6
7	8	9	10	11	12	13
14	15	16	17	18	19	20
21	22	23	24	25	26	27
28	29	30	31			

This semimonthly pay period covers the first half of a month; the subsequent pay period covers the second half of the same month.

July 2019						
Sun.	Mon.	Tues.	Wed.	Thurs.	Fri.	Sat.
	1	2	3	4	5	6
7	8	9	10	11	12	13
14	15	16	17	18	19	20
21	22	23	24	25	26	27
28	29	30	31			

This monthly pay period covers a full month, regardless of the days on which it begins and ends.

July 2019						
Sun.	Mon.	Tues.	Wed.	Thurs.	Fri.	Sat.
	1	2	3	4	5	6
7	8	9	10	11	12	13
14	15	16	17	18	19	20
21	22	23	24	25	26	27
28	29	30	31			

Payroll processing can be time consuming, particularly if employees are paid on an hourly basis. In many instances, when employees are paid on any of the above schedules, they are not being paid for the most recent week(s). Therefore, it is common for a lag to exist between the dates during which employees earn their pay, and the date on which they receive a paycheck.

For example, a weekly schedule could call for employees to be paid every Friday. If employees earn a total of $1,000 from Monday (4/8) through Friday (4/12), they would not receive the $1,000 until the following Friday (4/19). The check they receive on Friday, 4/12, would compensate them for the time that they worked during the prior week (Monday, 4/1, through Friday, 4/5).

TIP!   In some states laws have been enacted that require certain classes of employees to be paid on a specific basis. For example, New York State Labor Law Section 191 dictates that manual workers are to be paid weekly. Employers must be careful to comply with all such applicable regulations.

Defining the Workweek

As mentioned in Chapter 1, a workweek, as defined in the Fair Labor Standards Act (FLSA), is any consecutive seven-day period. It can differ from a calendar week (it does not need to run from Sunday through Saturday), and can begin at any hour. For example, an acceptable workweek could begin at 8:00 a.m. on Tuesday and run through the following Tuesday at 7:59 a.m.

It is important that a business clearly define its workweek so that payroll is properly calculated. For example, if an employee receives overtime pay for any hours worked after the first 40 in a given week, there must be a clear beginning and end to the workweek so that overtime hours are accurately determined.

WARNING!   The workweek must be consistent from one week to another. It may be altered only if the change is intended to be permanent, and if it is not made in order to circumvent overtime requirements.

Case in Point 2-1	**Evaluate Pay Periods and Workweeks**

In these examples, we will review a number of pay periods and determine whether certain specified workweeks are acceptable under the FLSA:

1. Jason Ivory receives two paychecks every month, each of which compensates him for half of the current month. What type of pay period is Jason's employer utilizing?

    This employer is compensating Jason on a semimonthly basis. This is the only pay period type under which an employee consistently receives two paychecks every month.

2. Lance Quigley receives 52 paychecks every year. What type of pay period is Lance's employer utilizing?

   This employer is compensating Lance on a weekly basis. As a result, Lance receives one paycheck for each of the 52 weeks in a given year.

3. Drew Graham began working for his employer on Monday, 9/2. He receives his first paycheck on Wednesday, 9/11, and his second paycheck on Wednesday, 9/25. The second paycheck was twice as large as the first, and every paycheck after the 9/25 check compensates Drew for the same period of time. What type of pay period is Drew's employer utilizing?

   This employer is compensating Drew on a biweekly basis. The 9/11 paycheck compensated Drew for his first week of employment (Monday, 9/2, through Friday, 9/6). The 9/25 paycheck compensated Drew for his second and third weeks of employment (Monday, 9/9, through Friday, 9/20). We know that Drew is not paid on a semimonthly basis because each paycheck compensates him for the same period of time. Because the number of days within each month differs, semimonthly paychecks do not all compensate employees for the same number of days.

4. Vincent Meacham's employer has traditionally utilized a workweek running from Monday morning through Sunday evening. During the summer months, the company experiences an increased workload over the weekends. Vincent's employer has decided to alter the workweek so that it begins on Saturday morning each week. The employer expects to return to the Monday through Sunday schedule at the end of the summer. Is Vincent's employer in violation of the Fair Labor Standards Act?

   Yes, the employer is in violation of the FLSA. While it is acceptable for an employer to change a workweek, there must be an expectation that the change is permanent. Temporary changes are not permissible under the FLSA.

5. Gino Lofton's employer pays employees on a biweekly basis. As a result, the employer defines a workweek as the two-week period running from Monday through the second Sunday of the period. Is Gino's employer in violation of the Fair Labor Standards Act?

   Yes, the employer is in violation of the FLSA. Regardless of the pay period in use, a workweek must be defined as a consistent seven-day period. Defining a workweek like this means that, regardless of the frequency of paychecks, a number of payroll-related items, such as overtime hours, are determined on a week-by-week basis.

Wage Determination Issues

When establishing the wage rate for an employee, several considerations should be made. An employer must ensure compliance with the Equal Pay Act. Additionally, in certain states there are mandated minimum wages that exceed the current federal minimum wage. Employers are required to pay employees no less than these higher state minimum wage rates. Lastly, employers must establish time cards for each employee, which may then be used to track all hours worked.

The Equal Pay Act of 1963 (EPA)

On the Web

eeoc.gov/laws/statutes/epa.cfm

The **Equal Pay Act of 1963 (EPA)** is one of the most prominent amendments to the Fair Labor Standards Act. It dictates that no employer may discriminate against any employee by paying a lower wage than is paid to an employee of the other gender for a similar job. While the Equal Pay Act prohibits discrimination against employees of either gender, it was enacted primarily to protect female employees.

WARNING! Employers cannot reduce the wage rate of any employee in an effort to comply with the Equal Pay Act. If a wage disparity exists, the lower wage must be increased so that it equals the higher wage.

According to the U.S. Department of Labor, in 1963 women earned, on average, 59 cents for every dollar earned by a man in a similar job. In 2013, 50 years after the enactment of the Equal Pay Act, this figure had risen to 81 cents. This statistic underscores the fact that gender-based wage discrimination is still prevalent today, and employers must be vigilant to ensure that it does not exist in their organizations.

The Equal Pay Act allows for a disparity in pay between employees of different genders under a small number of prescribed circumstances. These include the existence of:

- a seniority system
- a merit system
- a system based on quantity or quality of output produced
- any other non-gender-based system that results in a pay differential

State Minimum Wages

On the Web

dol.gov/whd/minwage
/america.htm

Under the FLSA, if an employee's state mandates a higher minimum wage than the current federal minimum wage of $7.25/hour, the employee is required to be paid at least the higher state rate. Such state minimum wages can be significantly higher than the federal minimum wage, as in Washington, where the state minimum wage is currently $12/hour.

NOTE! Some municipalities have enacted minimum wage rates that are higher than the applicable federal and state rates. For example, as of 7/1/2019 the San Francisco minimum wage was set at $15.59.

Time Cards

For employees who are paid on an hourly basis, an employee **time card** offers a method by which hours worked may be tracked. Since employee pay is often based on hours worked, this is a vital component of the payroll process.

This employee time card allows employees to enter hours worked for a one-week period.

Employee Time Card

Employee Name _____

Employee SS# _____

Day	Date	Morning		Afternoon		Daily Total
		Time In	Time Out	Time In	Time Out	
Monday						
Tuesday						
Wednesday						
Thursday						
Friday						
Saturday						
Sunday						
					Weekly Total:	

Employee Signature _____

Note that the Daily Total column displays the total hours worked by the employee each day. Per the FLSA, employers are permitted to round employee time worked to the nearest 15-minute increment. This rounding is completed based on consecutive hours worked, not total hours worked in a single day. For example, if an employee works 4 hours and 2 minutes in the morning and then 3 hours and 6 minutes in the afternoon, an additional 15-minute increment is not credited to the employee for the extra 8 minutes worked (2 in the morning + 6 in the afternoon). However, if all 8 additional minutes are worked in the morning, then the employee would receive credit for an additional 15-minute increment. Furthermore, employee time cards must be verified by at least one supervisor prior to calculating employee pay.

NOTE! In many work environments, even salaried employees complete time cards so that the employer has verification of hours worked.

Alternative Timekeeping Methods

While many employers continue to use time cards, an increasing number are turning to electronic timekeeping methods. Examples include badge terminals (at which employees swipe badges), and biometric terminals (at which employees apply handprints, fingerprints, or other biological data). In both instances, the computer system logs employee hours based on the entries at these terminals.

| Case in Point 2-2 | **Complete Time Cards for Two Employees** |

In this example, we'll complete a time card for two different employees. Note that this employer rounds employee time to the nearest 15-minute increment.

1. Angelo Dorsett (SSN 444-44-4444) worked five days for Lucky Ties Apparel during the week of 11/25/2019 through 12/1/2019 (he had Monday and Sunday off). Each working day he arrived at 8:00 a.m. (except Wednesday, when he was three minutes early, and Friday, when he arrived at 6:59 a.m.). He left for lunch at 12:00 p.m. each day (except Tuesday, when he left at 12:07 p.m.), and arrived back at 1:00 p.m. (except Friday and Saturday, when he arrived back at 12:57 p.m. and 1:02 p.m., respectively). He left each day at 5:00 p.m. (except Wednesday and Thursday, when he stayed until 7:10 p.m. and 8:42 p.m., respectively). His completed time card appears as follows:

Employee Time Card

Employee Name   **Angelo Dorsett**

Employee SS#   **444-44-4444**

Day	Date	Morning		Afternoon		Daily
		Time In	Time Out	Time In	Time Out	Total
Monday	11/25/19	--	--	--	--	--
Tuesday	11/26/19	8:00	12:07	1:00	5:00	8
Wednesday	11/27/19	7:57	12:00	1:00	7:10	10.25
Thursday	11/28/19	8:00	12:00	1:00	8:42	11.75
Friday	11/29/19	6:59	12:00	12:57	5:00	9
Saturday	11/30/19	8:00	12:00	1:02	5:00	8
Sunday	12/1/19	--	--	--	--	--
					Weekly Total:	47

Employee Signature   *Angelo Dorsett*

Notice that the *Daily Total* column lists whole, not partial, hours for each day except Wednesday and Thursday. Since this employer rounds employee time to the nearest 15-minute increment, Angelo is credited with an extra quarter hour (15 minutes) on Wednesday and an extra three-quarters of an hour (45 minutes) on Thursday. Rounding resulted in full hours worked for all other workdays. For example, instead of listing 7 hours and 58 minutes for Saturday, the employer rounded to 8 hours.

2. Lucy Marshall (SSN 777-77-7777) worked six days for Lucky Ties Apparel during the week of 11/25/2019 through 12/1/2019 (she had Wednesday off). Each working day she arrived at 6:00 a.m. (except Monday, when she was five minutes early, and Friday, when she arrived at 9:32 a.m.). She left for lunch at 11:00 a.m. each day (except Thursday, when she left at 10:58 a.m., and Sunday, when she left at 11:29 a.m.), and arrived back at 12:00 p.m. (except Saturday, when she arrived back at 1:06 p.m.). She left work each day at 4:00 p.m. (except for Tuesday and Friday, when she stayed until 2:54 p.m. and 4:01 p.m., respectively). Her completed time card appears as follows:

Employee Time Card

Employee Name **Lucy Marshall**

Employee SS# **777-77-7777**

Day	Date	Morning		Afternoon		Daily Total
		Time In	Time Out	Time In	Time Out	
Monday	11/25/19	5:55	11:00	12:00	4:00	9
Tuesday	11/26/19	6:00	11:00	12:00	2:54	8
Wednesday	11/27/19	--	--	--	--	--
Thursday	11/28/19	6:00	10:58	12:00	4:00	9
Friday	11/29/19	9:32	11:00	12:00	4:01	5.5
Saturday	11/30/19	6:00	11:00	1:06	4:00	8
Sunday	12/1/19	6:00	11:29	12:00	4:00	9.5
					Weekly Total:	49

Employee Signature *Lucy-Marshall*

Because this employee worked an extra half hour on both Friday and Sunday, the Daily Total column displays 5.5 hours and 9.5 hours, respectively. Since it's common to credit an employee with an extra quarter hour for time worked in excess of at least eight extra minutes, the employer calculated the gross pay based on this additional time. Therefore, Lucy receives credit for two additional 15-minute increments on both Friday and Sunday as a result of her extra time worked.

Salaries and Wages

Employees are most commonly paid either wages or salaries by their employers.

- A **wage** is an amount typically paid to employees on an hourly basis.
- A **salary** is typically an annual pay amount (monthly or semimonthly may also be used) agreed upon by the employer and the employee.

NOTE!   Alternative base wages may also be used, such as daily wage rates and rates based on employee output (such as for the number of products assembled).

Regular wages are calculated by multiplying an employee's wage rate by the number of hours worked. For example, an employee earning $8.00/hour, who works 38 hours a week, earns $304 ($8 × 38 hours). If the employee didn't earn any other type of pay (such as overtime), the $304 total also represents the employee's **gross wages**. Gross wages are earned wages that, as we will see later, are not equal to the amount actually paid to employees in their paychecks.

Regular earnings for salaried employees are calculated differently. For these employees, the employer must divide the annual salary by 52 weeks. For example, if an employer earns a salary of $52,000/year, then the employee's regular weekly earnings are $1,000 ($52,000/52 weeks).

Weekly Regular Earnings Calculation	
Wage-earning employee	Regular wage rate × regular hours worked
Salaried employee	Annual salary/52 weeks

Calculating Overtime Pay

As discussed previously, the Fair Labor Standards Act requires that overtime be paid for any hours employees work after the first 40 in a workweek. This pay must equal at least 1.5 times the regular wages paid to the employee (referred to as *time and a half*).

TIP!   While the FLSA mandates that overtime pay cannot be below 1.5 times the regular wages, it is acceptable for an employer to offer overtime pay that is more than 1.5 times regular pay.

One common misconception is that overtime must be paid to employees who work nights and/or weekends. The FLSA does not require that employers pay overtime during these work shifts, as long as the 40 hours/week threshold has not yet been met.

When an employee earns overtime pay, total gross wages (which include both regular and overtime earnings) may be calculated in two different ways:

- First method—the employer adds the regular wages to the overtime wages (overtime wage rate × overtime hours worked).

- Second method—the employer first determines a total for all hours worked based on the regular wage rate (total hours worked × regular rate). To this the employer adds the additional pay earned for working overtime hours ([overtime rate – regular rate] × overtime hours worked).

Total Gross Wages Calculation	
Method 1	Regular wages + overtime wages
Method 2	Total regular wages for all hours worked + additional pay earned for overtime hours worked

Total gross wages are the same regardless of which method is used to calculate them.

TIP! In some circumstances, it's possible for an employee to have a workweek in which regular hours diverge from the 40-hour standard. Assume throughout this book, unless otherwise noted, that all employees operate with a regular 40-hour workweek.

Case in Point 2-3	Calculate Employee Regular and Overtime Earnings

In these examples, we'll review calculations for both regular and overtime earnings for Lucky Ties Apparel employees. We will also determine gross pay.

NOTE! For simplicity, all calculations shown throughout the textbook, both intermediate and final, have been rounded to two decimal places at each calculation. As you calculate amounts, you should round to two decimal places as well; for example, 81.574 is rounded to 81.57, whereas 81.575 is rounded to 81.58.

1. Paul Rogers has worked for Lucky Ties Apparel for four years. During the most recent year he was paid regular wages of $11.50/hour. In the most recent week, he worked 35 hours. Calculate his gross pay for the week.

   As Paul did not work any overtime hours, his regular earnings are equal to his gross pay. These regular earnings are calculated as follows:

   $11.50 (regular wage rate) × 35 hours (regular hours worked) = $402.50

2. Lucky Ties Apparel hired Maryanne Sherman at the beginning of the current year at an annual salary of $40,000. Calculate her gross pay for the most recent week, assuming that she's paid on a weekly basis.

   Maryanne earns the same gross pay every week, since her annual salary is evenly divided over all 52 weeks of each year. Her regular earnings for a single week are calculated as follows:

   $40,000 (annual salary) / 52 weeks = $769.23

3. Bill Novak has worked for Lucky Ties Apparel for 10 years. He currently earns regular wages of $14.75/hour and overtime wages of $22.50/hour. During a recent week, Bill worked 46 hours. Calculate his gross pay using both methods.

Bill's gross pay is the same for both methods. Remember that the FLSA dictates that any hours worked beyond the first 40 in a week must be compensated at the overtime wage rate. Bill's gross pay is calculated as follows:

Method 1: $14.75 (regular wage rate) ×
40 hours (regular hours worked) = $590

$22.50 (overtime wage rate) ×
6 hours (overtime hours worked) = $135

$590 (regular wages) +
$135 (overtime wages) = $725 (gross pay)

Method 2: $14.75 (regular wage rate) ×
46 hours (total hours worked) = $678.50

$22.50 (overtime rate) −
$14.75 (regular rate) = $7.75

$7.75 (calculated above) ×
6 hours (overtime hours worked) = $46.50

$678.50 (calculated above) +
$46.50 (calculated above) = $725 (gross pay)

Converting to Hourly Rates

It's common for employers to comply with the FLSA by compensating employees with an overtime pay rate of 1.5 times the regular rate (the minimum requirement). If an employee is not compensated with an hourly wage, his/her compensation must be converted to an hourly rate in order to calculate the applicable overtime earned.

As discussed previously, certain employees are exempt from the provisions of the FLSA, and employers are not compelled to compensate these employees at the standard overtime rate. While many salaried employees (such as executive, administrative, and professional employees) fit this description, others are non-exempt and must be compensated at the overtime rate for any overtime hours worked. The following conversion process may be used to calculate overtime wages for employees not paid on an hourly basis.

Weekly Wage Conversions

If an employee earns $820/week and works 44 hours during one week, the employee is owed overtime pay (for working more than 40 hours in a week). Since the employee is not paid on an hourly basis, how can the employer determine the proper amount of overtime pay? Assuming that the employer offers overtime pay at 1.5 times regular pay, the overtime pay can be calculated by converting the weekly rate to an hourly rate.

Use this four-step process to make the conversion, and then calculate total gross pay.

Process for Determining Weekly Gross Pay Based on Weekly Wages	
Step 1:	Determine the hourly regular wage rate.
Step 2:	Convert to an hourly overtime wage rate.
Step 3:	Calculate overtime wages earned.
Step 4:	Determine gross pay by adding regular earnings to overtime earnings.

Based on the above example, gross pay is calculated as follows:

Step 1: Determine the hourly regular wage rate by dividing the weekly rate by 40 hours (total number of regular hours worked during the week). In this instance, $820 / 40 hours = $20.50/hour.

Step 2: Multiply the regular hourly rate by 1.5 to convert it to the overtime hourly rate. Here, that is $20.50 × 1.5 = $30.75/hour.

Step 3: Multiply the overtime hourly rate by the number of overtime hours worked. In this example, $30.75 × 4 hours = $123.

Step 4: Add the weekly wage rate to the overtime earnings. The total gross pay for this employee is $820 + $123 = $943.

TIP! If an employee receives a biweekly wage, you must begin the conversion process by dividing the biweekly wage by two (to convert it to a weekly wage). The above four-step process may then be followed as shown.

Annual Salary Conversions

A similar series of calculations is required when converting an annual salary to an hourly rate. For annual salary conversions, use a five-step process.

Conversion of Annual Salary to Weekly Gross Pay	
Step 1:	Determine the weekly salary.
Step 2:	Determine the hourly regular wage rate.
Step 3:	Convert to an hourly overtime wage rate.
Step 4:	Calculate overtime wages earned.
Step 5:	Determine gross pay by adding regular earnings to overtime earnings.

To put these steps in concrete terms, assume that an employee receives $58,000/year, worked 48 hours in a recent week, and is paid 1.5 times the regular wage rate for overtime hours. This employee's gross pay is calculated as follows:

Step 1: Divide the annual salary by 52 weeks to determine the weekly salary. Here, the weekly salary is calculated as $58,000 / 52 weeks = $1,115.38/week.

Step 2: Determine the hourly regular wage rate by dividing the weekly rate by 40 hours (total number of regular hours worked during the week). In this instance, $1,115.38 / 40 hours = $27.88/hour.

Step 3: Multiply the regular hourly rate by 1.5 to convert it to the overtime hourly rate. Here, that is $27.88 × 1.5 = $41.82/hour.

Step 4: Multiply the overtime hourly rate by the number of overtime hours worked. In this example, $41.82 × 8 hours = $334.56.

Step 5: Add the weekly wage rate to the overtime earnings. The total gross pay for this employee is $1,115.38 + $334.56 = $1,449.94.

TIP! If an employee receives a monthly or semimonthly salary, you must begin the conversion process by multiplying either the monthly salary by 12 months or the semimonthly salary by 24 (to convert them to an annual salary). The above five-step process may then be followed as shown.

Case in Point 2-4   ## Convert to Hourly Rates and Calculate Weekly Gross Pay

In these examples, we will review five independent circumstances, and determine both the hourly wage rates and gross pay for each employee:

1. Angelo Dorsett is a salesman for Lucky Ties Apparel. He earns regular wages of $700/week, does not receive commission, and worked 47 hours during the most recent week. Assuming that Lucky Ties Apparel pays him an overtime rate of 1.5 times his regular rate, what should Angelo's gross pay be for the week?

    Step 1: Angelo's hourly regular wage rate is $700 / 40 regular hours = $17.50/hour.

    Step 2: Angelo's hourly overtime wage rate is $17.50 × 1.5 = $26.25/hour.

    Step 3: Angelo's overtime wages earned are $26.25 × 7 overtime hours = $183.75/hour.

    Step 4: Angelo's gross pay for the week is $700 + $183.75 = $883.75.

2. Melissa Kubiak has worked in the warehouse of Lucky Ties Apparel for two years. She earns a biweekly wage of $1,200 and worked 41 hours during the most recent week. Assuming that Lucky Ties Apparel pays her an overtime rate of 1.5 times her regular rate, what should Melissa's gross pay be for the week?

    Pre-Step: Melissa's weekly salary is $1,200 / 2 weeks = $600/week.

    Step 1: Melissa's hourly regular wage rate is $600 / 40 regular hours = $15/hour.

    Step 2: Melissa's hourly overtime wage rate is $15 × 1.5 = $22.50/hour.

    Step 3: Melissa's overtime wages earned are $22.50 × 1 overtime hour = $22.50.

    Step 4: Melissa's gross pay for the week is $600 + $22.50 = $622.50.

3. Stacie Martin works in the warehouse of Lucky Ties Apparel and is paid an annual salary of $43,992. During the most recent week, she worked 51 hours and is paid overtime wages of 1.5 times her regular wage rate. What should Stacie's gross pay be for the week?

    Step 1: Stacie's weekly salary is $43,992 / 52 weeks = $846/week.

    Step 2: Stacie's hourly regular wage rate is $846 / 40 regular hours = $21.15/hour.

    Step 3: Stacie's hourly overtime wage rate is $21.15 × 1.5 = $31.73/hour.

    Step 4: Stacie's overtime wages earned are $31.73 × 11 overtime hours = $349.03.

    Step 5: Stacie's gross pay for the week is $846 + $349.03 = $1,195.03.

4. Lucy Marshall has been a member of the janitorial staff at Lucky Ties Apparel for six years and earns a monthly salary of $2,730. During the most recent week, she worked 49 hours and is paid overtime wages of 1.5 times her regular wage rate. What should Lucy's gross pay be for the week?

   Pre-Step: Lucy's annual salary is $2,730 × 12 months = $32,760.

   Step 1: Lucy's weekly salary is $32,760 / 52 = $630/week.

   Step 2: Lucy's hourly regular wage rate is $630 / 40 regular hours = $15.75/hour.

   Step 3: Lucy's hourly overtime wage rate is $15.75 × 1.5 = $23.63/hour.

   Step 4: Lucy's overtime wages earned are $23.63 × 9 overtime hours = $212.67.

   Step 5: Lucy's gross pay for the week is $630 + $212.67 = $842.67.

5. Donald McHenry has been a member of the janitorial staff at Lucky Ties Apparel for four years and earns a semimonthly salary of $1,326. During the most recent week, he worked 45 hours and is paid overtime wages of 1.5 times his regular wage rate. What should Donald's gross pay be for the week?

   Pre-Step: Donald's annual salary is $1,326 × 24 semimonthly periods = $31,824.

   Step 1: Donald's weekly salary is $31,824 / 52 = $612/week.

   Step 2: Donald's hourly regular wage rate is $612 / 40 regular hours = $15.30/hour.

   Step 3: Donald's hourly overtime wage rate is $15.30 × 1.5 = $22.95/hour.

   Step 4: Donald's overtime wages earned are $22.95 × 5 overtime hours = $114.75.

   Step 5: Donald's gross pay for the week is $612 + $114.75 = $726.75.

Commissions, Bonuses, and Incentive Plans

Wages and salaries are not the only types of compensation an employee may receive. Employers can also compensate employees through **commissions** (a percentage of each sale), **bonuses** (either planned or unplanned additional amounts), and **incentive plans** (more pay for increased productivity).

Paying Commissions

Commissions are typically paid to employees as a percentage of sales. For example, if an employee sells a product for $2,000 and earns a 10% commission on every sale, that employee is paid a $200 ($2,000 × 10%) commission. Commissions can be the only form of income earned by an employee, or they can be earned in conjunction with a wage or salary.

Commissions are considered to be a component of an employee's regular pay. To calculate the overtime pay of an employee who earns commissions, the regular hourly wages and the commissions must be combined to determine an overall hourly rate. This combined rate is then multiplied by 1.5 (or the higher applicable rate of compensation offered by the employer) to arrive at the overtime hourly rate.

For example, if an employee works 44 hours, earns a regular hourly wage of $10/hour, and earns commissions of $220, a combined regular hourly wage rate (which takes the commission into account) must be determined. Use the following three-step process to arrive at this figure:

Calculation of Regular Hourly Wage Rate Including Commission	
Step 1:	Determine total regular wages. ($10 × 44 hours = $440)
Step 2:	Add the commission to the above amount. ($440 + $220 = $660)
Step 3:	Divide the combined total by the regular hours worked. ($660 / 44 hours = $15)

If this employer offers an overtime wage rate that is 1.5 times the regular rate, the overtime wage rate is $22.50 ($15 × 1.5). As the above calculation includes regular wages for overtime hours, we now must add the additional overtime pay to the above total. The additional overtime hourly wage rate is $7.50 per hour ($22.50 overtime wage rate minus $15 regular wage rate); therefore, additional overtime earnings are $30 ($7.50 per hour additional overtime hourly wage rate × 4 overtime hours). Total gross wages are $690 ($660 combined regular earnings and commissions + $30 additional overtime earnings).

NOTE! Employees of retail and service businesses who are paid commissions and who meet certain requirements set by the FLSA are exempt from the mandate that overtime pay exceed regular pay by at least 1.5 times.

Awarding Bonuses

A bonus is an amount awarded to an employee outside of regular and overtime pay. There are two types of bonuses: discretionary and nondiscretionary:

- A **discretionary bonus** is one that is unplanned and not contingent on the employee reaching specific goals. An example is a surprise holiday bonus given to employees at the end of the year.
- A **nondiscretionary bonus** is one that is planned and that an employer pays as a result of a specific metric being met. An example is a longevity bonus paid to an employee on his/her tenth anniversary with a company.

The distinction between these two bonus types is important, because nondiscretionary bonuses are considered part of regular pay, while discretionary bonuses are not. Similar to commissions, nondiscretionary bonuses must be combined with regular hourly wages prior to determining an employee's overtime pay.

Offering Incentive Plans

An employer may offer a variety of incentive plans to employees, which are designed to reward employees for their performance and/or loyalty to the company. The most common types of incentive plans are:

- Cash paid for reaching specified sales or production goals.
- Profit-sharing plans in which employees receive a share of profits once they exceed a predetermined level of productivity.
- Stock option plans in which employees who meet predetermined goals may purchase shares of stock with pre-tax dollars.
- Additional vacation days for employees whose tenure with the company surpasses preset lengths.
- Sabbaticals, common in academic institutions, that provide employees with paid leave after working for a predetermined number of years.

When a cash incentive is offered, it may be paid in a lump sum or as an increase in the hourly (or per-unit) rate paid. In the case of an increased pay rate, the increase is typically earned upon employee performance exceeding a preset, quantifiable level.

TIP! For the purposes of the FLSA, cash paid for reaching specified goals is considered a nondiscretionary bonus and therefore is a component of regular pay. This must be considered when calculating overtime pay.

Case in Point 2-5	Calculate Employee Commissions, Bonuses, and Incentive Pay

In these examples, we'll review four independent circumstances and will calculate the total earnings for each employee:

1. An employee who sells automobiles is paid $8/hour in regular wages. In addition, he earns another $300 for every car he sells. During the most recent week, he works 46 hours and sells five cars. His employer pays overtime wages of 1.5 times regular hourly wages.

   Step 1: Total regular wages are $8 × 46 hours = $368.

   Step 2: Total combined regular earnings are $1,500 (5 cars × $300) + $368 = $1,868.

   Step 3: The regular earnings hourly rate is $1,868 / 46 hours = $40.61/hour.

   Now that the regular earnings hourly rate is determined, the overtime hourly rate can be calculated as follows: $40.61 × 1.5 = $60.92/hour.

   The additional overtime hourly rate therefore is $60.92 – $40.61 = $20.31.

   Using this additional overtime hourly rate, the additional overtime earnings are $20.31 × 6 hours = $121.86.

   This results in total earnings of $1,868 + $121.86 = $1,989.86.

2. After his company made a particularly large sale, an employee is awarded a discretionary bonus of $2,000. During this same week, the employee works 42 hours, earning regular wages of $13/hour, with overtime pay calculated as 1.5 times the regular wage rate.

   Since a discretionary bonus is not considered to be part of regular earnings, overtime pay is calculated using the standard 1.5 × regular hourly wages formula.

   Regular pay therefore is $13 × 40 hours = $520. The overtime hourly rate is $13 × 1.5 = $19.50/hour, which results in overtime pay of $19.50 × 2 hours = $39.

   Total earnings for the week are $520 (regular earnings) + $39 (overtime earnings) + $2,000 (discretionary bonus) = $2,559.

3. An employee who earns regular wages of $9.50/hour and overtime pay of 1.5 times his regular wage rate works 53 hours during the most recent week. As a result of total company sales exceeding $1,000,000 for the year, the employee also received a predetermined bonus of $1,500.

Because this bonus was planned and paid out once company sales reached $1,000,000, it's considered to be a nondiscretionary bonus. As a result, it's considered part of regular earnings. The three-step process for combining regular wages and commissions outlined previously may be used to combine regular wages and nondiscretionary bonuses as well.

Step 1: Total regular wages are $9.50 × 53 hours = $503.50.

Step 2: Total combined regular earnings are $1,500 + $503.50 = $2,003.50.

Step 3: The regular earnings hourly rate is $2,003.50 / 53 hours = $37.80/hour.

The overtime hourly rate, based on the above calculation, is $37.80 × 1.5 = $56.70/hour.

The additional overtime hourly rate therefore is $56.70 − $37.80 = $18.90.

Using this additional overtime hourly rate, the additional overtime earnings are $18.90 × 13 hours = $245.70.

Therefore, total earnings are $2,003.50 + $245.70 = $2,249.20.

4. An employee works in a factory where she earns regular wages of $8/hour, with overtime pay calculated as 1.5 times regular earnings. If, during any week, she is able to assemble more than 1,000 product units, her regular rate increases to $9/hour for the week. Her rate similarly increases to $10/hour if she assembles more than 1,200 units and $11/hour if she assembles more than 1,400 units. During the most recent week she worked 44 hours and assembled 1,352 units.

This employee has earned incentive pay, since she assembled more than 1,000 product units. For her level of production (1,352 units), she has earned an increased regular wage rate of $10/hour.

Regular wages are calculated as follows: $10 × 40 hours = $400.

Her overtime hourly wage rate is $10 × 1.5 = $15/hour.

Therefore, her overtime pay is calculated as follows: $15 × 4 hours = $60.

Her total earnings for the week are $400 + $60 = $460.

Alternative Pay Considerations

In certain instances, based on an employee's job duties, it's appropriate to use alternative methods of compensation.

- For individuals who are their own boss (such as Certified Public Accountants who earn income outside of a large organization), **self-employment income** must be determined.
- For employees who regularly receive tips from customers (such as waiters and waitresses), special minimum wage and overtime rules apply.
- For employees who produce a measurable output (such as seamstresses creating dresses), compensation may be based on the number of units produced. This is referred to as a **piecework system**.

Self-Employment Income

Individuals who operate a sole proprietorship or partnership must account for and report annual self-employment income. This consists of the revenue an owner may claim based on the company operations, minus expenses incurred. These individuals do not have to be concerned with the minimum wage and overtime provisions of the FLSA; however, they still must track total income to ensure that appropriate taxes are paid. We'll examine the tax implications of self-employment income in further detail in Chapter 5.

Tipped Employees

Employees who receive tips are covered by the FLSA and therefore must be paid the applicable hourly minimum wage. A tipped employee is someone who typically receives more than $30/month in tips. Employers can take advantage of a maximum tip credit of $5.12, which results in employees receiving an hourly wage of $2.13 ($7.25 minimum wage minus $5.12 tip credit). Employers who elect to take advantage of this tip credit must inform employees of their intention to do so, and must use a consistent tip credit for both regular and overtime hours. Additionally, if the applicable state tip credit is lower than $5.12, the employer may take advantage only of this lower amount.

Employers cannot use an employee's tips for any purpose other than a tip credit against wages owed, or as part of a **tip pool**. A tip pool, in which all employee tips are added together (pooled) and then divided amongst employees, is permissible under the FLSA. However, these employees each must receive the applicable hourly minimum wage, and the pool must include only employees who regularly receive tips.

WARNING! Regardless of whether an employer elects to utilize a tip credit, under no circumstance may that employer retain an employee's tips.

If the employee's total hourly wage (the sum of the hourly wage received and employee tips) does not exceed the applicable minimum wage, the employer must compensate the employee for the difference. In addition, the employer must use the overtime factor (1.5 for time and a half) to calculate the overtime hourly rate for a tipped employee based on the applicable minimum wage. No tip credit may be factored into this calculation.

Tipped Employees Overtime Calculation	
Step 1:	Regular hourly rate × regular hours worked = regular earnings
Step 2:	Minimum wage – regular hourly rate = hourly tip credit
Step 3:	(Minimum wage × overtime factor) – hourly tip credit = overtime hourly rate
Step 4:	Overtime hourly rate × overtime hours worked = overtime earnings
Step 5:	Total hours worked × hourly tip credit = total tip credit
Step 6:	Regular earnings + overtime earnings + total tips = total earnings

NOTE!   The tip credit cannot exceed total tips received, so the employer should compare these figures after completing Step 5 above. If the tip credit is too high, the employer must reduce the tip credit such that it does not exceed total tips received. This reduction is calculated as *current tip credit* minus *total tips received*.

Utilizing Piecework Systems

In certain instances it's logical to compensate employees based on their output, rather than on hours worked. Under this *piecework* system, an employee receives a fixed amount for each unit of output. These units can take many forms, such as products assembled, telemarketing phone calls made, or packages filled.

One important element that the employer must remember is that the minimum wage requirements of the FLSA apply to employees compensated under a piece-work system. To confirm compliance with the FLSA, an employer must determine each piecework employee's hourly rate. This may be done by dividing total weekly compensation by the number of hours worked.

Piecework Overtime Calculation	
Step 1:	Piece rate × units of output = regular earnings for all hours
Step 2:	Regular earnings for all hours / total hours worked = regular hourly rate
Step 3:	Regular hourly rate × additional overtime factor = additional overtime hourly rate
Step 4:	Additional overtime hourly rate × overtime hours worked = additional overtime earnings
Step 5:	Regular earnings for all hours + additional overtime earnings = total earnings

NOTE!   The additional overtime factor is typically 0.5 (1.5 overtime rate minus 1.0 regular rate).

The additional overtime hourly rate, in Step 3 above, is often also called the **premium rate**, because it represents the premium over the regular hourly rate to which the piecework employee is entitled for overtime hours worked.

NOTE! An alternative to the calculation shown above is to pay an employee at least 1.5 times the regular piece rate for all units of output produced during overtime hours (all hours after the first 40). In this approach, the employer must ensure that the regular hourly rate exceeds the applicable minimum wage rate.

| Case in Point 2-6 | Calculate Earnings for Tipped and Piecework Employees |

In these examples, we'll examine three independent circumstances and will determine how total compensation is calculated for each employee.

1. Eric Parker works for a small restaurant chain as a waiter. He is paid $2.13/hour by his employer and receives $150 in tips during a 35-hour workweek. What is Eric's total compensation for the week?

    Eric's employer pays regular wages of $74.55 ($2.13 regular wage rate × 35 regular hours worked). As a result, if the FLSA were ignored, Eric's total compensation would be $224.55 ($74.55 regular wages + $150 tips).

    Because this is less than the FLSA-mandated minimum of $253.75 ($7.25 minimum wage × 35 hours worked), the employer must compensate Eric for the difference. Therefore, Eric receives an additional $29.20 ($253.75 − $224.55) to increase his total compensation to $253.75.

2. Meredith Baer works as an automobile valet at a steak house. She is paid $3/hour by her employer and received $310 in tips during the most recent 44-hour workweek. Meredith's employer pays overtime hourly wages at a rate of 1.5 times regular hourly wages. What is Meredith's total compensation for the week?

    Using the six-step process detailed previously (in the Tipped Employees Overtime Calculation table on page 60), total compensation is calculated as follows:

    Step 1: Meredith's employer pays regular earnings of $120 ($3 regular wage rate × 40 regular hours worked).

    Step 2: This is the result of her employer taking a tip credit of $4.25 ($7.25 minimum wage − $3 regular wage rate).

    Step 3: When calculating overtime compensation, this tip credit must be maintained at the same level. Therefore, total overtime compensation is based on an hourly rate of $6.63 ($7.25 minimum wage × 1.5 overtime factor − $4.25 tip credit).

    Step 4: This results in overtime earnings totaling $26.52 ($6.63 overtime hourly rate × 4 overtime hours worked).

Step 5: Before total compensation is finalized, the employer must ensure that the total tip credit does not exceed tips received by the employee. In this instance, the total tip credit of $187 ($4.25 tip credit × 44 hours worked) does not exceed total tips received of $310, and therefore the employer owes no additional compensation.

Step 6: Total compensation is then calculated as $456.52 ($120 regular earnings + $26.52 overtime earnings + $310 tips).

3. Nancy Winchester assembles children's toys and is paid $0.06 for each unit assembled. During the most recent week, Nancy worked 48 hours and assembled 8,528 units. Nancy's employer pays overtime hourly wages at a rate of 1.5 times regular hourly wages. What is Nancy's total compensation for the week?

Using the five-step process detailed previously (in the Piecework Overtime Calculation table on page 60), total compensation is calculated as follows:

Step 1: Regular earnings for all hours are calculated as $0.06 (piece rate) × 8,528 (units of output) = $511.68.

Step 2: The regular hourly rate is then calculated as $511.68 (regular earnings) / 48 (hours worked) = $10.66.

Step 3: The additional overtime hourly rate is then calculated as $10.66 (regular hourly rate) × 0.5 (additional overtime rate) = $5.33.

Step 4: Additional overtime earnings are calculated as $5.33 (additional overtime hourly rate) × 8 (overtime hours worked) = $42.64.

Step 5: Total earnings are then calculated as $511.68 (regular earnings) + $42.64 (additional overtime earnings) = $554.32.

4. Andrew Fitzpatrick is a telemarketer who is paid $0.32 for every telemarketing phone call he places. During the most recent week, Andrew worked 43 hours and placed 1,722 calls, 124 of which were placed during the final three hours he worked. Andrew's employer pays an overtime piece rate 1.5 times the regular rate. Using the alternative method outlined earlier, determine Andrew's total compensation for the week.

During regular hours Andrew placed 1,598 (1,722 − 124) calls, and therefore earned $511.36 (1,598 × $0.32) in regular earnings. As the overtime hourly piece rate is $0.48 ($0.32 × 1.5), Andrew earns overtime pay of $59.52 (124 × $0.48). Therefore, total earnings are $570.88 ($511.36 + $59.52).

Payroll Register

Unlike the employee earnings record, which displays the earnings for a single employee over a range of pay periods, the **payroll register** shows each employee's pay for a single period. Ordinarily the payroll register is completed prior to the employee earnings record, as the payroll register summarizes all payroll data for a single period. This data is then taken from the payroll register and entered within each individual employee earnings record.

The payroll register displays both total earnings (gross pay) and each employee's paycheck amount (net pay).

Payroll Register

Pay Period _____

Pay Date _____

Employee Name	Earnings							Deductions					Check Number	Net Pay
	Regular Hours	Regular Rate	Regular Earnings	Overtime Hours	Overtime Rate	Overtime Earnings	Total Earnings	FWT	SWT	Social Security	Medicare	Vol. With.		
Totals:														

As discussed earlier, the net pay is calculated by subtracting all deductions from the gross pay (total earnings) in the payroll register. Depending on the business, other columns may appear in the payroll register. For example, if a business's employees are unionized, the *Deductions* section may contain a separate column for *Union Dues* that are withheld from each employee's gross pay. Additionally, for some employees not all columns are necessary. For example, a salaried executive is exempt from the minimum wage provision of the FLSA, and therefore no hourly rate information is necessary.

Note that in some instances a company will choose not to display identical columns within the employee earnings records and the payroll register. For example, here the payroll register includes a *voluntary withholdings* column that summarizes the *retirement contribution, life insurance, charitable contributions,* and *additional withholding* columns within the employee earnings records. Be aware of this potential structural difference when transferring figures from the payroll register to the employee earnings records.

TIP! Just as with the employee earnings record, the payroll register is typically completed within a computerized payroll system. However, we'll work with manual versions of the payroll register throughout the textbook.

Case in Point 2-7   Complete a Payroll Register

In this example, we will complete a payroll register for Lucky Ties Apparel. We will then transfer the information from the payroll register to the employee earnings records for each employee. Earlier we calculated the weekly pay for eight different employees of Lucky Ties Apparel. The partially completed payroll register for the most recent week appears below. The pay period ends on 12/1/2019, with checks distributed on the subsequent Thursday. Note that you must determine the totals within the Regular, Overtime, and Total Earnings columns after entering individual employee data.

NOTE!   We'll return to this example in the next chapter, where we'll complete the *Deductions* and *Net Pay* sections of both the payroll register and the employee earnings records.

Payroll Register

Pay Period   **12/1/2019**

Pay Date   **12/5/2019**

Employee Name	Regular Hours	Regular Rate	Regular Earnings	Overtime Hours	Overtime Rate	Overtime Earnings	Total Earnings	FWT	SWT	Social Security	Medicare	Vol. With.	Check Number	Net Pay
Rogers, P	35	$ 11.50	$ 402.50	0	n/a	$ -	$ 402.50							
Sherman, M	n/a	n/a	$ 769.23	0	n/a	$ -	$ 769.23							
Novak, B	40	$ 14.75	$ 590.00	6	$ 22.50	$ 135.00	$ 725.00							
Dorsett, A	40	$ 17.50	$ 700.00	7	$ 26.25	$ 183.75	$ 883.75							
Kubiak, M	40	$ 15.00	$ 600.00	1	$ 22.50	$ 22.50	$ 622.50							
Martin, S	40	$ 21.15	$ 846.00	11	$ 31.73	$ 349.03	$ 1,195.03							
Marshall, L	40	$ 15.75	$ 630.00	9	$ 23.63	$ 212.67	$ 842.67							
McHenry, D	40	$ 15.30	$ 612.00	5	$ 22.95	$ 114.75	$ 726.75							
Totals:			$5,149.73			$1,017.70	$ 6,167.43							

To complete the *Earnings* portion of the employee earnings records, simply transfer the payroll information from the payroll register. Note that each employee's address, Social Security number, marital status, and withholding allowances have also been entered into the employee earnings records.

Employee Earnings Record

Name   Paul Rogers

Address   657 Flicker Lane
Brockport, NY 14420

SS#   111-11-1111

Marital Status   Single

Fed. Withholding Allow.   1

State Withholding Allow.   1

Pay Period Ending	Regular Hours Worked	Regular Pay Rate	Regular Wages	Overtime Hours Worked	Overtime Pay Rate	Overtime Wages	Gross Pay	Federal Withholding Tax	State Withholding Tax	Social Security Tax	Medicare Tax	Retirement Contribution	Life Insurance	Charitable Contribution	Additional Withholding	Check Number	Net Pay
12/1/19	35	$ 11.50	$ 402.50	0	n/a	$ -	$ 402.50										

Employee Earnings Record

Name   Maryanne Sherman   Marital Status   Single

Address   8171 Winston Court   Fed. Withholding Allow.   2

            Rochester, NY 14604   State Withholding Allow.   1

SS#   222-22-2222

	Earnings							Deductions									
Pay Period Ending	Regular Hours Worked	Regular Pay Rate	Regular Wages	Overtime Hours Worked	Overtime Pay Rate	Overtime Wages	Gross Pay	Federal Withholding Tax	State Withholding Tax	Social Security Tax	Medicare Tax	Retirement Contribution	Life Insurance	Charitable Contribution	Additional Withholding	Check Number	Net Pay
12/1/19	n/a	n/a	$ 769.23	0	n/a	$ -	$ 769.23										

Employee Earnings Record

Name   Bill Novak   Marital Status   Married

Address   536A North Yellow Lake Avenue   Fed. Withholding Allow.   4

            Hamlin, NY 14464   State Withholding Allow.   3

SS#   333-33-3333

	Earnings							Deductions									
Pay Period Ending	Regular Hours Worked	Regular Pay Rate	Regular Wages	Overtime Hours Worked	Overtime Pay Rate	Overtime Wages	Gross Pay	Federal Withholding Tax	State Withholding Tax	Social Security Tax	Medicare Tax	Retirement Contribution	Life Insurance	Charitable Contribution	Additional Withholding	Check Number	Net Pay
12/1/19	40	$ 14.75	$ 590.00	6	$ 22.50	$ 135.00	$ 725.00										

Employee Earnings Record

Name   Angelo Dorsett   Marital Status   Single

Address   400 Hillside Court   Fed. Withholding Allow.   2

            Hilton, NY 14468   State Withholding Allow.   2

SS#   444-44-4444

	Earnings							Deductions									
Pay Period Ending	Regular Hours Worked	Regular Pay Rate	Regular Wages	Overtime Hours Worked	Overtime Pay Rate	Overtime Wages	Gross Pay	Federal Withholding Tax	State Withholding Tax	Social Security Tax	Medicare Tax	Retirement Contribution	Life Insurance	Charitable Contribution	Additional Withholding	Check Number	Net Pay
12/1/19	40	$ 17.50	$ 700.00	7	$ 26.25	$ 183.75	$ 883.75										

Employee Earnings Record

Name	Melissa Kubiak	Marital Status	Married
Address	254 Cheesehead Drive	Fed. Withholding Allow.	4
	Pittsford, NY 14534	State Withholding Allow.	4
SS#	555-55-5555		

	Earnings							Deductions									
Pay Period Ending	Regular Hours Worked	Regular Pay Rate	Regular Wages	Overtime Hours Worked	Overtime Pay Rate	Overtime Wages	Gross Pay	Federal Withholding Tax	State Withholding Tax	Social Security Tax	Medicare Tax	Retirement Contribution	Life Insurance	Charitable Contribution	Additional Withholding	Check Number	Net Pay
12/1/19	40	$ 15.00	$ 600.00	1	$ 22.50	$ 22.50	$ 622.50										

Employee Earnings Record

Name	Stacie Martin	Marital Status	Married
Address	2 Lava Lane	Fed. Withholding Allow.	2
	Brockport, NY 14420	State Withholding Allow.	1
SS#	666-66-6666		

	Earnings							Deductions									
Pay Period Ending	Regular Hours Worked	Regular Pay Rate	Regular Wages	Overtime Hours Worked	Overtime Pay Rate	Overtime Wages	Gross Pay	Federal Withholding Tax	State Withholding Tax	Social Security Tax	Medicare Tax	Retirement Contribution	Life Insurance	Charitable Contribution	Additional Withholding	Check Number	Net Pay
12/1/19	40	$ 21.15	$ 846.00	11	$ 31.73	$ 349.03	$ 1,195.03										

Employee Earnings Record

Name	Lucy Marshall	Marital Status	Single
Address	232 Muscle Road	Fed. Withholding Allow.	3
	Hamlin, NY 14464	State Withholding Allow.	2
SS#	777-77-7777		

	Earnings							Deductions									
Pay Period Ending	Regular Hours Worked	Regular Pay Rate	Regular Wages	Overtime Hours Worked	Overtime Pay Rate	Overtime Wages	Gross Pay	Federal Withholding Tax	State Withholding Tax	Social Security Tax	Medicare Tax	Retirement Contribution	Life Insurance	Charitable Contribution	Additional Withholding	Check Number	Net Pay
12/1/19	40	$ 15.75	$ 630.00	9	$ 23.63	$ 212.67	$ 842.67										

Employee Earnings Record

Name	Donald McHenry	
Address	22 Iceberg Lane	
	Fairport, NY 14450	
SS#	888-88-8888	

Marital Status	Married
Fed. Withholding Allow.	6
State Withholding Allow.	5

Pay Period Ending	Regular Hours Worked	Regular Pay Rate	Regular Wages	Overtime Hours Worked	Overtime Pay Rate	Overtime Wages	Gross Pay	Federal Withholding Tax	State Withholding Tax	Social Security Tax	Medicare Tax	Retirement Contribution	Life Insurance	Charitable Contribution	Additional Withholding	Check Number	Net Pay
12/1/19	40	$ 15.30	$ 612.00	5	$ 22.95	$ 114.75	$ 726.75										

Self-Assessment

Complete the Self-Assessment as directed by your instructor, whether that is in the book or your eLab course, if applicable.

True/False Questions

1. Per the FLSA, a workweek is any nonconsecutive seven-day period designated by the employer.   *True   False*

2. An employer may change its workweek, as long as the change is meant to be permanent and is not designed to circumvent overtime requirements.   *True   False*

3. The Equal Pay Act protects only female employees from wage discrimination.   *True   False*

4. An employee time card lists total hours worked for all employees during a single workweek.   *True   False*

5. An employee's overtime wage rate must always be at least 1.5 times his/her regular wage rate.   *True   False*

6. The FLSA does not mandate that employees be compensated at the overtime wage rate for hours worked during nights and weekends, unless the 40-hour threshold has been reached.   *True   False*

7. Commissions are considered to be a component of an employee's regular pay.   *True   False*

8. A discretionary bonus is one that is planned and paid out upon an employee reaching a specific milestone.   *True   False*

9. The maximum tip credit that an employer may take advantage of is $2.13.   *True   False*

10. A payroll register displays compensation information for a single pay period.   *True   False*

Multiple Choice Questions

11. Which of the following is not a common pay period used by employers?
    A. Semimonthly
    B. Monthly
    C. Biweekly
    D. Daily

12. Under the provisions of the Equal Pay Act, employers may compensate employees differently for the same job based on each of the following except:
    A. Gender
    B. Seniority
    C. Output quantity
    D. A merit system

13. When different minimum wage rates are in effect, which rate takes precedence, and therefore must be met by an employer?
    A. Federal minimum wage
    B. The highest applicable minimum wage
    C. Local (municipality) minimum wage
    D. State minimum wage

14. An employee who worked 38 hours during the current workweek and receives $11.25/hour has earned gross pay of:
    A. $450
    B. $427.50
    C. $1,125
    D. $380

15. An employee who worked 44 hours during the current workweek, receives regular wages of $9.50/hour, and is paid overtime wages of 1.5 times his regular wage rate has earned gross pay of:
    A. $418
    B. $380
    C. $437
    D. $627

16. What is the hourly wage rate of an employee who typically has a 40-hour workweek and who earns a monthly salary of $1,768?
    A. $10.20
    B. $20.40
    C. $442
    D. $408

17. Each of the following is a type of incentive plan except:
    A. Stock options
    B. Sabbaticals
    C. Overtime compensation
    D. Profit sharing plans

18. Under which of the following circumstances may an employer retain an employee's tips?
    A. The full tip credit is utilized by the employer.
    B. No tip credit is utilized by the employer.
    C. A tip pool is utilized by all employees.
    D. Under no circumstance may an employer retain an employee's tips.

19. A tipped employee is paid $2.13/hour during a week in which he works 40 hours. During this week he receives $195 in tips from customers. How much additional compensation (beyond the hourly rate and tips) must his employer remit in order to comply with the FLSA?
    A. $0
    B. $92.87
    C. $290
    D. $9.80

20. An employee works 44 hours during a week in which he produces 3,057 units at a piece rate of $0.14/unit. What is the employee's regular hourly rate across all hours worked?
    A. $69.48
    B. $9.73
    C. $4.96
    D. $10.70

Practice Set A

The IRS forms and Excel templates needed for these assignments are included in the Student Exercise Files download for this course. If directed to do so, complete these assignments in Homework Grader.

PSa 2-1 Identify Pay Periods and Evaluate Workweeks

Examine each of the following independent circumstances and identify the type of pay period (weekly, biweekly, semimonthly, or monthly) being utilized. Then indicate whether the specified workweek is FLSA *compliant* or *noncompliant*.

1. Touchdown Corporation's most recent pay period ended on Wednesday, 7/31/2019, with paychecks printed and distributed one week later. The subsequent pay period ended on Thursday, 8/15/2019. To coincide with the pay periods, the employer's last workweek ran from Thursday, 8/1/2019, through Thursday, 8/15/2019.

2. Dachshund, Inc., recently changed its pay period such that it now runs from Wednesday through Tuesday each week. The workweek also begins on Wednesday; however, it starts at 8:00 a.m. and runs through the following Wednesday at 7:59 a.m.

3. Electronics Depot compensates its employees 26 times each year. Its workweek begins on Monday at 12:00 a.m. and runs through Sunday at 11:59 p.m.

PSa 2-2 Complete a Time Card

Complete a time card for each employee below. Note that this employer rounds employee time to the nearest 15-minute increment.

1. Audra Moyer (SSN 888-22-4444) worked seven days during the week of 10/7/2019 through 10/13/2019. She arrived at 8:00 a.m. each day (except Monday when she was six minutes early and Tuesday when she arrived at 6:57 a.m.). She left for lunch at 12:00 p.m. each day (except Tuesday, when she left at 11:58 a.m., and Saturday, when she left at 12:03 p.m.) and arrived back at 1:00 p.m. (except for Friday, when she arrived back at 1:02 p.m.). She left work at 4:00 p.m. each day (except for Tuesday, Wednesday, and Sunday, when she stayed until 5:02 p.m., 3:58 p.m., and 5:31 p.m., respectively).

2. Stephen Fitzpatrick (SSN 333-99-7777) worked four days during the week of 5/20/2019 through 5/26/2019 (he was off work on Monday, Wednesday, and Friday). He arrived at 7:00 a.m. each day (except Tuesday, when he arrived at 5:58 a.m.). He left for lunch at 11:00 a.m. each day (except Tuesday, when he left at 11:03 a.m., and Saturday, when he did not take a lunch break), and arrived back at 12:00 p.m. (except for Thursday, when he arrived back at 12:32 p.m., and Saturday, when he did not take a lunch break). He left work at 5:00 p.m. each day (except for Sunday, when he stayed until 6:04 p.m.).

PSa 2-3 Calculate Weekly Regular Earnings

Calculate the weekly regular earnings for each of the following employees:

1. Jason Richards earns $8.45/hour and worked 37 hours during the most recent week.

2. Drew Johnson earns an annual salary of $72,000.

3. Lucas Short earns $10.20/hour and worked 40 hours during the most recent week.

4. Anna Graham earns an annual salary of $122,500.

5. Molly Mitchell earns $13/hour and worked 38 hours during the most recent week.

PSa 2-4 Calculate Weekly Gross Pay

Calculate gross pay (regular earnings + overtime earnings) for each of the following employees. Every employee earns hourly overtime wages that are 1.5 times greater than his/her regular wage rate.

1. Luisa Williams earns $7.50/hour and worked 44 hours during the most recent week.

2. Jonathan Olsen earns $9.10/hour and worked 47 hours during the most recent week.

3. Nathan Upton earns $11.80/hour and worked 42 hours during the most recent week.

4. Juan Rodriguez earns $14/hour and worked 48 hours during the most recent week.

5. Drew Painter earns $16.60/hour and worked 51 hours during the most recent week.

PSa 2-5 Determine Hourly Regular and Overtime Wage Rates

Determine both the regular and overtime wage rates for each of the following employees. All are paid overtime wage rates that are 1.5 times their respective regular wage rates.

1. Nancy Bowie earns a weekly wage of $950. During the most recent week, she worked 46 hours.

2. Ronald McHenry earns a biweekly wage of $2,100. During the most recent week, he worked 48 hours.

3. Frank Wayne earns an annual salary of $62,000. During the most recent week, he worked 52 hours.

4. Michelle Connolly earns a monthly salary of $5,000. During the most recent week, she worked 43 hours.

5. Howie Gillette earns a semimonthly salary of $1,900. During the most recent week, he worked 41 hours.

PSa 2-6 Calculate Gross Pay

Calculate gross pay for each of the five employees listed in the prior exercise.

PSa 2-7 Calculate Gross Pay with Commissions

Calculate gross pay for each of the following employees. All are paid overtime wage rates that are 1.5 times their respective regular wage rates.

1. Samuel Worthy earns both $7.25/hour and a 10% commission on all sales. During the most recent week, he worked 42 hours and made total sales of $11,000.

2. Charlotte Denning earns both $9/hour and $25 for every sale she completes. During the most recent week, she worked 48 hours and made a total of 62 sales.

3. James Finch earns both $11.70/hour and a 12% commission on all sales. During the most recent week, he worked 45 hours and made total sales of $7,200.

4. Keri Weinberg earns both $10/hour, $10 for every sale of Product A, and $14 for every sale of Product B. During the most recent week, she worked 54 hours and sold 26 units of Product A and 41 units of Product B.

5. Tom Wilson earns both $16.20/hour and a 15% commission on all sales. During the most recent week, he worked 47 hours and made total sales of $13,000.

PSa 2-8 Calculate Gross Pay with Bonuses

Calculate gross pay for each of the following employees. All are paid overtime wage rates that are 1.5 times their respective regular wage rates.

1. Jefferson Dodge earns $8.50/hour. During the most recent week, he received a discretionary bonus of $1,000 and worked 47 hours.

2. Julia Jones earns $12/hour. During the most recent week, she received a nondiscretionary bonus of $3,100 and worked 42 hours.

3. Joseph Marshall earns $7.40/hour. During the most recent week, he received a nondiscretionary bonus of $720 and worked 50 hours.

4. Philip Lucas earns $10/hour. During the most recent week, he received a nondiscretionary bonus of $2,200 and worked 49 hours.

PSa 2-9 Calculate Gross Pay Based on an Incentive Plan

Calculate gross pay for each of the following employees of Launchpad Co. The company offers a regular wage rate of $8.20/hour to all employees. Under an incentive plan in place for all employees, this rate increases for any employee who can meet weekly production goals. The increased rates and corresponding thresholds that must be met are as follows:

- $9.40/hour for producing at least 2,000 units
- $10.60/hour for producing at least 2,800 units
- $11.80/hour for producing at least 3,700 units
- $13/hour for producing at least 4,700 units

All employees are paid overtime wage rates that are 1.5 times their respective regular wage rates.

1. Bronson Chau worked 45 hours and produced 3,251 units.

2. Pauline Myers worked 48 hours and produced 2,054 units.

3. Angela Smith worked 54 hours and produced 5,157 units.

4. Angelo Balducci worked 48 hours and produced 3,986 units.

PSa 2-10 Calculate Gross Pay for a Tipped Employee

Calculate gross pay for each of the following employees. All are paid overtime wage rates that are 1.5 times their respective regular wage rates.

1. Anita Workman receives tips from customers as a standard component of her weekly pay. She was paid $2.50/hour by her employer and received $284 in tips during the most recent 46-hour workweek.

2. Cole Earnhardt receives tips from customers as a standard component of his weekly pay. He was paid $2.13/hour by his employer and received $442 in tips during the most recent 42-hour workweek.

3. Calista Flood receives tips from customers as a standard component of her weekly pay. She was paid $4.10/hour by her employer and received $350 in tips during the most recent 38-hour workweek.

4. Bethany Pugh receives tips from customers as a standard component of her weekly pay. She was paid $3.60/hour by her employer and received $162 in tips during the most recent 51-hour workweek.

PSa 2-11 Calculate Gross Pay for a Piecework Employee

Calculate gross pay for each of the following employees. All are paid overtime wage rates that are 1.5 times their respective regular wage rates.

1. Walter Pinkman assembles merchandise and is paid $0.11 for each unit assembled. During the most recent week, he worked 46 hours and assembled 5,628 units.

2. Sidney Darling is a telemarketer who is paid $0.34 for every telemarketing call he places. During the most recent week, he worked 41 hours and placed 1,642 calls.

3. Pete Brees assembles merchandise and is paid $0.04 for each unit assembled. During the most recent week, he worked 52 hours and assembled 13,284 units.

4. Roy Carter is a telemarketer who is paid $0.30 for every telemarketing phone call he places. During the most recent week, he worked 51 hours and placed 1,536 calls.

PSa 2-12 Populate a Payroll Register

Complete the top portion and earnings section of a payroll register for the five employees in PSa 2-4. The associated pay period ends on 9/8/2019, with paychecks being printed and distributed six days later.

PSa 2-13 Populate Employee Earnings Records

Complete the top portion and earnings section of an employee earnings record for each employee from PSa 2-4 and PSa 2-12. Additional data for each employee is as follows:

- Luisa Williams (SSN 678-90-1111) lives at 345 Mountain View Lane, Juneau, AK 99801; is single; and claims one withholding allowance for both federal and state taxes.

- Jonathan Olsen (SSN 123-45-6789) lives at 25 Harvard Path, Winston-Salem, NC 27101; is single; and claims two federal withholding allowances and one state withholding allowance.

- Nathan Upton (SSN 232-23-2323) lives at 5672 Hillside Lane, St. Louis, MO 63101; is married; and claims three withholding allowances for both federal and state taxes.

- Juan Rodriguez (SSN 343-43-3434) lives at 432B Main Street, Baton Rouge, LA 70801; is single; and claims one withholding allowance for both federal and state taxes.

- Drew Painter (SSN 454-45-4545) lives at 12 State Road, Dallas, TX 75201; is married; and claims five federal withholding allowances and four state withholding allowances.

Practice Set B

The IRS forms and Excel templates needed for these assignments are included in the Student Exercise Files download for this course. If directed to do so, complete these assignments in Homework Grader.

PSb 2-1 Identify Pay Periods and Evaluate Workweeks

Examine each of the following independent circumstances and identify the type of pay period (weekly, biweekly, semimonthly, or monthly) being utilized. Then indicate whether the specified workweek is FLSA *compliant* or *noncompliant*.

1. Carpets 'r Us pays its employees 24 times each year. Its workweek is based on activity level and varies from week to week but never exceeds a seven-day period.

2. Flagpole Enterprises distributes paychecks to employees every other week on Friday afternoon. These pay dates fall exactly seven days after the end of every pay period. The workweek begins Monday at 8:00 a.m. and ends Friday afternoon at 6:00 p.m.

3. Radio World prints and distributes checks for its employees 12 times each year. Its workweek begins Tuesday at 2:43 p.m. and ends a week later on Tuesday at 2:42 p.m.

PSb 2-2 Complete a Time Card

Complete a time card for each employee below. Note that this employer rounds employee time to the nearest 15-minute increment.

1. Adam Spruce (SSN 565-56-5656) worked six days during the week of 1/14/2019 through 1/20/2019 (he was off work on Tuesday). He arrived at 9:00 a.m. each day (except Friday, when he was four minutes early, and Sunday, when he was two minutes late). He left for lunch at 12:30 p.m. each day (except Wednesday, when he left at 12:28 p.m., and Thursday, when he left at 1:01 p.m.), and arrived back at 1:30 p.m. (except Friday, when he arrived back at 2:02 p.m.). He left work at 5:00 p.m. each day (except Monday, when he stayed until 6:28 p.m.).

2. Tyson Newton (SSN 676-67-6767) worked five days during the week of 4/8/2019 through 4/14/2019 (he was off work on Saturday and Sunday). He arrived at 8:30 a.m. each day (except Monday, when he was 30 minutes early, and Tuesday, when he was one hour late). He left for lunch at 12:00 p.m. each day (except Wednesday, when he left at 12:04 p.m., and Thursday, when he didn't take a lunch break), and arrived back at 1:00 p.m. (except Friday, when he arrived back at 1:04 p.m., and Thursday, when he did not take a lunch break). He left work at 6:00 p.m. each day (except Friday, when he left work at 4:31 p.m.).

PSb 2-3 Calculate Weekly Regular Earnings

Calculate the weekly regular earnings for each of the following employees:

1. Phillip Hilton earns $9.05/hour and worked 34 hours during the most recent week.

2. Suzanne Milliner earns an annual salary of $51,000.

3. Sally Russell earns $11.55/hour and worked 38 hours during the most recent week.

4. Wendy Parker earns an annual salary of $91,500.

5. Robert Norton earns $18.20/hour and worked 40 hours during the most recent week.

PSb 2-4 Calculate Weekly Gross Pay

Calculate gross pay (regular earnings + overtime earnings) for each of the following employees. Each of them earns hourly overtime wages 1.5 times greater than his/her regular wage rate.

1. Jimmy Troffa earns $7.80/hour and worked 41 hours during the most recent week.

2. Tyler Thomas earns $10.90/hour and worked 45 hours during the most recent week.

3. Ryan Brown earns $14.60/hour and worked 48 hours during the most recent week.

4. Michael Kaminski earns $16/hour and worked 55 hours during the most recent week.

5. Tina Baldwin earns $17.10/hour and worked 50 hours during the most recent week.

PSb 2-5 Determine Hourly Regular and Overtime Wage Rates

Determine both the regular and overtime wage rates for each of the following employees. All are paid overtime wage rates that are 1.5 times their respective regular wage rates.

1. Kevin Williams earns a weekly wage of $740. During the most recent week, he worked 42 hours.

2. Charles Joyner earns a biweekly wage of $2,720. During the most recent week, he worked 45 hours.

3. Julio Valdez earns an annual salary of $81,000. During the most recent week, he worked 44 hours.

4. Bridget Stein earns a monthly salary of $6,200. During the most recent week, she worked 56 hours.

5. Betsy Cranston earns a semimonthly salary of $2,200. During the most recent week, she worked 49 hours.

PSb 2-6 Calculate Gross Pay

Calculate gross pay for each of the five employees listed in the prior exercise.

PSb 2-7 Calculate Gross Pay with Commissions

Calculate gross pay for each of the following employees. All are paid overtime wage rates that are 1.5 times their respective regular wage rates.

1. Billy Fortuna earns both $11.45/hour and a 10% commission on all sales. During the most recent week, he worked 47 hours and made total sales of $8,800.

2. Emily Robinson earns both $8.10/hour and $35 for every sale she completes. During the most recent week, she worked 55 hours and made a total of 49 sales.

3. Richard Eisenhower earns both $14.90/hour and a 14% commission on all sales. During the most recent week, he worked 43 hours and made total sales of $5,700.

4. Zoey Jefferson earns $19.10/hour, $5 for every sale of Product A, and $18 for every sale of Product B. During the most recent week, she worked 50 hours and sold 37 units of Product A and 29 units of Product B.

5. Bruce Wright earns both $13.50/hour and a 20% commission on all sales. During the most recent week, he worked 41 hours and made total sales of $15,200.

PSb 2-8 Calculate Gross Pay with Bonuses

Calculate gross pay for each of the following employees. All are paid overtime wage rates that are 1.5 times their respective regular wage rates.

1. Neil Mitchell earns $11/hour. During the most recent week, he received a discretionary bonus of $7,200 and worked 43 hours.

2. Francine Palmer earns $7.90/hour. During the most recent week, she received a nondiscretionary bonus of $2,450 and worked 45 hours.

3. Martin Green earns $11.10/hour. During the most recent week, he received a nondiscretionary bonus of $1,360 and worked 51 hours.

4. Melvin Waxman earns $17.60/hour. During the most recent week, he received a nondiscretionary bonus of $440 and worked 56 hours.

PSb 2-9 Calculate Gross Pay Based on an Incentive Plan

Calculate gross pay for each of the following four employees of Person Mover Corp. The company offers a regular wage rate of $7.90/hour to all employees. Under an incentive plan in place for all employees, this rate increases for any employee who can meet weekly production goals. The increased rates and corresponding thresholds that must be met are as follows:

- $8.30/hour for producing at least 550 units
- $10.70/hour for producing at least 720 units
- $13.20/hour for producing at least 1,000 units
- $17.70/hour for producing at least 1,310 units

All employees are paid overtime wage rates that are 1.5 times their respective regular wage rates.

1. Willy Tripp worked 42 hours and produced 882 units.

2. Louise Franklin worked 49 hours and produced 591 units.

3. Maya James worked 44 hours and produced 1,302 units.

4. Mason Winston worked 53 hours and produced 302 units.

PSb 2-10 Calculate Gross Pay for a Tipped Employee

Calculate gross pay for each of the following employees. All are paid overtime wage rates that are 1.5 times their respective regular wage rates.

1. Stanley Smothers receives tips from customers as a standard component of his weekly pay. He is paid $5.10/hour by his employer and received $305 in tips during the most recent 41-hour workweek.

2. Arnold Weiner receives tips from customers as a standard component of his weekly pay. He is paid $4.40/hour by his employer and received $188 in tips during the most recent 47-hour workweek.

3. Katherine Shaw receives tips from customers as a standard component of her weekly pay. She is paid $2.20/hour by her employer and received $553 in tips during the most recent 56-hour workweek.

4. Tracey Houseman receives tips from customers as a standard component of her weekly pay. She is paid $3.90/hour by her employer and received $472 in tips during the most recent 45-hour workweek.

PSb 2-11 Calculate Gross Pay for a Piecework Employee

Calculate gross pay for each of the following employees. All are paid overtime wage rates that are 1.5 times their respective regular wage rates.

1. Shane Bryan is a telemarketer who is paid $0.28 for every telemarketing phone call he places. During the most recent week, he worked 47 hours and placed 2,084 calls.

2. Zeke Saunders assembles merchandise and is paid $0.18 for each unit assembled. During the most recent week, he worked 48 hours and assembled 3,436 units.

3. Luke Hernandez is a telemarketer who is paid $0.41 for every telemarketing phone call he places. During the most recent week, he worked 42 hours and placed 1,374 calls.

4. Quincy Finkelstein assembles merchandise and is paid $0.08 for each unit assembled. During the most recent week, he worked 42 hours and assembled 6,209 units.

PSb 2-12 Populate a Payroll Register

Complete the top portion and earnings section of a payroll register for the five employees in PSb 2-4. The associated pay period ends on 7/21/2019, with paychecks being printed and distributed six days later.

PSb 2-13 Populate Employee Earnings Records

Complete the top portion and earnings section of an employee earnings record for each employee from PSb 2-4 and PSb 2-12. Additional data for each employee is as follows:

- Jimmy Troffa (SSN 787-78-7878) lives at 81 Jackson Road, Berkeley, CA 94701; is married; and claims three withholding allowances for both federal and state taxes.
- Tyler Thomas (SSN 898-89-8989) lives at 4004 Dartmouth Court, Reno, NV 89501; is single; and claims three federal withholding allowances and two state withholding allowances.
- Ryan Brown (SSN 100-00-0000) lives at 3 Fireside Avenue, Bentonville, AR 72716; is single; and claims two withholding allowances for both federal and state taxes.
- Michael Kaminski (SSN 200-00-0000) lives at 881 Sawmill Street, Nashville, TN 37201; is single; and claims three withholding allowances for both federal and state taxes.
- Tina Baldwin (SSN 300-00-0000) lives at 91845 Village Path, Trenton, NJ 08601; is married; and claims four federal withholding allowances and three state withholding allowances.

Continuing Payroll Problem

The IRS forms and Excel templates needed for these assignments are included in the Student Exercise Files download for this course. If directed to do so, complete these assignments in Homework Grader.

CPP 2-1 Calculate and Document Gross Pay

Calculate gross pay for a number of employees of TCLH Industries, a manufacturer of cleaning products. Then complete a payroll register based on your calculations. Recall that all calculations, both intermediate and final, should be rounded to two decimal places.

1. Complete a time card for each employee below. Note that this employer rounds employee time to the nearest 15-minute increment.

   - Zachary Fox (SSN 121-21-2121) worked five days for TCLH Industries during the week of 12/9/2019 through 12/15/2019 (he had both Saturday and Sunday off that week). On each working day he arrived at 7:00 a.m. (except Tuesday, when he was four minutes early, and Wednesday, when he arrived at 8:02 a.m.). He left for lunch at 11:00 a.m. each day (except Tuesday and Friday, when he left at 10:59 a.m.), and arrived back at 12:00 p.m. (except Friday, when he arrived back at 11:53 a.m.). He left at 4:00 p.m. each day (except Monday and Thursday, when he stayed until 6:02 p.m. and 4:01 p.m., respectively).

   - Calvin Bell (SSN 500-00-0000) worked six days for TCLH Industries during the week of 12/9/2019 through 12/15/2019 (he had Wednesday off that week). On each working day he arrived at 8:00 a.m. (except Monday and Saturday, when he was seven minutes early and two minutes late, respectively). He left for lunch each day at noon (except Tuesday, when he left at 11:56 a.m., and Saturday, when he didn't take lunch), and arrived back (except Saturday) at 1:00 p.m. He left at 5:00 p.m. each day (except Monday, when he stayed until 6:00 p.m., and Friday, when he stayed until 6:29 p.m.).

2. Complete the earnings section of the payroll register for the week of 12/9/2019 through 12/15/2019. TCLH Industries prints and distributes paychecks each week on the Thursday following the completion of the pay period. Then, complete an employee earnings record for each of the four employees of TCLH Industries. (Recall that you began this record for Zachary Fox in Chapter 1.)

   - Zachary Fox (SSN 121-21-2121), whose time card you completed above, lives at 1483 Independence Road, Durham, NC 27701. He is married, claims two withholding allowances for both federal and state, earns regular wages of $28/hour, and earns overtime wages of $42/hour.

   - Calvin Bell (SSN 500-00-0000), whose time card you completed above, lives at 2222 Sacker Place, Durham, NC 27701. He is single, claims two federal withholding allowances and one state withholding allowance, earns regular wages of $7.30/hour, and earns overtime wages of 1.5 times his regular wage rate.

   - David Alexander (SSN 454-54-5454) earns an annual salary of $210,600 and is exempt from the overtime provisions of the FLSA. He lives at 1 Freedom Boulevard, Durham, NC 27701; is single; and claims one withholding allowance for both federal and state taxes.

   - Michael Sierra (SSN 232-32-3232) earns an annual salary of $127,400 and is exempt from the overtime provisions of the FLSA. He lives at 200 Mississippi Road, Durham, NC 27701; is married; and claims four federal withholding allowances and three state withholding allowances.

Critical Thinking

CT 2-1 Review Various Incentive Plans

You were introduced earlier to some of the most common incentive plans used by employers. In all cases, these plans are designed to encourage specific employee behaviors that align with the goals of the organization. In this exercise, you'll use the Internet to research alternate incentive plans beyond those listed earlier.

Incentive plans can be divided into monetary (providing employees with the opportunity to earn additional money) and nonmonetary (incentivizing employees with a benefit other than money). Use the Internet to identify four employee incentives (two monetary and two nonmonetary) not listed in this chapter. For each incentive, write at least three sentences in which you describe the incentive and discuss the circumstance in which it is most appropriate. Lastly, write at least two sentences in which you select the one of these incentives that you deem to be most effective, and discuss your reasoning.

Submit your final file based on the guidelines provided by your instructor.

CT 2-2 Research State Minimum Wages

In states in which the state minimum wage exceeds the federal minimum wage, employers must comply with the higher state wage. In this exercise, you'll research current state minimum wages, identifying those states that currently require a minimum wage higher than the federal requirement.

Begin by researching state minimum wages on the Internet, and then identify those states that require higher minimum wages than the current federal rate. Write a paragraph of at least five sentences in which you list these states, identify the state(s) with the highest current state minimum wage, identify the current state minimum wage in your state, and discuss reasons why you believe that certain states have mandated higher minimum wage rates.

Submit your final file based on the guidelines provided by your instructor.

Federal and State Income Tax Withholding

LEARNING OBJECTIVES

- Identify and distinguish between mandatory and voluntary deductions

- Determine taxable earnings

- Calculate federal income tax withholding using the wage-bracket method

- Calculate federal income tax withholding using the percentage method

- Discuss state and local income tax withholding

Once an employee's earnings are determined, the next step is to calculate the amounts withheld from the earnings. While some of these deductions are mandatory (such as Medicare tax), others are voluntary and may be elected by the employee. In this chapter, you will identify a wide range of both mandatory and voluntary deductions. Next, you will examine federal income tax withholding more closely and learn two methods for calculating the tax. You will then review state and local income tax withholding, and will conclude by entering both federal and state income tax withholding figures in the payroll register.

Videos available! Check out the Video Launch Pad in your student exercise file download to access videos associated with this chapter. One video presents a chapter overview, and the other provides more detail on a key chapter topic.

CASE STUDY

Determining Federal and State Income Tax Withholding for Lucky Ties Apparel

Lucky Ties Apparel is required to withhold a variety of taxes from each employee's pay. Among these are federal and state income tax withholdings. As not all employees of Lucky Ties Apparel earn the same amount, and all have a different number of federal and state withholding allowances, the applicable calculations differ from one employee to the next.

Because these deductions from gross pay are among your payroll-related responsibilities, you decide that a thorough examination of each is warranted. You begin by examining both the federal and state income tax withholding, so that you understand the different methods that may be used to calculate each. You then fill out the payroll register with these newly calculated deductions.

Federal, state, and local income tax withholding (where applicable) are some of the mandatory deductions withheld from employee pay.

MY CONSTRUCTION COMPANY
1001 Fifth Avenue
New York, NY 10022

| Period ending: | 12/8/2019 |
| Pay date: | 12/10/2019 |

CLARK MITCHELL
547 Smith Street
New York, NY 10033

Earnings	Rate	Hours	This Period	Year to Date
Regular	$14.00	40.00	$560.00	$28,000.00
Overtime	$21.00	4.00	$84.00	$6,615.00
Holiday	$30.00	0.00	$0.00	$2,250.00
		Gross Pay	$644.00	$36,865.00

Deductions			
Statutory		This Period	Year to Date
Federal Income Tax		$19.00	$1,350.00
Social Security Tax		$39.93	$2,285.63
Medicare Tax		$9.34	$534.54
NYS Income Tax		$12.67	$783.33
NYC Income Tax		$8.44	$472.22
NYSDI Tax		$0.60	$30.00
Other			
401(k)		$32.20*	$1,843.25
Life Insurance		$10.00	$500.00

Federal Income Tax Withholding

State Income Tax Withholding

Local Income Tax Withholding

| Net Pay | $511.82 |

* Excluded from federal taxable wages

Social Security Number: ***-**-1119
Taxable Marital Status: Married
Exemptions/Allowances:
Federal: 4, $25 Additional Tax
State: 3
Local: 3

Other Benefits and Information	This Period	Year to Date
Vacation Hrs.		64.00
Sick Hrs.		24.00

Deductions from Employee Earnings

Once an employee's gross pay is calculated, certain amounts are withheld by the employer and are not included in the employee's paycheck. These amounts are referred to as **deductions**. Some of these amounts must be withheld, and these are called **mandatory deductions**. Others may be requested by the employee, and these are referred to as **voluntary deductions**.

Mandatory Deductions

Employees are subject to a number of mandatory deductions that their employers are required to withhold from each paycheck. Among these deductions are the following:

- **Federal income tax withholding**—This tax (also called *federal income tax*) is collected by the federal government to fund a wide range of government agencies. A small percentage of employees are exempt from this tax, as you will see later in this chapter.

- **State income tax withholding**—The majority of states collect this tax (also called *state income tax*) to fund state operations. As of 2019, nine states (Alaska, Florida, Nevada, New Hampshire, South Dakota, Tennessee, Texas, Washington, and Wyoming) did not collect state taxes on individual incomes.

NOTE! In 2019 New Hampshire and Tennessee did collect taxes on dividend and interest income.

- **Local income tax withholding**—Some municipalities, such as Manhattan in New York State, require that local income tax withholding (also called *local income tax*) be deducted from employee earnings to fund government operations in their respective municipalities.

- **Social Security tax (OASDI)**—This tax is withheld from employee earnings to fund the Social Security system, which pays benefits to retired or disabled workers, as well as their dependents and survivors. This tax is subject to an income threshold, and therefore (in 2019) was only calculated as 6.2% of the first $132,900 earned during the year. This will be discussed in detail in Chapter 4.

- **Medicare tax (HI)**—This tax (in 2019) was calculated as 1.45% of all employee earnings. These funds operate the Medicare federal health insurance program that covers individuals 65 years of age or older and certain disabled individuals. This will be discussed in detail in Chapter 4.

TIP! Social Security tax and Medicare tax, in conjunction, are referred to as FICA (Federal Insurance Contributions Act) taxes.

- **State disability insurance tax**—Five states (California, Hawaii, New Jersey, New York, and Rhode Island) and the territory of Puerto Rico require that disability insurance be withheld from employee pay. With these funds, the states provide benefits to temporarily disabled employees who are unable to work as a result of a non-work-related circumstance. This will be discussed in detail in Chapter 4.

Voluntary Deductions

In addition to the items that must be withheld from an employee's pay, there are a number of amounts that an employee may elect to have withheld. Common examples of these voluntary deductions, which will be examined further in Chapter 4, are as follows:

- **Union dues**—For those employees who are unionized, the associated dues may be withheld from their earnings and remitted directly to the union.
- **Retirement plans**—Employees may elect to have monies withheld for retirement plans, some of which can be tax-deferred (no federal income tax is paid on these funds when they are withheld). These are called *defined contribution plans*, as the employee's contribution percentage (portion of gross pay deducted) is fixed.
- **Medical plans**—Depending on various criteria, employees may realize a tax benefit from having funds withheld and directed to a medical savings plan. These plans differ from flexible spending accounts (discussed next) in that the funds roll over and can be used in subsequent years.

NOTE! Medical plans differ from health insurance premiums, which employees can elect to have withheld from gross earnings and which pay for (either in part or entirely) the employee's health insurance coverage.

- **Cafeteria plans**—Offered by some employers, these plans can provide a variety of benefits, and designated funds are not subject to federal income tax withholding. One common type of cafeteria plan is a **flexible spending account**, through which employees may be reimbursed for qualified benefits such as dependent care and medical expenses.

Not technically a voluntary deduction for the employee to whom it is applied, a *wage garnishment* represents monies withheld from pay as a result of a court order. These amounts may fund a wide range of monetary obligations, including child support. Individual states have varying requirements regarding the reporting of newly hired employees, in large part to identify those employees for whom garnishments should be made.

Distinguishing Between Gross Pay and Taxable Pay

As you saw in the previous chapter, gross pay encompasses all earnings of an employee for a given period. However, each of the above-listed taxes is not necessarily calculated based on this gross pay. For example, since dependent care expenses and cafeteria plans are tax-deferred, the amount contributed to these must be subtracted from gross pay before determining federal income tax withholding. Additionally, 401(k) and 403(b) plans are both tax-deferred retirement plans that are exempt from federal income tax. Taxable pay (also called taxable income) represents the portion of gross pay used to calculate each of the mandatory deductions.

Note that taxable pay used to calculate federal income tax withholding can be different from taxable pay used to calculate Social Security or Medicare tax. For example, deductions for a 401(k) or 403(b) retirement plan are not taxable for federal income tax withholding but are taxable for Social Security and Medicare taxes. The following chart summarizes the taxes for which different employee payments are either taxable (T) or nontaxable (N). Contrary to the information displayed below, when offered as part of a cafeteria plan, group-term life insurance benefits exceeding $50,000 are subject to FICA taxes, and adoption assistance benefits are subject to both FICA and FUTA taxes.

	Federal Withholding Tax	FICA Taxes	FUTA Taxes
401(k) retirement plan	N	T	T
403(b) retirement plan	N	T	T
Cafeteria plan	N	N	N
Charitable contribution	T	T	T
Dependent care benefit	N	N	N
Flexible spending account	N	N	N
Medical savings plan	N	N	N
SIMPLE IRA retirement plan	N	T	T
Union dues	T	T	T
Wage garnishment	T	T	T

life insurance   *T*

Depending on the regulations in place, taxable income for both state and local income tax withholdings can also differ from that for federal income tax withholding. For simplicity, we will assume throughout the text that, for every employee, taxable income is the same for federal, state, and local income tax withholding.

Case in Point 3-1	**Determine Gross and Taxable Pay**

Based on the information provided below, determine the gross pay for each employee. Then calculate taxable pay for federal income tax withholding, Social Security tax, and Medicare tax.

1. An employee works 37 regular hours during the first workweek of 2019 and earns $8.25/hour. He has requested that his employer withhold 8% of gross pay, which is to be contributed to a 401(k) plan.

   Gross pay for this employee, who did not work any overtime hours, was $305.25 (37 hours × $8.25).

As 401(k) contributions are tax-deferred for the purposes of federal income tax withholding, this employee's contribution must be subtracted from gross pay in order to determine taxable pay for federal income tax withholding. The 401(k) contribution is $24.42 ($305.25 × 8%); therefore, taxable pay for federal income tax withholding is $280.83 ($305.25 – $24.42).

For this employee, there are no amounts that must be subtracted from gross pay in order to arrive at taxable pay for Social Security tax or Medicare tax (401(k) contributions are taxable for these two taxes). Therefore, taxable pay for both Social Security tax and Medicare tax is $305.25.

2. An employee works 43 hours (3 of which were overtime hours) during a workweek in November of 2019. The employee earns $37.50/hour, with his employer paying 1.5 times the regular rate of pay for overtime hours. To date, he has earned $132,100 during the year (these earnings include hourly wages, as well as bonus payments, which are also subject to FICA tax). He has requested that his employer withhold 10% of gross pay, which is to be contributed to a 403(b) plan.

    Regular earnings for this employee were $1,500 (40 hours × $37.50/hour). The overtime rate of pay is $56.25/hour ($37.50/hour × 1.5), and the overtime earnings were $168.75 (3 hours × $56.25/hour). Therefore, gross pay for the week was $1,668.75 ($1,500 regular earnings + $168.75 overtime earnings).

    Taxable earnings for federal income tax withholding must exclude the 403(b) contribution. This contribution was $166.88 ($1,668.75 gross pay × 10%); therefore, the taxable earnings for federal income tax withholding were $1,501.87 ($1,668.75 gross pay – $166.88 403(b) contribution).

    The previous annual earnings of $132,100, when added to the gross pay of $1,668.75, total $133,768.75. As this exceeds the 2019 Social Security tax threshold of $132,900, only a portion of the gross pay is taxable for Social Security tax. The portion of gross pay that falls below the threshold totals $800 ($132,900 threshold – $132,100 previous annual earnings), and therefore this $800 represents the taxable pay for Social Security tax.

    Medicare tax is not subject to an earnings threshold. In addition, 403(b) contributions are not exempt from Medicare tax. Therefore, taxable pay for Medicare tax is the same as the gross pay of $1,668.75.

Federal Income Tax Withholding

The manner in which federal income tax withholding is remitted to the United States government is referred to as a **pay-as-you-go** system. Under this system, income tax must be paid as the income is earned.

The pay-as-you-go system was established as a result of the **Current Tax Payment Act of 1943**. This act modified the federal income tax system such that payments could no longer be made in the subsequent year, but instead must be paid in the year that the income is earned. To facilitate the collection of these taxes, the act stipulated that employers must withhold these taxes from employee pay and remit the withholdings to the federal government. Over the next few pages we will review two methods by which these taxes may be calculated. In Chapter 6 we will then examine how these taxes are reported on a quarterly basis within Form 941 and on an annual basis within Forms W-2 and W-3.

Under limited circumstances, employees may be exempted from paying federal income tax withholding. Typically, an employee who qualifies for exemption did not owe federal income tax during the prior year and does not expect to owe it in the current year. In this instance, the employee must file a W-4 Form with the employer indicating the exempt status. These qualifying employees are often low-income earners who, in many instances, qualify for the Earned Income Credit, which reduces the tax burden on their year-end personal tax returns.

For the employer to withhold the correct amount of federal income tax for each non-exempt employee, a number of calculation methods may be utilized. The two primary methods are the wage-bracket method and the percentage method.

The Wage-Bracket Method

Under the **wage-bracket method**, an employee's marital status, withholding allowances, and taxable pay are used to locate the correct amount of withholding on a federal income tax withholding table. This is one of the primary instances in which key information from the employee's W-4 Form (marital status and federal with-holding allowances) is utilized to determine applicable taxes.

Updated Federal Income Tax Withholding Tables are published each year in Circular E.

SINGLE Persons—WEEKLY Payroll Period												
(For Wages Paid through December 2019)												
And the wages are–		And the number of withholding allowances claimed is—										
At least	But less than	0	1	2	3	4	5	6	7	8	9	10
		The amount of income tax to be withheld is—										
$ 0	$73	$0	$0	$0	$0	$0	$0	$0	$0	$0	$0	$0
73	84	1	0	0	0	0	0	0	0	0	0	0
84	95	2	0	0	0	0	0	0	0	0	0	0
95	106	3	0	0	0	0	0	0	0	0	0	0
106	117	4	0	0	0	0	0	0	0	0	0	0
117	128	5	0	0	0	0	0	0	0	0	0	0
128	139	6	0	0	0	0	0	0	0	0	0	0
139	150	7	0	0	0	0	0	0	0	0	0	0
150	161	8	0	0	0	0	0	0	0	0	0	0
161	172	9	1	0	0	0	0	0	0	0	0	0
172	183	10	2	0	0	0	0	0	0	0	0	0
183	194	12	3	0	0	0	0	0	0	0	0	0
194	205	13	5	0	0	0	0	0	0	0	0	0
205	216	14	6	0	0	0	0	0	0	0	0	0
216	227	15	7	0	0	0	0	0	0	0	0	0
227	238	16	8	0	0	0	0	0	0	0	0	0
238	249	17	9	1	0	0	0	0	0	0	0	0
249	260	18	10	2	0	0	0	0	0	0	0	0
260	271	19	11	3	0	0	0	0	0	0	0	0
271	282	21	12	4	0	0	0	0	0	0	0	0
282	293	22	13	5	0	0	0	0	0	0	0	0
293	304	23	14	6	0	0	0	0	0	0	0	0
304	315	25	16	7	0	0	0	0	0	0	0	0
315	326	26	17	9	1	0	0	0	0	0	0	0
326	337	27	18	10	2	0	0	0	0	0	0	0
337	348	29	19	11	3	0	0	0	0	0	0	0
348	359	30	20	12	4	0	0	0	0	0	0	0
359	370	31	22	13	5	0	0	0	0	0	0	0
370	381	33	23	14	6	0	0	0	0	0	0	0
381	392	34	24	15	7	0	0	0	0	0	0	0
392	403	35	26	16	8	0	0	0	0	0	0	0
403	414	37	27	17	9	1	0	0	0	0	0	0
414	425	38	28	18	10	2	0	0	0	0	0	0
425	436	39	29	20	12	3	0	0	0	0	0	0
436	447	40	31	21	13	5	0	0	0	0	0	0
447	458	42	32	22	14	6	0	0	0	0	0	0
458	469	43	33	24	15	7	0	0	0	0	0	0
469	480	44	35	25	16	8	0	0	0	0	0	0
480	491	46	36	26	17	9	1	0	0	0	0	0
491	502	47	37	28	18	10	2	0	0	0	0	0
502	513	48	39	29	19	11	3	0	0	0	0	0
513	524	50	40	30	21	12	4	0	0	0	0	0
524	535	51	41	32	22	13	5	0	0	0	0	0
535	546	52	43	33	23	14	6	0	0	0	0	0
546	557	54	44	34	25	16	7	0	0	0	0	0
557	568	55	45	36	26	17	9	0	0	0	0	0
568	579	56	47	37	27	18	10	2	0	0	0	0
579	590	58	48	38	29	19	11	3	0	0	0	0
590	601	59	49	40	30	20	12	4	0	0	0	0
601	612	60	51	41	31	22	13	5	0	0	0	0
612	623	62	52	42	33	23	14	6	0	0	0	0
623	634	63	53	44	34	24	15	7	0	0	0	0
634	645	64	55	45	35	25	16	8	0	0	0	0
645	656	66	56	46	36	27	17	9	1	0	0	0
656	667	67	57	47	38	28	18	10	2	0	0	0
667	678	68	59	49	39	29	20	11	3	0	0	0
678	689	70	60	50	40	31	21	13	5	0	0	0
689	700	71	61	51	42	32	22	14	6	0	0	0
700	711	72	62	53	43	33	24	15	7	0	0	0
711	722	73	64	54	44	35	25	16	8	0	0	0
722	733	75	65	55	46	36	26	17	9	1	0	0
733	744	76	66	57	47	37	28	18	10	2	0	0
744	755	77	68	58	48	39	29	19	11	3	0	0
755	766	79	69	59	50	40	30	21	12	4	0	0
766	777	80	70	61	51	41	32	22	13	5	0	0
777	788	81	72	62	52	43	33	23	14	6	0	0

The withholding table shown above is for an employee whose marital status is single and who is paid on a weekly basis. Weekly wage ranges are provided on the left of the table, and federal withholding allowances are at the top. To determine an employee's federal income tax withholding, an employer locates the intersection of the applicable wage range of the employee's taxable pay and the number of withholding allowances (found on the employee's W-4 Form).

For example, if a single employee is paid on a weekly basis and claims one federal withholding allowance and earns wages of $312, that employee is subject to $16 of federal income tax withholding. This employee would look at the intersection of the $304 to $315 wages row and the 1 withholding allowance column to determine this tax amount.

If this same employee earned wages of $330, the $326 to $337 row is applicable, resulting in federal income tax withholding of $18. The wage increments represent *at least… but less than*; therefore, wages of $326 correspond with the $326 to $337 row. Using the $315 to $326 row, in this instance, would be incorrect.

TIP!   Notice that, as the number of withholding allowances increases, the federal income tax withholding decreases. To ensure that sufficient tax is withheld during the year, employees may elect to claim fewer withholding allowances than they are permitted, thus increasing total withholding.

On the Web

irs.gov/pub/irs-pdf
/p15.pdf

Many different withholding tables are published by the Internal Revenue Service (IRS) in Circular E. Aside from the *Single: Weekly* table, a portion of which is shown above, the following tables are also available:

- Married: Weekly
- Single: Biweekly
- Married: Biweekly
- Single: Semimonthly
- Married: Semimonthly
- Single: Monthly
- Married: Monthly
- Single: Daily
- Married: Daily

These tables can all be viewed in Appendix A. Each table is two pages long and displays the appropriate federal income tax withholding for an employee with up to 10 withholding allowances. Circular E provides instruction regarding the federal income tax withholding calculation (under the wage-bracket method) for employees claiming more than 10 withholding allowances. However, in the event that an employee earns more than the largest wage range on the appropriate table, the percentage method must be used instead of the wage-bracket method.

The Percentage Method

An alternative method for determining federal income tax withholding is the **percentage method**. To use this method, the employer completes a three-step process:

Step 1: Multiply the employee's number of federal withholding allowances by the applicable figure shown in the table below.

This *One Withholding Allowance* table is published each year in Circular E.

Payroll Period	One Withholding Allowance
Weekly	$ 80.80
Biweekly	161.50
Semimonthly	175.00
Monthly	350.00
Quarterly	1,050.00
Semiannually	2,100.00
Annually	4,200.00
Daily or miscellaneous (each day of the payroll period)	16.20

Step 2: Subtract the Step 1 result from the employee's taxable pay.

Step 3: Use the percentage method tables (provided annually in Circular E) to calculate the federal income tax withholding, based on the result from Step 2.

This percentage method table provides calculation instruction for both single and married employees earning weekly pay.

(For Wages Paid in 2019)

TABLE 1—WEEKLY Payroll Period

(a) SINGLE person (including head of household)—

If the amount of wages (after subtracting withholding allowances) is: The amount of income tax to withhold is:

Not over $73 . . . . $0

Over—	But not over—		of excess over—
$73	—$260 . .	$0.00 plus 10%	—$73
$260	—$832 . .	$18.70 plus 12%	—$260
$832	—$1,692 . .	$87.34 plus 22%	—$832
$1,692	—$3,164 . .	$276.54 plus 24%	—$1,692
$3,164	—$3,998 . .	$629.82 plus 32%	—$3,164
$3,998	—$9,887 . .	$896.70 plus 35%	—$3,998
$9,887		$2,957.85 plus 37%	—$9,887

(b) MARRIED person—

If the amount of wages (after subtracting withholding allowances) is: The amount of income tax to withhold is:

Not over $227 . . . . $0

Over—	But not over—		of excess over—
$227	—$600 . .	$0.00 plus 10%	—$227
$600	—$1,745 . .	$37.30 plus 12%	—$600
$1,745	—$3,465 . .	$174.70 plus 22%	—$1,745
$3,465	—$6,409 . .	$553.10 plus 24%	—$3,465
$6,409	—$8,077 . .	$1,259.66 plus 32%	—$6,409
$8,077	—$12,003 . .	$1,793.42 plus 35%	—$8,077
$12,003		$3,167.52 plus 37%	—$12,003

For example, if a single employee has $1,080.80 of taxable pay, is paid weekly, and claims one federal withholding allowance, Step 1 results in $80.80 (1 allowance × $80.80 weekly figure in table). Step 2 results in $1,000 ($1,080.80 taxable pay minus the $80.80 Step 1 result). Step 3 results in the employee having federal income tax withholding of $87.34 + (22% × [$1,000 - $832]) = $124.30. Based on the third row of the *single* portion of the table, the excess of the $1,000 wages over $832 must be multiplied by 22%. This is how we determine the amount that is added to the $87.34 starting point to arrive at federal income tax withholding.

NOTE! The percentage method often yields a different withholding amount than the wage-bracket method for the same circumstance. In spite of this difference, both methods are acceptable.

Seven other versions of the percentage method table are also provided in Circular E. These allow for the calculation of federal income tax withholding for employees paid on the following bases: biweekly, semimonthly, monthly, quarterly, semiannually, annually, and daily.

TIP! More types of tables are provided under the percentage method than the wage-bracket method. For this reason, the wage-bracket method cannot be used for employees with quarterly, semiannual, or annual pay periods.

Case in Point 3-2	Calculate Federal Income Tax Withholding

For each of the following employees of Lucky Ties Apparel, let's calculate the federal income tax withholding for the current weekly pay period. We'll use the wage-bracket method for the first three employees and the percentage method for the final two employees.

Before You Begin: Federal withholding tax tables for both the wage-bracket method and the percentage method can be found in Appendix A.

1. Paul Rogers (single; one federal withholding allowance) earned gross pay of $402.50. For each period, he makes a 401(k) contribution of 8% of gross pay.

    Wage-Bracket Method:

    Taxable pay for federal income tax withholding excludes the 401(k) contribution. This retirement plan contribution totals $32.20 ($402.50 × 8%), and therefore taxable pay is $370.30 ($402.50 − $32.20).

    Using the Single: Weekly withholding table, this taxable pay falls in the $370 to $381 range. The intersection of this row and the one withholding allowance column yields federal income tax withholding of $23.

2. Maryanne Sherman (single; two federal withholding allowances) earned gross pay of $769.23. She does not make any retirement plan contributions.

    Wage-Bracket Method:

    All of the gross pay is taxable for federal income tax withholding purposes; therefore, taxable pay is $769.23.

    Using the Single: Weekly withholding table, this taxable pay falls in the $766 to $777 range. The intersection of this row and the two withholding allowances column yields federal income tax withholding of $61.

3. Bill Novak (married; four federal withholding allowances) earned gross pay of $725. For each period, he makes a flexible spending account contribution of 6% of gross pay.

    Wage-Bracket Method:

    Taxable pay for federal income tax withholding excludes the flexible spending account contribution. This contribution totals $43.50 ($725 × 6%), and therefore taxable pay is $681.50 ($725 – $43.50).

    Using the Married: Weekly withholding table, this taxable pay falls in the $678 to $689 range. The intersection of this row and the four withholding allowances column yields federal income tax withholding of $13.

4. Angelo Dorsett (single; two federal withholding allowances) earned gross pay of $883.75. For each period, he makes a dependent care flexible spending account contribution of 10% of gross pay.

    Percentage Method:

    Before undertaking the three-step process for the percentage method, taxable pay must first be determined. Taxable pay for federal income tax withholding excludes the dependent care flexible spending account contribution. This dependent care flexible spending account contribution totals $88.38 ($883.75 × 10%), and therefore taxable pay is $795.37 ($883.75 – $88.38).

    Step 1: Two withholding allowances × $80.80 (weekly one withholding allowance amount) = $161.60.

    Step 2: $795.37 (taxable pay) – $161.60 = $633.77.

    Step 3: Using the *single* side of the *weekly* table, the step 2 result falls in the $260 to $832 range. Therefore, federal income tax withholding is calculated as $18.70 + (12% x [$633.77 – $260]), which equals $63.55.

5. Melissa Kubiak (married; four federal withholding allowances) earned gross pay of $622.50. She does not make any retirement plan contributions.

    Percentage Method:

    Before undertaking the three-step process for the percentage method, taxable pay must first be determined. All of the gross pay is taxable for federal income tax withholding purposes; therefore, taxable pay is $622.50.

    Step 1: Four withholding allowances × $80.80 (weekly one withholding allowance amount) = $323.20.

    Step 2: $622.50 (taxable pay) – $323.20 = $299.30.

    Step 3: Using the *married* side of the *weekly* table, the step 2 result falls in the $227 to $600 range. Therefore, federal income tax withholding is calculated as $0 + (10% x [$299.30 – $227]), which equals $7.23.

Other Federal Income Tax Withholding Considerations

An employee's federal income tax withholding can be impacted by a number of other circumstances. Among the most common are the passing away or termination of an employee, and changes in the number of dependents (or other similar changes) that require the submission of an updated W-4 Form.

Deceased and Terminated Employees

In the event that an employee dies, it is likely that a portion of the employee's earnings will be paid by the employer after death. Any such payments are not subject to federal income tax withholding and should be excluded from the calculation of taxable pay.

When an individual's employment ends, either voluntarily or involuntarily, that person is entitled to all compensation earned prior to termination. The required timing of this payment differs from state to state and ranges from immediately upon involuntary termination to the time of the subsequent pay date. These earnings are subject to federal income tax withholding in the same manner as were the employee's prior earnings.

Changing the W-4 Form

Employees may need to change their W-4 Forms for a variety of reasons, including marriage, divorce, the birth of children, or change of job status for the employee or his/her spouse.

WARNING! For changes that either reduce the number of withholding allowances, or alter the status from *married* to *single*, the employee is required to complete a new W-4 Form within 10 days. No time limit exists for other changes; the employee may submit a new W-4 Form for other changes at his/her discretion.

When an updated W-4 Form is submitted by the employee, the employer must process the change (and therefore adjust the federal income tax withholding) no later than the start of the first payroll period that ends at least 30 days after submission of the new form. Although there is no limit to the number of W-4 Form changes that may be submitted by an employee, this time frame over which an employer is permitted to implement the change effectively limits the total number of changes that can be processed in a given year.

TIP! Accepting an updated W-4 Form is not optional for an employer. New W-4 Forms resulting from circumstances described earlier must be processed by the employer.

Case in Point 3-3	**Determine Timing of Employer Responsibilities**

For each of the following circumstances, determine the date on which the referenced action must take place:

1.   Samuel Wildhorn's divorce was finalized on Sunday, June 9. When must he submit a revised W-4 Form to his employer?

     When an employee's divorce is finalized, that employee has 10 days to provide the employer with a revised W-4 Form. Therefore, Samuel must furnish a new W-4 Form no later than Wednesday, June 19.

2.   Maggie Yang decides on Monday, March 4, that she would like to increase her number of federal withholding allowances from three to five. When must she submit a revised W-4 Form to her employer?

     In this instance, there is no time limit for submitting a new W-4 Form, as this is not one of the circumstances under which notification must be made within 10 days. Maggie is free to submit the new form whenever she would like.

3.   Brandon Rosenberg decides on Tuesday, October 15, that he would like to reduce his number of federal withholding allowances from five to three. He makes this change on a revised W-4 Form and submits it on Friday, October 18. Brandon is compensated on a semimonthly basis (at the middle and end of each month), and receives his paycheck five days after the end of each pay period. By which pay date must this change be in effect?

     The next two pay periods that end after submission of the new form have end dates of October 31 and November 15, neither of which is 30 days after submission. The pay period ending on November 30 is the first pay period that ends at least 30 days after submission; therefore, the W-4 Form must be processed prior to the beginning of this pay period (which starts on November 16). The associated pay date, which is five days after the end of the period, is December 5. The W-4 Form change must be in effect for this pay date.

State Income Tax Withholding

On the Web

sba.gov/business-guide
/manage-your-business
/pay-taxes

In addition to federal income tax withholding, the majority of employees are also subject to state income tax withholding. These taxes are calculated based on state taxable income, which in many states is the same as federal taxable income.

As was noted previously, nine states do not collect state income tax on employee taxable income. The tax rates imposed in the other 41 states vary widely from one to the next. Furthermore, while some states levy a flat tax on all employee earnings, others levy a graduated tax, which increases as the employee's earnings increase. Refer to your eLab course or Appendix C for links to state taxing authorities in each of the 50 states, in addition to all United States territories. Further details regarding each state's specific withholding tax provisions can be found there. You may also refer to Appendix D for State Tax/Revenue Department addresses.

Due to the variability in state income tax withholding rates and methods, we will utilize a flat 5% state tax rate throughout the textbook.

Local Income Tax Withholding

In addition to both federal and state income tax withholding, employees living and/or working in certain jurisdictions are subject to local income tax withholding. These taxes vary widely in terms of the tax rates applied and the form in which the taxes are levied. For example, some local jurisdictions (such as cities or towns) impose local income tax withholding as a percentage of gross pay, whereas others do so as a percentage of federal or state income tax withholding, while still others impose a simple flat tax (specific, identical dollar amount for each employee) on a weekly basis.

Local jurisdictions may also elect to impose different local income tax withholding on residents and nonresidents. The justification for this practice is that residents utilize the services of the jurisdiction to a greater extent than nonresidents and therefore should bear a greater tax burden.

| Case in Point 3-4 | ## Calculate State and Local Income Tax Withholding |

For each of the following employees, calculate the applicable state and local income tax withholding.

Before You Begin: Assume a state income tax withholding rate of 5% of taxable earnings.

1. Julio Ordonez earned gross pay of $847, all of which is taxable for state and local income tax withholding. The city in which he both lives and works levies a tax of 2% of an employee's gross pay.

   State income tax withholding for this employee is $42.35 ($847 gross pay × 5% state tax rate). Local income tax withholding is $16.94 ($847 gross pay × 2% local tax rate).

2. Alyona Gaponovitch earned gross pay of $1,620. Of this amount, $1,598 is taxable for state and local income tax withholding. The city in which she works (she lives elsewhere) levies a tax of 1.5% of an employee's gross pay on residents and 0.8% of an employee's gross pay on nonresidents.

   State income tax withholding for this employee is $79.90 ($1,598 taxable pay × 5% state tax rate). Local income tax withholding is based on a rate of 0.8%, as Alyona is a nonresident. Therefore, her local income tax withholding is $12.78 ($1,598 taxable pay × 0.8% local tax rate).

3. Lucy Farmington earned gross pay of $1,100. Of this amount, $1,065 is taxable for state and local income tax withholding. The city in which she lives and works levies a tax of 2.1% of an employee's gross pay on residents and 0.5% of an employee's gross pay on nonresidents.

   State income tax withholding for this employee is $53.25 ($1,065 taxable pay × 5% state tax rate). Local income tax withholding is based on a rate of 2.1%, as Lucy is a resident. Therefore, her local income tax withholding is $22.37 ($1,065 taxable pay × 2.1% local tax rate).

4. Gabrielle Fernandez earned weekly gross pay of $740, all of which is taxable for state and local income tax withholding. The city in which she lives and works levies a tax of $10/week on employees who work within city limits.

   State income tax withholding for this employee is $37 ($740 taxable pay × 5% state tax rate). Local income tax withholding is unrelated to Gabrielle's gross pay and is $10.

The Payroll Register

As you saw in the last chapter, the payroll register is completed based on the earnings and deductions that are subsequently transferred to the employee earnings records. Note that the city of Rochester, NY, in which Lucky Ties Apparel is located, does not levy local income tax withholding. As a result, there is no column in either the employee earnings record or the payroll register in which local income tax withholding can be entered. Both of these forms may be modified by the employer in this manner to suit a company's circumstance.

As with the employee earnings record, the payroll register columns can be modified to add columns for such voluntary deductions as health insurance and union dues.

Payroll Register

Pay Period _____

Pay Date _____

Employee Name	Regular Hours	Regular Rate	Regular Earnings	Overtime Hours	Overtime Rate	Overtime Earnings	Total Earnings	FWT	SWT	Social Security	Medicare	Health Ins.	Union Dues	Check Number	Net Pay
Totals:															

Earnings columns span: Regular Hours, Regular Rate, Regular Earnings, Overtime Hours, Overtime Rate, Overtime Earnings, Total Earnings. Deductions columns span: FWT, SWT, Social Security, Medicare, Health Ins., Union Dues.

Case in Point 3-5   Complete a Payroll Register

In this example, we'll complete a payroll register for Lucky Ties Apparel. Earlier we calculated the federal income tax withholding for five different employees of Lucky Ties Apparel. Their federal withholding tax for the most recent week has been entered into the payroll register below (federal income tax withholding for Angelo Dorsett and Melissa Kubiak differ slightly from earlier calculations, as Lucky Ties Apparel has elected to use the wage-bracket method for all employees).

Additionally, the federal income tax withholding for three other employees (whose earnings were determined in the last chapter) has been entered within the payroll register below. The state income tax withholding has been completed for all employees based on the previously assumed 5% tax rate. Based on the payroll register, we will complete a portion of the deductions section of each employee earnings record.

Assume that any deductions that are exempt from federal income tax withholding are also exempt from state income tax withholding. Further note that Lucy Marshall has requested that a voluntary deduction of 8% of gross earnings be contributed to a 401(k) retirement plan.

Payroll Register

Pay Period **12/1/2019**

Pay Date **12/5/2019**

Employee Name	Regular Hours	Regular Rate	Regular Earnings	Overtime Hours	Overtime Rate	Overtime Earnings	Total Earnings	FWT	SWT	Social Security	Medicare	Vol. With.	Check Number	Net Pay
					Earnings					Deductions				
Rogers, P	35	$ 11.50	$ 402.50	0	n/a	$ -	$ 402.50	$ 23.00	$ 18.52					
Sherman, M	n/a	n/a	$ 769.23	0	n/a	$ -	$ 769.23	$ 61.00	$ 38.46					
Novak, B	40	$ 14.75	$ 590.00	6	$ 22.50	$ 135.00	$ 725.00	$ 13.00	$ 34.08					
Dorsett, A	40	$ 17.50	$ 700.00	7	$ 26.25	$ 183.75	$ 883.75	$ 63.00	$ 39.77					
Kubiak, M	40	$ 15.00	$ 600.00	1	$ 22.50	$ 22.50	$ 622.50	$ 7.00	$ 31.13					
Martin, S	40	$ 21.15	$ 846.00	11	$ 31.73	$ 349.03	$ 1,195.03	$ 90.00	$ 59.75					
Marshall, L	40	$ 15.75	$ 630.00	9	$ 23.63	$ 212.67	$ 842.67	$ 51.00	$ 38.76					
McHenry, D	40	$ 15.30	$ 612.00	5	$ 22.95	$ 114.75	$ 726.75	$ 2.00	$ 36.34					
Totals:			$5,149.73			$1,017.70	$ 6,167.43	$310.00	$296.81					

Note that totals for the FWT and SWT columns have been calculated within the payroll register. As was done in the previous chapter when transferring earnings amounts, all federal income tax withholding and state income tax withholding figures from the payroll register are now transferred to the employee earnings records.

Employee Earnings Record

Name	Paul Rogers	Marital Status	Single
Address	657 Flicker Lane	Fed. Withholding Allow.	1
	Brockport, NY 14420	State Withholding Allow.	1
SS#	111-11-1111		

Pay Period Ending	Regular Hours Worked	Regular Pay Rate	Regular Wages	Overtime Hours Worked	Overtime Pay Rate	Overtime Wages	Gross Pay	Federal Withholding Tax	State Withholding Tax	Social Security Tax	Medicare Tax	Retirement Contribution	Life Insurance	Charitable Contribution	Additional Withholding	Check Number	Net Pay
			Earnings							Deductions							
12/1/19	35	$ 11.50	$ 402.50	0	n/a	$ -	$ 402.50	$ 23.00	$ 18.52								

Employee Earnings Record

Name	Maryanne Sherman	Marital Status	Single
Address	8171 Winston Court	Fed. Withholding Allow.	2
	Rochester, NY 14604	State Withholding Allow.	1
SS#	222-22-2222		

Pay Period Ending	Regular Hours Worked	Regular Pay Rate	Regular Wages	Overtime Hours Worked	Overtime Pay Rate	Overtime Wages	Gross Pay	Federal Withholding Tax	State Withholding Tax	Social Security Tax	Medicare Tax	Retirement Contribution	Life Insurance	Charitable Contribution	Additional Withholding	Check Number	Net Pay
			Earnings							Deductions							
12/1/19	n/a	n/a	$ 769.23	0	n/a	$ -	$ 769.23	$ 61.00	$ 38.46								

Employee Earnings Record

Name	Bill Novak	Marital Status	Married
Address	536A North Yellow Lake Avenue	Fed. Withholding Allow.	4
	Hamlin, NY 14464	State Withholding Allow.	3
SS#	333-33-3333		

			Earnings								Deductions						
Pay Period Ending	Regular Hours Worked	Regular Pay Rate	Regular Wages	Overtime Hours Worked	Overtime Pay Rate	Overtime Wages	Gross Pay	Federal Withholding Tax	State Withholding Tax	Social Security Tax	Medicare Tax	Retirement Contribution	Life Insurance	Charitable Contribution	Additional Withholding	Check Number	Net Pay
12/1/19	40	$ 14.75	$ 590.00	6	$ 22.50	$ 135.00	$ 725.00	$ 13.00	$ 34.08								

Employee Earnings Record

Name	Angelo Dorsett	Marital Status	Single
Address	400 Hillside Court	Fed. Withholding Allow.	2
	Hilton, NY 14468	State Withholding Allow.	2
SS#	444-44-4444		

			Earnings								Deductions						
Pay Period Ending	Regular Hours Worked	Regular Pay Rate	Regular Wages	Overtime Hours Worked	Overtime Pay Rate	Overtime Wages	Gross Pay	Federal Withholding Tax	State Withholding Tax	Social Security Tax	Medicare Tax	Retirement Contribution	Life Insurance	Charitable Contribution	Additional Withholding	Check Number	Net Pay
12/1/19	40	$ 17.50	$ 700.00	7	$ 26.25	$ 183.75	$ 883.75	$ 63.00	$ 39.77								

Employee Earnings Record

Name	Melissa Kubiak	Marital Status	Married
Address	254 Cheesehead Drive	Fed. Withholding Allow.	4
	Pittsford, NY 14534	State Withholding Allow.	4
SS#	555-55-5555		

			Earnings								Deductions						
Pay Period Ending	Regular Hours Worked	Regular Pay Rate	Regular Wages	Overtime Hours Worked	Overtime Pay Rate	Overtime Wages	Gross Pay	Federal Withholding Tax	State Withholding Tax	Social Security Tax	Medicare Tax	Retirement Contribution	Life Insurance	Charitable Contribution	Additional Withholding	Check Number	Net Pay
12/1/19	40	$ 15.00	$ 600.00	1	$ 22.50	$ 22.50	$ 622.50	$ 7.00	$ 31.13								

Employee Earnings Record

Name	Stacie Martin	Marital Status	Married
Address	2 Lava Lane	Fed. Withholding Allow.	2
	Brockport, NY 14420	State Withholding Allow.	1
SS#	666-66-6666		

	Earnings							Deductions									
Pay Period Ending	Regular Hours Worked	Regular Pay Rate	Regular Wages	Overtime Hours Worked	Overtime Pay Rate	Overtime Wages	Gross Pay	Federal Withholding Tax	State Withholding Tax	Social Security Tax	Medicare Tax	Retirement Contribution	Life Insurance	Charitable Contribution	Additional Withholding	Check Number	Net Pay
12/1/19	40	$ 21.15	$ 846.00	11	$ 31.73	$ 349.03	$ 1,195.03	$ 90.00	$ 59.75								

Employee Earnings Record

Name	Lucy Marshall	Marital Status	Single
Address	232 Muscle Road	Fed. Withholding Allow.	3
	Hamlin, NY 14464	State Withholding Allow.	2
SS#	777-77-7777		

	Earnings							Deductions									
Pay Period Ending	Regular Hours Worked	Regular Pay Rate	Regular Wages	Overtime Hours Worked	Overtime Pay Rate	Overtime Wages	Gross Pay	Federal Withholding Tax	State Withholding Tax	Social Security Tax	Medicare Tax	Retirement Contribution	Life Insurance	Charitable Contribution	Additional Withholding	Check Number	Net Pay
12/1/19	40	$ 15.75	$ 630.00	9	$ 23.63	$ 212.67	$ 842.67	$ 51.00	$ 38.76								

Employee Earnings Record

Name	Donald McHenry	Marital Status	Married
Address	22 Iceberg Lane	Fed. Withholding Allow.	6
	Fairport, NY 14450	State Withholding Allow.	5
SS#	888-88-8888		

	Earnings							Deductions									
Pay Period Ending	Regular Hours Worked	Regular Pay Rate	Regular Wages	Overtime Hours Worked	Overtime Pay Rate	Overtime Wages	Gross Pay	Federal Withholding Tax	State Withholding Tax	Social Security Tax	Medicare Tax	Retirement Contribution	Life Insurance	Charitable Contribution	Additional Withholding	Check Number	Net Pay
12/1/19	40	$ 15.30	$ 612.00	5	$ 22.95	$ 114.75	$ 726.75	$ 2.00	$ 36.34								

Self-Assessment

Complete the Self-Assessment as directed by your instructor, whether that is in the book or your eLab course, if applicable.

True/False Questions

1. State income tax withholding must be deducted from gross pay for employees of every state. *True False*

2. Social Security tax is subject to an income threshold, and therefore is levied on an employee's wages only until he/she has earned more than the threshold level in a single year. *True False*

3. Taxable pay used to calculate federal income tax withholding can differ from taxable pay used to calculate Social Security tax. *True False*

4. The current pay-as-you-go system of remitting federal income tax withholding was established by the Current Tax Payment Act of 1943. *True False*

5. Employees who are exempt from federal income tax withholding are only required to verbally inform their employer of this status. *True False*

6. The number of federal withholding allowances impacts the withholding amount calculated under the wage-bracket method but not under the percentage method. *True False*

7. Employers who utilize quarterly pay periods must use the percentage method to determine federal income tax withholdings. *True False*

8. Employees are either subject to both federal and state income tax withholding or to neither of these. *True False*

9. State income tax withholding calculations differ from one state to another. *True False*

10. Because not all employees are subject to local income tax withholding, this amount never appears in the payroll register. *True False*

Multiple Choice Questions

11. Which of the following is not a mandatory deduction from gross pay?
    A. Federal income tax withholding
    B. Union dues
    C. Social Security tax
    D. Medicare tax

12. Which of the following was not a result of the Current Tax Payment Act of 1943?
    A. Use of a pay-as-you-go system
    B. Requirement that taxes no longer be paid in the year after the associated taxable pay is earned
    C. Employer withholding of federal income tax
    D. One federal income tax withholding rate that was consistent for all employees

13. Which of the following is not a withholding table available for use with the wage-bracket method of calculating federal income tax withholding?
    A. Married; Biweekly
    B. Single; Semimonthly
    C. Single; Daily
    D. Married; Semiannually

14. Under the wage-bracket method, what would the federal income tax withholding be for a married employee with three federal withholding allowances who has weekly taxable earnings of $786?
    A. $0
    B. $15
    C. $31
    D. $52

15. For which of the following employees may the wage-bracket method not be used?
    A. A single employee who claims 6 withholding allowances and earns weekly pay of $1,047
    B. A married employee who claims 11 withholding allowances and earns monthly pay of $3,420
    C. A single employee who claims 4 withholding allowances and earns biweekly pay of $1,320
    D. A married employee who claims 9 withholding allowances and earns semimonthly pay of $3,350

16. When using the wage-bracket method, which of the following employees is subject to federal income tax withholding of $0 for the specified period?
    A. A married employee who claims two withholding allowances and earns weekly pay of $434
    B. A single employee who claims one withholding allowance and earns weekly pay of $40
    C. A married employee who claims three withholding allowances and earns weekly pay of $481
    D. A single employee who claims two withholding allowances and earns weekly pay of $252

17. Under the percentage method, what is the federal income tax withholding for a single employee with one federal withholding allowance who has biweekly taxable pay of $862?
    A. $24.35
    B. $49.36
    C. $59.08
    D. $71.56

18. When an employee gets a divorce, how many days does he/she have to file a new W-4 Form with his/her employer?
    A. 10
    B. 30
    C. 45
    D. Unlimited

19. Which of the following statements about state income tax withholding is inaccurate?
    A. State income tax withholding is not levied in all 50 states.
    B. Some states charge higher state income tax withholding to employees with high earnings, as compared with employees whose earnings are smaller.
    C. State income tax withholding cannot be levied on an employee who is subject to local income tax withholding.
    D. For those states that levy a flat state income tax withholding, the applicable rate varies from state to state.

20. Which of the following is not considered a municipality from which local income tax withholding could be levied?
    A. West Virginia
    B. Manhattan
    C. San Francisco
    D. Yonkers

Practice Set A

The IRS forms and Excel templates needed for these assignments are included in the Student Exercise Files download for this course. If directed to do so, complete these assignments in Homework Grader.

PSa 3-1 Identify Deductions

For each of the deductions listed, indicate whether it is a mandatory deduction or a voluntary deduction:

1. Medicare tax

2. State income tax withholding

3. Union dues

4. Federal income tax withholding

5. Medical plans

PSa 3-2 Calculate Gross Pay and Taxable Pay

For each employee, first calculate gross pay. Then determine taxable income used to calculate federal income tax withholding, Social Security tax, and Medicare tax.

1. An employee works 47 hours (seven were overtime hours) during a workweek in December of 2019. He earns $39/hour, with his employer paying 1.5 times the regular rate of pay for overtime hours. To date, he has earned $131,050 during the year. He has requested that his employer withhold 6% of gross pay, which is to be contributed to a 401(k) plan.

2. An employee works 39 regular hours during a workweek in August of 2019. He was hired six years ago, earns a salary of $116,500/year, and is exempt from the overtime provisions of the FLSA. To date, he has received no compensation beyond his annual salary. He has requested that his employer withhold 12% of gross pay, which is to be contributed to a 403(b) plan.

3. An employee works 51 hours (11 were overtime hours) during a workweek in December of 2019. He earns $10,000/month, with his employer paying 1.5 times the regular rate of pay for overtime hours. To date, he has earned $134,200 during the year. He has requested that his employer withhold 9% of gross pay, which is to be contributed to a 401(k) plan.

PSa 3-3 Calculate Federal Income Tax Withholding Using the Wage-Bracket Method

Refer to the Federal Tax Tables in Appendix A.

For each employee listed, use the wage-bracket method to calculate federal income tax withholding:

1. Sam Coleridge (married; four federal withholding allowances) earned weekly gross pay of $565.

2. Michael Kolk (single; two federal withholding allowances) earned biweekly gross pay of $975. He participates in a flexible spending account, to which he contributed $100 during the period.

3. Anita McLachlan (single; no federal withholding allowances) earned monthly gross pay of $2,440. For each period, she makes a 401(k) contribution of 9% of gross pay.

4. Stacey Williamson (married; three federal withholding allowances) earned semimonthly gross pay of $1,250. She participates in a cafeteria plan, to which she contributed $150 during the period.

PSa 3-4 Calculate Federal Income Tax Withholding Using the Percentage Method

Refer to the Federal Tax Tables in Appendix A.

For each employee listed, use the percentage method to calculate federal income tax withholding:

1. Billy Rainer (married; two federal withholding allowances) earned weekly gross pay of $602.

2. Angel Rodriguez (married; three federal withholding allowances) earned biweekly gross pay of $1,020. He participates in a flexible spending account, to which he contributed $50 during the period.

3. Julie Smithers (single; two federal withholding allowances) earned monthly gross pay of $2,170. For each period, she makes a 401(k) contribution of 10% of gross pay.

4. Anna Marquez (single; no federal withholding allowances) earned semimonthly gross pay of $1,700. She participates in a cafeteria plan, to which she contributed $110 during the period.

PSa 3-5 Calculate Federal Income Tax Withholding Using Two Methods

Refer to the Federal Tax Tables in Appendix A.

For each employee listed, use both the wage-bracket method and the percentage method to calculate federal income tax withholding. Show all work for each method.

1. Thomas Fortuna (married; four federal withholding allowances) earned weekly gross pay of $745. For each period, he makes a 401(k) retirement plan contribution of 10% of gross pay.

2. Barbara Houlihan (single; one federal withholding allowance) earned daily gross pay of $320. For each period, she makes a 401(k) contribution of 12% of gross pay.

3. Marcus Xavier (married; five federal withholding allowances) earned monthly gross pay of $3,650. He participates in a flexible spending account, to which he contributed $200 during the period.

PSa 3-6 Calculate Federal (Wage-Bracket Method), State, and Local Income Tax Withholding

Refer to the Federal Tax Tables in Appendix A.

For each employee listed, use the wage-bracket method to calculate federal income tax withholding. Then calculate both the state income tax withholding (assuming a state tax rate of 5% of taxable pay, with taxable pay being the same for federal and state income tax withholding), and the local income tax withholding.

1. Paul Bronson (single; one federal withholding allowance) earned weekly gross pay of $1,247. For each period, he makes a 401(k) retirement plan contribution of 10% of gross pay. The city in which he works (he lives elsewhere) levies a tax of 1.5% of an employee's taxable pay (which is the same for federal and local income tax withholding) on residents, and 0.8% of an employee's taxable pay on nonresidents.

2. Stephen McPherson (married; five federal withholding allowances) earned weekly gross pay of $980. He participates in a flexible spending account, to which he contributed $75 during the period. The city in which he lives and works levies a tax of 2.3% of an employee's taxable pay (which is the same for federal and local income tax withholding) on residents, and 1.6% of an employee's taxable pay on nonresidents.

3. Tyler Howard (married; four federal withholding allowances) earned weekly gross pay of $1,310. For each period, he makes a 403(b) retirement plan contribution of 7% of gross pay. The city in which he lives and works levies a tax of 1.4% of an employee's taxable pay (which is the same for federal and local income tax withholding) on both residents and nonresidents.

4. Alejandro Garcia (single; three federal withholding allowances) earned weekly gross pay of $1,110. He participates in a cafeteria plan, to which he paid $50 during the period. The city in which he works levies a tax of $12/week on employees who work within city limits.

PSa 3-7 Calculate Federal (Percentage Method), State, and Local Income Tax Withholding

Refer to the Federal Tax Tables in Appendix A.

For each employee listed, use the percentage method to calculate federal income tax withholding. Then calculate both the state income tax withholding (assuming a state tax rate of 5% of taxable pay, with taxable pay being the same for federal and state income tax withholding), and the local income tax withholding.

1. Walter Ferrell (married; four federal withholding allowances) earned weekly gross pay of $1,030. For each period, he makes a 401(k) retirement plan contribution of 14% of gross pay. The city in which he works (he lives elsewhere) levies a tax of 1.3% of an employee's taxable pay (which is the same for federal and local income tax withholding) on residents and 1.1% of an employee's taxable pay on nonresidents.

2. Lucas Sedaris (married; three federal withholding allowances) earned weekly gross pay of $2,800. He participates in a flexible spending account, to which he contributed $150 during the period. The city in which he lives and works levies a tax of 3.1% of an employee's taxable pay (which is the same for federal and local income tax withholding) on residents and 2.4% of an employee's taxable pay on nonresidents.

3. Darrell Roper (married; six federal withholding allowances) earned weekly gross pay of $1,540. He does not request that any voluntary deductions be made from his gross pay. The city in which he lives and works levies a tax of 2.5% of an employee's taxable pay (which is the same for federal and local income tax withholding) on both residents and nonresidents.

4. Giuseppe Fortuna (single; two federal withholding allowances) earned weekly gross pay of $3,820. He participates in a cafeteria plan, to which he paid $175 during the period. The city in which he works levies a tax of $13/week on employees who work within city limits.

PSa 3-8 Populate a Payroll Register

This problem is a continuation of exercise PSa 2-12 from Chapter 2.

Complete the Federal Withholding Tax (wage-bracket method) and State Withholding Tax columns of the payroll register for the five employees whose information was provided in PSa 2-4 and PSa 2-12. The state income tax withholding rate is 5% of taxable pay, with taxable pay being the same for federal and state income tax withholding. Additional information for each employee is provided below.

- Luisa Williams makes a 401(k) retirement plan contribution of 14% of gross pay each period.
- Jonathan Olsen participates in a cafeteria plan, to which he pays $100 each period.
- Nathan Upton does not make any voluntary deductions each period.
- Juan Rodriguez makes a 403(b) retirement plan contribution of 13% of gross pay.
- Drew Painter participates in a flexible spending account, to which he contributes $50 each period.

Although you will further modify the Voluntary Withholdings column in the next chapter, you should complete this column (along with the FWT and SWT columns) based on the information provided above.

PSa 3-9 Populate Employee Earnings Records

This problem is a continuation of exercise PSa 2-13 from Chapter 2.

Complete the Federal Income Tax Withholding (FWT) and State Income Tax Withholding (SWT) columns of the employee earnings records for the five employees from PSa 3-8. The earnings section of the employee earnings records was previously completed in PSa 2-13. Although you will further modify the Retirement Contribution and Additional Withholding columns in the next chapter, you should complete these columns (along with the FWT and SWT columns) based on the information provided in PSa 3-8.

Practice Set B

The IRS forms and Excel templates needed for these assignments are included in the Student Exercise Files download for this course. If directed to do so, complete these assignments in Homework Grader.

PSb 3-1 Identify Deductions

For each of the deductions listed, indicate whether it is a mandatory deduction or a voluntary deduction:

1. Cafeteria plans

2. Social Security tax

3. State disability insurance

4. Local income tax withholding

5. Retirement plans

PSb 3-2 Calculate Gross Pay and Taxable Pay

For each employee, first calculate gross pay. Then determine taxable income used to calculate federal income tax withholding, Social Security tax, and Medicare tax.

1. An employee works 42 hours (two were overtime hours) during a workweek in December of 2019. He earns $40.50/hour, with his employer paying 1.5 times the regular rate of pay for overtime hours. To date, he has earned $132,300 during the year. He has requested that his employer withhold 7% of gross pay to contribute to a 403(b) plan.

2. An employee works 37 regular hours during a workweek in August of 2019. He was hired four years ago, earns a salary of $135,100/year, and is exempt from the overtime provisions of the FLSA. To date, he has received no compensation beyond his annual salary. He has requested that his employer withhold 8% of gross pay to contribute to a 401(k) plan.

3. An employee works 50 hours (10 of which were overtime hours) during a workweek in December of 2019. He earns $9,500/month, with his employer paying 1.5 times the regular rate of pay for overtime hours. To date, he has earned $109,700 during the year. He has requested that his employer withhold 13% of gross pay to contribute to a 403(b) plan.

PSb 3-3 Calculate Federal Income Tax Withholding Using the Wage-Bracket Method

Refer to the Federal Tax Tables in Appendix A.

For each employee listed, use the wage-bracket method to calculate federal income tax withholding:

1. Paul Yount (married; seven federal withholding allowances) earned weekly gross pay of $605.

2. Paulina Robinson (single; three federal withholding allowances) earned biweekly gross pay of $1,245. She contributed $75 to a flexible spending account during the period.

3. Lacey Kunis (single; two federal withholding allowances) earned monthly gross pay of $3,090. For each period, she makes a 401(k) contribution of 18% of gross pay.

4. Francine Stewart (married; four federal withholding allowances) earned semimonthly gross pay of $1,420. She contributed $125 to a cafeteria plan during the period.

PSb 3-4 Calculate Federal Income Tax Withholding Using the Percentage Method

Refer to the Federal Tax Tables in Appendix A.

For each employee listed, use the percentage method to calculate federal income tax withholding:

1. Juan Hoffman (single; two federal withholding allowances) earned weekly gross pay of $445.

2. William Harrison (single; one federal withholding allowance) earned biweekly gross pay of $990. He contributed $75 to a flexible spending account during the period.

3. Loretta Goulet (married; three federal withholding allowances) earned monthly gross pay of $2,800. For each period, she makes a 401(k) contribution of 14% of gross pay.

4. Louise Simpson (married; nine federal withholding allowances) earned semimonthly gross pay of $2,300. She contributed $100 to a cafeteria plan during the period.

PSb 3-5 Calculate Federal Income Tax Withholding Using Two Methods

Refer to the Federal Tax Tables in Appendix A.

For each employee listed, use both the wage-bracket method and the percentage method to calculate federal income tax withholding. Show all work for each method.

1. Warren Cavanagh (single; no federal withholding allowances) earned weekly gross pay of $620. For each period, he makes a 401(k) retirement plan contribution of 5% of gross pay.

2. Stacey Vaughn (married; four federal withholding allowances) earned daily gross pay of $275. For each period, she makes a 401(k) contribution of 8% of gross pay.

3. Jordan Peters (single; three federal withholding allowances) earned monthly gross pay of $2,300. He contributed $150 to a flexible spending account during the period.

PSb 3-6 Calculate Federal (Wage-Bracket Method), State, and Local Income Tax Withholding

Refer to the Federal Tax Tables in Appendix A.

For each employee listed, use the wage-bracket method to calculate federal withholding tax. Then calculate both the state withholding tax (assuming a state tax rate of 5% of taxable pay, with taxable pay being the same for federal and state income tax withholding) and the local withholding tax.

1. Jay Monroe (single; two federal withholding allowances) earned weekly gross pay of $1,145. For each period, he makes a 401(k) retirement plan contribution of 12% of gross pay. The city in which he works (he lives elsewhere) levies a tax of 2% of an employee's taxable pay (which is the same for federal and local income tax withholding) on residents and 1.7% of an employee's taxable pay on nonresidents.

2. Gus Damon (married; nine federal withholding allowances) earned weekly gross pay of $1,200. He contributed $125 to a flexible spending account during the period. The city in which he lives and works levies a tax of 3% of an employee's taxable pay (which is the same for federal and local income tax withholding) on residents and 0.4% of an employee's taxable pay on nonresidents.

3. Kenneth Riley (single; no federal withholding allowances) earned weekly gross pay of $1,000. For each period, he makes a 403(b) retirement plan contribution of 5% of gross pay. The city in which he lives and works levies a tax of 1.7% of an employee's taxable pay (which is the same for federal and local income tax withholding) on both residents and nonresidents.

4. Ross McMichael (married; two federal withholding allowances) earned weekly gross pay of $970. He paid $60 to a cafeteria plan during the period. The city in which he works levies a tax of $8/week on employees who work within city limits.

PSb 3-7 Calculate Federal (Percentage Method), State, and Local Income Tax Withholding

Refer to the Federal Tax Tables in Appendix A.

For each employee listed, use the percentage method to calculate federal income tax withholding. Then calculate both the state income tax withholding (assuming a state tax rate of 5% of taxable pay, with taxable pay being the same for federal and state income tax withholding), and the local income tax withholding.

1. Armand Giroux (single; no federal withholding allowances) earned weekly gross pay of $1,500. For each period, he makes a 401(k) retirement plan contribution of 8% of gross pay. The city in which he works (he lives elsewhere) levies a tax of 1% of an employee's taxable pay (which is the same for federal and local income tax withholding) on residents and 0.6% of an employee's taxable pay on nonresidents.

2. Peter Quigley (married; eight federal withholding allowances) earned weekly gross pay of $2,350. He contributed $100 to a flexible spending account during the period. The city in which he lives and works levies a tax of 2.7% of an employee's taxable pay (which is the same for federal and local income tax withholding) on residents and 1.9% of an employee's taxable pay on nonresidents.

3. Eric Belanger (married; four federal withholding allowances) earned weekly gross pay of $1,275. He does not request that any voluntary deductions be made from his gross pay. The city in which he lives and works levies a tax of 1.5% of an employee's taxable pay (which is the same for federal and local income tax withholding) on both residents and nonresidents.

4. Christopher Martin (single; four federal withholding allowances) earned weekly gross pay of $2,780. He paid $85 to a cafeteria plan during the period. The city in which he works levies a tax of $7/week on employees who work within city limits.

PSb 3-8 Populate a Payroll Register

This problem is a continuation of exercise PSb 2-12 from Chapter 2.

Complete the Federal Withholding Tax (wage-bracket method) and State Withholding Tax columns of the payroll register for the five employees whose information was provided in PSb 2-4 and PSb 2-12. Note that the state income tax withholding rate is 5% of taxable pay, with taxable pay being the same for federal and state income tax withholding. Additional information for each employee is provided below:

- Jimmy Troffa makes a 401(k) retirement plan contribution of 9% of gross pay each period.

- Tyler Thomas pays $75 to a cafeteria plan during each period.

- Ryan Brown does not make any voluntary deductions each period.

- Michael Kaminski makes a 403(b) retirement plan contribution of 10% of gross pay.

- Tina Baldwin contributes $110 to a flexible spending account each period.

Although you will further modify the Voluntary Withholdings column in the next chapter, you should complete this column (along with the FWT and SWT columns) based on the information provided above.

PSb 3-9 Populate Employee Earnings Records

This problem is a continuation of exercise PSb 2-13 from Chapter 2.

Complete the Federal Income Tax Withholding (FWT) and State Income Tax Withholding (SWT) columns of the employee earnings records for the five employees from PSb 3-8. Note that the earnings section of the employee earnings records was previously completed in PSb 2-13. Although you will further modify the Retirement Contribution and Additional Withholding columns in the next chapter, you should complete these columns (along with the FWT and SWT columns) based on the information provided in PSb 3-8.

Continuing Payroll Problem

The IRS forms and Excel templates needed for these assignments are included in the Student Exercise Files download for this course. If directed to do so, complete these assignments in Homework Grader.

CPP 3-1 Calculate and Document Federal and State Income Tax Withholding

Calculate federal and state income tax withholding for a number of employees of TCLH Industries, a manufacturer of cleaning products. Use the wage-bracket method when it is possible to do so, and use the percentage method in all other instances. Assume the state income tax withholding rate to be 5% of taxable pay (which is the same for federal and state income tax withholding). Then, continue to fill out the payroll register and the employee earnings records based on your calculations.

1. Calculate the federal and state income tax withholdings for each employee based on information from the prior chapters' Continuing Payroll Problem, as well as the following:
   - Zachary Fox does not make any voluntary deductions that impact earnings subject to federal income tax withholding.
   - Calvin Bell makes a 401(k) retirement plan contribution of 6% of gross pay.
   - David Alexander makes a 401(k) retirement plan contribution of 12% of gross pay.
   - Michael Sierra contributes $50 to a flexible spending account each period.

2. Complete the Federal (FWT) and State (SWT) Income Tax Withholding columns of the payroll register (which you established during an earlier Continuing Payroll Problem) for TCLH Industries. Note that although the Voluntary Withholdings column will require additional updating in subsequent chapters, you should populate this column with any appropriate figures given above. Then complete the Federal and State Withholding Tax columns of the employee earnings record (which you established during an earlier Continuing Payroll Problem) for each of the four employees of TCLH Industries. Also complete the Retirement Contribution and Additional Withholding columns based on the information provided. The Additional Withholding column will require further updating in the next chapter.

Critical Thinking

CT 3-1 Investigate Federal Withholding Allowances

As you have seen, the number of federal withholding allowances claimed by an employee has a significant impact on the amount of federal income tax withheld from each paycheck. In Chapter 1 you examined the W-4 Form and learned that an employee claims his/her desired number of federal withholding allowances on this form. But how does an employee determine the optimal number of allowances? While the Personal Allowances Worksheet, which you reviewed in Chapter 1, provides guidance on this topic, an employee may still choose to alter the suggested number of allowances from this worksheet. In this exercise, you will use the Internet to research common reasons why employees may choose to either increase or decrease the number of allowances claimed.

Begin by researching different reasons why an employee may choose to alter his/her number of federal withholding allowances. Next, write a paragraph of at least five sentences, in which you discuss the two most compelling reasons you identified for reducing the number of allowances. Then, write a second paragraph of at least five sentences, in which you discuss the two most compelling reasons you identified for increasing the number of allowances.

Submit your final file based on the guidelines provided by your instructor.

CT 3-2 Examine State Income Tax Withholding

Earlier you learned that, as of 2019, nine states do not levy state income tax withholdings on their residents. Two of these (New Hampshire and Tennessee) collect tax on dividend and interest income, but how do the other seven states (Alaska, Florida, Nevada, South Dakota, Texas, Washington, and Wyoming) raise funds to run government operations? In this exercise, you will use the Internet to research the manner in which some of these states generate revenues.

Select three of the seven states listed above to research. If you either live or work in one of these states, include it in your selection. Use the Internet to research the alternative methods utilized by these states to generate funds. These may include different tax types, state-specific revenue-generating activities, or other methods. For each state, write a paragraph of at least four sentences in which you discuss the manner in which these funds are raised.

Submit your final file based on the guidelines provided by your instructor.

FICA Taxes and Voluntary Deductions

4

LEARNING OBJECTIVES

- Calculate Social Security tax

- Calculate Medicare tax

- Identify states in which state disability insurance is withheld

- Apply various voluntary deductions

- Record employee payroll journal entries

Having calculated federal and state tax withholdings in the last chapter, you're now ready to examine the remaining mandatory deductions from gross earnings. These include Social Security tax and Medicare tax, which are collectively referred to as FICA taxes. In this chapter, you'll review the purpose and application of FICA taxes. You'll also examine state disability insurance and voluntary deductions in detail. After completing the payroll register and employee earnings records, you'll conclude by examining the journal entries related to the deductions discussed in Chapter 3 and this chapter.

Videos available! Check out the Video Launch Pad in your student exercise file download to access videos associated with this chapter. One video presents a chapter overview, and the other provides more detail on a key chapter topic.

CASE STUDY

Determining FICA Taxes and Voluntary Deductions for Lucky Ties Apparel

After having deducted federal and state income tax withholding from employee earnings, Lucky Ties Apparel must then calculate further deductions. FICA taxes include Social Security and Medicare tax, both of which must be withheld from employee pay. While the applicable rates for these taxes are the same for each employee, there is an annual per-employee ceiling on Social Security taxes that must be taken into consideration.

To complete your understanding of employee deductions, you review both Social Security and Medicare tax. You then examine state disability insurance (which is applicable only in some states), and further review a number of voluntary deductions. After including these tax calculations in both the payroll register and the employee earnings records, you finish by reviewing the required journal entry to account for both deductions and net pay.

Social Security and Medicare taxes are mandatory for all employees, while state disability insurance and voluntary deductions are also withheld for some employees.

Social Security Tax

Medicare Tax

State Disability Insurance

Voluntary Deductions

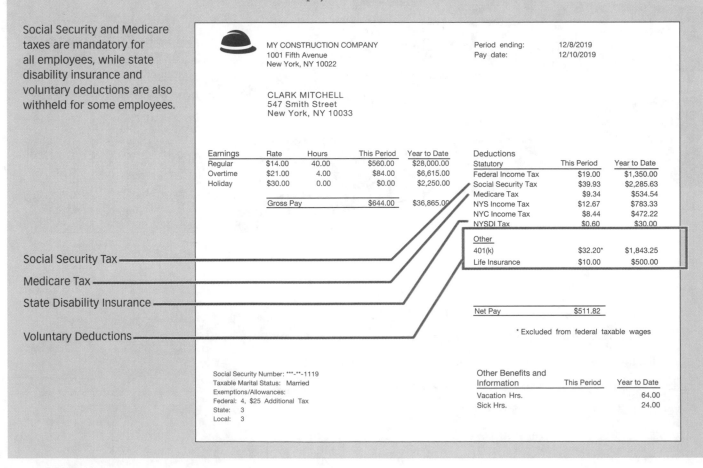

MY CONSTRUCTION COMPANY
1001 Fifth Avenue
New York, NY 10022

Period ending: 12/8/2019
Pay date: 12/10/2019

CLARK MITCHELL
547 Smith Street
New York, NY 10033

Earnings	Rate	Hours	This Period	Year to Date
Regular	$14.00	40.00	$560.00	$28,000.00
Overtime	$21.00	4.00	$84.00	$6,615.00
Holiday	$30.00	0.00	$0.00	$2,250.00
		Gross Pay	$644.00	$36,865.00

Deductions		
Statutory	This Period	Year to Date
Federal Income Tax	$19.00	$1,350.00
Social Security Tax	$39.93	$2,285.63
Medicare Tax	$9.34	$534.54
NYS Income Tax	$12.67	$783.33
NYC Income Tax	$8.44	$472.22
NYSDI Tax	$0.60	$30.00
Other		
401(k)	$32.20*	$1,843.25
Life Insurance	$10.00	$500.00

Net Pay	$511.82

* Excluded from federal taxable wages

Social Security Number: ***-**-1119
Taxable Marital Status: Married
Exemptions/Allowances:
Federal: 4, $25 Additional Tax
State: 3
Local: 3

Other Benefits and Information	This Period	Year to Date
Vacation Hrs.		64.00
Sick Hrs.		24.00

Social Security Tax

Also referred to as OASDI (old age, survivors, and disability insurance), Social Security tax was initially established to provide employees with retirement benefits. Over time the program was expanded to provide financial support to employees' survivors and to disabled employees.

Initially, the Social Security tax rate was 1% of taxable earnings. This rate was in place from 1937–1949, after which it has steadily increased over the years. A number of credits have, for certain years, been passed into law, and have reduced the effective Social Security tax rate remitted on the employee's behalf. The most recent tax rates (before taking these credits into account) are shown here.

Year(s)	Social Security Tax Rate		Year(s)	Social Security Tax Rate
1974–1977	4.95%		1982–1983	5.40%
1978	5.05%		1984–1987	5.70%
1979–1980	5.08%		1988–1989	6.06%
1981	5.35%		1990–2019	6.20%

NOTE! Whereas employees are permitted to increase federal and state income tax withholdings by a set amount each pay period, this is neither necessary nor permissible for Social Security tax.

The Social Security Wage Base

Aside from the applicable Social Security tax rate, which is presently 6.2%, you must also consider the earnings threshold over which Social Security tax is not levied. Once an employee's year-to-date taxable earnings reaches this threshold (referred to as the Social Security wage base), no further Social Security tax is withheld until the beginning of the following year. The result is that no Social Security tax is paid by the employee after that employee earns a specified amount during the year. From 1937–1950, the first wage base was $3,000. Therefore, Social Security tax was levied on the first $3,000 earned by each employee during these years. Annual earnings above $3,000 for each employee were not subject to the tax. Similar to the Social Security tax rate, the wage base has increased steadily since that time. As of 2019, the wage base is $132,900.

Year(s)	Social Security Wage Base		Year(s)	Social Security Wage Base
2007	$97,500		2014	$117,000
2008	$102,000		2015–2016	$118,500
2009–2011	$106,800		2017	$127,200
2012	$110,100		2018	$128,400
2013	$113,700		2019	$132,900

Taxable Earnings for Social Security Tax

Similar to the taxable earnings for federal and state income tax withholding, taxable earnings for Social Security tax also exclude certain portions of gross pay. Among the amounts that must be subtracted from gross pay to arrive at taxable earnings for Social Security tax are those deducted for cafeteria plans (including flexible spending accounts, such as those for dependent care expenses). Refer to the chart provided in Chapter 3 for a review of those payments that are both taxable and nontaxable for FICA taxes (Social Security and Medicare taxes).

WARNING!   Retirement plan contributions (such as those for 401(k) and 403(b) plans) are taxable for Social Security tax and should not be subtracted from gross pay when calculating taxable earnings for Social Security tax.

Calculating Social Security Tax

Here we will review how to calculate Social Security tax. In Chapter 6 we will examine how Social Security tax is reported on a quarterly basis within Form 941 and on an annual basis within Forms W-2 and W-3. To calculate an employee's Social Security tax, the employer must undertake a four-step process, outlined below:

Step 1:   Determine current period taxable earnings for Social Security tax.

Step 2:   Add the Step 1 result to the year-to-date taxable earnings for Social Security tax.

Step 3:   • If the Step 2 result exceeds the Social Security wage base, determine the amount by which it is higher and subtract this amount from the Step 1 result. Your new amount (if it is positive) is used to determine Social Security tax in Step 4 (a negative result indicates that $0 should be used in Step 4).

• If the Step 2 result does not exceed the Social Security wage base, use the Step 1 result when determining Social Security tax in Step 4.

Step 4:   Multiply the current 6.2% tax rate by the Step 3 result.

An alternate overview of the Social Security tax calculation can be seen in the flow-chart below:

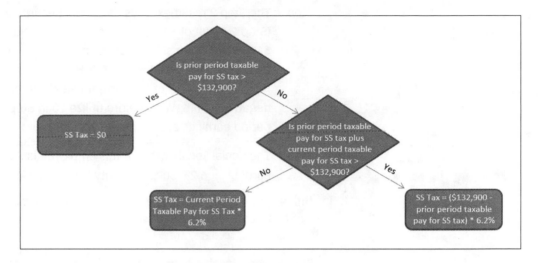

Case in Point 4-1	# Calculate Social Security Tax

For each of the following employees of Lucky Ties Apparel, we'll calculate the Social Security tax for the current weekly pay period:

1. Paul Rogers earned gross pay of $402.50. Each period he makes a 401(k) contribution of 8% of gross pay. His current year taxable earnings for Social Security tax, to date, are $83,900.

   Step 1: Here, taxable earnings for Social Security tax are the same as gross pay. The only voluntary deduction is the retirement plan, which is taxable for the purposes of Social Security. Therefore, the current period taxable earnings are $402.50.

   Step 2: When the current period taxable earnings of $402.50 are added to the year-to-date earnings of $83,900, the result is $84,302.50.

   Step 3: The Step 2 result does not exceed the taxable wage base of $132,900, and therefore all of the current week's taxable earnings of $402.50 (the Step 1 result) are subject to Social Security tax.

   Step 4: The Social Security tax for this employee is $24.96 ($402.50 current period taxable earnings × 6.2% Social Security tax rate).

2. Maryanne Sherman earned gross pay of $769.23. She does not make any retirement plan contributions. Her current year taxable earnings for Social Security tax (which include a nondiscretionary bonus), to date, are $135,750.

   Step 1: Here, taxable earnings for Social Security tax are the same as gross pay. There are no voluntary deductions that would reduce taxable earnings for Social Security tax. Therefore, the current period taxable earnings are $769.23.

Step 2: When the current period taxable earnings of $769.23 are added to the year-to-date earnings of $135,750, the result is $136,519.23.

Step 3: The Step 2 result exceeds the Social Security wage base by $3,619.23 (Step 2 result of $136,519.23 minus the Social Security wage base of $132,900). When subtracted from the current period taxable earnings of $769.23, the result is –$2,850. Because the wage base was exceeded before adding any of the current week's earnings, we arrive here at a negative result. We therefore utilize $0 in Step 4, as none of the current period earnings are subject to Social Security tax.

Step 4: The Social Security tax for this employee is $0 ($0 current period taxable earnings × 6.2% Social Security tax rate).

3. Bill Novak earned gross pay of $725. Each period he contributes 6% of gross pay to a flexible spending account. His current year taxable earnings for Social Security tax, to date, are $128,900.

Step 1: Here, taxable earnings for Social Security tax are less than gross pay. The employee contributes $43.50 ($725 gross pay × 6% rate) to a flexible spending account. This amount is not taxable for Social Security tax, and therefore taxable earnings are $681.50 ($725 gross pay – $43.50 nontaxable portion).

Step 2: When the current period taxable earnings of $681.50 are added to the year-to-date earnings of $128,900, the result is $129,581.50.

Step 3: The Step 2 result does not exceed the Social Security wage base of $132,900, and therefore all of the current week's taxable earnings of $681.50 (the Step 1 result) are subject to Social Security tax.

Step 4: The Social Security tax for this employee is $42.25 ($681.50 current period taxable earnings × 6.2% Social Security tax rate).

4. Angelo Dorsett earned gross pay of $883.75. Each period he designates 10% of gross pay for a dependent care flexible spending account. His current year taxable earnings for Social Security tax, to date, are $132,800.

Step 1: Here, taxable earnings for Social Security tax are less than gross pay. The employee designates $88.38 ($883.75 gross pay × 10% rate) for a dependent care flexible spending account. This amount is not taxable for Social Security tax, and therefore taxable earnings are $795.37 ($883.75 gross pay – $88.38 nontaxable portion).

Step 2: When the current period taxable earnings of $795.37 are added to the year-to-date earnings of $132,800, the result is $133,595.37.

Step 3: The Step 2 result exceeds the Social Security wage base by $695.37 (Step 2 result of $133,595.37 minus the Social Security wage base of $132,900). When subtracted from the current period taxable earnings of $795.37, the result is $100. We therefore utilize $100 in Step 4, as this is the only portion of current period earnings that are subject to Social Security tax.

Step 4: The Social Security tax for this employee is $6.20 ($100 current period taxable earnings × 6.2% Social Security tax rate).

Medicare Tax

Also referred to as HI (hospital insurance), Medicare tax funds health-care coverage for individuals 65 or older. Taxable earnings for Medicare tax are calculated in the same manner as taxable earnings for Social Security tax.

TIP! Because they are both mandated under the Federal Insurance Contributions Act, Social Security tax and Medicare tax are collectively referred to as FICA taxes.

Initially, the Medicare tax rate was 0.35% of taxable earnings. This rate was in place in 1966, after which it increased repeatedly before reaching the current rate of 1.45%. A complete history of Medicare tax rates is shown here.

Year(s)	Medicare Tax Rate	Year(s)	Medicare Tax Rate
1966	0.35%	1978	1.00%
1967	0.50%	1979–1980	1.05%
1968–1972	0.60%	1981–1984	1.30%
1973	1.00%	1985	1.35%
1974–1977	0.90%	1986–2019	1.45%

As with Social Security tax earlier, we review the calculation of Medicare tax here, and in Chapter 6 we will examine how Medicare tax is reported on a quarterly basis within Form 941 and on an annual basis within Forms W-2 and W-3.

Additional Medicare Tax

Beginning in 2013, an Additional Medicare Tax of 0.9% was imposed on individuals whose earnings exceeded specified levels. This tax was implemented as a result of the Patient Protection and Affordable Care Act, which was signed into law in 2010. The extra revenue generated by the Additional Medicare Tax is designed to fund the expanded health-care coverage that is provided through this legislation.

The income threshold over which Additional Medicare Tax is levied is based on an individual's filing status. The filing status that an individual elects on his/her year-end tax return, while primarily impacted by marital status, can be influenced by other factors (such as a desire to file separately from one's spouse or the payment of at least half of the cost of keeping up a home for an unmarried individual). The applicable thresholds for Additional Medicare Tax are shown here.

Filing Status	Earnings Threshold
Single/head of household/qualifying widower	$200,000
Married filing jointly	$250,000
Married filing separately	$125,000

WARNING! Unlike for Social Security tax, there is no upper earnings limit above which Medicare tax is not levied. All employee earnings are subject to standard Medicare tax, while Additional Medicare Tax is also levied on high-income individuals.

During the pay period in which an employee reaches the Additional Medicare Tax threshold of $200,000, only the portion of taxable earnings that exceeds the threshold is subject to the Additional Medicare Tax rate.

Although the earnings threshold over which Additional Medicare Tax is levied differs based on filing status, the IRS simplifies the process of withholding this tax by instructing employers to collect Additional Medicare Tax from all earnings exceeding $200,000 for every employee, regardless of filing status. While this can result in either too much or too little tax being withheld for certain employees, that is resolved when the employee files their tax return at year-end.

An overview of the Medicare tax calculation is shown in the flowchart below:

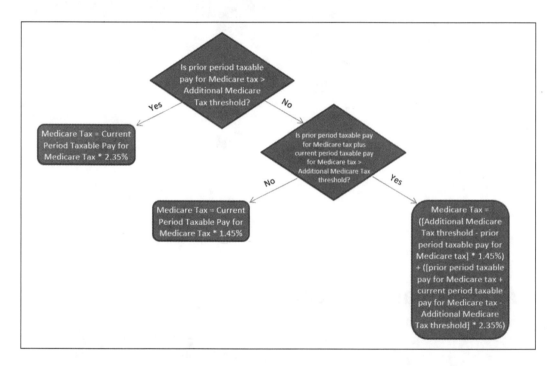

Case in Point 4-2   Calculate Medicare Tax

For each of the following employees, we will calculate the Medicare tax for the current weekly pay period:

1. Beverly Itzin's filing status is married filing jointly, and she has earned gross pay of $3,525. Each period she makes a 401(k) contribution of 8% of gross pay and contributes $100 to a flexible spending account. Her current year taxable earnings for Medicare tax, to date, are $122,400.

   Beverly's taxable earnings for Medicare tax do not include her contribution to the flexible spending account and therefore are $3,425 ($3,525 gross pay – $100 flexible spending account contribution). Note that the 401(k) payment is fully taxable for Medicare tax. She has not yet reached the earnings threshold over which the Additional Medicare Tax is assessed, so her Medicare tax is $49.66 ($3,425 taxable earnings × 1.45% Medicare tax rate).

2. Willard Poe's filing status is single, and he has earned gross pay of $4,100. Each period he makes a 403(b) contribution of 10% of gross pay and contributes $200 to a cafeteria plan. His current year taxable earnings for Medicare tax, to date, are $207,400.

   Willard's taxable earnings for Medicare tax do not include his contribution to the cafeteria plan and therefore are $3,900 ($4,100 gross pay – $200 cafeteria plan contribution). Note that the 403(b) payment is fully taxable for Medicare tax. He has reached the earnings threshold of $200,000, and therefore Additional Medicare Tax is assessed on these earnings. The total Medicare tax rate on these earnings is 2.35% (1.45% standard tax rate + 0.90% additional tax rate). Therefore, his resulting Medicare tax is $91.65 ($3,900 taxable earnings × 2.35% total Medicare tax rate).

3. Yelena Phillips' filing status is single, and she has earned gross pay of $2,000. Her current year taxable earnings for Medicare tax, to date, are $199,600.

   Yelena reached the $200,000 earnings threshold during the current period. The portion of her earnings that does not exceed the threshold is $400 ($200,000 threshold – $199,600 earnings to date), while the portion of her earnings that does exceed the threshold is $1,600 ($2,000 gross pay – $400 portion not exceeding threshold). While $400 is subject only to Medicare tax of 1.45%, $1,600 is subject to both regular and Additional Medicare Tax (2.35% rate). Therefore, total Medicare tax owed is $43.40 ($400 × 1.45% + $1,600 × 2.35%).

Additional Withholding Tax Considerations

Aside from the mandatory deductions that you have examined thus far, there are a wide variety of other amounts that may be withheld from gross pay. Among these are state disability insurance, wage garnishments, retirement plans, cafeteria plans, union dues, and charitable contributions.

State Disability Insurance

Disability insurance programs provide short-term benefits to employees who are unable to work as a result of an off-the-job circumstance. Presently there are five states (California, Hawaii, New Jersey, New York, and Rhode Island), as well as the commonwealth of Puerto Rico, that require employers to carry disability insurance for their employees. Depending on each state's regulations, employees may be required to contribute toward the insurance coverage through payroll withholding. For example, in New York State an employer may require that 0.5% of an employee's earnings (not to exceed $0.60/week) be withheld for this purpose.

Wage Garnishments

A **wage garnishment** is the withholding of a portion of an employee's earnings in compliance with a court order or other legal proceeding. Among the most common reasons for the levying of a wage garnishment are child support, alimony payments, bankruptcy, federal or state tax payments, student loans, and creditors to whom amounts are owed.

Title III of the Consumer Credit Protection Act (CCPA) dictates both that employers may not discharge an employee as a result of a wage garnishment and that the amount of the garnishment may not exceed a prescribed level. Wage garnishments are limited to the lesser of 25% of disposable earnings (gross pay minus mandatory deductions) or the amount of disposable earnings that exceed 30 times the federal minimum wage (disposable earnings – [30 × federal minimum wage]). This limit may be increased in certain instances, such as garnishments for child support, bankruptcy, and federal or state tax payments.

Although the CCPA does not address the order in which garnishments are satisfied, other federal and state laws can be examined to determine which garnishments to pay when an employee is subject to two or more. Typically the order in which multiple garnishments are satisfied is based on when each garnishment order is received, with the earlier garnishments receiving priority. However, this order is not always followed, as child support payments and federal tax levies are typically satisfied before other garnishments. Federal student loans are satisfied next, then state and local tax levies and student loans, and finally commercial garnishments. Remember that multiple garnishments cannot result in total garnishments exceeding the limits prescribed within the CCPA, so it is possible for lower-priority garnishments to be reduced or postponed until higher-priority garnishments are fully satisfied.

One additional item to keep in mind is that bankruptcy proceedings will stop the majority of wage garnishments; however, child support payments continue concurrently with bankruptcy proceedings.

NOTE! If the state regulations applicable to an employee limit wage garnishments to a smaller amount than is permissible under federal regulations (as described above), the smaller state regulations take precedence.

Contributing to Retirement Plans

Depending on the circumstance, an employee may choose from a wide variety of retirement plans. Contributions to these plans constitute voluntary deductions from gross earnings. Some of the most common retirement plans, as well as the federal law regulating these plans, are discussed here.

401(k) Plan

A **401(k) plan** (named after the associated subsection of the Internal Revenue Code) is a defined-contribution retirement plan under which a set amount may be withheld from gross earnings each pay period. These funds are tax deferred, meaning that they are not subject to federal income tax withholding when earned but are taxed when the employee withdraws the funds subsequent to retirement.

Some employers choose to match employee contributions to a 401(k) plan. Additionally, an employee is permitted to contribute only up to a specified amount ($19,000 in 2019) to the plan each year.

403(b) Plan

A **403(b) plan** (named after the associated subsection of the Internal Revenue Code) is also referred to as a tax-sheltered annuity (TSA) plan. It is very similar to a 401(k) plan; however, 403(b) plans are available only to certain employees of the following institution types:

- public education institutions
- certain tax-exempt organizations

Ministers can also be eligible for a 403(b) plan. For all of these eligible individuals, the annual contribution limit in 2019 is the same $19,000 as it is for a 401(k) plan.

TIP! Both 401(k) and 403(b) plans allow for *catch-up* withholdings, which are additional annual withholdings (above the initial $19,000) based on employee age and/or years of service.

SIMPLE IRA Plan

A **SIMPLE IRA** (Individual Retirement Arrangement) is a retirement plan designed for employees of small businesses (fewer than 100 employees). SIMPLE stands for *Savings Incentive Match Plan for Employees*. Although these retirement plans are relatively easy for an employer to establish, a significant drawback is that the contribution limit ($13,000 in 2019) is lower than that for a 401(k) or 403(b) plan. Another difference is that the employer is required to contribute to a SIMPLE IRA plan, while employer contributions are optional for a 401(k) or 403(b) plan. The employee may choose to have amounts withheld from gross earnings for a SIMPLE IRA plan but is not required to do so. If the employee does choose to contribute, the deduction from gross earnings is exempt from federal income tax withholding.

Payroll Deduction IRA

A **Payroll Deduction IRA** is perhaps the simplest retirement plan option. For this reason, it is often utilized by individuals who are self-employed. Only the employee may contribute to a Payroll Deduction IRA, and the 2019 annual contribution is limited to the lesser of $6,000 ($7,000 for employees age 50 or older) or taxable earnings. Although contributions to Payroll Deduction IRAs are subject to federal income tax withholding, the employee may receive a tax deduction on his/her year-end tax return for contributions made during the year.

NOTE! A number of other retirement plans are often utilized, including a traditional IRA and a Roth IRA; however, as these do not involve deductions from employee earnings, they are not discussed here.

The Employee Retirement Income Security Act of 1974

On the Web

webapps.dol.gov
/dolfaq/go-dol-faq.asp?
faqid=225

Commonly referred to as ERISA, the **Employee Retirement Income Security Act of 1974** regulates retirement plans offered by employers. While it does not require that employers offer such plans, for those that do, ERISA sets forth a number of requirements.

Employees must be provided with pertinent retirement plan information, such as the manner in which it is funded. Secondly, fiduciaries of the retirement plan (individuals who can make investment decisions) may be held accountable for breaches of responsibility. This results in more conscientious investing of the funds. Additionally, ERISA sets forth requirements for retirement plan participation, the accumulation of benefits, and the time frame over which plan benefits become nonforfeitable.

Cafeteria Plans

A cafeteria plan is a group of benefits offered by an employer. To offer a cafeteria plan, the employer must give each employee a choice of at least one taxable option (compensation on which tax is levied; this is typically cash) and one nontaxable option. The voluntary nontaxable deductions afforded to employees through a cafeteria plan can include:

- Medical care reimbursements
- Adoption assistance
- Group-term life insurance
- Health savings account
- Flexible spending account

A flexible spending account is a type of cafeteria plan that sets aside funds to be used for health-care expenses during the year. Some of these plans are designated for a specific purpose, such as a dependent care flexible spending account. These plans contain a *use it or lose it* feature that traditionally prevented employees from carrying over the contributed funds for use in the subsequent year, although this provision has been relaxed in recent years.

If desired, an employee may choose from any of the available options. With a few notable exceptions (such as for adoption assistance and group-term life insurance coverage exceeding $50,000), cafeteria plans are exempt from both federal income tax withholding and FICA tax.

Dependent Care Benefits

Dependent care benefits, which can be offered as part of a cafeteria plan, are among the most common benefits taken advantage of by employees. Employees may receive up to $5,000 per year in dependent care benefits that are not subject to federal withholding tax, Social Security tax, or Medicare tax (this amount is reduced to $2,500 for employees who file tax returns under Married Filing Separately status). These benefits are to be used to care for a qualifying individual so that the employee may work.

Charitable Contributions, Union Dues, and Insurance Premiums

Employees may choose to have charitable contributions voluntarily deducted from gross earnings and remitted directly to the charity by the employer. Some employers choose to match employee charitable contributions, thereby magnifying the impact of the employee's donation. Although these amounts are subject to federal income tax withholding, the employee typically may claim a deduction on his/her year-end tax return for the contribution amount.

Many different types of employees, such as college faculty members and auto workers, may be eligible to join a union. These organizations negotiate a variety of employment terms on behalf of their members. Union dues are typically withheld from gross earnings as a voluntary deduction but are subject to federal income tax withholding. Similar to charitable contributions, union dues may be claimed as a deduction on the employee's year-end tax return.

Insurance premiums, such as those for health insurance and life insurance, may also be withheld and remitted to the insurance company on behalf of the employee as a voluntary deduction. Except when it is associated with a cafeteria plan, health insurance is subject to federal income tax withholding when it is paid by the employee through a deduction. In this instance, the amount spent may be claimed as a deduction on the employee's year-end tax return.

Case in Point 4-3	Identify Miscellaneous Deductions

See if you can match each of the voluntary deduction types listed in the left column to the corresponding withholding description in the right column. Answers are below.

1.	Wage garnishment	A.	An employee elects to withhold amounts to fund multiple benefits on a pre-tax basis.
2.	401(k)	B.	An amount is withheld as a result of a court order.
3.	Charitable contribution	C.	An employee working for a public university withholds funds for a retirement plan.
4.	Cafeteria plan	D.	A steelworker elects to withhold funds that are remitted to an organization that advocates on his behalf for work-related issues.
5.	Union dues	E.	An employee chooses to withhold funds that are remitted directly to a local soup kitchen.
6.	403(b)	F.	An employee (who is not eligible for a 403(b) plan) withholds the maximum permissible amount ($19,000) for a retirement plan.

The items match up as follows:

1 → B   2 → F   3 → E
4 → A   5 → D   6 → C

Remember the following:

- Wage garnishments are required as a result of a legal proceeding.

- The maximum 401(k) contribution is $19,000.

- Charitable contributions can be made to both large and small organizations.

- A cafeteria plan allows for the selection of multiple options.

- Union dues are paid to a union that advocates on the employee's behalf.

- 403(b) plans are available only to certain employees (such as those who are employed by a public university).

Completing the Payroll Register

Once the withholding amounts identified throughout this chapter have been properly calculated, both the payroll register and the employee earnings records can be completed. The final figure in both the payroll register and the employee earnings records is the net pay. As you have seen, this is the amount for which each employee's paycheck is written. To facilitate the tracking of employee paychecks, the check number is included beside net pay for each pay period.

Recall that Lucky Ties Apparel combines the voluntary deductions on each employee earnings record into a *single voluntary* withholdings column on the payroll register. As a result, each voluntary withholdings figure within the payroll register must be broken out across multiple columns when transferred to the respective employee earnings records.

Case in Point 4-4	**Complete a Payroll Register**

In this example, we will complete a payroll register for Lucky Ties Apparel. Earlier we calculated the Social Security tax for four different employees of Lucky Ties Apparel. The below payroll register for the most recent week reflects these employees' deductions. Additionally, the payroll register has been populated with information for four other employees (whose earnings were determined in Chapter 2).

Note that none of these remaining four employees exceed the Social Security wage base as of the end of the current pay period. Additionally, Medicare deductions have been entered for each employee. Lastly, the Voluntary Withholdings column contains appropriate withholdings for life insurance, charitable contributions, cafeteria plans, and state disability insurance (Lucky Ties Apparel conducts business in New York State, which allows for the withholding of disability insurance). Based on this payroll register, we will complete the employee earnings records for each employee.

Payroll Register

Pay Period   12/1/2019

Pay Date   12/5/2019

Employee Name	Regular Hours	Regular Rate	Regular Earnings	Overtime Hours	Overtime Rate	Overtime Earnings	Total Earnings	FWT	SWT	Social Security	Medicare	Vol. With.	Check Number	Net Pay
				Earnings						*Deductions*				
Rogers, P	35	$ 11.50	$ 402.50	0	n/a	$ -	$ 402.50	$ 23.00	$ 18.52	$ 24.96	$ 5.84	$ 42.80	1462	$ 287.38
Sherman, M	n/a	n/a	$ 769.23	0	n/a	$ -	$ 769.23	$ 61.00	$ 38.46	$ -	$ 11.15	$ 10.60	1463	$ 648.02
Novak, B	40	$ 14.75	$ 590.00	6	$ 22.50	$ 135.00	$ 725.00	$ 13.00	$ 34.08	$ 42.25	$ 9.88	$ 69.10	1464	$ 556.69
Dorsett, A	40	$ 17.50	$ 700.00	7	$ 26.25	$ 183.75	$ 883.75	$ 63.00	$ 39.77	$ 6.20	$ 11.53	$ 113.98	1465	$ 649.27
Kubiak, M	40	$ 15.00	$ 600.00	1	$ 22.50	$ 22.50	$ 622.50	$ 7.00	$ 31.13	$ 38.60	$ 9.03	$ 35.60	1466	$ 501.14
Martin, S	40	$ 21.15	$ 846.00	11	$ 31.73	$ 349.03	$ 1,195.03	$ 90.00	$ 59.75	$ 74.09	$ 17.33	$ 60.60	1467	$ 893.26
Marshall, L	40	$ 15.75	$ 630.00	9	$ 23.63	$ 212.67	$ 842.67	$ 51.00	$ 38.76	$ 52.25	$ 12.22	$ 78.01	1468	$ 610.43
McHenry, D	40	$ 15.30	$ 612.00	5	$ 22.95	$ 114.75	$ 726.75	$ 2.00	$ 36.34	$ 45.06	$ 10.54	$ 0.60	1469	$ 632.21
Totals:			$5,149.73			$1,017.70	$6,167.43	$310.00	$296.81	$283.41	$ 87.52	$411.29		$4,778.40

The employee earnings records can now be completed in full. Although not explicitly discussed earlier, a number of deductions (life insurance, charitable contributions, and state disability insurance) were entered for each employee. When these, as well as the previously discussed withholding amounts, are subtracted from gross pay, each employee's net pay is determined.

Employee Earnings Record

Name   Paul Rogers   Marital Status   Single

Address   657 Flicker Lane   Fed. Withholding Allow.   1

Brockport, NY 14420   State Withholding Allow.   1

SS#   111-11-1111

Pay Period Ending	Regular Hours Worked	Regular Pay Rate	Regular Wages	Overtime Hours Worked	Overtime Pay Rate	Overtime Wages	Gross Pay	Federal Withholding Tax	State Withholding Tax	Social Security Tax	Medicare Tax	Retirement Contribution	Life Insurance	Charitable Contribution	Additional Withholding	Check Number	Net Pay
				Earnings							*Deductions*						
12/1/19	35	$ 11.50	$ 402.50	0	n/a	$ -	$ 402.50	$ 23.00	$ 18.52	$ 24.96	$ 5.84	$ 32.20	$ -	$ 10.00	$ 0.60	1462	$ 287.38

Employee Earnings Record

Name   Maryanne Sherman   Marital Status   Single

Address   8171 Winston Court   Fed. Withholding Allow.   2

Rochester, NY 14604   State Withholding Allow.   1

SS#   222-22-2222

Pay Period Ending	Regular Hours Worked	Regular Pay Rate	Regular Wages	Overtime Hours Worked	Overtime Pay Rate	Overtime Wages	Gross Pay	Federal Withholding Tax	State Withholding Tax	Social Security Tax	Medicare Tax	Retirement Contribution	Life Insurance	Charitable Contribution	Additional Withholding	Check Number	Net Pay
				Earnings							*Deductions*						
12/1/19	n/a	n/a	$ 769.23	0	n/a	$ -	$ 769.23	$ 61.00	$ 38.46	$ -	$ 11.15	$ -	$ -	$ 10.00	$ 0.60	1463	$ 648.02

Employee Earnings Record

Name	Bill Novak	Marital Status	Married
Address	536A North Yellow Lake Avenue	Fed. Withholding Allow.	4
	Hamlin, NY 14464	State Withholding Allow.	3
SS#	333-33-3333		

	Earnings							Deductions									
Pay Period Ending	Regular Hours Worked	Regular Pay Rate	Regular Wages	Overtime Hours Worked	Overtime Pay Rate	Overtime Wages	Gross Pay	Federal Withholding Tax	State Withholding Tax	Social Security Tax	Medicare Tax	Retirement Contribution	Life Insurance	Charitable Contribution	Additional Withholding	Check Number	Net Pay
12/1/19	40	$ 14.75	$ 590.00	6	$ 22.50	$ 135.00	$ 725.00	$ 13.00	$ 34.08	$ 42.25	$ 9.88	$ -	$ 25.00	$ -	$ 44.10	1464	$ 556.69

Employee Earnings Record

Name	Angelo Dorsett	Marital Status	Single
Address	400 Hillside Court	Fed. Withholding Allow.	2
	Hilton, NY 14468	State Withholding Allow.	2
SS#	444-44-4444		

	Earnings							Deductions									
Pay Period Ending	Regular Hours Worked	Regular Pay Rate	Regular Wages	Overtime Hours Worked	Overtime Pay Rate	Overtime Wages	Gross Pay	Federal Withholding Tax	State Withholding Tax	Social Security Tax	Medicare Tax	Retirement Contribution	Life Insurance	Charitable Contribution	Additional Withholding	Check Number	Net Pay
12/1/19	40	$ 17.50	$ 700.00	7	$ 26.25	$ 183.75	$ 883.75	$ 63.00	$ 39.77	$ 6.20	$ 11.53	$ -	$ 20.00	$ 5.00	$ 88.98	1465	$ 649.27

Employee Earnings Record

Name	Melissa Kubiak	Marital Status	Married
Address	254 Cheesehead Drive	Fed. Withholding Allow.	4
	Pittsford, NY 14534	State Withholding Allow.	4
SS#	555-55-5555		

	Earnings							Deductions									
Pay Period Ending	Regular Hours Worked	Regular Pay Rate	Regular Wages	Overtime Hours Worked	Overtime Pay Rate	Overtime Wages	Gross Pay	Federal Withholding Tax	State Withholding Tax	Social Security Tax	Medicare Tax	Retirement Contribution	Life Insurance	Charitable Contribution	Additional Withholding	Check Number	Net Pay
12/1/19	40	$ 15.00	$ 600.00	1	$ 22.50	$ 22.50	$ 622.50	$ 7.00	$ 31.13	$ 38.60	$ 9.03	$ -	$ -	$ 15.00	$ 20.60	1466	$ 501.14

Employee Earnings Record

Name	Stacie Martin	Marital Status	Married
Address	2 Lava Lane	Fed. Withholding Allow.	2
	Brockport, NY 14420	State Withholding Allow.	1
SS#	666-66-6666		

	Earnings							Deductions									
Pay Period Ending	Regular Hours Worked	Regular Pay Rate	Regular Wages	Overtime Hours Worked	Overtime Pay Rate	Overtime Wages	Gross Pay	Federal Withholding Tax	State Withholding Tax	Social Security Tax	Medicare Tax	Retirement Contribution	Life Insurance	Charitable Contribution	Additional Withholding	Check Number	Net Pay
12/1/19	40	$ 21.15	$ 846.00	11	$ 31.73	$ 349.03	$ 1,195.03	$ 90.00	$ 59.75	$ 74.09	$ 17.33	$ -	$ 35.00	$ 25.00	$ 0.60	1467	$ 893.26

Employee Earnings Record

Name	Lucy Marshall	Marital Status	Single
Address	232 Muscle Road	Fed. Withholding Allow.	3
	Hamlin, NY 14464	State Withholding Allow.	2
SS#	777-77-7777		

	Earnings							Deductions									
Pay Period Ending	Regular Hours Worked	Regular Pay Rate	Regular Wages	Overtime Hours Worked	Overtime Pay Rate	Overtime Wages	Gross Pay	Federal Withholding Tax	State Withholding Tax	Social Security Tax	Medicare Tax	Retirement Contribution	Life Insurance	Charitable Contribution	Additional Withholding	Check Number	Net Pay
12/1/19	40	$ 15.75	$ 630.00	9	$ 23.63	$ 212.67	$ 842.67	$ 51.00	$ 38.76	$ 52.25	$ 12.22	$ 67.41	$ -	$ 10.00	$ 0.60	1468	$ 610.43

Employee Earnings Record

Name	Donald McHenry	Marital Status	Married
Address	22 Iceberg Lane	Fed. Withholding Allow.	6
	Fairport, NY 14450	State Withholding Allow.	5
SS#	888-88-8888		

	Earnings							Deductions									
Pay Period Ending	Regular Hours Worked	Regular Pay Rate	Regular Wages	Overtime Hours Worked	Overtime Pay Rate	Overtime Wages	Gross Pay	Federal Withholding Tax	State Withholding Tax	Social Security Tax	Medicare Tax	Retirement Contribution	Life Insurance	Charitable Contribution	Additional Withholding	Check Number	Net Pay
12/1/19	40	$ 15.30	$ 612.00	5	$ 22.95	$ 114.75	$ 726.75	$ 2.00	$ 36.34	$ 45.06	$ 10.54	$ -	$ -	$ -	$ 0.60	1469	$ 632.21

Accounting for Payroll (Employee Portion)

Before You Begin: This section assumes prior knowledge of the transaction recording process. Consult with your instructor to determine if you are required to review this material.

Once each employee's earnings, deductions, and net pay are determined, the employer must record a journal entry to account for each element in the payroll register. For the purposes of this journal entry, all gross pay is considered to be either salaries expense or wages expense. These two amounts are not in any way impacted by the breakdown of deductions.

A journal entry to account for employee payroll and its associated withholding amounts would appear as follows:

12/5	Salaries Expense	XXXXX	
	Wages Expense	XXXXX	
	Federal Income Tax Payable		XXXXX
	State Income Tax Payable		XXXXX
	Social Security Tax Payable		XXXXX
	Medicare Tax Payable		XXXXX
	Retirement Plan Payable		XXXXX
	Health Insurance Payable		XXXXX
	Union Dues Payable		XXXXX
	Charitable Contribution Payable		XXXXX
	Cash		XXXXX
	Payment of Salaries & Wages to Employees		

Because the total of salaries expense and wages expense increases as a result of the employee's earnings (employee earnings are seen as a payroll expense by the employer), these accounts are debited for a total amount equal to gross pay.

The corresponding credits in this journal entry account for each of the amounts owed by the employer, as well as the cash paid to the employees in their paychecks. When the employer withholds amounts from employee paychecks, these amounts are immediately owed to the corresponding entities. For example, once federal income tax withholding is withheld from employee gross pay, it is immediately owed to the U.S. government.

The same holds true for a voluntary deduction, so an amount withheld for a charitable contribution is immediately owed to the intended charity. For this reason, every withheld amount is displayed as a credit to a liability account within the necessary journal entry. The credits to payable accounts in this journal entry can change, depending on the types of payroll withholding that a business has during any given pay period. The credit to the Cash account represents the net pay earned by employees. This is the only amount that is actually paid by the employer on the pay date and therefore the only amount displayed as a reduction (credit) to cash.

WARNING! As with every journal entry, total debits must always equal total credits in the employee payroll journal entry.

| Case in Point 4-5 | **Record a Payroll Journal Entry** |

In this example, we will record a journal entry for Lucky Ties Apparel, in which we account for employee gross pay, payroll withholdings, and net pay. Each employee was subject to $0.60 of state disability insurance, and the only other additional withholding amount on the employee earnings records are contributions to cafeteria plans. Refer to the payroll register and employee earnings records at the end of the previous Case in Point to either calculate or locate the figures included in this journal entry.

TIP! Recall that salaries are compensation typically paid on an annual basis, while wages are compensation typically paid on an hourly basis.

12/5	Salaries Expense	3,533.68	
	Wages Expense	2,633.75	
	Federal Income Tax Payable		310.00
	State Income Tax Payable		296.81
	Social Security Tax Payable		283.41
	Medicare Tax Payable		87.52
	Retirement Plan Payable		99.61
	Life Insurance Payable		80.00
	Charitable Contribution Payable		75.00
	Disability Insurance Payable		4.80
	Cafeteria Plan Payable		151.88
	Cash		4,778.40
	Payment of Salaries & Wages to Employees		

Many of the amounts listed in the journal entry were taken directly from the payroll register. This is one of the primary reasons why it is beneficial to summarize payroll activity for a single pay period in the payroll register.

Also, the debits for gross pay are divided between two accounts. These amounts are the sum of the gross pay for employees who earn a salary (Sherman, Martin, Marshall, and McHenry) and the gross pay for employees who earn wages (Rogers, Novak, Dorsett, and Kubiak).

Self-Assessment

Complete the Self-Assessment as directed by your instructor, whether that is in the book or your eLab course, if applicable.

True/False Questions

1. The sole purpose of Social Security taxes is to provide retirement benefits to employees.   *True   False*

2. The Social Security wage base for 2019 is $132,900.   *True   False*

3. Taxable earnings for Social Security tax are always the same as taxable earnings for federal income tax withholding.   *True   False*

4. Collectively, Social Security tax and Medicare tax are referred to as FICA taxes.   *True   False*

5. The income threshold for Medicare tax indicates the income level above which no Medicare taxes are levied.   *True   False*

6. Employees are required to contribute toward the purchase of disability insurance in all 50 states.   *True   False*

7. The contribution limit for a SIMPLE IRA is lower than that for a 401(k) or 403(b).   *True   False*

8. ERISA is a set of regulations that dictate the manner in which a cafeteria plan may be administered.   *True   False*

9. Flexible spending accounts contain a use it or lose it feature that, although relaxed in recent years, limits the time over which the account's funds may be utilized.   *True   False*

10. Certain withholding amounts are disregarded when determining net pay.   *True   False*

Multiple Choice Questions

11. Which of the following statements regarding Social Security tax is false?
    A. Social Security tax is also referred to as OASDI tax because it was initially established to benefit retired employees, survivors of employees, and disabled employees.
    B. Social Security tax was first levied on employees in 1937.
    C. All earnings of an employee that exceed the taxable wage base in a single year are not subject to Social Security tax.
    D. Contributions to cafeteria plans are not taxable for Social Security tax.

12. Which of the following is taxable for Social Security tax?
    A. Contributions to a 403(b) plan
    B. Contributions to a flexible spending account
    C. Contributions to a dependent care flexible spending account
    D. Contributions to a cafeteria plan

13. How much Social Security tax would be owed by an employee who has taxable earnings for Social Security tax of $2,000, and who, prior to the current pay period, has earned $132,600 of taxable earnings for Social Security tax?
    A. $0
    B. $18.60
    C. $105.40
    D. $124.00

14. The Additional Medicare Tax is paid on a portion of employee earnings by which of the following individuals?
    A. Joe Stinson's filing status is married filing jointly. He earns $174,000 during the year.
    B. Jeanette Yancy's filing status is head of household. She earns $194,000 during the year.
    C. Keanu Levine's filing status is married filing separately. He earns $132,000 during the year.
    D. Carolyn Hughes' filing status is qualifying widow. She earns $187,000 during the year.

15. If an individual whose filing status is single earns $256,000 during the year, what portion of the earnings are subject to Additional Medicare Tax, and what is the total (standard and Additional) Medicare Tax rate that will be applied to these earnings?
    A. $6,000 and 0.9%
    B. $6,000 and 2.35%
    C. $56,000 and 0.9%
    D. $56,000 and 2.35%

16. Contributions to which of the following retirement plans are subject to federal income tax withholding?
    A. 401(k)
    B. 403(b)
    C. SIMPLE IRA
    D. Payroll Deduction IRA

17. Which of the following is not a retirement plan?
    A. 401(k)
    B. Flexible spending account
    C. 403(b)
    D. SIMPLE IRA

18. Which of the following is not a voluntary deduction from gross earnings?
    A. Union dues
    B. State disability insurance
    C. Payroll deduction IRA
    D. Cafeteria plan

19. Assuming that taxable earnings are $51,200 for a 44-year-old individual, which of the following is the contribution limit applicable to a Payroll Deduction IRA?
    A. $6,000
    B. $7,000
    C. $13,000
    D. $19,000

20. Which of the following payroll register columns can contain a combination of multiple withholding amounts?
    A. State Income Tax Withholding
    B. Social Security
    C. Medicare
    D. Voluntary Withholdings

Practice Set A

The IRS forms and Excel templates needed for these assignments are included in the Student Exercise Files download for this course. If directed to do so, complete these assignments in Homework Grader.

PSa 4-1 Calculate Taxable Earnings for Social Security Tax

For each employee listed below, calculate the taxable earnings for Social Security tax for the described pay period. Note that none of these employees exceeded the Social Security wage base during the year.

1. Devin Moody earned gross pay of $1,450 during a recent pay period. He contributes 11% of gross pay to a 403(b) retirement plan and $100 each pay period to a cafeteria plan.

2. Jaclyn Connor earned gross pay of $1,820 during a recent pay period. She contributes 7% of gross pay to a 401(k) retirement plan and 3% of gross pay to a dependent care flexible spending account.

3. Amy Williams earned gross pay of $990 during a recent pay period. She contributes $75 to a flexible spending account and 5% of gross pay to a separate dependent care flexible spending account.

4. Edward Sorkin earned gross pay of $850 during a recent pay period. He contributes 10% of gross pay to a 401(k) retirement plan.

PSa 4-2 Calculate Social Security Tax

For each of the following employees, calculate the Social Security tax for the weekly pay period described:

1. Alfred Morneau earned gross pay of $820. Each period he makes a 401(k) contribution of 5% of gross pay, and his current year taxable earnings for Social Security tax, to date, are $37,200.

2. Rachel Schillo earned gross pay of $1,900. She does not make any retirement plan contributions, and her current year taxable earnings for Social Security tax, to date, are $105,000.

3. Rudolph Fabrizio earned gross pay of $3,200. Each period he contributes 3% of gross pay to a flexible spending account, and his current year taxable earnings for Social Security tax, to date, are $131,400.

4. Michael Frank earned gross pay of $2,650. Each period he designates 6% of gross pay for a dependent care flexible spending account, and his current year taxable earnings for Social Security tax, to date, are $224,300.

PSa 4-3 Calculate Medicare Tax

For each of the following employees, calculate the Medicare tax for the weekly pay period described:

1. Paul Robinson's filing status is married filing jointly, and he has earned gross pay of $2,650. Each period he makes a 403(b) contribution of 8% of gross pay. His current year taxable earnings for Medicare tax, to date, are $274,000.

2. Stephen Belcher's filing status is single, and he has earned gross pay of $1,840. Each period he makes a 401(k) contribution of 6% of gross pay and contributes 3% of gross pay to a dependent care flexible spending plan. His current year taxable earnings for Medicare tax, to date, are $198,950.

3. Sidney Black's filing status is head of household, and he has earned gross pay of $970. Each period he contributes $50 to a flexible spending plan. His current year taxable earnings for Medicare tax, to date, are $86,400.

4. Bill Clay's filing status is married filing separately, and he has earned gross pay of $1,900. Each period he makes a 403(b) contribution of 10% of gross pay and contributes $75 to a cafeteria plan. His current year taxable earnings for Medicare tax, to date, are $199,600.

PSa 4-4 Calculate FICA Taxes

For each of the following employees, calculate both the Social Security tax and the Medicare tax for the weekly pay period described:

1. Bradley Banks' filing status is qualifying widower, and he has earned gross pay of $1,570. Each period he makes a 401(k) contribution of 6% of gross pay and makes a contribution of 2% of gross pay to a flexible spending account. His current year taxable earnings for Social Security tax and Medicare tax, to date, are $212,900.

2. Kyle Struck's filing status is single, and he has earned gross pay of $2,400. Each period he makes a 403(b) contribution of 9% of gross pay and makes a contribution of 1.5% of gross pay to a cafeteria plan. His current year taxable earnings for Social Security tax and Medicare tax, to date, are $199,500.

3. Sebastian Wayne's filing status is married filing jointly, and he has earned gross pay of $3,820. Each period he makes a 401(k) contribution of 10% of gross pay and contributes $150 to a dependent care flexible spending account. His current year taxable earnings for Social Security tax and Medicare tax, to date, are $92,500.

4. Lukas Douglas' filing status is married filing separately, and he has earned gross pay of $2,000. Each period he makes a 403(b) contribution of 12% of gross pay and contributes $75 to a cafeteria plan. His current year taxable earnings for Social Security tax and Medicare tax, to date, are $132,600.

PSa 4-5 Define Miscellaneous Deductions

For each of the voluntary deductions listed, write a definition of at least two sentences:

1. 403(b)

2. SIMPLE IRA

3. Flexible spending account

4. Union dues

5. Insurance premiums

PSa 4-6 Populate a Payroll Register

This problem is a continuation of exercise PSa 3-8 from Chapter 3.

Complete the remaining columns of the payroll register for the five employees whose information was provided in PSa 2-4, PSa 2-12, and PSa 3-8. All employees work in a state that does not require the withholding of disability insurance. Additional information for each employee is provided below:

- Luisa Williams voluntarily deducts life insurance of $15 and a charitable contribution of $5 each pay period. Her year-to-date taxable earnings for Social Security tax, prior to the current pay period, are $82,600, and she is paid with check #0500.

- Jonathan Olsen voluntarily deducts a charitable contribution of $10 each pay period. His year-to-date taxable earnings for Social Security tax, prior to the current pay period, are $31,550, and he is paid with check #0501.

- Nathan Upton does not make any voluntary deductions each period. His year-to-date taxable earnings for Social Security tax, prior to the current pay period, are $132,420, and he is paid with check #0502.

- Juan Rodriguez voluntarily deducts life insurance of $25 each pay period. His year-to-date taxable earnings for Social Security tax, prior to the current pay period, are $134,500, and he is paid with check #0503.

- Drew Painter voluntarily deducts life insurance of $20 and a charitable contribution of $25 each pay period. His year-to-date taxable earnings for Social Security tax, prior to the current pay period, are $51,750, and he is paid with check #0504.

PSa 4-7 Populate Employee Earnings Records

This problem is a continuation of exercise PSa 3-9 from Chapter 3.

Complete the remainder of the employee earnings records for the five employees from PSa 4-6. The earnings section of the employee earnings records was previously completed in PSa 2-13 and PSa 3-9. Note that voluntary withholdings on the payroll register must be divided across the appropriate columns within the employee earnings records.

PSa 4-8 Record an Employee Payroll Journal Entry

Based on the payroll register and the employee earnings records that you completed in the prior two exercises, record the necessary journal entry to account for employee payroll. All employees' earnings are determined on an hourly basis.

PSa 4-9 Record an Employee Payroll Journal Entry

Based on the following figures for all employees during the most recent pay period, record the necessary journal entry to account for employee payroll as of 10/11/2019. A template to be used with this problem is among the Student Exercise Files.

Account Name	Amount
Retirement Plan Payable	$127.10
Social Security Tax Payable	$356.30
Medicare Tax Payable	$110.43
Cafeteria Plan Payable	$193.80
Wages Expense	$4,605.67

Account Name	Amount
Charitable Contribution Payable	$101.82
State Income Tax Payable	$345.23
Salaries Expense	$3,263.98
Life Insurance Payable	$102.08
Federal Income Tax Payable	$516.78

Practice Set B

The IRS forms and Excel templates needed for these assignments are included in the Student Exercise Files download for this course. If directed to do so, complete these assignments in Homework Grader.

PSb 4-1 Calculate Taxable Earnings for Social Security Tax

For each employee listed below, calculate the taxable earnings for Social Security tax for the described pay period. Note that none of these employees exceeded the Social Security wage base during the year.

1. Dustin Woodward earned gross pay of $2,200 during a recent pay period. He contributes 8% of gross pay to a 403(b) retirement plan and $50 each pay period to a cafeteria plan.

2. Olivia Sutter earned gross pay of $950 during a recent pay period. She contributes 5% of gross pay to a 401(k) retirement plan and 1% of gross pay to a dependent care flexible spending account.

3. Ana Grantham earned gross pay of $1,420 during a recent pay period. She contributes $40 to a flexible spending account and 2.5% of gross pay to a separate dependent care flexible spending account.

4. Paul Bernstein earned gross pay of $1,100 during a recent pay period. He contributes 14% of gross pay to a 401(k) retirement plan.

PSb 4-2 Calculate Social Security Tax

For each of the following employees, calculate the Social Security tax for the weekly pay period described:

1. Mortimer Klein earned gross pay of $1,340. Each period he makes a 401(k) contribution of 3% of gross pay. His current year taxable earnings for Social Security tax, to date, are $184,600.

2. Helena Smith earned gross pay of $2,000. She does not make any retirement plan contributions. Her current year taxable earnings for Social Security tax, to date, are $132,700.

3. Kasey Wolfe earned gross pay of $1,140. Each period he contributes 1.5% of gross pay to a flexible spending account. His current year taxable earnings for Social Security tax, to date, are $71,900.

4. Matthew Pugh earned gross pay of $880. Each period he designates 2% of gross pay for a dependent care flexible spending account. His current year taxable earnings for Social Security tax, to date, are $132,900.

PSb 4-3 Calculate Medicare Tax

For each of the following employees, calculate the Medicare tax for the weekly pay period described:

1. Caleb Griffin's filing status is married filing jointly, and he has earned gross pay of $3,100. Each period he makes a 401(k) contribution of 7% of gross pay. His current year taxable earnings for Medicare tax, to date, are $198,400.

2. Anderson Fowler's filing status is single, and he has earned gross pay of $2,220. Each period he makes a 403(b) contribution of 11% of gross pay and contributes 2.5% of gross pay to a dependent care flexible spending plan. His current year taxable earnings for Medicare tax, to date, are $124,375.

3. Rick Portnoy's filing status is head of household, and he has earned gross pay of $1,300. Each period he contributes $40 to a flexible spending plan. His current year taxable earnings for Medicare tax, to date, are $206,100.

4. Shawn Buffett's filing status is married filing separately, and he has earned gross pay of $2,680. Each period he makes a 401(k) contribution of 14% of gross pay and contributes $60 to a cafeteria plan. His current year taxable earnings for Medicare tax, to date, are $210,300.

PSb 4-4 Calculate FICA Taxes

For each of the following employees, calculate both the Social Security tax and the Medicare tax for the weekly pay period described:

1. Tyler Samuels' filing status is qualifying widower, and he has earned gross pay of $830. Each period he makes a 401(k) contribution of 9% of gross pay and makes a contribution of 1% of gross pay to a flexible spending account. His current year taxable earnings for Social Security tax and Medicare tax, to date, are $199,720.

2. Jacob Finney's filing status is single, and he has earned gross pay of $1,240. Each period he makes a 403(b) contribution of 8% of gross pay and makes a contribution of 0.8% of gross pay to a cafeteria plan. His current year taxable earnings for Social Security tax and Medicare tax, to date, are $132,100.

3. Charlie Lilly's filing status is married filing jointly, and he has earned gross pay of $1,850. Each period he makes a 401(k) contribution of 15% of gross pay and contributes $60 to a dependent care flexible spending account. His current year taxable earnings for Social Security tax and Medicare tax, to date, are $84,200.

4. Desmond Carroll's filing status is married filing separately, and he has earned gross pay of $4,120. Each period he makes a 403(b) contribution of 5% of gross pay and contributes $90 to a cafeteria plan. His current year taxable earnings for Social Security tax and Medicare tax, to date, are $97,200.

PSb 4-5 Define Miscellaneous Deductions

For each of the voluntary deductions listed, write a definition of at least two sentences:

1. State disability insurance

2. 401(k)

3. Payroll deduction IRA

4. Cafeteria plan

5. Charitable contribution

PSb 4-6 Populate a Payroll Register

This problem is a continuation of exercise PSb 3-8 from Chapter 3.

Complete the remaining columns of the payroll register for the five employees whose information was provided in PSb 2-4, PSb 2-12, and PSb 3-8. All employees work in a state that does not require the withholding of disability insurance. Additional information for each employee is provided below:

- Jimmy Troffa voluntarily deducts life insurance of $10 and a charitable contribution of $15 each pay period. His year-to-date taxable earnings for Social Security tax, prior to the current pay period, are $71,300, and he is paid with check #0800.

- Tyler Thomas voluntarily deducts a charitable contribution of $35 each pay period. His year-to-date taxable earnings for Social Security tax, prior to the current pay period, are $132,150, and he is paid with check #0801.

- Ryan Brown does not make any voluntary deductions each period. His year-to-date taxable earnings for Social Security tax, prior to the current pay period, are $22,400, and he is paid with check #0802.

- Michael Kaminski voluntarily deducts life insurance of $30 each pay period. His year-to-date taxable earnings for Social Security tax, prior to the current pay period, are $79,560, and he is paid with check #0803.

- Tina Baldwin voluntarily deducts life insurance of $5 and a charitable contribution of $3 each pay period. Her year-to-date taxable earnings for Social Security tax, prior to the current pay period, are $133,700, and she is paid with check #0804.

PSb 4-7 Populate Employee Earnings Records

This problem is a continuation of exercise PSb 3-9 from Chapter 3.

Complete the remainder of the employee earnings records for the five employees from PSb 4-6. The earnings section of the employee earnings records was previously completed in PSb 2-13 and PSb 3-9. Note that voluntary withholdings on the payroll register must be divided across the appropriate columns within the employee earnings records.

PSb 4-8 Record an Employee Payroll Journal Entry

Based on the payroll register and the employee earnings records that you completed in the prior two exercises, record the necessary journal entry to account for employee payroll. All employees' earnings are determined on an hourly basis.

PSb 4-9 Record an Employee Payroll Journal Entry

Based on the following figures for all employees during the most recent pay period, record the necessary journal entry to account for employee payroll as of 5/3/2019. A template to be used with this problem is included in the Student Exercise Files.

Account Name	Amount
State Income Tax Payable	$175.32
Salaries Expense	$3,589.82
Cafeteria Plan Payable	$98.42
Medicare Tax Payable	$56.08
Federal Income Tax Payable	$262.44

Account Name	Amount
Charitable Contributions Payable	$51.71
Life Insurance Payable	$51.84
Retirement Plan Payable	$64.55
Social Security Tax Payable	$180.94
Wages Expense	$406.67

Continuing Payroll Problem

The IRS forms and Excel templates needed for these assignments are included in the Student Exercise Files download for this course. If directed to do so, complete these assignments in Homework Grader.

CPP 4-1 Complete the Payroll Register and Record the Employee Payroll Journal Entry

Calculate Social Security and Medicare tax for a number of employees of TCLH Industries, a manufacturer of cleaning products. None of the employees files as married filing separately on their year-end tax return. Then complete the payroll register using these calculations and the additional information provided below. Lastly, complete the employee earnings records and record the necessary journal entry for employee payroll.

1. Calculate the Social Security Tax and Medicare Tax columns of the payroll register based on information from the prior chapters' Continuing Payroll Problems, as well as the following:

   - Calvin Bell's current year taxable earnings for FICA taxes, prior to the current pay period, are $20,478.57.

   - David Alexander's current year taxable earnings for FICA taxes, prior to the current pay period, are $198,450.

   - Michael Sierra's current year taxable earnings for FICA taxes, prior to the current pay period, are $117,600.

2. Next, complete the remainder of the payroll register for each employee based on the following information:

   - Zachary Fox has authorized voluntary deductions each pay period of $10 for charitable contributions, $15 for life insurance, and $7 for union dues. He receives check #092.

   - Calvin Bell has authorized voluntary deductions each pay period of $15 for charitable contributions and $7 for union dues. He receives check #093.

   - David Alexander has authorized voluntary deductions each pay period of $20 for charitable contributions. He receives check #094.

   - Michael Sierra has authorized voluntary deductions each pay period of $5 for charitable contributions and $20 for life insurance. He receives check #095.

3. Complete the employee earnings records based on the completed payroll register. Note that voluntary withholdings on the payroll register must be divided across the appropriate columns within the employee earnings records.

4. Record the journal entry to account for employee payroll based on the employee earnings records and the totals in the payroll register. Book the entry on the date paychecks are distributed.

Critical Thinking

CT 4-1 Evaluate the Patient Protection and Affordable Care Act

President Obama signed the Patient Protection and Affordable Care Act into law on March 23, 2010. Commonly referred to as Obamacare, this legislation was designed to ensure that all Americans receive adequate health care. As there is an increased cost associated with providing this medical coverage, the federal government needed a method by which it could raise additional funds. The Additional Medicare Tax, which is levied only after an employee has earned a specified amount of income in a single year, is one such method. In this exercise, you will use the Internet to evaluate this legislation and decide whether you are in favor of its enactment.

First, research the legislation to learn about its most important elements. While you should focus on all aspects of the act, pay particular attention to the implications of the Additional Medicare Tax. Write a paragraph of at least four sentences in which you highlight these vital components. Continue your research by examining both the arguments in favor of the act and those against it. Write two more paragraphs (of at least three sentences each) in which you outline these arguments. Lastly, write a concluding paragraph of at least four sentences in which you explain your opinion regarding the effectiveness of this law. Be certain to provide adequate support for your opinion.

Submit your final file based on the guidelines provided by your instructor.

CT 4-2 Review Cafeteria Plan Benefits

A cafeteria plan can provide a wide variety of benefits to an employee. These plans are desirable to both the employer and the employee, as both parties can reduce their tax burden by participating. For this reason, these plans are relatively common. For an employee to derive maximum benefit from a cafeteria plan, that employee must understand the different benefits provided. In this exercise, you will use the Internet to research the most common cafeteria plan features, and then you will describe a number of them.

Begin by researching the possible elements of a cafeteria plan. Identify three components that you believe would be most beneficial for you, either now or in the future. Write a paragraph of at least six sentences in which you discuss your three selected elements. Ensure that you both define the benefit and discuss why you believe it would be helpful to you.

Submit your final file based on the guidelines provided by your instructor.

Federal and State Unemployment Taxes

The payroll process is not complete once each employee's check has been written. In addition to remitting employee withholdings to the appropriate government entity, the employer must pay additional taxes (based on this payroll) that are not withheld from gross earnings. While some of these employer taxes mirror those that were withheld from the employees, others are specific to the employer. These employer taxes represent an additional expense that the employer must bear as a result of compensating employees. In this chapter, you will first examine the manner in which federal unemployment and state unemployment taxes are calculated. You will then examine the matching Social Security and Medicare taxes that are paid by the employer. After reviewing the journal entry to account for these employer taxes, you'll finish by examining nonemployee compensation and self-employment tax.

Videos available! Check out the Video Launch Pad in your student exercise file download to access videos associated with this chapter. One video presents a chapter overview, and the other provides more detail on a key chapter topic.

Determining Employer Taxes for Lucky Ties Apparel

Lucky Ties has now successfully withheld all necessary amounts from the employees' earnings. The next step is for the company to determine the proper amount of employer taxes to remit. These taxes are not withheld from employee pay and therefore are entirely satisfied by the employer. Although these taxes are all based on employees' taxable earnings, some are matched by the employer, while others are paid solely by the employer.

As part of your examination of these employer taxes, you first look at federal unemployment tax, and the extent to which it is reduced as a result of paying state unemployment tax. You then review state unemployment tax and the different effective rates in different states. You next examine the manner in which Social Security tax and Medicare tax are matched by the employer and conclude by reviewing the manner in which the employer payroll taxes are recorded on the company's books.

FUTA and SUTA taxes are not withheld from employee pay (in most states) and therefore do not appear on the check stub.

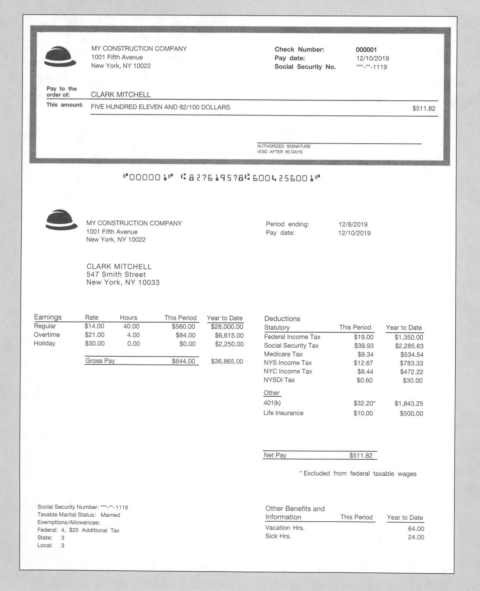

MY CONSTRUCTION COMPANY		Check Number:	000001
1001 Fifth Avenue		Pay date:	12/10/2019
New York, NY 10022		Social Security No.	***-**-1119

Pay to the order of: **CLARK MITCHELL**

This amount: FIVE HUNDRED ELEVEN AND 82/100 DOLLARS $511.82

AUTHORIZED SIGNATURE
VOID AFTER 60 DAYS

⑈000001⑈ ⑆8276I9578⑆ 6004256001⑈

MY CONSTRUCTION COMPANY
1001 Fifth Avenue
New York, NY 10022

Period ending: 12/8/2019
Pay date: 12/10/2019

CLARK MITCHELL
547 Smith Street
New York, NY 10033

Earnings	Rate	Hours	This Period	Year to Date
Regular	$14.00	40.00	$560.00	$28,000.00
Overtime	$21.00	4.00	$84.00	$6,615.00
Holiday	$30.00	0.00	$0.00	$2,250.00
		Gross Pay	$644.00	$36,865.00

Deductions		
Statutory	This Period	Year to Date
Federal Income Tax	$19.00	$1,350.00
Social Security Tax	$39.93	$2,285.63
Medicare Tax	$9.34	$534.54
NYS Income Tax	$12.67	$783.33
NYC Income Tax	$8.44	$472.22
NYSDI Tax	$0.60	$30.00
Other		
401(k)	$32.20*	$1,843.25
Life Insurance	$10.00	$500.00
Net Pay	$511.82	

* Excluded from federal taxable wages

Social Security Number: ***-**-1119
Taxable Marital Status: Married
Exemptions/Allowances:
Federal: 4, $25 Additional Tax
State: 3
Local: 3

Other Benefits and Information	This Period	Year to Date
Vacation Hrs.		64.00
Sick Hrs.		24.00

Federal Unemployment Tax (FUTA)

Federal unemployment tax (also referred to as FUTA, from the Federal Unemployment Tax Act) is levied on the employer, based on the taxable earnings of the employees. The federal government uses these taxes to provide unemployment compensation to individuals who are out of work.

TIP!   Certain compensation, such as that paid to agricultural workers, government employees, and employees of religious organizations, is exempt from FUTA tax.

As of 2018 the tax is levied on only the first $7,000 of taxable wages for federal income tax withholding. Once an employee has earned $7,000 in a single year, no further FUTA tax is levied on the employer for this employee. As of 2018 the FUTA tax rate is 6%. However, employers may take advantage of a credit against this 6% rate for having paid state unemployment tax (which we will examine in detail later in this chapter). This credit is 5.4%, resulting in an actual FUTA tax rate of 0.6% (6% − 5.4%).

WARNING!   The credit of 5.4% is not based on the state unemployment tax rate in an employer's state (this specific rate is dictated by the federal government). The full credit may be used even when the state unemployment tax rate is below 5.4%.

Credit Reduction States

In some instances, states must take out loans from the federal government in order to provide unemployment benefits to all eligible individuals in the state. These loans are referred to as **Title XII advances** (named after Title XII of the Social Security Act), and they must be repaid in a timely manner.

If a state maintains an outstanding loan balance as of January 1 for two consecutive years and has not fully repaid the loan as of November 1 of the second year, it is subject to a credit reduction. Instead of a 5.4% credit, these states receive a lower credit, and therefore their employers must pay a higher FUTA tax rate than the 0.6% that would otherwise be in place. These credit reductions can increase from one year to the next if a state remains in default for consecutive years.

2018 Credit Reduction States

Credit Reduction; FUTA Rate	State/Territory
2.4%; 3.0%	U.S. Virgin Islands

Here we will review how to calculate FUTA tax. In Chapter 6 we will examine how FUTA tax is commonly reported on an annual basis within Form 940. Regardless of whether or not an employer operates in a credit-reduction state, the same five-step process may be used to determine FUTA tax owed:

Step 1:   Determine the applicable FUTA tax rate based on whether the employee works in a credit-reduction state.

Step 2:   Determine current period taxable earnings for FUTA tax.

Step 3:   Add the Step 2 result to the year-to-date taxable earnings for FUTA tax.

Step 4:   • If the Step 3 result exceeds the taxable wage base, determine the amount by which it is higher, and subtract this amount from the Step 2 result. Your new amount (if it is positive) is used to determine FUTA tax in Step 5 (a negative result here indicates that $0 should be used in Step 5).

　　　　　• If the Step 3 result does not exceed the taxable wage base, use the Step 2 result when determining FUTA tax in Step 5.

Step 5:   Multiply the tax rate from Step 1 by the Step 4 result.

WARNING!   Employers may also be subject to a reduction of the FUTA tax credit if they do not remit state unemployment tax payments (SUTA tax, which will be discussed shortly) in a timely manner.

Making FUTA Tax Payments

FUTA tax must be remitted by the employer on a quarterly basis. One exception to this occurs when total FUTA tax owed by the employer is less than $500. In this instance, the employer may postpone payment of applicable FUTA tax either until the total tax owed exceeds $500 or until the end of the year. When FUTA taxes exceed $500 at the end of a quarter, they must be paid by the final day of the first month after the end of the quarter. As a result, the four payment dates for FUTA tax during the year are as follows:

Quarter	FUTA Tax Due Date
1st quarter	April 30
2nd quarter	July 31
3rd quarter	October 31
4th quarter	January 31

If the total FUTA tax owed for the 4th quarter exceeds $500, it must be deposited by the due date of January 31. However, if 4th quarter FUTA tax does not exceed $500, the employer may mail payment with the year-end Form 940 (which will be examined in detail in Chapter 6).

Case in Point 5-1	# Calculate FUTA Tax

For each of the following businesses, calculate the FUTA tax that is owed for the pay period described. Base your answers on the 2018 FUTA rate information and 2018 credit-reduction state information provided earlier.

1. Caramia Company employs three workers in Colorado Springs, CO. As of the beginning of the current pay period, these employees have earned $42,500, $6,800, and $2,000. Calculate FUTA tax for the current pay period if these employees earn taxable pay of $3,140, $1,470, and $1,500, respectively.

   Step 1: Colorado is not a credit-reduction state. Therefore, Caramia Company is entitled to claim the entire 5.4% credit, resulting in a FUTA tax rate of 0.6% (6% minus 5.4%).

   Step 2: Taxable earnings for the three employees are provided above as $3,140, $1,470, and $1,500.

   Step 3: The first employee earned $3,140 during the current period, with year-to-date earnings of $42,500, for a total of $45,640.

   The second employee earned $1,470 during the current period, with year-to-date earnings of $6,800, for a total of $8,270.

   The third employee earned $1,500 during the current period, with year-to-date earnings of $2,000, for a total of $3,500.

   Step 4: The Step 3 result for the first employee exceeds the wage base of $7,000 by $38,640. When subtracted from the Step 2 result of $3,140, we arrive at –$35,500. As this is a negative amount, none of the current year taxable earnings are subject to FUTA tax.

   The Step 3 result for the second employee exceeds the wage base of $7,000 by $1,270. When subtracted from the Step 2 result of $1,470, we arrive at $200. This positive amount is subject to FUTA tax.

   The Step 3 result for the third employee does not exceed the wage base of $7,000; therefore, all $1,500 of current period taxable earnings are subject to FUTA tax.

   Step 5: With total earnings subject to FUTA tax of $1,700 ($0 + $200 + $1,500), the FUTA tax owed by the employer is $10.20 ($1,700 × 0.6%).

2. Perfect Painting employs 17 workers in Des Moines, IA. For the current pay period, the employees earn total taxable pay of $24,500. Of this amount, only $3,250 is subject to FUTA tax, as this is the portion of individual employees' earnings that does not exceed the $7,000 threshold. Calculate FUTA tax based on these earnings.

   Step 1: Iowa is not a credit-reduction state, and therefore Perfect Painting is entitled to the full credit of 5.4%, resulting in a FUTA tax rate of 0.6% (6% − 5.4%).

   Step 2: Taxable earnings are given above as $24,500.

   Steps 3 and 4: Although year-to-date earnings are not provided here, the goal of Steps 3 and 4 is to determine the portion of current period taxable earnings on which FUTA tax should be calculated. This amount is given as $3,250.

   Step 5: With total earnings subject to FUTA tax of $3,250, the FUTA tax owed by the employer is $19.50 ($3,250 × 0.6%).

3. CJ Industries employs two workers in the U.S. Virgin Islands. As of the beginning of the current pay period, these employees have earned, to date, $16,300 and $4,100, respectively. Calculate FUTA tax for the current pay period if these employees earn taxable pay of $1,275 and $840, respectively.

   Step 1: Employers in the U.S. Virgin Islands are subject to a credit reduction, in which the credit is reduced by 2.4%, the FUTA tax rate for CJ Industries is 3.0% (6.0% − 3.0%).

   Step 2: Taxable earnings are given above as $1,275 and $840.

   Step 3: The first employee earned $1,275 during the current period, with year-to-date earnings of $16,300, for a total of $17,575.

   The second employee earned $840 during the current period, with year-to-date earnings of $4,100, for a total of $4,940.

   Step 4: The Step 3 result for the first employee exceeds the wage base of $7,000 by $10,575. When subtracted from the Step 2 result of $1,275, we arrive at −$9,300. As this is a negative amount, none of the current year taxable earnings are subject to FUTA tax.

   The Step 3 result for the second employee does not exceed the wage base of $7,000; therefore, all $840 of current period taxable earnings are subject to FUTA tax.

   Step 5: When the taxable earnings of $840 are multiplied by the applicable tax rate from Step 1 of 3.0% (recall that the FUTA tax rate is higher in this credit-reduction state), total FUTA tax owed by the employer is $25.20.

State Unemployment Tax (SUTA)

Similar to FUTA, state unemployment tax (also referred to as SUTA, from the State Unemployment Tax Act) is levied on the employer based on the taxable earnings of the employees. Unemployment programs are run through the efforts of both the federal and individual state governments. The majority of unemployment taxes are paid not to the federal government but to the states through the collection of SUTA tax.

NOTE! As of 2019 there are three states (Alaska, New Jersey, and Pennsylvania) that levy SUTA tax on the employee as well as the employer.

As with FUTA tax, there is a threshold in most states over which SUTA tax is not levied on taxable earnings. The SUTA tax rate applicable to an employer varies from state to state and in most cases is dependent on the number of employees who have been laid off by the employer. As an employer lays off more employees and therefore creates more workers who are eligible for unemployment benefits, the employer must contribute more to the unemployment program through higher SUTA taxes.

SUTA Experience Rating

Employers are assigned an appropriate SUTA tax rate (resulting from multiple factors, including employee turnover) by their state at the beginning of each year. These SUTA tax rates are determined by the employer's **experience rating**, which is based on a calculation that differs from state to state. Some states will permit an employer to make a voluntary contribution to its unemployment tax account (a one-time, lump sum payment) in order to reduce its SUTA tax rate. This approach could yield tax savings for the employer if the lump-sum payment is ultimately less than the additional SUTA taxes that would have been paid at the otherwise higher SUTA tax rate.

The SUTA tax rates prescribed by individual states for 2019 range from a low of 0% to a high of 14.37%. The wage threshold over which SUTA tax is not assessed ranges from a low of $7,000 to a high of $49,800. As discussed in Chapter 1, unless noted otherwise, we assume a state unemployment tax rate of 3.4% and a threshold of $8,500 throughout this book.

The *new employer* SUTA tax rate in each state is lower than the maximum SUTA tax rate that may be assigned. As a result, years ago some employers that experienced significant employee turnover, and therefore were subject to high SUTA tax rates, circumvented the application of this high rate by forming new companies and transferring all employees to these new businesses. The result was that the new employer SUTA tax rate was applied to the employees in these newly formed businesses, in spite of the fact that employee turnover for this group of employees was high. To prevent employers from artificially avoiding high SUTA tax rates in this manner, the SUTA Dumping Prevention Act of 2004 was enacted by President George W. Bush. The act requires states to ensure that prior employee turnover impacts the SUTA tax rate, even when a new business is formed by an employer.

The majority of states allow employers to claim a credit for SUTA tax paid for an employee who has already worked (and been subject to SUTA tax) in a different state during the same year. The intent is to ensure that employers do not pay more than a reasonable amount of SUTA tax in a given year as a result of an employee working in multiple states.

To calculate applicable SUTA tax, the following four-step process may be utilized:

Step 1:   Determine current period taxable earnings for SUTA tax.

Step 2:   Add the Step 1 result to the year-to-date taxable earnings for SUTA tax.

Step 3:   • If the Step 2 result exceeds the taxable wage base, determine the amount by which it is higher, and subtract this amount from the Step 1 result. Your new amount (if it is positive) will be used to determine SUTA tax in Step 4 (a negative result here indicates that $0 should be used in Step 4).

   • If the Step 2 result does not exceed the taxable wage base, use the Step 1 result when determining SUTA tax in Step 4.

Step 4:   Multiply the SUTA tax rate by the Step 3 result.

Case in Point 5-2   Calculate SUTA Tax

For each of the following businesses, calculate the SUTA tax for the pay period described. Assume a SUTA tax rate of 3.4% and a taxable earnings threshold of $8,500.

1.   Blast, Inc., employs two workers who, as of the beginning of the current pay period, have earned $2,450 and $8,100. Calculate SUTA tax for the current pay period if these employees earn taxable pay of $725 and $640, respectively.

   Step 1: Current period taxable earnings for the two employees are given above as $725 and $640.

   Step 2: When current period taxable earnings are added to year-to-date taxable earnings, the first employee totals $3,175 ($725 + $2,450), and the second employee totals $8,740 ($640 + $8,100).

   Step 3: The first employee's Step 2 total does not exceed the taxable wage base. Therefore, the entire current period taxable earnings of $725 are subject to SUTA tax.

   The second employee's Step 2 total exceeds the taxable wage base of $8,500 by $240. When subtracted from the Step 1 result of $640, we arrive at $400, which is subject to SUTA tax.

   Step 4: When total taxable earnings of $1,125 ($725 + $400) are multiplied by the SUTA tax rate of 3.4%, total SUTA tax owed by the employer is $38.25.

2. Football Enterprises employs 43 workers who, for the current pay period, earn total taxable pay of $57,220. Of this amount, only $10,400 is subject to SUTA tax, as this is the portion of individual employee earnings that does not exceed the $8,500 threshold. Calculate SUTA tax based on these earnings.

Step 1: Current period taxable earnings are given above as $57,220.

Steps 2 and 3: Although year-to-date earnings are not provided here, the goal of Steps 2 and 3 is to determine the portion of current period taxable earnings on which SUTA tax should be calculated. This amount is given as $10,400.

Step 4: When total taxable earnings of $10,400 are multiplied by the SUTA tax rate of 3.4%, total SUTA tax owed by the employer is $353.60.

Matching Social Security and Medicare Tax

In the last chapter you learned how Social Security and Medicare taxes are withheld from employee gross pay. In this way, employees indirectly pay both of these taxes to the federal government. In addition to these withholdings, as of 2019 the employer must then pay an equal amount of Social Security and Medicare tax. For example, if an employer withholds $450 in Social Security and Medicare tax from an employee's earnings, the employer must then pay an additional $450 for the employer portion of these taxes. The resulting total tax remitted by the employer is $900 ($450 employee portion + $450 employer portion). In this instance, the employer is said to be *matching* the employee's taxes.

Similar to FUTA and SUTA tax, these employer Social Security and Medicare taxes are an expense of the employer. As they are matched to the amounts owed by the employee, these taxes are based on the level of employee earnings.

WARNING! Note that although employers are typically said to be matching Social Security tax, the Social Security tax rate has at certain times been different for the employee and the employer. For example, a temporary tax cut from 2011 to 2012 dictated that the employee's portion of Social Security tax was reduced to 4.2%, while the employer portion remained at 6.2%.

Keep in mind that while standard Medicare tax is matched by the employer, Additional Medicare Tax is not. Therefore, even if an employee's earnings exceed the applicable Additional Medicare Tax threshold, the employer is only responsible for matching Medicare tax at the standard 1.45% rate for all taxable earnings.

Case in Point 5-3	## Calculate Employer Social Security and Medicare Tax

For the following circumstance, determine the employer's matching Social Security and Medicare taxes:

1. For the most recent pay period, total Social Security and Medicare taxes withheld from all employee earnings totaled $601.40 and $140.65, respectively. Note that no single employee has, to date, exceeded his/her Additional Medicare Tax threshold.

    Since the employer is required to match all Social Security and Medicare taxes withheld from employee gross pay, the employer's Social Security and Medicare taxes are $601.40 and $140.65, respectively.

2. Rodney Alford files as single on his tax return and had taxable earnings for FICA of $2,000 during the most recent pay period. His earnings to date, prior to the current pay period, were $199,000.

    Rodney previously exceeded the Social Security wage base of $132,900, and therefore neither he nor his employer is responsible for Social Security tax on the current period earnings. Although Rodney did exceed the Additional Medicare Tax threshold of $200,000 for an individual who files as single on his tax return ($199,000 previous earnings + $2,000 current period taxable earnings = $201,000 total year-to-date earnings), his employer must match only regular Medicare tax, not Additional Medicare Tax. As a result, Rodney's employer must pay matching Medicare tax on the current period taxable earnings of $29 ($2,000 taxable earnings × 1.45% regular Medicare tax rate).

Accounting for Payroll (Employer Portion)

Before You Begin: This section assumes prior knowledge of the transaction-recording process. Consult with your instructor to determine if you are required to review this material.

As you saw in the prior chapter, all payroll activity must be recorded in journal entries. Employee gross pay and its associated withholding amounts are recorded first. The second journal entry that must be recorded is designed to record the employer taxes we have examined in this chapter.

The first journal entry recorded both salaries expense and wages expense, because all of the amounts discussed in that journal entry (both the withholding amounts and the net pay) had been earned by the employees. This second journal entry instead records payroll tax expense, which is incurred by the employer as a result of maintaining employees. This entry does not include those amounts earned by the employees. Instead, all amounts in this journal entry are paid by the employer.

12/5	Payroll Tax Expense	XXXXX	
	Federal Unemployment Tax Payable		XXXXX
	State Unemployment Tax Payable		XXXXX
	Social Security Tax Payable		XXXXX
	Medicare Tax Payable		XXXXX
	Recording of Employer Payroll Tax Expenses		

The credits to Social Security Tax Payable and Medicare Tax Payable are identical in this journal entry to those that we recorded in the prior journal entry (they are *matched* to the earlier figures). It is important to record these items separately from the first journal entry, so that the different types of expenses are properly debited.

Case in Point 5-4	**Record an Employer Payroll Journal Entry**

In this example, we will record a journal entry for Lucky Ties Apparel, in which we account for employer payroll taxes. The only employee who had not exceeded the FUTA and SUTA taxable wage bases prior to the current period was Donald McHenry, whose year-to-date earnings prior to the current period were $5,200.

12/5	Payroll Tax Expense	400.00	
	Federal Unemployment Tax Payable		4.36
	State Unemployment Tax Payable		24.71
	Social Security Tax Payable		283.41
	Medicare Tax Payable		87.52
	Recording of Employer Payroll Tax Expenses		

The debit to Payroll Tax Expense of $400 is the sum of the credited amounts below. We have already determined the Social Security Tax Payable and Medicare Tax Payable amounts from the prior journal entry in Chapter 4.

When Donald's taxable earnings of $726.75 are added to year-to-date earnings of $5,200, neither the $7,000 FUTA taxable wage base nor the $8,500 SUTA taxable wage base is exceeded, and therefore all of the current period's taxable earnings are subject to FUTA and SUTA tax. The FUTA tax amount of $4.36 is calculated as 0.6% × $726.75, while the SUTA tax amount of $24.71 is calculated as 3.4% × $726.75.

TIP!   As in the previous journal entry, all taxes are credited to liability accounts because they are immediately owed to the respective government entities.

Nonemployee Compensation

Throughout the textbook thus far, you have examined only the manner in which payroll-related topics impact employees. However, a wide variety of individuals perform services for employers without qualifying as employees. The general rule that employers use to define these individuals as **independent contractors**, instead of employees, is that these workers determine how the employer's work is completed and what is to be done. For example, a lawyer can provide legal services through whatever method desired, as long as the legal representation is sufficient. Because the employer can't exert control over the method used by the lawyer, the *employee* classification does not apply. This lawyer would be considered an independent contractor.

When an employer utilizes the services of an independent contractor, a number of forms that are specific to this circumstance must be completed. These include Form W-9 (Request for Taxpayer Identification Number and Certification), Form 1099-MISC (Miscellaneous Income), and Form 1096 (Annual Summary and Transmittal of U.S. Information Returns).

Independent Contractors

On the Web

irs.gov/pub/irs-pdf
/fss8.pdf

Independent contractors, who perform services for employers without qualifying as employees, can do so both with or without having formed a business of their own. Among those professionals who most frequently work as independent contractors are accountants, lawyers, doctors, and subcontractors. The determination of whether an individual is an employee or an independent contractor can be unclear at times, but it essentially comes down to whether the employer can control how the work is performed. If the employer is unable to make this determination, Form SS-8 (Determination of Worker Status for Purposes of Federal Employment Taxes and Income Tax Withholding) may be filed. The IRS, upon receipt and review of this form, will render a decision as to the worker's employment classification.

Statutory Employees

Statutory employees, for whom FICA taxes must be withheld, are those individuals who would otherwise be considered independent contractors but who meet certain requirements that dictate that they be categorized as employees. Among those who may qualify as statutory employees are drivers who deliver food or who pick up and deliver laundry/dry cleaning, life insurance sales agents, individuals who work on goods/materials from home and subsequently return them to a designated person, and full-time traveling or city salespeople. An employer must ensure that workers should not be classified as statutory employees prior to treating them as independent contractors.

Form W-9

On the Web

irs.gov/pub/irs-pdf
/fw9.pdf

Although employers (in many instances) are not responsible for withholding taxes from the compensation of independent contractors, they are obligated to report the individual's annual compensation to the federal government. They must also inform the independent contractor of his/her annual compensation at year-end. To accurately complete these forms, the employer must obtain either the independent contractor's Social Security number or the applicable Employer Identification Number (for the business under which the independent contractor operates, or for a resident alien, for example). This may be done through the use of Form W-9 (Request for Taxpayer Identification Number and Certification). Upon receipt of Form W-9, the employer retains the form and does not submit it to the IRS.

Examine the Form: W-9

Form W-9 primarily contains the independent contractor's demographic information.

1. **Top portion of form:** *Name* (either of the individual or business), *Business Name* (if applicable; typically the Doing Business As name), *Federal Tax Classification* (Individual/Sole Proprietor is typically checked by an independent contractor), and *Address* should be completed.

2. **Exemptions:** Not typically completed by U.S.-based independent contractors. Enter the applicable code from the Form W-9 instructions if you are exempt from backup withholding or Foreign Account Tax Compliance Act (FATCA) reporting.

3. **List account number(s) here:** Typically left blank (accounts already established with the IRS to pay back taxes can be entered here).

4. **Requester's name and address:** This item does not need to be completed for the form to be valid. If utilized, it should include information for the entity requesting that the independent contractor complete the form.

5. **Taxpayer Identification Number:** Either the Social Security number or Employer Identification Number of the independent contractor should be entered here.

6. **Certification:** Form must be signed and dated to be valid.

Form 1099-MISC

On the Web

irs.gov/pub/irs-pdf
/f1099msc.pdf

At the end of the year, the employer must both furnish the independent contractor with a copy of Form 1099-MISC and remit a copy of the form to the IRS. Form 1099-MISC displays total annual earnings for the independent contractor. The form must be provided to the independent contractor no later than January 31 of the following year. This is necessary so that the independent contractor has sufficient time to complete his/her individual tax return (due on April 15) after receiving the form.

TIP! For many items in Form 1099-MISC (such as rents, other income, medical and health-care benefits, nonemployee compensation, crop-insurance proceeds, and gross proceeds paid to an attorney), only annual compensation exceeding $600 must be reported.

Examine the Form: 1099-MISC

Form 1099-MISC reports many different types of income and withholding amounts.

☐ VOID ☐ CORRECTED			
PAYER'S name, street address, city or town, state or province, country, ZIP or foreign postal code, and telephone no.	**1** Rents $	OMB No. 1545-0115 **2019** Form **1099-MISC**	**Miscellaneous Income**
	2 Royalties $		
	3 Other income $	**4** Federal income tax withheld $	Copy 1 **For State Tax Department**
PAYER'S TIN	RECIPIENT'S TIN	**5** Fishing boat proceeds $	**6** Medical and health care payments $
RECIPIENT'S name		**7** Nonemployee compensation $	**8** Substitute payments in lieu of dividends or interest $
Street address (including apt. no.) City or town, state or province, country, and ZIP or foreign postal code		**9** Payer made direct sales of $5,000 or more of consumer products to a buyer (recipient) for resale ▶ ☐	**10** Crop insurance proceeds $
		11	**12**
Account number (see instructions)	FATCA filing requirement ☐	**13** Excess golden parachute payments $	**14** Gross proceeds paid to an attorney $
15a Section 409A deferrals $	**15b** Section 409A income $	**16** State tax withheld $	**17** State/Payer's state no.	**18** State income $

Form **1099-MISC**   www.irs.gov/Form1099MISC   Department of the Treasury - Internal Revenue Service

Void/Corrected: The Void box is checked when an employer determines that a partially completed electronic form contains an inaccuracy. Checking the box ensures that the form is disregarded when submitted. The Corrected box is checked when newly submitted forms are completed to correct a previous error.

Left side of form: Payer and recipient information should be fully completed. The account number box is optional and may be used by the payer to assign unique numbers to different 1099-MISC forms. The FATCA filing requirement box is checked only if the organization completing the form is required to report that a foreign financial account is associated with the 1099-MISC.

Boxes 1–15: Income and withholding amounts are entered in these boxes. The majority of independent contractors' earnings are considered to be nonemployee compensation and therefore are reported in box 7.

Boxes 16–18: These boxes are not completed for federal tax purposes. In some instances, these boxes are completed in order to report state earnings and withholding amounts for up to two states.

Form 1096

On the Web

irs.gov/pub/irs-pdf
/f1096.pdf

So that the federal government possesses a record of the compensation paid to independent contractors, the employer must complete and submit both Form 1096 (Annual Summary and Transmittal of U.S. Information Returns) and copies of all 1099-MISC forms at the end of each year. Note that Form 1096 must accompany only paper versions of Form 1099-MISC. When electronic versions of Form 1099-MISC are submitted, the due date is extended to March 31 (unless this date is impacted by a weekend or holiday) and Form 1096 is not required. When Form 1099-MISC is completed, paper versions of these two forms must then be submitted to the IRS by March 1 of the following year (this date changes by a day or two during leap years and when it falls on a weekend). Form 1096 provides a total of all compensation paid to every independent contractor during the year.

WARNING!   Form 1096 is used to report compensation that has been entered on a wide variety of forms. If an employer has completed multiple types of these forms (such as at least one Form 1099-MISC and one Form 1099-INT, which is used to report interest earned), then the company must submit a separate Form 1096 for each type.

Examine the Form: 1096

Form 1096 provides an annual summary of compensation for one of the form types listed at the bottom of the form.

Do Not Staple 6969		
Form **1096** Department of the Treasury Internal Revenue Service	**Annual Summary and Transmittal of U.S. Information Returns**	OMB No. 1545-0108 20**19**

FILER'S name

Street address (including room or suite number)

City or town, state or province, country, and ZIP or foreign postal code

Name of person to contact	Telephone number	**For Official Use Only**
Email address	Fax number	

1 Employer identification number	2 Social security number	3 Total number of forms	4 Federal income tax withheld $	5 Total amount reported with this Form 1096 $

6 Enter an "X" in only one box below to indicate the type of form being filed.   7 Form 1099-MISC with NEC in box 7, check . . . . . . ▶ ☐

W-2G 32	1097-BTC 50	1098 81	1098-C 78	1098-E 84	1098-F 03	1098-Q 74	1098-T 83	1099-A 80	1099-B 79	1099-C 85	1099-CAP 73	1099-DIV 91	1099-G 86	1099-INT 92	1099-K 10	1099-LS 16
☐	☐	☐	☐	☐	☐	☐	☐	☐	☐	☐	☐	☐	☐	☐	☐	☐

1099-LTC 93	1099-MISC 95	1099-OID 96	1099-PATR 97	1099-Q 31	1099-QA 1A	1099-R 98	1099-S 75	1099-SA 94	1099-SB 43	3921 25	3922 26	5498 28	5498-ESA 72	5498-QA 2A	5498-SA 27	
☐	☐	☐	☐	☐	☐	☐	☐	☐	☐	☐	☐	☐	☐	☐	☐	

Return this entire page to the Internal Revenue Service. Photocopies are not acceptable.

Under penalties of perjury, I declare that I have examined this return and accompanying documents and, to the best of my knowledge and belief, they are true, correct, and complete.

Signature ▶   Title ▶   Date ▶

Top of the form: Company name, address, contact person, telephone number, email address, and fax number should be completed.

Examine the Form: 1096 (continued)

Boxes 1–2: Either the Employer Identification Number or the Social Security number of the company's owner should be entered. Only one of these boxes should be completed.

Box 3: The total number of completed forms (not pages) that are being submitted with Form 1096 should be entered here.

Box 4: Total federal income tax withheld from Form 1099-MISC (or other form type being reported) is entered here.

Box 5: Total compensation for all independent contractors is entered here.

Box 6: Only one box should contain an "X," as Form 1096 can report on only one form type. For independent contractors, the Form 1099-MISC box is checked.

Box 7: Unless this is the company's final return (due to the ceasing of operations), this box is left blank.

Signature line: The contact person's signature and title, as well as the date, must be entered for the form to be valid.

Case in Point 5-5   # Complete Form 1099-MISC and Form 1096

In this example, we will complete Form 1099-MISC for Blaine Freemont (SSN 444-44-4444), an independent contractor of Fallen Bear Company (745 Alpine Way, Rapid City, SD 57703). Blaine (who lives at 84 Mountain Avenue, Rapid City, SD 57702) earns nonemployee compensation of $21,000 during the year. Fallen Bear Company (Federal Tax Identification #33-3333333) does not use account numbers and does not report state data.

We will then complete Form 1096 for Fallen Bear Company, which, in addition to Blaine Freemont's Form 1099-MISC, issues three other 1099-MISC forms. Total compensation across these four forms is $62,500, on which no federal income tax was withheld. The CFO of Fallen Bear Company, Jaime Vargas (telephone #605-555-8271, fax #605-555-8270, email address jvargas@fbc.com), signs and submits the form on the due date.

☐ VOID ☐ CORRECTED		

PAYER'S name, street address, city or town, state or province, country, ZIP or foreign postal code, and telephone no.	**1** Rents $	OMB No. 1545-0115	
	2 Royalties $	**2019**	**Miscellaneous Income**
Fallen Bear Company **745 Alpine Way** **Rapid City, SD 57703**		Form **1099-MISC**	
	3 Other income $	**4** Federal income tax withheld $	**Copy 1** **For State Tax Department**
PAYER'S TIN RECIPIENT'S TIN	**5** Fishing boat proceeds	**6** Medical and health care payments	
33-3333333 444-44-4444	$	$	
RECIPIENT'S name	**7** Nonemployee compensation	**8** Substitute payments in lieu of dividends or interest	
Blaine Freemont Street address (including apt. no.)	$ 21,000	$	
	9 Payer made direct sales of $5,000 or more of consumer products to a buyer (recipient) for resale ▶ ☐	**10** Crop insurance proceeds $	
84 Mountain Avenue City or town, state or province, country, and ZIP or foreign postal code	**11**	**12**	
Rapid City, SD 57702			
Account number (see instructions)	FATCA filing requirement ☐	**13** Excess golden parachute payments $	**14** Gross proceeds paid to an attorney $
15a Section 409A deferrals $	**15b** Section 409A income $	**16** State tax withheld $ -------- $	**17** State/Payer's state no.	**18** State income $ -------- $

Form **1099-MISC**   www.irs.gov/Form1099MISC   Department of the Treasury - Internal Revenue Service

All company information and independent contractor information is entered on the left of the form. As the company does not enter state information, box 7 is the only other box that is populated. No signature (either from the employer or the independent contractor) is included on Form 1099-MISC.

Do Not Staple   6969

Form **1096**

Department of the Treasury
Internal Revenue Service

Annual Summary and Transmittal of
U.S. Information Returns

OMB No. 1545-0108

20**19**

FILER'S name

Fallen Bear Company

Street address (including room or suite number)

745 Alpine Way

City or town, state or province, country, and ZIP or foreign postal code

Rapid City, SD 57703

Name of person to contact	Telephone number
Jaime Vargas	605-555-8271
Email address	Fax number
jvargas@fbc.com	605-555-8270

For Official Use Only

1 Employer identification number	2 Social security number	3 Total number of forms	4 Federal income tax withheld	5 Total amount reported with this Form 1096
33-3333333		4	$ 0	$ 62,500

6 Enter an "X" in only one box below to indicate the type of form being filed.   **7 Form 1099-MISC with NEC in box 7, check . . . . ▶ ☐**

W-2G 32	1097-BTC 50	1098 81	1098-C 78	1098-E 84	1098-F 03	1098-Q 74	1098-T 83	1099-A 80	1099-B 79	1099-C 85	1099-CAP 73	1099-DIV 91	1099-G 86	1099-INT 92	1099-K 10	1099-LS 16
☐	☐	☐	☐	☐	☐	☐	☐	☐	☐	☐	☐	☐	☐	☐	☐	☐

1099-LTC 93	1099-MISC 95	1099-OID 96	1099-PATR 97	1099-Q 31	1099-QA 1A	1099-R 98	1099-S 75	1099-SA 94	1099-SB 43	3921 25	3922 26	5498 28	5498-ESA 72	5498-QA 2A	5498-SA 27	
☐	☒	☐	☐	☐	☐	☐	☐	☐	☐	☐	☐	☐	☐	☐	☐	

Return this entire page to the Internal Revenue Service. Photocopies are not acceptable.

Under penalties of perjury, I declare that I have examined this return and accompanying documents and, to the best of my knowledge and belief, they are true, correct, and complete.

Signature ▶ *Jaime Vargas*   Title ▶ CFO   Date ▶ 3/1/20

Instructions   **When to file.** File Form 1096 as follows.

In this instance, Form 1096 is issued by a company that possesses an Employer Identification Number (EIN). Therefore, box 1 is populated, while box 2 (which would contain the Social Security number if the form were completed by an individual employer) is left blank. The 1099-MISC box is checked, while all other boxes remain unchecked.

The Self-Employment Contributions Act (SECA)

On the Web

irs.gov/businesses/small
-businesses-self
-employed

The **Self-Employment Contributions Act of 1954** established that self-employed individuals must pay self-employment taxes (SE taxes). These taxes are very similar to Social Security and Medicare taxes, which aren't paid by self-employed individuals. SE taxes serve to ensure that self-employed individuals are taxed in a manner similar to standard employees.

As you have seen, an employee pays Social Security tax of 6.2% of taxable earnings, while the employer matches the same 6.2%. This results in total Social Security tax of 12.4% being remitted to the federal government. Similarly, for Medicare, 1.45% of taxable earnings are paid by both the employee and the employer, resulting in a total of 2.9% being remitted. Since a self-employed individual takes on the role of both employer and employee, self-employment taxes total 15.3% (12.4% + 2.9%) of **net self-employment income**.

Similar to Social Security tax, there is a taxable earnings threshold applied to the 12.4% portion of self-employment taxes. While the full 15.3% self-employment tax is levied on the first $132,900 of net self-employment income (the same 2019 taxable earnings wage base as for Social Security tax), only the 2.9% Medicare portion of the self-employment tax rate is levied on net self-employment income above that level.

Additionally, there is an income floor below which self-employment taxes need not be paid. Self-employment taxes must be remitted by any individual whose net self-employment income totals $400 or more for the year.

NOTE!   Net self-employment income represents income after certain business expenses are subtracted.

If an individual is both self-employed and receives earnings that are subject to FICA taxes from a second job, that person must be sure to pay the full 15.3% tax on only the first $132,900 earned. This threshold applies to all earnings in a single year, whether they are self-employment earnings or earnings from a second job that are subject to FICA taxes.

Similarly, an individual who is both self-employed and receives earnings that are subject to FICA taxes from a second job must combine these earnings to determine if the applicable Additional Medicare Tax threshold has been exceeded in a single year. The employee is subject to Additional Medicare Tax of 0.9% on all earnings that exceed the applicable threshold.

Statutory Nonemployees

Certain workers are considered to be self-employed by virtue of their professions. These individuals are referred to as **statutory nonemployees**, and they include direct sellers, real-estate agents, and companion sitters (who are not employees of a companion sitting placement service). For direct sellers and real-estate agents to be treated as statutory nonemployees, they must be compensated based on sales (not hours worked), and they must have a written contract that dictates that they are not employees.

Case in Point 5-6	Calculate Self-Employment Taxes

For each of the following individuals, calculate the applicable self-employment tax. Assume that each individual files tax returns under married filing jointly status.

1. Samuel Henner earns net self-employment income of $97,200. He does not work a second job.

   As Samuel's net self-employment income has not yet exceeded the $132,900 threshold, the entire amount is subject to self-employment tax.

   When the earnings of $97,200 are multiplied by the 15.3% self-employment tax rate, the self-employment taxes are $14,871.60.

2. Lisa Coleman earns net self-employment income of $119,200. Aside from this self-employment, she works a second job from which she receives FICA taxable earnings of $19,400.

   Lisa's FICA taxable earnings from her second job must be considered when determining the portion of her earnings subject to the full 15.3% self-employment tax. When these FICA taxable earnings of $19,400 are subtracted from the $132,900 threshold, we find that $113,500 is subject to the full 15.3% tax, resulting in taxes on these earnings of $17,365.50.

   The remaining $5,700 of self-employment income ($119,200 total self-employment income – $113,500 determined above) is subject to only the 2.9% tax rate, resulting in taxes on these earnings of $165.30. Therefore, total taxes owed are $17,530.80 ($17,365.50 + $165.30).

3. Penelope Woods earns net self-employment income of $136,400. Aside from this self-employment, she works a second job from which she receives FICA taxable earnings of $23,900.

   Penelope's FICA taxable earnings from her second job must be considered when determining the portion of her earnings subject to the full 15.3% self-employment tax. When these FICA taxable earnings of $23,900 are subtracted from the $132,900 threshold, we find that $109,000 is subject to the full 15.3% tax, resulting in taxes on these earnings of $16,667.

   The remaining $27,400 of self-employment income ($136,400 total self-employment income – $109,000 determined above) is subject to only the 2.9% tax rate, resulting in taxes on these earnings of $794.60. Therefore, total taxes owed are $17,471.60 ($16,677 + $794.60).

Self-Assessment

Complete the Self-Assessment as directed by your instructor, whether that is in the book or your eLab course, if applicable.

True/False Questions

1. FUTA tax is paid solely by the employer.   *True   False*

2. The credit for FUTA tax must equal the applicable SUTA tax rate for the employer.   *True   False*

3. FUTA credit reductions are assessed as a result of individual states neglecting to repay
    federal loans in a timely manner.   *True   False*

4. There are a few states in which SUTA tax is levied on both the employer and the employee.   *True   False*

5. Employers who have experienced significant employee turnover can be levied SUTA tax as
    high as 25% of taxable earnings.   *True   False*

6. For employers who do not have a track record with employees, a New Employer SUTA tax
    rate is assigned.   *True   False*

7. It is possible for an employer to pay FUTA tax on a specific employee's pay, while not paying
    SUTA tax on the same employee's pay.   *True   False*

8. For 2019 the employer's matching Social Security and Medicare tax may equal those taxes
    withheld from employee earnings, but will not always do so.   *True   False*

9. An independent contractor is considered to be an employee of the business for which he/she
    performs work.   *True   False*

10. The self-employment tax rate is the same as the combined employee and employer
    FICA tax rates.   *True   False*

Multiple Choice Questions

11. The taxable earnings threshold over which FUTA tax is not levied is:
    A. $7,000
    B. $132,900
    C. $200,000
    D. $250,000

12. The FUTA credit applicable to a non-credit-reduction state is:
    A. 3%
    B. 3.6%
    C. 5.4%
    D. 6%

13. How much FUTA tax would an employer in a non-credit-reduction state owe if an employee has earned $6,400 to date and has current period taxable pay of $1,500?
    A. $3.60
    B. $9
    C. $36
    D. $90

14. Which of the following is an accurate statement about SUTA tax?
    A. Every state designates a taxable earnings threshold below which SUTA tax is not levied.
    B. SUTA tax paid by an employer is typically less than FUTA tax paid for the same period.
    C. SUTA tax rates differ from one employer to another but do not change from year to year.
    D. The SUTA tax rate is based on the number of layoffs that an employer has experienced.

15. Based on the range of possible SUTA tax rates and thresholds, which of the following circumstances could occur?
    A. An employee who has year-to-date earnings of $50,600 pays 5.2% SUTA tax on the current period taxable pay.
    B. An employee who has year-to-date earnings of $21,400 pays 17.2% SUTA tax on the current period taxable pay.
    C. An employee who has year-to-date earnings of $26,300 pays 0% SUTA tax on the current period taxable pay.
    D. An employee who has year-to-date earnings of $4,300 pays 14.5% SUTA tax on the current period taxable pay.

16. Which of the following states does not levy SUTA tax on employees?
    A. South Dakota
    B. Alaska
    C. New Jersey
    D. Pennsylvania

17. Which of the following employee taxes is matched by the employer?
    A. State unemployment tax
    B. Federal income tax
    C. Medicare tax
    D. Federal unemployment tax

18. Currently the employer's Social Security tax:
    A. is greater than the employee's Social Security tax
    B. is the same as the employee's Social Security tax
    C. is less than the employee's Social Security tax
    D. can be any of the above

19. Which of the following is accurate regarding self-employment tax?
    A. The taxable wage base (threshold) is the same as that for Social Security tax.
    B. If an individual receives compensation from a business, he/she is not required to pay self-employment tax on net self-employment income.
    C. Self-employment tax is designed such that the self-employed individual pays the equivalent of only the employee portion of FICA taxes.
    D. Self-employment tax must be paid by all self-employed individuals, regardless of income level.

20. What is the self-employment tax rate levied on the first $132,900 of 2019 net self-employment income?
    A. 2.9%
    B. 12.4%
    C. 15.3%
    D. 18.2%

Practice Set A

The IRS forms and Excel templates needed for these assignments are included in the Student Exercise Files download for this course. If directed to do so, complete these assignments in Homework Grader.

PSa 5-1 Determine the Applicable FUTA Tax Rate

For each of the following businesses, determine the applicable FUTA tax rate for 2018 based on the locations listed below:

1. A business operating in Seattle, WA

2. A business operating in Charlotte, NC

3. A business operating in Sacramento, CA

4. A business operating in Bangor, ME

5. A business operating in the U.S. Virgin Islands

PSa 5-2 Determine the Taxable Earnings Subject to FUTA Tax

For each of the described pay periods, determine the taxable earnings subject to FUTA tax:

1. A business employs three individuals, whose taxable earnings to date (prior to the current pay period) are $5,700, $8,000, and $1,000. During the current pay period, these employees earn $1,800, $3,140, and $2,500, respectively.

2. A business employs two individuals, whose taxable earnings to date (prior to the current pay period) are $2,400 and $7,200. During the current pay period, these employees earn $1,250 and $750, respectively.

3. A business employs three individuals, whose taxable earnings to date (prior to the current pay period) are $26,700, $4,400, and $6,850. During the current pay period, these employees earn $2,320, $2,550, and $3,100, respectively.

PSa 5-3 **Calculate FUTA Tax**

For each of the following independent circumstances, calculate the FUTA tax owed by the employer:

1. An employer in Albany, NY, employs two individuals, whose taxable earnings to date (prior to the current pay period) are $8,100 and $6,200. During the current pay period, these employees earn $750 and $1,620, respectively.

2. An employer in Bloomington, IL, employs three individuals, whose taxable earnings to date (prior to the current pay period) are $51,500, $32,420, and $7,550. During the current pay period, these employees earn $1,800, $2,250, and $740, respectively.

3. An employer in the U.S. Virgin Islands employs two individuals, whose taxable earnings to date (prior to the current pay period) are $920 and $5,150. During the current pay period, these employees earn $2,200 and $3,000, respectively.

4. An employer in Essex, CT, employs three individuals, whose taxable earnings to date (prior to the current pay period) are $7,000, $6,100, and $9,400. During the current pay period, these employees earn $650, $980, and $1,100, respectively.

PSa 5-4 **Calculate SUTA Tax**

For each of the following independent circumstances, calculate the SUTA tax owed by the employer. Assume a SUTA tax rate of 3.4% and a taxable earnings threshold of $8,500.

1. Hometown Bakery employs three workers who, as of the beginning of the current pay period, have earned $16,200, $7,150, and $4,000. Calculate SUTA tax for the current pay period if these employees earn taxable pay of $1,450, $2,100, and $960, respectively.

2. Electronics Outlet employs two workers who, as of the beginning of the current pay period, have earned $8,400 and $7,200. Calculate SUTA tax for the current pay period if these employees earn taxable pay of $3,450 and $2,250, respectively.

3. Delivery, Inc., employs 127 workers who, for the current pay period, earn total taxable pay of $347,540. Of this amount, only $31,400 is subject to SUTA tax, as this is the portion of individual employee earnings that does not exceed the $8,500 threshold. Calculate SUTA tax based on these earnings.

PSa 5-5 Calculate FUTA and SUTA Tax

For each of the following independent circumstances, calculate both the FUTA and SUTA tax owed by the employer:

1. An employer in the U.S. Virgin Islands employs two individuals, whose taxable earnings to date (prior to the current pay period) are $5,100 and $6,900. During the current pay period, these employees earn $1,700 and $2,650, respectively. The applicable SUTA tax rate is 1.5%, and the U.S. Virgin Islands SUTA threshold is $26,500.

2. An employer in Newark, NJ, employs three individuals, whose taxable earnings to date (prior to the current pay period) are $26,900, $32,300, and $6,850. During the current pay period, these employees earn $3,200, $2,950, and $1,620, respectively. The applicable SUTA tax rate is 3.4%, and the New Jersey SUTA threshold is $34,400.

3. An employer in Cincinnati, OH, employs two individuals, whose taxable earnings to date (prior to the current pay period) are $4,900 and $8,200. During the current pay period, these employees earn $2,800 and $1,900, respectively. The applicable SUTA tax rate is 2.5%, and the Ohio SUTA threshold is $9,500.

4. An employer in Juneau, AK, employs three individuals, whose taxable earnings to date (prior to the current pay period) are $36,000, $41,400, and $5,200. During the current pay period, these employees earn $3,600, $4,200, and $1,200, respectively. The applicable SUTA tax rate is 2.5%, and the Alaska SUTA threshold is $39,900.

PSa 5-6 Record an Employer Payroll Tax Journal Entry

Based on the following figures for the most recent pay period, record the necessary journal entry to account for employer payroll taxes as of 1/18/2019:

Account Name	Amount
Medicare Tax Payable	$31.90
State Unemployment Tax Payable	$74.80
Social Security Tax Payable	$136.40
Federal Unemployment Tax Payable	$13.20

PSa 5-7 Complete Form 1099-MISC

Complete Form 1099-MISC for William Porter (SSN 222-22-2222), an independent contractor of Pronespeed, Inc., (6 Snowcap Lane, Jefferson City, MO 65101). William (who lives at 55 Rounding Place, Jefferson City, MO 65101) earns nonemployee compensation of $13,400 during the year. Pronespeed, Inc., (Federal Tax Identification #99-9999999) does not use account numbers and does not report state data.

PSa 5-8 Complete Form 1096

Complete Form 1096 for Pronespeed, Inc., based on the information from PSa 5-7 and the following. In addition to William Porter's Form 1099-MISC, the company issued seven other 1099-MISC forms. Total compensation across these eight forms is $101,400, on which no federal income tax was withheld. The controller of Pronespeed, Inc., William Mancuso (telephone #573-555-2320, fax #573-555-2321, email address wmancuso@PSI.com), signs and submits a paper version of the form on the due date.

PSa 5-9 Calculate Self-Employment Tax

For each of the following individuals, calculate the applicable self-employment tax. Assume that each individual files tax returns under married filing jointly status.

1. Annabelle Jefferson earns net self-employment income of $43,500. She does not work a second job.

2. Alexander Ryan earns net self-employment income of $115,000. He works a second job from which he receives FICA taxable earnings of $48,500.

3. Morgan Cruise earns net self-employment income of $221,000. She works a second job from which she receives FICA taxable earnings of $108,200.

Practice Set B

The IRS forms and Excel templates needed for these assignments are included in the Student Exercise Files download for this course. If directed to do so, complete these assignments in Homework Grader.

PSb 5-1 Determine the Applicable FUTA Tax Rate

For each of the following businesses, determine the applicable FUTA tax rate for 2018 based on the locations listed below:

1. A business operating in the U.S. Virgin Islands

2. A business operating in Columbus, OH

3. A business operating in Austin, TX

4. A business operating in Oakland, CA

5. A business operating in Birmingham, AL

PSb 5-2 Determine the Taxable Earnings Subject to FUTA Tax

For each of the described pay periods, determine the taxable earnings subject to FUTA tax:

1. A business employs three individuals, whose taxable earnings to date (prior to the current pay period) are $12,200, $5,250, and $3,000. During the current pay period, these employees earn $2,400, $2,000, and $1,350, respectively.

2. A business employs two individuals, whose taxable earnings to date (prior to the current pay period) are $3,000 and $31,400. During the current pay period, these employees earn $3,300 and $1,450, respectively.

3. A business employs three individuals, whose taxable earnings to date (prior to the current pay period) are $5,200, $46,700, and $500. During the current pay period, these employees earn $2,100, $1,140, and $920, respectively.

PSb 5-3 Calculate FUTA Tax

For each of the following independent circumstances, calculate the FUTA tax owed by the employer:

1. An employer in Cleveland, OH, employs two individuals, whose taxable earnings to date (prior to the current pay period) are $5,000 and $12,000. During the current pay period, these employees earn $1,800 and $2,000, respectively.

2. An employer in Nesconset, NY, employs three individuals, whose taxable earnings to date (prior to the current pay period) are $6,900, $1,000, and $24,200. During the current pay period, these employees earn $2,400, $1,750, and $3,000, respectively.

3. An employer in the U.S. Virgin Islands employs two individuals, whose taxable earnings to date (prior to the current pay period) are $8,500 and $3,400. During the current pay period, these employees earn $880 and $675, respectively.

4. An employer in Cary, NC, employs three individuals, whose taxable earnings to date (prior to the current pay period) are $5,900, $8,900, and $6,600. During the current pay period, these employees earn $940, $1,020, and $850, respectively.

PSb 5-4 Calculate SUTA Tax

For each of the following independent circumstances, calculate the SUTA tax owed by the employer. Assume a SUTA tax rate of 3.4% and a taxable earnings threshold of $8,500.

1. A-1 Framing employs three workers who, as of the beginning of the current pay period, have earned $8,550, $8,200, and $7,400. Calculate SUTA tax for the current pay period if these employees earn taxable pay of $1,000, $1,350, and $1,800, respectively.

2. Mrs. Fix-It Corp. employs two workers who, as of the beginning of the current pay period, have earned $4,200 and $6,500. Calculate SUTA tax for the current pay period if these employees earn taxable pay of $2,700 and $2,400, respectively.

3. Burger Bites Restaurant employs 51 workers who, for the current pay period, earn total taxable pay of $87,450. Of this amount, only $11,000 is subject to SUTA tax, as this is the portion of individual employee earnings that does not exceed the $8,500 threshold. Calculate SUTA tax based on these earnings.

PSb 5-5 Calculate FUTA and SUTA Tax

For each of the following independent circumstances, calculate both the FUTA and SUTA tax owed by the employer:

1. An employer in Delaware City, DE, employs two individuals, whose taxable earnings to date (prior to the current pay period) are $6,100 and $8,800. During the current pay period, these employees earn $1,450 and $2,000, respectively. The applicable SUTA tax rate is 2.1%, and the Delaware SUTA threshold is $16,500.

2. An employer in Bridgeport, CT, employs three individuals, whose taxable earnings to date (prior to the current pay period) are $5,500, $12,900, and $14,200. During the current pay period, these employees earn $2,200, $1,950, and $2,400, respectively. The applicable SUTA tax rate is 4.9%, and the Connecticut SUTA threshold is $15,000.

3. An employer in the U.S. Virgin Islands employs two individuals, whose taxable earnings to date (prior to the current pay period) are $1,420 and $26,100. During the current pay period, these employees earn $3,350 and $1,700, respectively. The applicable SUTA tax rate is 3%, and the U.S. Virgin Islands SUTA threshold is $26,500.

4. An employer in Durham, NC, employs three individuals, whose taxable earnings to date (prior to the current pay period) are $6,000, $21,700, and $34,900. During the current pay period, these employees earn $980, $1,600, and $1,150, respectively. The applicable SUTA tax rate is 1.2%, and the North Carolina SUTA threshold is $24,300.

PSb 5-6 Record an Employer Payroll Tax Journal Entry

Based on the following figures for the most recent pay period, record the necessary journal entry to account for employer payroll taxes as of 6/28/2019:

Account Name	Amount
Social Security Tax Payable	$217.00
Federal Unemployment Tax Payable	$21.00
Medicare Tax Payable	$50.75
State Unemployment Tax Payable	$119.00

PSb 5-7 Complete Form 1099-MISC

Complete Form 1099-MISC for Emma Jamison (SSN 777-77-7777), an independent contractor of SingleStep Industries (993 Valley Court, Detroit, MI 48126). Emma (who lives at 12 Handsome Place, Detroit, MI 48126) earns nonemployee compensation of $32,900 during the year. SingleStep Industries (Federal Tax Identification #88-8888888) does not use account numbers and does not report state data.

PSb 5-8 Complete Form 1096

Complete Form 1096 for SingleStep Industries, based on the information from PSb 5-7 and the following. In addition to Emma Jamison's Form 1099-MISC, the company issued one other Form 1099-MISC. Total compensation across these two forms is $44,000, on which no federal income tax was withheld. The president of SingleStep Industries, George Borstein (telephone #313-555-8880, fax #313-555-8881, email address gborstein@ sstep.com), signs and submits a paper version of the form on the due date.

PSb 5-9 Calculate Self-Employment Tax

For each of the following individuals, calculate the applicable self-employment tax. Assume that each individual files tax returns under married filing jointly status.

1. Allison Wilson earns net self-employment income of $74,200. She does not work a second job.

2. Martin Hughes earns net self-employment income of $152,000. He works a second job from which he receives FICA taxable earnings of $100,300.

3. Elisa Grant earns net self-employment income of $198,000. She works a second job from which she receives FICA taxable earnings of $78,200.

Continuing Payroll Problem

The IRS forms and Excel templates needed for these assignments are included in the Student Exercise Files download for this course. If directed to do so, complete these assignments in Homework Grader.

CPP 5-1 Calculate and Record Employer Payroll Taxes

Calculate the FUTA and SUTA tax payable for a number of employees of TCLH Industries, a manufacturer of cleaning products. Conclude by recording the necessary journal entry for employer payroll taxes. As TCLH Industries operates in North Carolina, assume a SUTA tax rate of 1.2% and a taxable earnings threshold of $24,300.

1. Calculate the employer's total FUTA and SUTA taxes. Current period taxable earnings for FUTA and SUTA taxes are the same as those for FICA taxes. Year-to-date taxable earnings for FUTA and SUTA taxes, prior to the current pay period, are as follows:

   - Zachary Fox: $0

   - Calvin Bell: $20,478.57

   - David Alexander: $198,450

   - Michael Sierra: $117,600

2. Record the journal entry to account for employer payroll taxes based on the totals in the payroll register and the above calculations. Book the entry on the date paychecks are distributed.

Critical Thinking

CT 5-1 Compare the Federal and State Unemployment Programs

The federal and state unemployment programs are designed to work in conjunction to ensure that all eligible workers receive appropriate unemployment benefits. Naturally, as part of this process, certain elements are handled by the federal government, while others are controlled by the individual states. In this exercise, you will use the Internet to research the manner in which the federal government and individual states divide responsibility for distributing unemployment benefits.

Begin by researching the manner in which unemployment benefits are distributed to workers. Continue by examining the elements of the program that are handled by the federal government and those responsibilities that typically fall to the individual states. Write a paragraph of at least five sentences in which you discuss what you have learned about the division of responsibilities in the unemployment program.

Submit your final file based on the guidelines provided by your instructor.

CT 5-2 Research Self-Employment Taxes

Self-employment taxes are levied to ensure that the equivalent of Social Security and Medicare taxes are paid by individuals who are self-employed. As you have seen, these taxes were established by the Self-Employment Contributions Act of 1954 (SECA). In this exercise, you will use the Internet to research both the historical evolution of SECA and the current impact of the act.

First research the components of SECA and the historical SECA tax rates. Then examine the primary objections to the act. Write a paragraph of at least five sentences in which you discuss the tax rate trend since the act was established and the arguments against this taxation. Then write whether you agree with the levying of SECA tax, and provide your reasoning.

Submit your final file based on the guidelines provided by your instructor.

Periodic and Year-End Payroll Reporting

LEARNING OBJECTIVES

- Record the necessary payroll journal entries

- Complete quarterly Form 941

- Complete year-end Form 940

- Complete year-end Form W-2

- Complete year-end Form W-3

At this stage, you've completed all steps for a single payroll cycle. However, you're not done yet, as there are a number of remaining payroll reporting requirements. While some of the necessary forms are completed on a quarterly basis, others are submitted annually. Similarly, there are a number of payroll accounting journal entries that must be recorded as a given year progresses. In this chapter, you'll begin by examining the remaining payroll accounting that must be performed. You'll then review a number of required forms, including Forms 941, 940, W-2, and W-3. As you work through this chapter, note that a calendar of IRS filing due dates may be found in Appendix B in the back of the book.

Videos available! Check out the Video Launch Pad in your student exercise file download to access videos associated with this chapter. One video presents a chapter overview, and the other provides more detail on a key chapter topic.

CASE STUDY

Completing Payroll Recording for Lucky Ties Apparel

Although Lucky Ties Apparel has now accounted for the different payroll taxes that must be remitted, it has not yet completed all payroll-related requirements. The company has a number of federal and state payroll reporting requirements that must be met in order to avoid financial penalties. Lucky Ties Apparel also must record journal entries when payroll-related payments are made.

To meet these requirements, you first examine the remaining journal entries that are necessary when both deducted amounts and employer payroll taxes are paid to the appropriate organization (federal government, insurance provider, etc.). You then review a number of federal payroll-related forms such as Forms 941, 940, W-2, and W-3.

Employers must report payroll-related activity by filing Form 941 on a quarterly basis.

Form **941 for 2019:** **Employer's QUARTERLY Federal Tax Return**
(Rev. January 2019)   Department of the Treasury — Internal Revenue Service

950117
OMB No. 1545-0029

Employer identification number (EIN) [ ] [ ] – [ ] [ ] [ ] [ ] [ ] [ ] [ ]

Name *(not your trade name)*

Trade name *(if any)*

Address

Number   Street   Suite or room number

City   State   ZIP code

Foreign country name   Foreign province/county   Foreign postal code

Report for this Quarter of 2019
(Check one.)

- [ ] 1: January, February, March
- [ ] 2: April, May, June
- [ ] 3: July, August, September
- [ ] 4: October, November, December

Go to *www.irs.gov/Form941* for instructions and the latest information.

Read the separate instructions before you complete Form 941. Type or print within the boxes.

Part 1:   Answer these questions for this quarter.

1   Number of employees who received wages, tips, or other compensation for the pay period including: *Mar. 12* (Quarter 1), *June 12* (Quarter 2), *Sept. 12* (Quarter 3), or *Dec. 12* (Quarter 4)   **1** [ ]

2   Wages, tips, and other compensation . . . .   **2** [ ]

3   Federal income tax withheld from wages, tips, and other compensation . . . . . .   **3** [ ]

4   If no wages, tips, and other compensation are subject to social security or Medicare tax   [ ] Check and go to line 6.

		Column 1		Column 2	
5a	Taxable social security wages . .	[ ]	× 0.124 =	[ ]	
5b	Taxable social security tips . . .	[ ]	× 0.124 =	[ ]	
5c	Taxable Medicare wages & tips . .	[ ]	× 0.029 =	[ ]	
5d	Taxable wages & tips subject to Additional Medicare Tax withholding	[ ]	× 0.009 =	[ ]	

5e   Add Column 2 from lines 5a, 5b, 5c, and 5d . . . .   **5e** [ ]

5f   Section 3121(q) Notice and Demand—Tax due on unreported tips (see instructions) . .   **5f** [ ]

6   Total taxes before adjustments. Add lines 3, 5e, and 5f . . . .   **6** [ ]

7   Current quarter's adjustment for fractions of cents . . . .   **7** [ ]

8   Current quarter's adjustment for sick pay . . . .   **8** [ ]

9   Current quarter's adjustments for tips and group-term life insurance . . . . .   **9** [ ]

10   Total taxes after adjustments. Combine lines 6 through 9 . . . .   **10** [ ]

11   Qualified small business payroll tax credit for increasing research activities. Attach Form 8974   **11** [ ]

12   Total taxes after adjustments and credits. Subtract line 11 from line 10 . . . .   **12** [ ]

13   Total deposits for this quarter, including overpayment applied from a prior quarter and overpayments applied from Form 941-X, 941-X (PR), 944-X, or 944-X (SP) filed in the current quarter   **13** [ ]

14   Balance due. If line 12 is more than line 13, enter the difference and see instructions . . .   **14** [ ]

15   Overpayment. If line 13 is more than line 12, enter the difference [ ]   Check one: [ ] Apply to next return. [ ] Send a refund.

▶ You MUST complete both pages of Form 941 and SIGN it.   Next ▶

For Privacy Act and Paperwork Reduction Act Notice, see the back of the Payment Voucher.   Cat. No. 17001Z   Form **941** (Rev. 1-2019)

Accounting for Payroll (Periodic Entries)

Before You Begin: This section assumes prior knowledge of the transaction-recording process. Consult with your instructor to determine if you are required to review this material.

You have learned how to record journal entries for employee payroll and employer payroll taxes. In each of these journal entries, multiple liability accounts were credited because, as of the payroll date, none of the deductions from employee pay or employer taxes were actually remitted to the organization to which they were owed. When these liabilities are paid, a different journal entry is booked to account for the payment.

Federal income tax withholding, Social Security tax (employee and employer portions), and Medicare tax (employee and employer portions) must be paid by the employer on either a monthly or semiweekly basis. The applicable payment increment is determined by reviewing the employer's **lookback period**.

The lookback period for a given year is the previous July 1 through June 30. For example, the lookback period for 2019 runs from July 1, 2017, through June 30, 2018. If an employer reports less than $50,000 in combined taxes (the three taxes listed above) during the lookback period, the company is a **monthly depositor**. Alternatively, if the reported taxes exceed $50,000, the employer is a **semiweekly depositor**.

Monthly depositors must submit each month's payment by the 15th of the following month. Semiweekly depositors whose pay date falls from Wednesday to Friday must submit payment by the following Wednesday, while those whose pay date falls from Saturday to Tuesday must submit payment by the following Friday.

Type of Depositor	Payment Dates
Monthly	15th of the following month
Semiweekly (pay date Wed–Fri)	Following Wednesday
Semiweekly (pay date Sat–Tues)	Following Friday

When payment is made, the journal entry appears as follows:

9/15	Federal Income Tax Payable	XXXXX	
	Social Security Tax Payable	XXXXX	
	Medicare Tax Payable	XXXXX	
	Cash		XXXXX
	Monthly Payment of Federal Taxes		

The liability (payable) accounts are debited to reduce their balances. This is appropriate as the amounts are no longer owed. The corresponding credit is to the *Cash* account, to illustrate that the employer now has less cash than it did before. Since Social Security tax and Medicare tax are both matched by the employer, the amounts of these taxes in the journal entry will combine the employee and employer portions.

NOTE!   State income tax payments are usually made on schedules similar to those for federal payments. In those cases the state payment is included as part of the earlier journal entry. Check your individual state's regulations to determine the exact payment requirements.

Submitting Unemployment Tax Payments

FUTA Tax Payment Schedule

Quarter	Payment Date
1st Quarter (Jan.–Mar.)	April 30
2nd Quarter (Apr.–Jun.)	July 31
3rd Quarter (Jul.–Sept.)	October 31
4th Quarter (Oct.–Dec.)	January 31

While federal unemployment tax is paid on a quarterly basis, many small businesses are permitted to remit payment once at the end of each year. Employers whose FUTA tax owed does not exceed $500 at the end of a quarter are permitted to delay payment. In these instances, the employer must remit payment either when total FUTA tax owed exceeds $500 at the end of a quarter or after the 4th quarter of the year, whichever comes first. Stated differently, an employer must remit payment by the due dates listed at left only if the total FUTA tax owed exceeds $500 at the end of a quarter. State unemployment taxes are also typically remitted on a quarterly basis, with specific regulations differing from state to state.

For those quarters in which FUTA tax must be paid, the payment is due at a different time than the other federal taxes and therefore is typically paid separately. As such, the associated journal entry is as follows:

10/31	FUTA Tax Payable	XXXXX	
	Cash		XXXXX
	Quarterly Payment of Unemployment Taxes		

SUTA tax typically follows a similar payment schedule (depending on the individual state's regulations), and when paid at the same time as FUTA tax would be included in the above journal entry.

TIP!   When a payment date for any of the previously listed taxes falls on either a weekend or a holiday, the employer is permitted to remit payment on the next business day.

Voluntary Withholding Payments

The payments for voluntary deductions are typically made at set intervals during the year. These intervals differ based on the deduction in question and the employer. For example, when withheld charitable contributions are remitted to the designated organization, the associated journal entry appears as follows:

10/1	Charitable Contribution Payable	XXXXX	
	Cash		XXXXX
	Payment of Withheld Charitable Contributions		

Case in Point 6-1   ## Record Monthly and Quarterly Journal Entries

In this example, we'll record the following:

- One journal entry to account for the month-end payment of federal taxes

- One journal entry to account for the payment of federal unemployment taxes

- One journal entry to account for the payment of the voluntary deductions of Lucky Ties Apparel

The company is a monthly depositor whose December federal taxes, 4th quarter FUTA taxes, and 4th quarter voluntary deductions are displayed below. Assume that each voluntary deduction is remitted to the respective organization on a quarterly basis, on the last day of the first month after the end of the quarter. All tax payments are made in a timely manner on the payment due date (which, for this quarter, is not impacted by a weekend or holiday).

December Tax Totals	
Federal income tax	$1,942
Employee's Social Security tax	$1,215
Employee's Medicare tax	$395
Employer's Social Security tax	$1,215
Employer's Medicare tax	$395

4th Quarter Totals	
FUTA tax	$66
Retirement plan	$598
Health insurance	$480
Charitable contribution	$450
Cafeteria plan	$912

1.

1/15	Federal Income Tax Payable	1,942	
	Social Security Tax Payable	2,430	
	Medicare Tax Payable	790	
	Cash		5,162
	Monthly Payment of Federal Taxes		

Social Security and Medicare payments include both the employee and employer portions. The journal entry is recorded on January 15, as the December payment is due on the 15th day of the subsequent month (January).

2.

1/31	FUTA Tax Payable	66	
	Cash		66
	Quarterly Payment of Unemployment Taxes		

Based on the FUTA tax payment schedule, the 4th quarter unemployment tax payment is made on January 31.

3.

1/31	Retirement Plan Payable	598	
	Health Insurance Payable	480	
	Charitable Contribution Payable	450	
	Cafeteria Plan Payable	912	
	Cash		2,440
	Quarterly Payment of Voluntary Deductions		

In spite of the fact that these voluntary withholding amounts were paid on the same day as the FUTA tax, it is not advisable to include FUTA tax with these items in one journal entry. Writing two journal entries gives each one a more specific purpose. In fact, many companies would not combine these voluntary deductions into one journal entry, opting instead to write a separate entry for each one. Both the approach illustrated above and this alternate method are acceptable.

Form 941 (Employer's Quarterly Federal Tax Return)

On the Web

irs.gov/pub/irs-pdf
/f941.pdf

Employers are required to complete and submit Form 941 on a quarterly basis. This form summarizes the payroll activity (including wages, employee taxes, and employer taxes) of a business for the most recent quarter. The Federal Income Tax Payable, Social Security Tax Payable, and Medicare Tax Payable accounts are (for monthly depositors) debited each month in order to reduce their balances when the taxes are remitted. To enter the correct tax figures in Form 941, the employer may sum the amounts in these journal entries to arrive at the quarterly totals. Similar calculations, based on the payroll register totals, may be made to arrive at the quarterly wage figures.

The due dates for the quarterly Form 941s are the same as the due dates for FUTA payments. Therefore, Form 941 is due by the last day of the first month after each quarter has ended.

NOTE! If an employer's total annual tax liability for federal income tax withholding, Social Security tax, and Medicare tax is less than $1,000, the employer is not required to file quarterly Form 941 and may instead file Form 944 at the end of the year.

As you saw previously, employers typically make payments on either a monthly or semiweekly basis. However, if an employer owes total taxes of less than $2,500 for either the current or preceding quarter, the company is permitted to disregard the monthly or semiweekly schedule and instead submit payment either with Form 941 or use another method prior to the Form 941 due date.

WARNING! If total accumulated tax owed exceeds $100,000 at the end of any day, then the **next-day deposit rule** is triggered, and the employer must pay all taxes owed on the following business day.

The quarterly Form 941 payments and the amounts owed during the quarter will not necessarily be equal. One common cause of this discrepancy is the rounding of tax payments, resulting in differences of a few cents. Form 941 is designed to reconcile the federal tax payments that have been made with the federal taxes that are owed during a quarter. Any differences between these amounts are accounted for within the form or result in either a *Balance Due* or *Overpayment* amount that is reported at the bottom of page 1 of the form.

The Electronic Federal Tax Payment System

On the Web

eftps.gov

The **Electronic Federal Tax Payment System (EFTPS)** provides the simplest method for employers to submit federal tax payments. To use the system, an employer must enroll by acquiring a PIN that, when combined with the Employer Identification Number, identifies the employer in the system. The PIN may be requested either by phone or Internet and is mailed to the employer.

Once the PIN is established and the employer has linked the desired bank account, the employer may remit payment either by phone (1-800-555-3453) or Internet (a separate Internet password must be established to use this method).

TIP! The EFTPS is a free service and is therefore the most efficient method for remitting federal tax payments.

When using the EFTPS, payments must be submitted by 8:00 p.m. the day before the tax due date. Alternative payment methods (such as wire transfer) must be used when making a same-day payment. If the employer chooses not to use the EFTPS, other available payment methods include using a credit or debit card or mailing a check (which must be postmarked by the tax due date). When a check is mailed with Form 941, the employer must also mail Form 941-V, which is a payment voucher summarizing basic information related to the payment. The employer is subject to penalties and interest if federal tax payments are not remitted in a timely manner.

NOTE! State tax payments may typically be remitted in a manner similar to that described here for federal tax payments.

Examine the Form: 941

Part 1 of Form 941 summarizes quarterly federal tax liabilities and payments.

Form **941 for 2019:** **Employer's QUARTERLY Federal Tax Return**

(Rev. January 2019)   Department of the Treasury — Internal Revenue Service

950117

OMB No. 1545-0029

Employer identification number (EIN) ☐☐ – ☐☐☐☐☐☐☐

Name *(not your trade name)*

Trade name *(if any)*

Address

Number   Street   Suite or room number

City   State   ZIP code

Foreign country name   Foreign province/county   Foreign postal code

Report for this Quarter of 2019
(Check one.)

☐ 1: January, February, March

☐ 2: April, May, June

☐ 3: July, August, September

☐ 4: October, November, December

Go to *www.irs.gov/Form941* for instructions and the latest information.

Read the separate instructions before you complete Form 941. Type or print within the boxes.

Part 1:   Answer these questions for this quarter.

1   Number of employees who received wages, tips, or other compensation for the pay period including: *Mar. 12* (Quarter 1), *June 12* (Quarter 2), *Sept. 12* (Quarter 3), or *Dec. 12* (Quarter 4)   **1** ⬚

2   Wages, tips, and other compensation . . . .   **2** ⬚

3   Federal income tax withheld from wages, tips, and other compensation . . . . . .   **3** ⬚

4   If no wages, tips, and other compensation are subject to social security or Medicare tax   ☐ Check and go to line 6.

	Column 1		Column 2
5a Taxable social security wages . .	⬚	× 0.124 =	⬚
5b Taxable social security tips . . .	⬚	× 0.124 =	⬚
5c Taxable Medicare wages & tips. .	⬚	× 0.029 =	⬚
5d Taxable wages & tips subject to Additional Medicare Tax withholding	⬚	× 0.009 =	⬚

5e   Add Column 2 from lines 5a, 5b, 5c, and 5d . . . .   **5e** ⬚

5f   Section 3121(q) Notice and Demand—Tax due on unreported tips (see instructions) . .   **5f** ⬚

6   Total taxes before adjustments. Add lines 3, 5e, and 5f . . . .   **6** ⬚

7   Current quarter's adjustment for fractions of cents . . . .   **7** ⬚

8   Current quarter's adjustment for sick pay . . . .   **8** ⬚

9   Current quarter's adjustments for tips and group-term life insurance . . . . .   **9** ⬚

10   Total taxes after adjustments. Combine lines 6 through 9 . . . .   **10** ⬚

11   Qualified small business payroll tax credit for increasing research activities. Attach Form 8974   **11** ⬚

12   Total taxes after adjustments and credits. Subtract line 11 from line 10 . . . . . .   **12** ⬚

13   Total deposits for this quarter, including overpayment applied from a prior quarter and overpayments applied from Form 941-X, 941-X (PR), 944-X, or 944-X (SP) filed in the current quarter   **13** ⬚

14   Balance due. If line 12 is more than line 13, enter the difference and see instructions . . .   **14** ⬚

15   Overpayment. If line 13 is more than line 12, enter the difference ⬚   Check one: ☐ Apply to next return. ☐ Send a refund.

▶ **You MUST complete both pages of Form 941 and SIGN it.**   Next ▶

For Privacy Act and Paperwork Reduction Act Notice, see the back of the Payment Voucher.   Cat. No. 17001Z   Form **941** (Rev. 1-2019)

The top portion of the form (including Employer Identification Number, name, and address) must be completed in its entirety. The *Trade name* line is left blank unless a business has a *doing business as* (DBA) name (a name under which the company conducts its business and that differs from its legal name). The checkbox for the corresponding quarter should also be selected.

Part 1 of Form 941 should be completed as follows:

Line 1: Only employees who actually received compensation for the date listed here are counted when determining the number of employees to enter here.

Line 2: This box includes all compensation that would appear in box 1 of Form W-2. This includes all compensation that is subject to federal income tax withholding.

Line 3: Federal income tax withholding for the quarter is entered on this line.

Line 4: Compensation is typically subject to FICA taxes; therefore, this box is rarely checked.

Line 5a: Wages subject to Social Security tax, and their associated taxes, are entered here. If, prior to the beginning of the quarter, all employees have exceeded the Social Security wage base ($132,900 for 2019), then both columns are left blank. Social Security wages in Column 1 are multiplied by 0.124 (12.4%) to arrive at Social Security tax in Column 2. This is double the Social Security tax rate of 6.2%, to account for both the employee withholding and the employer match.

Line 5b: All employee tips that are subject to Social Security tax (namely, those earned prior to each employee reaching the Social Security wage base) are reported in Column 1, while the associated taxes are entered in Column 2.

Line 5c: All wages and tips subject to Medicare tax, and their associated taxes, are entered in Column 1. The employer then calculates Medicare tax and enters it in Column 2. Similar to the Social Security lines above, the Medicare tax rate of 1.45% is doubled (0.029, or 2.9%) to account for both the employee and employer portions.

Line 5d: All wages and tips subject to Additional Medicare Tax (those that exceed $200,000 for the year for a single employee), and their associated taxes, are entered on this line. Notice that the Additional Medicare Tax rate of 0.009 (0.9%) is displayed to assist in calculating the applicable Medicare tax. This figure is not doubled, as the employer does not match this tax.

Line 5e: This line totals all tax figures from lines 5a through 5d and therefore represents the total Social Security and Medicare tax for the quarter.

Line 5f: When an employer is informed by the IRS that taxes are owed on unreported employee tips, the associated taxes are displayed here.

Line 6: Total federal income tax withholding, Social Security tax, and Medicare tax combined are entered here.

Line 7: Cents may be added or subtracted here in order to eliminate any rounding-related differences between tax owed and deposits made. There is no penalty for entering these types of differences; however, the amount displayed should be only a few cents (either positive or negative). Although the IRS is unlikely to question slightly higher figures (such as $0.25 or $0.50), an amount that rounds up to a whole dollar (greater than $0.50) would constitute an additional amount owed to the IRS.

Line 8: If Social Security and Medicare taxes for sick pay were withheld by a third party, these taxes are entered here.

Examine the Form: 941 (continued)

Line 9: Uncollected Social Security and Medicare taxes related to tips and/or group-term life insurance are entered here.

Line 10: The sum of the prior four lines is entered here. The $2,500 threshold, below which total tax may be remitted with Form 941, is compared with this line.

Line 11: Certain small businesses that conduct qualified research and that elect to claim a payroll tax credit enter the amount of the credit here. This line will be left blank for the majority of companies.

Line 12: The credit on line 11 is subtracted from the total taxes on line 10 to arrive at the figure on this line.

Line 13: Actual federal tax deposits made by the employer are entered here.

Line 14: This line is populated only if total taxes on line 12 exceed total deposits on line 13. In this case, the difference between these two amounts is placed here, and payment is remitted for this amount.

Line 15: This line is populated only if total deposits on line 13 exceed total taxes on line 12. In this case, the difference between these two amounts is entered, and the employer must elect to either receive a check for the overpayment or apply it to the next return.

Parts 2 through 5 of Form 941 should be completed as follows:

Part 2; Line 16: The employer selects only one of these three options. If the employer qualifies for the first category, then the company does not check either the monthly or semiweekly box, regardless of the deposit schedule utilized. Monthly depositors also must enter monthly tax liability amounts in this section.

Part 3; Lines 17 and 18: Line 17 must be checked if wages will no longer be paid. Line 18 is checked by seasonal employers (those who do not pay wages year-round and therefore do not file Form 941 for all four quarters) on every Form 941 that is filed.

Part 4: To allow a third party (such as the employer's accountant) to discuss Form 941 with the IRS, this section must be completed. Note that the third party may not bind the employer to additional taxes, but instead may discuss the details only with the IRS. The third-party designation lasts for one year unless terminated early via written request. Additionally, if no PIN is selected by the employer, then the third-party designation will not be valid.

Part 5: The employer must sign and complete the top portion of this section for the form to be valid. If a paid preparer (such as the employer's accountant) completed the form, this individual is required to complete the *Paid Preparer Use Only* section.

Note: The *Name* and *Employer Identification Number* at the top of page 2 must be completed as well.

Parts 2–5 of Form 941 require additional information regarding both quarterly deposits and the company itself.

950217

Name *(not your trade name)*	Employer identification number (EIN)

Part 2: Tell us about your deposit schedule and tax liability for this quarter.

If you are unsure about whether you are a monthly schedule depositor or a semiweekly schedule depositor, see section 11 of Pub. 15.

16 Check one: ☐ Line 12 on this return is less than $2,500 or line 12 on the return for the prior quarter was less than $2,500, and you didn't incur a $100,000 next-day deposit obligation during the current quarter. If line 12 for the prior quarter was less than $2,500 but line 12 on this return is $100,000 or more, you must provide a record of your federal tax liability. If you are a monthly schedule depositor, complete the deposit schedule below; if you are a semiweekly schedule depositor, attach Schedule B (Form 941). Go to Part 3.

☐ **You were a monthly schedule depositor for the entire quarter.** Enter your tax liability for each month and total liability for the quarter, then go to Part 3.

Tax liability:	Month 1	.
	Month 2	.
	Month 3	.
Total liability for quarter		.	**Total must equal line 12.**

☐ **You were a semiweekly schedule depositor for any part of this quarter.** Complete Schedule B (Form 941), Report of Tax Liability for Semiweekly Schedule Depositors, and attach it to Form 941.

Part 3: Tell us about your business. If a question does NOT apply to your business, leave it blank.

17 If your business has closed or you stopped paying wages . . . . ☐ Check here, and

enter the final date you paid wages [/ /] .

18 If you are a seasonal employer and you don't have to file a return for every quarter of the year . . ☐ Check here.

Part 4: May we speak with your third-party designee?

Do you want to allow an employee, a paid tax preparer, or another person to discuss this return with the IRS? See the instructions for details.

☐ **Yes.** Designee's name and phone number [   ] [   ]

Select a 5-digit Personal Identification Number (PIN) to use when talking to the IRS. ☐ ☐ ☐ ☐ ☐

☐ **No.**

Part 5: Sign here. You MUST complete both pages of Form 941 and SIGN it.

Under penalties of perjury, I declare that I have examined this return, including accompanying schedules and statements, and to the best of my knowledge and belief, it is true, correct, and complete. Declaration of preparer (other than taxpayer) is based on all information of which preparer has any knowledge.

X Sign your name here [   ]

Print your name here [   ]

Print your title here [   ]

Date [/ /]

Best daytime phone [   ]

Paid Preparer Use Only

Check if you are self-employed . . . ☐

Preparer's name	[ ]	PTIN	[ ]
Preparer's signature	[ ]	Date	[/ /]
Firm's name (or yours if self-employed)	[ ]	EIN	[ ]
Address	[ ]	Phone	[ ]
City	[ ] State [ ]	ZIP code	[ ]

Form **941** (Rev. 1-2019)

Examine the Form: 941 (continued)

Form 941-V is submitted with Form 941 only when payment is included with the form.

✂	▼ **Detach Here and Mail With Your Payment and Form 941.** ▼	✂

Form **941-V**	**Payment Voucher**	OMB No. 1545-0029
Department of the Treasury Internal Revenue Service	▶ **Don't staple this voucher or your payment to Form 941.**	20**19**

1 Enter your employer identification number (EIN).	2 **Enter the amount of your payment.** ▶ Make your check or money order payable to "**United States Treasury**"	Dollars	Cents

3 Tax Period

- ○ 1st Quarter
- ○ 3rd Quarter
- ○ 2nd Quarter
- ○ 4th Quarter

4 Enter your business name (individual name if sole proprietor).

Enter your address.

Enter your city, state, and ZIP code; or your city, foreign country name, foreign province/county, and foreign postal code.

Form 941-V: The payment amount entered on line 2 must match the balance due displayed on line 14 of Form 941. All other information (Employer Identification Number, quarter, business name, and address) must also match Form 941.

Schedule B should be completed as follows:

The top portion of the form must be completed with the employer's identification number, company name, quarter, and year.

The body of the form contains boxes that correspond with each day of the prior quarter. Tax liabilities (not deposits) are entered in these boxes on those days when wages are paid. Monthly and quarterly totals are then entered in the boxes to the right. The total liability for the quarter, which is entered at the bottom right of the form, should equal line 12 of Form 941. Therefore, the purpose of Schedule B is to provide a breakdown of the total taxes owed for the quarter.

Schedule B must be submitted with Form 941 for all semiweekly depositors.

Schedule B (Form 941):

Report of Tax Liability for Semiweekly Schedule Depositors

(Rev. January 2017)   Department of the Treasury — Internal Revenue Service

960311

OMB No. 1545-0029

Employer identification number (EIN)

Name (not your trade name)

Calendar year   (Also check quarter)

Report for this Quarter...
(Check one.)

☐ **1:** January, February, March

☐ **2:** April, May, June

☐ **3:** July, August, September

☐ **4:** October, November, December

Use this schedule to show your TAX LIABILITY for the quarter; don't use it to show your deposits. When you file this form with Form 941 or Form 941-SS, don't change your tax liability by adjustments reported on any Forms 941-X or 944-X. You must fill out this form and attach it to Form 941 or Form 941-SS if you're a semiweekly schedule depositor or became one because your accumulated tax liability on any day was $100,000 or more. Write your daily tax liability on the numbered space that corresponds to the date wages were paid. See Section 11 in Pub. 15 for details.

Month 1

1	9	17	25	Tax liability for Month 1
2	10	18	26	
3	11	19	27	
4	12	20	28	
5	13	21	29	
6	14	22	30	
7	15	23	31	
8	16	24		

Month 2

1	9	17	25	Tax liability for Month 2
2	10	18	26	
3	11	19	27	
4	12	20	28	
5	13	21	29	
6	14	22	30	
7	15	23	31	
8	16	24		

Month 3

1	9	17	25	Tax liability for Month 3
2	10	18	26	
3	11	19	27	
4	12	20	28	
5	13	21	29	
6	14	22	30	
7	15	23	31	
8	16	24		

Fill in your total liability for the quarter (Month 1 + Month 2 + Month 3) ▶

Total must equal line 12 on Form 941 or Form 941-SS.

Total liability for the quarter

For Paperwork Reduction Act Notice, see separate instructions.   IRS.gov/form941   Cat. No. 11967Q   Schedule B (Form 941) (Rev. 1-2017)

WARNING! Be certain to enter tax liabilities in these boxes, not the actual deposits that are made. Schedule B is designed to summarize the liabilities incurred for a quarter, not the payments that are remitted.

Form 941 Rounding Considerations

Recall that line 7 of Form 941 displays an adjustment for fractions of cents. Why does this rounding issue occur? The answer is that total taxes before adjustment (line 6) are calculated using total compensation for the quarter, and therefore the result is rounded once. However, total deposits can represent multiple pay periods, and therefore these deposits are rounded at the time of each payment. This difference between the number of instances of rounding can result in total taxes showing slight discrepancies, which may be eliminated through the use of line 7 on the form.

For example, let's look at an employer who begins operations near the end of a quarter and therefore has two pay periods prior to the end of the quarter. If the employer has only one employee who earns $450.26 each period, then Social Security tax for each period is $27.92 ($450.26 taxable earnings × 6.2% Social Security tax rate). Total Social Security tax withheld from this employee's earnings for the quarter would therefore be $55.84 ($27.92 Social Security tax × 2 pay periods). However, when we calculate Social Security tax on line 5a, we use $900.52 in Column 1 ($450.26 taxable earnings × 2 pay periods) to arrive at $55.83 in Column 2 ($900.52 total Social Security wages × 6.2% Social Security tax rate). Total Social Security tax withheld of $55.84 differs from total Social Security tax calculated on the form of $55.83. This difference is the result of rounding and is the reason why line 7 on Form 941 is necessary.

Quarterly State Payroll Forms

For those states that levy a state income tax, forms must be submitted to summarize the employer's payroll activity. Similar to Form 941, these forms usually are submitted on a quarterly basis, and the taxes summarized in these forms typically must be deposited periodically during the quarter.

Case in Point 6-2   ## Complete Form 941

In this example, we will complete Form 941 for the 4th quarter of the year for Lucky Ties Apparel (Employer Identification #11-1111111). Assume that Lucky Ties Apparel (located at 77 Main Street, Rochester, NY 14602) chooses to complete and mail Form 941 on the due date. The form is signed by the president of the company, Harold Cameron (telephone #585-555-6281). Based on the lookback period, Lucky Ties Apparel is a monthly depositor and has deposited all tax amounts in a timely manner. All eight employees worked during each of the three months, and Lucky Ties Apparel does not choose to allow a third party to discuss the form with the IRS. Fourth quarter earnings and associated taxes withheld from employee earnings are as follows:

	October	November	December	Associated Earnings
FWT (federal withholding)	$1,845	$2,120	$1,942	$85,472
Social Security	$1,260	$1,305	$1,215	$60,968
Medicare	$420	$445	$395	$86,897

Form **941 for 2019:** Employer's QUARTERLY Federal Tax Return
(Rev. January 2019)   Department of the Treasury — Internal Revenue Service

950117

OMB No. 1545-0029

Employer identification number (EIN) 1 1 – 1 1 1 1 1 1 1 1

Name (not your trade name) Lucky Ties Apparel

Trade name (if any)

Address 77 Main Street
Number   Street   Suite or room number

Rochester   NY   14602
City   State   ZIP code

Foreign country name   Foreign province/county   Foreign postal code

Report for this Quarter of 2019
(Check one.)

☐ 1: January, February, March

☐ 2: April, May, June

☐ 3: July, August, September

☒ 4: October, November, December

Go to *www.irs.gov/Form941* for instructions and the latest information.

Read the separate instructions before you complete Form 941. Type or print within the boxes.

Part 1:   Answer these questions for this quarter.

1	Number of employees who received wages, tips, or other compensation for the pay period including: *Mar. 12* (Quarter 1), *June 12* (Quarter 2), *Sept. 12* (Quarter 3), or *Dec. 12* (Quarter 4)	1 — 8
2	Wages, tips, and other compensation	2 — 85,472 .
3	Federal income tax withheld from wages, tips, and other compensation	3 — 5,907 .
4	If no wages, tips, and other compensation are subject to social security or Medicare tax	☐ Check and go to line 6.

		Column 1		Column 2	
5a	Taxable social security wages . .	60,968 .	× 0.124 =	7,560 .	
5b	Taxable social security tips . . .	.	× 0.124 =	.	
5c	Taxable Medicare wages & tips . .	86,897 .	× 0.029 =	2,520 .	
5d	Taxable wages & tips subject to Additional Medicare Tax withholding	.	× 0.009 =	.	

5e	Add Column 2 from lines 5a, 5b, 5c, and 5d	5e — 10,080 .
5f	Section 3121(q) Notice and Demand—Tax due on unreported tips (see instructions) . .	5f — .
6	Total taxes before adjustments. Add lines 3, 5e, and 5f	6 — 15,987 .
7	Current quarter's adjustment for fractions of cents	7 — .
8	Current quarter's adjustment for sick pay	8 — .
9	Current quarter's adjustments for tips and group-term life insurance	9 — .
10	Total taxes after adjustments. Combine lines 6 through 9	10 — 15,987 .
11	Qualified small business payroll tax credit for increasing research activities. Attach Form 8974	11 — .
12	Total taxes after adjustments and credits. Subtract line 11 from line 10	12 — 15,987 .
13	Total deposits for this quarter, including overpayment applied from a prior quarter and overpayments applied from Form 941-X, 941-X (PR), 944-X, or 944-X (SP) filed in the current quarter	13 — 15,987 .
14	Balance due. If line 12 is more than line 13, enter the difference and see instructions . . .	14 — .
15	Overpayment. If line 13 is more than line 12, enter the difference [.] Check one: ☐ Apply to next return. ☐ Send a refund.	

▶ You MUST complete both pages of Form 941 and SIGN it.

Next ▶

For Privacy Act and Paperwork Reduction Act Notice, see the back of the Payment Voucher.   Cat. No. 17001Z   Form **941** (Rev. 1-2019)

Earnings for federal income tax withholding, Social Security tax, and Medicare tax are all reported in the first five lines of the form. In addition, the Social Security tax on line 5a and the Medicare tax on line 5c are displayed with the combined employee and employer portions.

		950217
Name *(not your trade name)*		**Employer identification number (EIN)**
Lucky Ties Apparel		11-1111111

Part 2:   **Tell us about your deposit schedule and tax liability for this quarter.**

If you are unsure about whether you are a monthly schedule depositor or a semiweekly schedule depositor, see section 11 of Pub. 15.

16   Check one: ☐ Line 12 on this return is less than $2,500 or line 12 on the return for the prior quarter was less than $2,500, and you didn't incur a $100,000 next-day deposit obligation during the current quarter. If line 12 for the prior quarter was less than $2,500 but line 12 on this return is $100,000 or more, you must provide a record of your federal tax liability. If you are a monthly schedule depositor, complete the deposit schedule below; if you are a semiweekly schedule depositor, attach Schedule B (Form 941). Go to Part 3.

☒ **You were a monthly schedule depositor for the entire quarter.** Enter your tax liability for each month and total liability for the quarter, then go to Part 3.

Tax liability:	Month 1	5,205.
	Month 2	5,620.
	Month 3	5,162.
Total liability for quarter		15,987.	**Total must equal line 12.**

☐ **You were a semiweekly schedule depositor for any part of this quarter.** Complete Schedule B (Form 941), Report of Tax Liability for Semiweekly Schedule Depositors, and attach it to Form 941.

Part 3:   **Tell us about your business. If a question does NOT apply to your business, leave it blank.**

17 If your business has closed or you stopped paying wages . . . . ☐ Check here, and

enter the final date you paid wages | / / | .

18 If you are a seasonal employer and you don't have to file a return for every quarter of the year   . . ☐ Check here.

Part 4:   **May we speak with your third-party designee?**

Do you want to allow an employee, a paid tax preparer, or another person to discuss this return with the IRS? See the instructions for details.

☐ Yes. Designee's name and phone number | | | |

Select a 5-digit Personal Identification Number (PIN) to use when talking to the IRS.   ☐ ☐ ☐ ☐ ☐

☒ No.

Part 5:   **Sign here. You MUST complete both pages of Form 941 and SIGN it.**

Under penalties of perjury, I declare that I have examined this return, including accompanying schedules and statements, and to the best of my knowledge and belief, it is true, correct, and complete. Declaration of preparer (other than taxpayer) is based on all information of which preparer has any knowledge.

✗   **Sign your name here**   *Harold Cameron*

Print your name here	Harold Cameron
Print your title here	President

Date | 1 31 20 |

Best daytime phone   585-555-6281

Paid Preparer Use Only   Check if you are self-employed . . . ☐

Preparer's name		PTIN	
Preparer's signature		Date	/ /
Firm's name (or yours if self-employed)		EIN	
Address		Phone	
City		State	ZIP code	

Page **2**   Form **941** (Rev. 1-2019)

As Lucky Ties Apparel is a monthly depositor, and line 12 exceeds $2,500, line 16 in Part 2 must display the monthly tax liabilities, which in this case are the same as the monthly deposits. Recall that these monthly tax liabilities include both the amounts withheld from employee pay (which were given earlier) as well as the matched employer taxes (Social Security tax and Medicare tax, which must be added to the previously provided figures). Lastly, the form is dated 1/31/20 in Part 5, as this is the due date for the form.

Now let's expand on this example to illustrate how rounding can require the use of line 7 (current quarter's adjustment for fractions of cents). Review the following page 1 of Form 941, in which the figures include the associated cents. Note that in this example, total deposits for the quarter equal $15,987.33.

Form **941 for 2019:** **Employer's QUARTERLY Federal Tax Return**
(Rev. January 2019)   Department of the Treasury — Internal Revenue Service

950117
OMB No. 1545-0029

Employer identification number (EIN) 1 1 – 1 1 1 1 1 1 1 1

Name *(not your trade name)* Lucky Ties Apparel

Trade name *(if any)*

Address 77 Main Street
Number   Street   Suite or room number

Rochester   NY   14602
City   State   ZIP code

Foreign country name   Foreign province/county   Foreign postal code

Report for this Quarter of 2019
(Check one.)

☐ **1:** January, February, March

☐ **2:** April, May, June

☐ **3:** July, August, September

☒ **4:** October, November, December

Go to *www.irs.gov/Form941* for instructions and the latest information.

Read the separate instructions before you complete Form 941. Type or print within the boxes.

Part 1:   **Answer these questions for this quarter.**

1	Number of employees who received wages, tips, or other compensation for the pay period including: *Mar. 12* (Quarter 1), *June 12* (Quarter 2), *Sept. 12* (Quarter 3), or *Dec. 12* (Quarter 4)	1	8
2	Wages, tips, and other compensation	2	85,472 . 45
3	Federal income tax withheld from wages, tips, and other compensation	3	5,907 . 20
4	If no wages, tips, and other compensation are subject to social security or Medicare tax	☐ Check and go to line 6.	

		Column 1		Column 2	
5a	Taxable social security wages	60,968 . 47	× 0.124 =	7,560 . 09	
5b	Taxable social security tips	.	× 0.124 =	.	
5c	Taxable Medicare wages & tips	86,897 . 06	× 0.029 =	2,520 . 01	
5d	Taxable wages & tips subject to Additional Medicare Tax withholding	.	× 0.009 =	.	

5e	Add Column 2 from lines 5a, 5b, 5c, and 5d	5e	10,080 . 10
5f	Section 3121(q) Notice and Demand—Tax due on unreported tips (see instructions)	5f	.
6	Total taxes before adjustments. Add lines 3, 5e, and 5f	6	15,987 . 30
7	Current quarter's adjustment for fractions of cents	7	. 03
8	Current quarter's adjustment for sick pay	8	.
9	Current quarter's adjustments for tips and group-term life insurance	9	.
10	Total taxes after adjustments. Combine lines 6 through 9	10	15,987 . 33
11	Qualified small business payroll tax credit for increasing research activities. Attach Form 8974	11	.
12	Total taxes after adjustments and credits. Subtract line 11 from line 10	12	15,987 . 33
13	Total deposits for this quarter, including overpayment applied from a prior quarter and overpayments applied from Form 941-X, 941-X (PR), 944-X, or 944-X (SP) filed in the current quarter	13	15,987 . 33
14	Balance due. If line 12 is more than line 13, enter the difference and see instructions	14	.
15	Overpayment. If line 13 is more than line 12, enter the difference [.] Check one: ☐ Apply to next return. ☐ Send a refund.		

▶ **You MUST complete both pages of Form 941 and SIGN it.**   Next ▶

For Privacy Act and Paperwork Reduction Act Notice, see the back of the Payment Voucher.   Cat. No. 17001Z   Form **941** (Rev. 1-2019)

Line 7 displays $0.03, as rounding of the monthly tax payments resulted in a difference between the quarter's deposits and tax owed. Entering this negligible amount on line 7 leads to the total taxes equaling total deposits on page 1 of Form 941.

TIP! Don't focus on how the above figures were derived. Instead, use this example to observe how rounding (which often creates issues within Form 941) can lead to the use of Line 7 within the form.

Form 940 (Employer's Annual Federal Unemployment Tax Return)

On the Web

irs.gov/pub/irs-pdf
/f940.pdf

Assuming that an employer has made timely federal tax deposits for each of the four quarters of the year, no payments for federal income tax withholding, Social Security tax, or Medicare tax are owed at year-end. Federal unemployment tax (FUTA tax) operates in the same manner; however, as you have seen, quarterly payments are made only when FUTA tax owed exceeds $500 at the end of a quarter. These quarterly payments may be made using the EFTPS.

Small businesses that employ only a few individuals often do not exceed $500 in FUTA tax for the year and therefore are not required to remit payment until Form 940 is submitted. When payment is included with Form 940, the form must be submitted by January 31 of the following year. When no payment is remitted with the form, the employer may wait until February 10 of the following year.

TIP! Just as with quarterly federal tax deposits on Form 941, annual FUTA tax payments remitted with Form 940 must be accompanied by a payment voucher (Form 940-V).

In instances when at least some of an employer's FUTA earnings are not subject to SUTA tax, or when an employer operates in a credit-reduction state, the resulting increase in FUTA tax must be calculated on Schedule A. The total for this form is then transferred to page 1 of Form 940.

One item that can cause confusion on Form 940 is the manner in which 401(k) contributions are recorded. Although box 4c lists "Retirement/Pension" as one item that may be exempt from FUTA tax, it is important to note that only those retirement payments made by the employer qualify for this exempt treatment. Therefore, if an employee requests that 401(k) contributions be withheld from gross earnings, this withheld amount is still subject to FUTA tax and should not be included within box 4 of the form.

The 2019 version of Form 940 was not released by the IRS prior to the publication of this text. When it is released, the 2019 version will be made available in the Learning Resource Center.

Examine the Form: 940

Form 940 requires both payroll and state information that allows for FUTA tax to be determined.

Form **940 for 2018:** **Employer's Annual Federal Unemployment (FUTA) Tax Return**

850113

Department of the Treasury — Internal Revenue Service

OMB No. 1545-0028

Employer identification number (EIN)

☐☐ – ☐☐☐☐☐☐☐

Name *(not your trade name)*

Trade name *(if any)*

Address

Number   Street   Suite or room number

City   State   ZIP code

Foreign country name   Foreign province/county   Foreign postal code

Type of Return
(Check all that apply.)

☐ **a.** Amended

☐ **b.** Successor employer

☐ **c.** No payments to employees in 2018

☐ **d.** Final: Business closed or stopped paying wages

Go to *www.irs.gov/Form940* for instructions and the latest information.

Read the separate instructions before you complete this form. Please type or print within the boxes.

Part 1: Tell us about your return. If any line does NOT apply, leave it blank. See instructions before completing Part 1.

1a If you had to pay state unemployment tax in one state only, enter the state abbreviation . **1a** ☐☐

1b If you had to pay state unemployment tax in more than one state, you are a multi-state employer . . . . **1b** ☐ Check here. Complete Schedule A (Form 940).

2 If you paid wages in a state that is subject to CREDIT REDUCTION . . . . **2** ☐ Check here. Complete Schedule A (Form 940).

Part 2: Determine your FUTA tax before adjustments. If any line does NOT apply, leave it blank.

3 Total payments to all employees . . . . **3** ☐ .

4 Payments exempt from FUTA tax . . . . . **4** ☐ .

Check all that apply: **4a** ☐ Fringe benefits   **4c** ☐ Retirement/Pension   **4e** ☐ Other
4b ☐ Group-term life insurance   **4d** ☐ Dependent care

5 Total of payments made to each employee in excess of $7,000 . . . . **5** ☐ .

6 Subtotal (line 4 + line 5 = line 6) . . . . **6** ☐ .

7 Total taxable FUTA wages (line 3 – line 6 = line 7). See instructions . . . . **7** ☐ .

8 FUTA tax before adjustments (line 7 × 0.006 = line 8) . . . . **8** ☐ .

Part 3: Determine your adjustments. If any line does NOT apply, leave it blank.

9 If ALL of the taxable FUTA wages you paid were excluded from state unemployment tax, multiply line 7 by 0.054 (line 7 × 0.054 = line 9). Go to line 12 . . . . **9** ☐ .

10 If SOME of the taxable FUTA wages you paid were excluded from state unemployment tax, OR you paid ANY state unemployment tax late (after the due date for filing Form 940), complete the worksheet in the instructions. Enter the amount from line 7 of the worksheet . . **10** ☐ .

11 If credit reduction applies, enter the total from Schedule A (Form 940) . . . . . . **11** ☐ .

Part 4: Determine your FUTA tax and balance due or overpayment. If any line does NOT apply, leave it blank.

12 Total FUTA tax after adjustments (lines 8 + 9 + 10 + 11 = line 12) . . . . **12** ☐ .

13 FUTA tax deposited for the year, including any overpayment applied from a prior year . **13** ☐ .

14 Balance due. If line 12 is more than line 13, enter the excess on line 14.
• If line 14 is more than $500, you must deposit your tax.
• If line 14 is $500 or less, you may pay with this return. See instructions . . . . **14** ☐ .

15 Overpayment. If line 13 is more than line 12, enter the excess on line 15 and check a box below **15** ☐ .

▶ You **MUST** complete both pages of this form and **SIGN** it.   Check one: ☐ Apply to next return. ☐ Send a refund.

Next ▶

For Privacy Act and Paperwork Reduction Act Notice, see the back of the Payment Voucher.   Cat. No. 112340   Form **940** (2018)

Examine the Form: 940 (continued)

The top portion of the form (including Employer Identification Number, name, and address) must be completed in its entirety. Boxes in the *Type of Return* section should be checked only if they apply, and may all be left blank when appropriate. Note that a *Successor Employer* is one who purchases the business during the year, and who therefore may be able to apply the FUTA taxes paid by the previous employer toward the $7,000 threshold.

Part 1 of Form 940 should be completed as follows:

Line 1: The two-letter abbreviation for the employer's state is entered on line 1a for employers who operate in only one state, while the checkbox on line 1b is checked when the employer operates in more than one state.

Line 2: The checkbox is checked when the employer operates in a credit-reduction state.

Part 2 of Form 940 should be completed as follows:

Line 3: Total employee compensation, including that which is not subject to FUTA tax, is entered here. Compensation in the payroll register may be summarized to arrive at this amount.

Line 4: Enter compensation exempt from FUTA tax here, and check all boxes that apply to the exempt compensation. Note that although Retirement/Pension is one item listed here, only those payments made by the employer for certain types of retirement plans (such as 401(k) and SIMPLE IRA plans) are exempt from FUTA tax. Contributions to retirement plans made by employees (amounts withheld from employee earnings) are not exempt from FUTA tax.

Line 5: Enter total compensation that exceeds $7,000 for each individual employee. This compensation should not include what was reported on line 4 above.

Line 6: This total represents all compensation on which FUTA tax will not be calculated.

Line 7: This total represents all compensation on which FUTA tax will be calculated.

Line 8: This total represents FUTA tax owed for the year.

Part 3 of Form 940 should be completed as follows:

Line 9: If all compensation is exempt from SUTA tax, this line accounts for the additional FUTA tax that results (as the FUTA rate cannot be reduced by 5.4% if SUTA tax is not applicable).

Line 10: The same as line 9; however, this line is utilized only when a portion of compensation is exempt from SUTA tax or a portion of SUTA tax has not been remitted in a timely manner.

Line 11: The additional tax attributable to the credit reduction for certain states is entered here.

Part 4 of Form 940 should be completed as follows:

Line 12: Total FUTA tax owed for the year, including adjustments from the prior three lines.

Line 13: Total actual FUTA tax payments made during the year are entered here.

Line 14: The amount due may be remitted with Form 940 if it is less than $500.

Line 15: If deposits exceed tax owed, the difference is entered here. If this line is completed, the employer must choose to either receive a check for the overpayment or apply it to the next quarter.

Note: The *Name* and *Employer Identification Number* at the top of page 2 must be completed as well.

Page 2 of Form 940 must be completed for the form to be valid.

850212

Name *(not your trade name)*	Employer identification number (EIN)

Part 5: Report your FUTA tax liability by quarter only if line 12 is more than $500. If not, go to Part 6.

16 Report the amount of your FUTA tax liability for each quarter; do NOT enter the amount you deposited. If you had no liability for a quarter, leave the line blank.

    16a **1st quarter** (January 1 – March 31) . . . . **16a** ☐ .

    16b **2nd quarter** (April 1 – June 30) . . . . **16b** ☐ .

    16c **3rd quarter** (July 1 – September 30) . . . . **16c** ☐ .

    16d **4th quarter** (October 1 – December 31) . . . . **16d** ☐ .

17 **Total tax liability for the year** (lines 16a + 16b + 16c + 16d = line 17) **17** ☐ . **Total must equal line 12.**

Part 6: May we speak with your third-party designee?

Do you want to allow an employee, a paid tax preparer, or another person to discuss this return with the IRS? See the instructions for details.

☐ **Yes.** Designee's name and phone number

    Select a 5-digit Personal Identification Number (PIN) to use when talking to IRS ☐ ☐ ☐ ☐ ☐

☐ **No.**

Part 7: Sign here. You MUST complete both pages of this form and SIGN it.

Under penalties of perjury, I declare that I have examined this return, including accompanying schedules and statements, and to the best of my knowledge and belief, it is true, correct, and complete, and that no part of any payment made to a state unemployment fund claimed as a credit was, or is to be, deducted from the payments made to employees. Declaration of preparer (other than taxpayer) is based on all information of which preparer has any knowledge.

X Sign your name here

    Print your name here

    Print your title here

Date / /

    Best daytime phone

Paid Preparer Use Only   Check if you are self-employed ☐

Preparer's name		PTIN	
Preparer's signature		Date / /	
Firm's name (or yours if self-employed)		EIN	
Address		Phone	
City	State	ZIP code	

Examine the Form: 940 (continued)

Parts 5–7 of Form 940 should be completed as follows:

Lines 16–17: The quarterly FUTA tax liabilities are reported here. These amounts should include any adjustments from lines 9 through 11, and therefore the total of the four amounts should equal line 12.

Part 6: Similar to Form 941, the third-party designee section is optional.

Part 7: The form must be signed by the employer in order to be valid.

The payment voucher (Form 940-V) must be submitted when payment is included with Form 940.

✂	▼ **Detach Here and Mail With Your Payment and Form 940.** ▼	✂

Form **940-V**	**Payment Voucher**	OMB No. 1545-0028
Department of the Treasury Internal Revenue Service	▶ **Don't staple or attach this voucher to your payment.**	2018

1 Enter your employer identification number (EIN).	2 **Enter the amount of your payment.** ▶ Make your check or money order payable to **"United States Treasury"**		Dollars	Cents
	3 Enter your business name (individual name if sole proprietor).			
	Enter your address.			
	Enter your city, state, and ZIP code or your city, foreign country name, foreign province/county, and foreign postal code.			

Form 940-V: This form is completed in the same manner as Form 941-V, with the exception that the quarter is not selected, as this is an annual form.

Schedule A (Form 940): After entering the Employer Identification Number and company name at the top of the form, the employer must then check all states in which the company paid SUTA tax. Then, in those credit-reduction states in which the employer operates, the employer must enter applicable FUTA taxable wages and use the adjacent percentage to calculate the total credit reduction.

Schedule A is completed only when a portion of an employer's FUTA earnings are exempt from SUTA tax or the employer operates in a credit-reduction state.

Schedule A (Form 940) for 2018:

Multi-State Employer and Credit Reduction Information
Department of the Treasury — Internal Revenue Service

860312

OMB No. 1545-0028

Employer identification number (EIN)

Name *(not your trade name)*

See the instructions on page 2. File this schedule with Form 940.

Place an "X" in the box of EVERY state in which you had to pay state unemployment tax this year. For each state with a credit reduction rate greater than zero, enter the FUTA taxable wages, multiply by the reduction rate, and enter the credit reduction amount. Don't include in the *FUTA Taxable Wages* **box wages that were excluded from state unemployment tax (see the instructions for Step 2). If any states don't apply to you, leave them blank.**

Postal Abbreviation	FUTA Taxable Wages	Reduction Rate	Credit Reduction	Postal Abbreviation	FUTA Taxable Wages	Reduction Rate	Credit Reduction
AK	.	× 0.000	.	NC	.	× 0.000	.
AL	.	× 0.000	.	ND	.	× 0.000	.
AR	.	× 0.000	.	NE	.	× 0.000	.
AZ	.	× 0.000	.	NH	.	× 0.000	.
CA	.	× 0.000	.	NJ	.	× 0.000	.
CO	.	× 0.000	.	NM	.	× 0.000	.
CT	.	× 0.000	.	NV	.	× 0.000	.
DC	.	× 0.000	.	NY	.	× 0.000	.
DE	.	× 0.000	.	OH	.	× 0.000	.
FL	.	× 0.000	.	OK	.	× 0.000	.
GA	.	× 0.000	.	OR	.	× 0.000	.
HI	.	× 0.000	.	PA	.	× 0.000	.
IA	.	× 0.000	.	RI	.	× 0.000	.
ID	.	× 0.000	.	SC	.	× 0.000	.
IL	.	× 0.000	.	SD	.	× 0.000	.
IN	.	× 0.000	.	TN	.	× 0.000	.
KS	.	× 0.000	.	TX	.	× 0.000	.
KY	.	× 0.000	.	UT	.	× 0.000	.
LA	.	× 0.000	.	VA	.	× 0.000	.
MA	.	× 0.000	.	VT	.	× 0.000	.
MD	.	× 0.000	.	WA	.	× 0.000	.
ME	.	× 0.000	.	WI	.	× 0.000	.
MI	.	× 0.000	.	WV	.	× 0.000	.
MN	.	× 0.000	.	WY	.	× 0.000	.
MO	.	× 0.000	.	PR	.	× 0.000	.
MS	.	× 0.000	.	VI	.	× 0.024	.
MT	.	× 0.000	.				

Total Credit Reduction. Add all amounts shown in the *Credit Reduction* boxes. Enter the total here and on Form 940, line 11   . . . .

.

For Privacy Act and Paperwork Reduction Act Notice, see the Instructions for Form 940.   Cat. No. 16997C   Schedule A (Form 940) 2018

Case in Point 6-3   Complete Form 940

In this example, we will complete Form 940 for Lucky Ties Apparel (Employer Identification #11-1111111). Assume that Lucky Ties Apparel (located at 77 Main Street, Rochester, NY 14602) chooses to complete and mail Form 940 on the due date. The form is signed by the president of the company, Harold Cameron (telephone #585-555-6281). Lucky Ties Apparel elects to delay remitting FUTA tax until the company is required to do so. Total employee compensation for the year was $510,236, annual retirement plan contributions totaled $7,646, and flexible spending account contributions totaled $6,905. All earnings subject to FUTA tax are also subject to SUTA tax. Lucky Ties Apparel does not choose to allow a third party to discuss the form with the IRS. Note that all eight employees of Lucky Ties Apparel earned more than $7,000 that was subject to FUTA tax during the 1st quarter of the year.

Form **940** for 2018: **Employer's Annual Federal Unemployment (FUTA) Tax Return**

850113

Department of the Treasury — Internal Revenue Service

OMB No. 1545-0028

Employer identification number (EIN) 1 1 - 1 1 1 1 1 1 1

Name *(not your trade name)* Lucky Ties Apparel

Trade name *(if any)*

Address 77 Main Street
Number   Street   Suite or room number

Rochester   NY   14602
City   State   ZIP code

Foreign country name   Foreign province/county   Foreign postal code

Type of Return
(Check all that apply.)

- [ ] **a.** Amended
- [ ] **b.** Successor employer
- [ ] **c.** No payments to employees in 2018
- [ ] **d.** Final: Business closed or stopped paying wages

Go to *www.irs.gov/Form940* for instructions and the latest information.

Read the separate instructions before you complete this form. Please type or print within the boxes.

Part 1:   Tell us about your return. If any line does NOT apply, leave it blank. See instructions before completing Part 1.

1a If you had to pay state unemployment tax in one state only, enter the state abbreviation .   **1a** N   Y

1b If you had to pay state unemployment tax in more than one state, you are a multi-state employer . . . .   **1b** [ ] Check here. Complete Schedule A (Form 940).

2 If you paid wages in a state that is subject to CREDIT REDUCTION . . . .   **2** [ ] Check here. Complete Schedule A (Form 940).

Part 2:   Determine your FUTA tax before adjustments. If any line does NOT apply, leave it blank.

3 Total payments to all employees . . . .   **3**   510,236.

4 Payments exempt from FUTA tax . . . .   **4**   6,905.

Check all that apply: **4a** [x] Fringe benefits   **4c** [ ] Retirement/Pension   **4e** [ ] Other
4b [ ] Group-term life insurance   **4d** [ ] Dependent care

5 Total of payments made to each employee in excess of $7,000 . . . .   **5**   447,331.

6 Subtotal (line 4 + line 5 = line 6) . . . .   **6**   454,236.

7 Total taxable FUTA wages (line 3 – line 6 = line 7). See instructions . . . .   **7**   56,000.

8 FUTA tax before adjustments (line 7 x 0.006 = line 8) . . . .   **8**   336.

Part 3:   Determine your adjustments. If any line does NOT apply, leave it blank.

9 If ALL of the taxable FUTA wages you paid were excluded from state unemployment tax, multiply line 7 by 0.054 (line 7 x 0.054 = line 9). Go to line 12 . . . .   **9**   .

10 If SOME of the taxable FUTA wages you paid were excluded from state unemployment tax, OR you paid ANY state unemployment tax late (after the due date for filing Form 940), complete the worksheet in the instructions. Enter the amount from line 7 of the worksheet . .   **10**   .

11 If credit reduction applies, enter the total from Schedule A (Form 940) . . . .   **11**   .

Part 4:   Determine your FUTA tax and balance due or overpayment. If any line does NOT apply, leave it blank.

12 Total FUTA tax after adjustments (lines 8 + 9 + 10 + 11 = line 12) . . . .   **12**   336.

13 FUTA tax deposited for the year, including any overpayment applied from a prior year .   **13**   0.

14 Balance due. If line 12 is more than line 13, enter the excess on line 14.
- If line 14 is more than $500, you must deposit your tax.
- If line 14 is $500 or less, you may pay with this return. See instructions . . . . . .   **14**   336.

15 Overpayment. If line 13 is more than line 12, enter the excess on line 15 and check a box below   **15**   .

▶ You **MUST** complete both pages of this form and **SIGN** it.   Check one: [ ] Apply to next return. [ ] Send a refund.

Next ▶

For Privacy Act and Paperwork Reduction Act Notice, see the back of the Payment Voucher.   Cat. No. 11234O   Form **940** (2018)

As all employees earned more than the $7,000 FUTA tax threshold for the year, total FUTA tax attributable to each employee is the $7,000 maximum. Therefore, total taxable FUTA wages on line 7 are calculated as $7,000 × 8 employees. Line 5 may then be calculated as total earnings ($510,236), minus flexible spending account contributions ($6,905), minus taxable FUTA wages ($56,000).

WARNING! As is discussed in the above calculation, Line 4 & Line 7 of Form 940 must be calculated before Line 5 can be determined.

850212

Name (not your trade name)	Employer identification number (EIN)
Lucky Ties Apparel	11-1111111

Part 5: Report your FUTA tax liability by quarter only if line 12 is more than $500. If not, go to Part 6.

16 Report the amount of your FUTA tax liability for each quarter; do NOT enter the amount you deposited. If you had no liability for a quarter, leave the line blank.

16a 1st quarter (January 1 – March 31) . . . . 16a [.]

16b 2nd quarter (April 1 – June 30) . . . . 16b [.]

16c 3rd quarter (July 1 – September 30) . . . . 16c [.]

16d 4th quarter (October 1 – December 31) . . . . 16d [.]

17 Total tax liability for the year (lines 16a + 16b + 16c + 16d = line 17) 17 [.] Total must equal line 12.

Part 6: May we speak with your third-party designee?

Do you want to allow an employee, a paid tax preparer, or another person to discuss this return with the IRS? See the instructions for details.

☐ Yes. Designee's name and phone number

Select a 5-digit Personal Identification Number (PIN) to use when talking to IRS

☒ No.

Part 7: Sign here. You MUST complete both pages of this form and SIGN it.

Under penalties of perjury, I declare that I have examined this return, including accompanying schedules and statements, and to the best of my knowledge and belief, it is true, correct, and complete, and that no part of any payment made to a state unemployment fund claimed as a credit was, or is to be, deducted from the payments made to employees. Declaration of preparer (other than taxpayer) is based on all information of which preparer has any knowledge.

X Sign your name here *Harold Cameron*

Print your name here Harold Cameron

Print your title here President

Date 1/31/20

Best daytime phone 585-555-6281

Paid Preparer Use Only Check if you are self-employed ☐

Preparer's name		PTIN	
Preparer's signature		Date	/ /
Firm's name (or yours if self-employed)		EIN	
Address		Phone	
City	State	ZIP code	

Page **2** Form **940** (2018)

Quarterly FUTA payments need not be displayed, as the total amount owed did not exceed $500. Because Lucky Ties Apparel remained below this threshold, it was also not required to remit FUTA tax until year-end. Therefore, the entire FUTA tax payment must now be made. When Form 940 is submitted with a payment, it is due by January 31. As Lucky Ties Apparel pays the FUTA tax on the due date, the form is submitted on this same day.

▼ **Detach Here and Mail With Your Payment and Form 940.** ▼

Form **940-V**	**Payment Voucher**	OMB No. 1545-0028
Department of the Treasury Internal Revenue Service	▶ **Don't staple or attach this voucher to your payment.**	20**18**

1 Enter your employer identification number (EIN).	**2** **Enter the amount of your payment.** ▶ Make your check or money order payable to "**United States Treasury**"	Dollars	Cents
11-1111111		336	

3 Enter your business name (individual name if sole proprietor).

Lucky Ties Apparel

Enter your address.

77 Main Street

Enter your city, state, and ZIP code or your city, foreign country name, foreign province/county, and foreign postal code.

Rochester, NY 14602

Form W-2 (Wage and Tax Statement)

For all employers whose compensation to employees exceeds $600 for the year (from which taxes are withheld), both Forms W-2 and W-3 must be completed. The employer is required to provide three copies of Form W-2, which displays annual earnings information, to each employee by January 31 of the following year. The copies provided to employees are as follows:

- Copy B: To be filed with the employee's federal tax return
- Copy C: To be maintained for the employee's records
- Copy 2: To be filed with the employee's state, city, or local tax return (typically employees receive two copies of this version)

The employer is also required to submit Copy A of Form W-2 to the Social Security Administration. This copy of the form must be submitted by March 1 (for paper copies) or March 31 (for e-filed copies). Form W-3 is a summary of all Form W-2s submitted by the employer and will be discussed shortly.

TIP! E-filing is an electronic method of submitting both federal and state tax forms. Whenever available, the federal and state governments encourage taxpayers to utilize this method (instead of submitting paper versions) due to its increased efficiency.

To arrive at the correct figures on Form W-2, the employer may use the employee earnings records, which when completed as of the end of the year will each summarize total compensation for a single employee. Although calculations may need to be performed based on the final totals in the employee earnings record, such as to determine the wages subject to federal income tax in box 1, all necessary figures are available therein.

Additionally, just as rounding issues impact Form 941, they also impact Form W-2. Boxes 4 and 6 on Form W-2 display Social Security tax withheld and Medicare tax withheld, respectively. These amounts must be determined by adding all withheld amounts during the year. They cannot be calculated by multiplying the box 3 (Social Security wages) and box 5 (Medicare wages and tips) amounts by their respective tax rates (6.2% and 1.45%), as rounding issues can result in the taxes from these calculations differing from the actual withheld amounts.

Examine the Form: W-2

While the IRS-approved W-2 Form appears here, employers may use alternative versions that convey the same information.

a Employee's social security number	
b Employer identification number (EIN)	**1** Wages, tips, other compensation / **2** Federal income tax withheld
c Employer's name, address, and ZIP code	**3** Social security wages / **4** Social security tax withheld
	5 Medicare wages and tips / **6** Medicare tax withheld
	7 Social security tips / **8** Allocated tips
d Control number	**9** / **10** Dependent care benefits
e Employee's first name and initial Last name Suff.	**11** Nonqualified plans / **12a** See instructions for box 12
	13 Statutory employee / Retirement plan / Third-party sick pay / **12b**
	14 Other / **12c** / **12d**
f Employee's address and ZIP code	

15 State Employer's state ID number	16 State wages, tips, etc.	17 State income tax	18 Local wages, tips, etc.	19 Local income tax	20 Locality name

OMB No. 1545-0008

Safe, accurate, FAST! Use IRS e-file Visit the IRS website at www.irs.gov/efile

Form **W-2** Wage and Tax Statement **2019** Department of the Treasury—Internal Revenue Service

Copy B—To Be Filed With Employee's FEDERAL Tax Return.
This information is being furnished to the Internal Revenue Service.

Parts a–f must be completed with employee and employer information. The control number in box d is an optional box that may be used by employers to track W-2 Forms.

Boxes 1–2: Earnings subject to federal income tax withholding and the associated tax are entered here.

Boxes 3–4: Earnings subject to Social Security tax (not to exceed the wage base) and the associated tax are entered here.

Boxes 5–6: Earnings subject to Medicare tax and the associated tax are entered here.

Box 7: Tips subject to Social Security tax are entered here. The sum of boxes 3 and 7 cannot exceed the Social Security wage base.

Box 8: Food and/or beverage companies enter tips allocated to employees here.

Box 9: This box is left blank.

Box 10: All dependent care expenses paid or incurred (which includes the value of health care provided to dependents) are entered here. This includes expenses related to dependent care flexible spending accounts.

Box 11: Contributions made to nonqualified retirement plans (for which taxes are not deferred and which are typically provided to highly compensated employees) are entered here.

Boxes 12a–12d: A wide variety of compensation types (identified by codes that are defined on the back of the form) are listed on the left side of these boxes when applicable. The corresponding compensation amount for each is listed to the right.

Examine the Form: W-2 (continued)

The following chart displaying the codes that may be entered within boxes 12a–12d can be used for reference when reviewing completed copies of Form W-2:

Code	Compensation Type
A	Uncollected Social Security or RRTA tax on tips
B	Uncollected Medicare tax on tips
C	Taxable cost of group-term life insurance over $50,000
D	Elective deferrals under a section 401(k) cash or deferred arrangement (plan)
E	Elective deferrals under a section 403(b) salary reduction agreement
F	Elective deferrals under a section 408(k)(6) salary reduction SEP
G	Elective deferrals and employer contributions (including nonelective deferrals) to any governmental or nongovernmental section 457(b) deferred compensation plan
H	Elective deferrals under a section 501(c)(18)(D) tax-exempt organization plan
J	Nontaxable sick pay
K	20% excise tax on excess golden parachute payments
L	Substantiated employee business-expense reimbursements
M	Uncollected Social Security or RRTA tax on taxable cost of group-term life insurance over $50,000 (for former employees)
N	Uncollected Medicare tax on taxable cost of group-term life insurance over $50,000 (for former employees)
P	Excludable moving expense reimbursements paid directly to the employee
Q	Nontaxable combat pay
R	Employer contributions to an Archer MSA
S	Employee salary-reduction contributions under a section 408(p) SIMPLE plan
T	Adoption benefits
V	Income from the exercise of nonstatutory stock option(s)
W	Employer contributions to a health savings account (HSA)
Y	Deferrals under a section 409A nonqualified deferred compensation plan
Z	Income under a nonqualified deferred compensation plan that fails to satisfy section 409A.
AA	Designated Roth contributions under a section 401(k) plan
BB	Designated Roth contributions under a section 403(b) plan
DD	Cost of employer-sponsored health coverage
EE	Designated Roth contributions under a section 457(b) plan

Box 13: Employers should check all boxes that apply here. **Statutory employees** are those for whom federal income tax is not withheld but Social Security and Medicare taxes are withheld (these include certain drivers of food and beverages and certain full-time life insurance sales agents). The *retirement plan* box is checked if the employee is an active participant in a wide variety of plans including a 401(k), 403(b), SEP plan, or

SIMPLE IRA account. The *third-party sick pay* box is checked if an employer is reporting third-party sick pay or a third party is reporting having remitted sick pay to an insured employee.

Box 14: Any additional information the employer wants to convey to the employee, such as state disability insurance withheld, union dues, and health insurance premiums deducted, is entered here.

Boxes 15–20: State and local taxes withheld, as well as the state names (and corresponding employer state ID numbers), are entered here.

| Case In Point 6-4 | **Complete Form W-2** |

In this example, we will complete two different W-2 Forms. We begin by completing the W-2 Form for Maryanne Sherman (8171 Winston Court, Rochester, NY 14604; SSN 222-22-2222), an employee of Lucky Ties Apparel (Employer Identification #11-1111111), which completes Form 941 on a quarterly basis. Lucky Ties Apparel (located at 77 Main Street, Rochester, NY 14602) does not use control or establishment numbers, and compensated eight employees during 2019. Maryanne's gross earnings for federal income tax withholding, Social Security tax, and Medicare tax was $139,580 for the year, while these taxes were $6,250, $8,239.80, and $1,907.98, respectively. State disability insurance for the year was $31.20, while the annual charitable contribution was $520. New York State income tax withholding was $1,999.92 (based on the same gross earnings amount as above) with no local taxes withheld. The employer's New York State ID number is the same as the federal Employer Identification Number.

Many of the above-provided figures can be found on the total row of Maryanne's employee earnings record. Note that this employee earnings record has been truncated to display only one week's payroll data along with the associated totals.

Employee Earnings Record

Name	Maryanne Sherman	Marital Status — Single
Address	8171 Winston Court, Rochester, NY 14604	Fed. Withholding Allow. — 2
SS#	222-22-2222	State Withholding Allow. — 1

			Earnings								Deductions							
Pay Period Ending	Regular Hours Worked	Regular Pay Rate	Regular Wages	Overtime Hours Worked	Overtime Pay Rate	Overtime Wages	Gross Pay	Federal Withholding Tax	State Withholding Tax	Social Security Tax	Medicare Tax	Retirement Contribution	Life Insurance	Charitable Contribution	Additional Withholding	Check Number	Net Pay
12/1/19	n/a	n/a	$ 769.23	0	n/a	$ -	$ 769.23	$ 61.00	$ 38.46	$ -	$ 11.15	$ -	$ -	$ 10.00	$ 0.60	1463	$ 648.02
Totals	n/a	n/a	$ 139,580.00	0	n/a	$ -	$ 139,580.00	$ 6,250.00	$ 1,999.92	$ 8,239.80	$ 1,907.98	$ -	$ -	$ 520.00	$ 31.20	n/a	$ 120,631.10

Upon reviewing the figures in the total row of the employee earnings record, the employer may then complete the Form W-2, as shown here.

22222	a Employee's social security number 222-22-2222	OMB No. 1545-0008		
b Employer identification number (EIN) 11-1111111			**1** Wages, tips, other compensation 139,580	**2** Federal income tax withheld 6,250
c Employer's name, address, and ZIP code Lucky Ties Apparel 77 Main Street Rochester, NY 14602			**3** Social security wages 132,900	**4** Social security tax withheld 8,239.80
			5 Medicare wages and tips 139,580	**6** Medicare tax withheld 1,907.98
			7 Social security tips	**8** Allocated tips
d Control number			**9**	**10** Dependent care benefits
e Employee's first name and initial Last name Suff. Maryanne Sherman 8171 Winston Court Rochester, NY 14604			**11** Nonqualified plans	**12a**
			13 Statutory employee ☐ Retirement plan ☐ Third-party sick pay ☐	**12b**
			14 Other SDI 31.20 Charity 520	**12c**
				12d
f Employee's address and ZIP code				

15 State Employer's state ID number	**16** State wages, tips, etc.	**17** State income tax	**18** Local wages, tips, etc.	**19** Local income tax	**20** Locality name
NY 11-1111111	139,580	1,999.92			

Form **W-2** Wage and Tax Statement   **2019**   Department of the Treasury—Internal Revenue Service
Copy 1—For State, City, or Local Tax Department

Notice that box 3 contains only $132,900, as Social Security tax is not levied on the full gross earnings of Maryanne Sherman but instead is levied only up to the 2019 Social Security wage base. Additionally, both state disability tax and charitable contributions are displayed in box 14, as these were withheld from gross earnings and are not listed elsewhere on the W-2 Form.

We will now complete the W-2 Form for Paul Rogers (657 Flicker Lane, Brockport, NY 14420; SSN 111-11-1111), an employee of Lucky Ties Apparel (Employer Identification #11-1111111), which completes Form 941 on a quarterly basis. Lucky Ties Apparel (located at 77 Main Street, Rochester, NY 14602) does not use control or establishment numbers and compensated eight employees during 2019. Paul's gross earnings for federal income tax withholding are $114,735, with an associated tax of $8,551.68. As a result of his total retirement contributions of $4,140, which were withheld from his gross pay starting in June and are not subject to federal income tax withholding, gross earnings subject to Social Security tax and Medicare tax were $118,875 ($114,735 + $4,140). The associated taxes were $7,370.25 and $1,723.69, respectively. State disability insurance for the year was $31.20, while the annual charitable contribution was $520. New York State income tax withholding was $3,420.67 (based on the gross earnings amount subject to federal income tax withholding provided above), with no local taxes withheld. The employer's New York State ID number is the same as the federal Employer Identification Number.

22222	**a** Employee's social security number 222-22-2222	OMB No. 1545-0008		
b Employer identification number (EIN) 11-1111111		**1** Wages, tips, other compensation 114,375		**2** Federal income tax withheld 8,551.68
c Employer's name, address, and ZIP code Lucky Ties Apparel 77 Main Street Rochester, NY 14602		**3** Social security wages 118,875		**4** Social security tax withheld 7,370.25
		5 Medicare wages and tips 118,875		**6** Medicare tax withheld 1,723.69
		7 Social security tips		**8** Allocated tips
d Control number		**9**		**10** Dependent care benefits
e Employee's first name and initial Last name Suff. Paul Rogers 657 Flicker Lane Brockport, NY 14420		**11** Nonqualified plans		**12a** D 4,140
		13 Statutory employee ☐ Retirement plan ☒ Third-party sick pay ☐		**12b**
		14 Other SDI 31.20 Charity 520		**12c**
				12d
f Employee's address and ZIP code				

15 State	Employer's state ID number	**16** State wages, tips, etc.	**17** State income tax	**18** Local wages, tips, etc.	**19** Local income tax	**20** Locality name
NY	11-1111111	114,735	3,420.67			

Form **W-2** Wage and Tax Statement   2019   Department of the Treasury—Internal Revenue Service

Copy 1—For State, City, or Local Tax Department

In this example, Paul Rogers' Form W-2 displays different wage amounts for federal income tax and FICA taxes. The federal income tax amount represents total gross earnings minus the 401(k) retirement contribution that is not subject to federal income tax.

The FICA tax amounts are equal to the total gross earnings for the year, as they are all subject to this tax.

Also note that the retirement plan contribution amount is entered in box 12a (code D indicates a 401(k) contribution).

Form W-3 (Transmittal of Wage and Tax Statements)

On the Web

irs.gov/pub/irs-pdf
/fw3.pdf

Form W-3 is an informational form that is submitted to the Social Security Administration by the employer at the same time as the W-2 Forms. The W-3 Form summarizes all of the information contained in the W-2 Forms and must agree with the totals of these. As the W-3 Form is submitted in conjunction with W-2 Forms, it is subject to the same due dates as those that apply to W-2 Forms (March 1 for paper filing; March 31 for e-filing).

TIP! Form W-3 is furnished to the Social Security Administration; it is not provided to the individual employees.

When completing Form W-3, the employer should not have a need to refer back to the payroll register or the employee earnings records, as all required compensation and tax information can be summarized from the individual W-2 Forms that have already been completed.

Examine the Form: W-3

DO NOT STAPLE

a Control number	For Official Use Only ▶ OMB No. 1545-0008
33333	

b **Kind of Payer** (Check one)	941 ☐ Military ☐ 943 ☐ 944 ☐ CT-1 ☐ Hshld. emp. ☐ Medicare govt. emp. ☐	**Kind of Employer** (Check one)	None apply ☐ 501c non-govt. ☐ State/local non-501c ☐ State/local 501c ☐ Federal govt. ☐	Third-party sick pay ☐ (Check if applicable)

c Total number of Forms W-2	d Establishment number	1 Wages, tips, other compensation	2 Federal income tax withheld
e Employer identification number (EIN)		3 Social security wages	4 Social security tax withheld
f Employer's name		5 Medicare wages and tips	6 Medicare tax withheld
		7 Social security tips	8 Allocated tips
		9	10 Dependent care benefits
		11 Nonqualified plans	12a Deferred compensation
g Employer's address and ZIP code			
h Other EIN used this year		13 For third-party sick pay use only	12b
15 State Employer's state ID number		14 Income tax withheld by payer of third-party sick pay	
16 State wages, tips, etc.	17 State income tax	18 Local wages, tips, etc.	19 Local income tax
Employer's contact person		Employer's telephone number	For Official Use Only
Employer's fax number		Employer's email address	

Under penalties of perjury, I declare that I have examined this return and accompanying documents, and, to the best of my knowledge and belief, they are true, correct, and complete.

Signature ▶   Title ▶   Date ▶

Form **W-3** Transmittal of Wage and Tax Statements   **2019**   Department of the Treasury Internal Revenue Service

Send this entire page with the entire Copy A page of Form(s) W-2 to the Social Security Administration (SSA). Photocopies are not acceptable. Do not send Form W-3 if you filed electronically with the SSA. Do not send any payment (cash, checks, money orders, etc.) with Forms W-2 and W-3.

Examine the Form: W-3 (continued)

Box a: Similar to box d on the W-2 Form, this control number box may be left blank, or an employer may assign a number.

Box b: One *Kind of Payer* box must be selected (941 applies to all companies examined in this text), and one *Kind of Employer* box must be selected (*None apply* would be applicable for all companies examined in this text). The *Third-party sick pay* box should also be selected where applicable.

Box c: This box displays the number of nonvoided W-2 Forms completed.

Box d: This optional box may be used by an employer to distinguish between different W-3 Forms that have been submitted for different establishments in the business.

Boxes e–g: These boxes must all be completed with the requested company information.

Box h: If another Employer Identification Number (such as that of a previous owner of the business) was used on a federally submitted form during the year, this number is entered here.

Boxes 1–11: These boxes require the same information as the W-2 Form but display the totals for all W-2s across the establishment (or business as a whole).

Box 12a: This displays one total for all deferred compensation codes entered on the individual W-2 Forms. No code is to be entered on the W-3 Form, as this is a combined amount across multiple codes.

Box 12b: This box is left blank.

Box 13: The phrase "Third-party sick pay recap" is entered here if a third-party payer of sick pay is completing the W-3 Form.

Box 14: Employers enter total income tax withheld from employee earnings for third-party sick pay here. Note that this amount is also included in the box 2 total.

Box 15: The two-letter state abbreviation and associated state ID number are entered here. This box is left blank if the employer completes W-2 Forms for more than one state.

Boxes 16–19: Totals from the corresponding boxes on the W-2 Forms are entered for each of these boxes, regardless of whether more than one state is represented in these W-2s.

The bottom portion of the form, including contact person, telephone, email, fax, signature, title, and date, should all be completed.

Case in Point 6-5   Complete Form W-3

In this example, we will complete the W-3 Form for Lucky Ties Apparel (Employer Identification #11-1111111). Lucky Ties Apparel (located at 77 Main Street, Rochester, NY 14602) does not use control numbers. Total employee compensation for the year was $510,236, annual retirement plan contributions totaled $7,646, and flexible spending account contributions totaled $6,904.56. Federal income tax withholding totaled $30,610 for the year. Only Maryanne Sherman (who did not contribute to a flexible spending account) earned more than the $132,900 Social Security wage base (see Case in Point 6-4 for this employee's earnings and tax totals). New York State earnings subject to income tax withholding were the same as those subject to federal income tax withholding. State income tax withholding totaled $17,892, with no local taxes withheld. The employer's New York State ID number is the same as the federal Employer Identification Number. The form is signed by the president of the company, Harold Cameron (telephone #585-555-6281), and is submitted on the due date for paper filings. Note that there are no rounding differences for Social Security tax or Medicare tax between withheld amounts and those that can be calculated by using the total taxable earnings for the year.

DO NOT STAPLE

a Control number	For Official Use Only ▶
33333	OMB No. 1545-0008

b Kind of Payer (Check one)	941 ✓ Military ☐ 943 ☐ 944 ☐ CT-1 ☐ Hshld. emp. ☐ Medicare govt. emp. ☐	Kind of Employer (Check one)	None apply ✓ 501c non-govt. ☐ State/local non-501c ☐ State/local 501c ☐ Federal govt. ☐	Third-party sick pay (Check if applicable) ☐

c Total number of Forms W-2 **8**	d Establishment number	1 Wages, tips, other compensation 495,685.44	2 Federal income tax withheld 30,610
e Employer identification number (EIN) 11-1111111		3 Social security wages 496,651.44	4 Social security tax withheld 30,792.39
f Employer's name Luck Ties Apparel		5 Medicare wages and tips 503,331.44	6 Medicare tax withheld 7,298.31
77 Main Street Rochester, NY 14602		7 Social security tips	8 Allocated tips
		9	10 Dependent care benefits
g Employer's address and ZIP code		11 Nonqualified plans	12a Deferred compensation 7,646
h Other EIN used this year		13 For third-party sick pay use only	12b

15 State NY	Employer's state ID number 11-1111111	14 Income tax withheld by payer of third-party sick pay	
16 State wages, tips, etc. 495,685.44	17 State income tax 17,892	18 Local wages, tips, etc.	19 Local income tax
Employer's contact person Harold Cameron		Employer's telephone number 585-555-6281	For Official Use Only
Employer's fax number		Employer's email address	

Under penalties of perjury, I declare that I have examined this return and accompanying documents, and, to the best of my knowledge and belief, they are true, correct, and complete.

Signature ▶ *Harold Cameron*   Title ▶ President   Date ▶ 3/1/20

Form **W-3** Transmittal of Wage and Tax Statements   2019   Department of the Treasury
Internal Revenue Service

Send this entire page with the entire Copy A page of Form(s) W-2 to the Social Security Administration (SSA).
Photocopies are not acceptable. Do not send Form W-3 if you filed electronically with the SSA.
Do not send any payment (cash, checks, money orders, etc.) with Forms W-2 and W-3.

The earnings subject to federal income tax in box 1 were calculated as total compensation of $510,236, minus retirement plan contributions of $7,646, minus flexible spending account contributions of $6,904.56 (these two amounts are not subject to federal income tax withholding).

The Social Security wages in box 3 are those on which Social Security tax is levied. One of the eight employees (Sherman) had earnings subject to Social Security tax that exceeded the Social Security wage base of $132,900; therefore, this threshold represents her Social Security wages. The other seven employees earned less than this amount; therefore, their entire compensation of $370,656 (total employee earnings of $510,236 minus Sherman's earnings of $139,580) less flexible spending account contributions of $6,904.56 (which are not subject to Social Security tax) represents the taxable Social Security earnings. Social Security wages of $496,651.44 are calculated as $132,900 + $370,656 minus $6,904.56. Social Security tax in box 4 is then calculated as Social Security wages of $496,651.44 × 6.2% (in this instance, no rounding issues exist that would result in this calculation being inaccurate).

Medicare wages in box 5 are calculated as total compensation of $510,236 minus flexible spending account contributions of $6,904.56. The resulting $503,331.44 is multiplied by 1.45% to arrive at $7,298.31 of Medicare taxes in box 6.

All other figures are taken from the information provided. The form is dated 3/1/20, as this is the due date for paper filing.

Self-Assessment

Complete the Self-Assessment as directed by your instructor, whether that is in the book or your eLab course, if applicable.

True/False Questions

1. The lookback period runs from July 1 through June 30.   *True*   *False*

2. FUTA tax must be remitted if the total FUTA tax owed exceeds $300 as of the end of the 2nd quarter.   *True*   *False*

3. Form 941 is due by the last day of the first month after each quarter has ended.   *True*   *False*

4. The Internal Revenue Service levies a small service fee for employers who utilize the Electronic Federal Tax Payment System.   *True*   *False*

5. When an employer remits a federal tax payment via a check sent through the United States Postal Service, the check must arrive by the form's due date.   *True*   *False*

6. Because Form 940 may not be remitted with a payment, no payment voucher can accompany the form.   *True*   *False*

7. The total for Schedule A (Form 940) also appears on the first page of Form 940.   *True*   *False*

8. Employers must furnish all employees with copies of the W-2 Form by January 31.   *True*   *False*

9. The W-3 Form is submitted to the Social Security Administration independent of all other federal forms.   *True*   *False*

10. Multiple due dates can apply to the W-3 Form, depending on whether a paper version is filed or the form is e-filed.   *True*   *False*

Multiple Choice Questions

11. What is the annual federal tax threshold above which an employer is deemed to be a semiweekly depositor?
    A. $500
    B. $7,000
    C. $50,000
    D. $132,900

12. Which of the following taxes, when required to be paid, is due by the last day of the first month after a quarter ends?
    A. Social Security tax
    B. Federal income tax
    C. FUTA tax
    D. Medicare tax

13. The next-day deposit rule is triggered when taxes owed at the end of a day are greater than what amount?
    A. $500
    B. $2,500
    C. $50,000
    D. $100,000

14. Total taxes owed, against which total deposits are compared, are reported on which line of Form 941?
    A. Line 2
    B. Line 12
    C. Line 13
    D. Line 14

15. Which of the following is the due date for Form 940 when it is submitted without a payment?
    A. January 1
    B. January 15
    C. January 31
    D. February 10

16. Schedule A (Form 940) is used in each of the following circumstances except when:
    A. The employer pays SUTA tax in two states.
    B. The employer does not pay FUTA tax until the 4th quarter of the year.
    C. The employer pays SUTA tax in four states.
    D. The employer operates in a credit-reduction state.

17. Which copy of the W-2 Form is submitted by the employer to the Social Security Administration?
    A. Copy A
    B. Copy B
    C. Copy C
    D. Copy 2

18. Which of the following items is not reported on the W-2 Form?
    A. Dependent care benefits
    B. Union dues
    C. Hours worked
    D. State income tax withheld

19. Which of the following is a true statement regarding the W-2 Form?
    A. Employers must submit the W-2 Form regardless of the amount of compensation paid to employees.
    B. Sending a copy of the W-2 Form to the employee is optional.
    C. The control number on the W-2 Form must be completed by the employer.
    D. The W-2 Form includes both federal and state tax information.

20. Which of the following appears on the W-3 Form but does not appear on the W-2 Form?
    A. Federal income tax withheld
    B. Kind of payer
    C. Social Security wages
    D. Dependent care benefits

Practice Set A

The IRS forms and Excel templates needed for these assignments are included in the Student Exercise Files download for this course. If directed to do so, complete these assignments in Homework Grader.

PSa 6-1 Examine the Lookback Period

For each of the following independent circumstances, examine the lookback period to determine whether the company is a monthly or semiweekly depositor for 2019:

1. A company's total taxes owed (federal income tax withholding, Social Security tax, and Medicare tax) for six consecutive quarters were as follows:

2017; 1st Quarter	$21,000	2017; 4th Quarter	$11,100
2017; 2nd Quarter	$13,200	2018; 1st Quarter	$14,800
2017; 3rd Quarter	$9,750	2018; 2nd Quarter	$13,000

2. A company's total taxes owed (federal income tax withholding, Social Security tax, and Medicare tax) for six consecutive quarters were as follows:

2017; 1st Quarter	$14,500	2017; 4th Quarter	$10,900
2017; 2nd Quarter	$10,000	2018; 1st Quarter	$14,000
2017; 3rd Quarter	$13,850	2018; 2nd Quarter	$11,700

3. A company's total taxes owed (federal income tax withholding, Social Security tax, and Medicare tax) for six consecutive quarters were as follows:

2017; 1st Quarter	$18,000	2017; 4th Quarter	$13,000
2017; 2nd Quarter	$15,500	2018; 1st Quarter	$11,800
2017; 3rd Quarter	$17,400	2018; 2nd Quarter	$9,000

PSa 6-2 Record a Monthly Federal Tax Payment Journal Entry

Walking Boots Company is a monthly depositor whose December federal taxes are displayed below. Record one journal entry to account for the payment of federal taxes. All tax payments are made in a timely manner on the payment due date (which, for this month, is not impacted by a weekend or holiday).

December Tax Totals			
Federal income tax	$604	Employer's Social Security tax	$575
Employee's Social Security tax	$575	Employer's Medicare tax	$178
Employee's Medicare tax	$178		

PSa 6-3 Record Quarterly FUTA and Voluntary Deduction Journal Entries

Cooking Cousins is a monthly depositor whose 4th quarter FUTA taxes and 4th quarter voluntary deductions are displayed below. Record one journal entry to account for the payment of federal unemployment taxes and one journal entry to account for the payment of the voluntary deductions. Assume that each voluntary deduction is remitted to the respective organization on a quarterly basis on the last day of the first month after the end of the quarter. All tax payments are made in a timely manner on the payment due date (which, for this quarter, is not impacted by a weekend or holiday).

4th Quarter Totals			
Federal unemployment tax	$26	Charitable contribution	$80
Retirement plan	$224	Cafeteria plan	$400
Health insurance	$350		

PSa 6-4 Complete Form 941

Complete Form 941 for the 2nd quarter of 2019 for Longneck Corp. (Employer Identification #22-2222222). Assume that Longneck Corp. (located at 518 State Street, Seattle, WA 98101) chooses to complete and mail Form 941 on the due date. Based on the lookback period, Longneck Corp. is a monthly depositor. Assume that all necessary deposits were made on a timely basis and that the employer made deposits equal to the total amount owed for the quarter. All six employees worked during each of the three months, and the company does not choose to allow a third party to discuss the form with the IRS. Note that the form is signed by the company's controller, Arnold Ming (telephone #206-555-0101), and that no employee is subject to Additional Medicare Tax during the quarter. Second quarter earnings and associated taxes withheld from employee earnings are as follows:

	April Taxes	May Taxes	June Taxes	2nd Quarter Earnings
FWT	$850.00	$910.00	$880.00	$11,291
Social Security	$225.06	$244.90	$230.08	$11,291
Medicare	$52.64	$57.28	$53.81	$11,291

PSa 6-5 Complete Form 940

Complete Form 940 for Blacklist Associates (Employer Identification #44-4444444). Assume that Blacklist Associates (located at 504 Cyprus Avenue, Providence, RI 02801) chooses to complete and mail Form 940 on the due date. Note that Blacklist Associates pays only SUTA tax in Rhode Island. The form is signed by the CEO of the company, James Scott (telephone #401-555-0492). The company elects to delay remitting FUTA tax until it is required to do so. Total employee compensation for the year was $452,870, and total charitable contributions totaled $18,500. All earnings subject to FUTA tax are also subject to SUTA tax. Blacklist Associates allows its accountant (Wally Gorman, telephone #401-555-9366, PIN #80515) to discuss the form with the IRS. Four employees of Blacklist Associates earned more than $7,000 that was subject to FUTA tax (each exceeded this threshold in the 1st quarter), while a fifth employee hired during the 4th quarter earned only $3,200 that was subject to FUTA tax.

PSa 6-6 Complete Form W-2

Complete Copy A of the W-2 Form for the two employees of Flywheel Outfitters, Inc. (Employer Identification #99-9999999). Flywheel Outfitters, Inc., (located at 909 Crispy Lane, Charleston, SC 29401) utilizes control numbers, and its South Carolina state ID number is the same as its federal Employer Identification Number.

Julio Estevez (766 Mixing Road, Charleston, SC 29401), whose Social Security number is 777-77-7777, is an employee of Flywheel Outfitters, Inc. (Julio's control number is #1045.) His gross earnings for federal income tax withholding, Social Security tax, and Medicare tax were $82,476.05 for the year, while these taxes were $8,645, $5,113.52, and $1,195.90, respectively. Annual union dues were $625. South Carolina income tax withholding was $5,773.32 (based on the above gross earnings for federal income tax), with no local taxes withheld.

Albert Ochie (73 Scaring Place, Charleston, SC 29401), whose Social Security number is 888-88-8888, is an employee of Flywheel Outfitters, Inc. (Albert's control number is #1055.) His gross earnings for federal income tax withholding, Social Security tax, and Medicare tax were $135,284.02 for the year, while these taxes were $15,270, $8,239.80, and $1,961.62, respectively. Annual union dues were $625, while Albert elects to have charitable contributions of $300 withheld. South Carolina income tax withholding was $7,944.03 (based on the above gross earnings for federal income tax), with no local taxes withheld.

PSa 6-7 Complete Form W-3

Complete the W-3 Form for Flywheel Outfitters, Inc., based on the W-2 Forms you completed in PSa 6-6 for the two employees of the company. The form is signed by the president of the company, Albert Ochie (telephone #843-555-8164), and is submitted on the due date for e-filing. The company files Form 941 during the year and selects "None apply" in the *Kind of Employer* section.

PSa 6-8 Complete Form W-3

Complete the W-3 Form for Belt Buckle Industries (Employer Identification #88-8888888). The company (located at 435 Georgia Lane, Clifton, NJ 07011) does not use control numbers. Total employee compensation (gross pay) for the year was $527,000, and annual retirement plan contributions totaled $15,200. Federal income tax withholding totaled $73,100 for the year. Of the company's four employees, only one had earnings subject to Social Security tax that did not exceed $132,900 (this employee earned $18,200). New Jersey state earnings subject to income tax withholding were the same as that subject to federal income tax withholding. State income tax withholding totaled $53,000, with no local taxes withheld. The employer's New Jersey State ID number is the same as its federal Employer Identification Number. The form is signed by the CEO of the company, Paul Goldstein (telephone #862-555-0052), and is submitted on the due date for e-filing. The company files Form 941 during the year and selects "None apply" in the *Kind of Employer* section. Note that there are no rounding differences for Social Security tax or Medicare tax between withheld amounts and those that can be calculated by using the total taxable earnings for the year, and no employee was subject to Additional Medicare Tax during the year.

Practice Set B

The IRS forms and Excel templates needed for these assignments are included in the Student Exercise Files download for this course. If directed to do so, complete these assignments in Homework Grader.

PSb 6-1 Examine the Lookback Period

For each of the following independent circumstances, examine the lookback period to determine whether the company is a monthly or semiweekly depositor for 2019:

1. A company's total taxes owed (federal income tax withholding, Social Security tax, and Medicare tax) for six consecutive quarters were as follows:

2017; 1st Quarter	$8,200	2017; 4th Quarter	$9,000
2017; 2nd Quarter	$11,500	2018; 1st Quarter	$12,100
2017; 3rd Quarter	$10,400	2018; 2nd Quarter	$18,200

2. A company's total taxes owed (federal income tax withholding, Social Security tax, and Medicare tax) for six consecutive quarters were as follows:

2017; 1st Quarter	$18,300	2017; 4th Quarter	$14,200
2017; 2nd Quarter	$15,700	2018; 1st Quarter	$11,400
2017; 3rd Quarter	$13,400	2018; 2nd Quarter	$7,200

3. A company's total taxes owed (federal income tax withholding, Social Security tax, and Medicare tax) for six consecutive quarters were as follows:

2017; 1st Quarter	$14,900	2017; 4th Quarter	$10,000
2017; 2nd Quarter	$8,700	2018; 1st Quarter	$16,200
2017; 3rd Quarter	$11,100	2018; 2nd Quarter	$15,100

PSb 6-2 Record a Monthly Federal Tax Payment Journal Entry

Decimal Corporation is a monthly depositor whose December federal taxes are displayed below. Record one journal entry to account for the payment of the federal taxes. All tax payments are made in a timely manner on the payment due date (which, for this month, is not impacted by a weekend or holiday).

December Tax Totals			
Federal income tax	$3,250	Employer's Social Security tax	$2,420
Employee's Social Security tax	$2,420	Employer's Medicare tax	$902
Employee's Medicare tax	$902		

PSb 6-3 Record Quarterly FUTA and Voluntary Deduction Journal Entries

Alton's Arboreal Association is a monthly depositor whose 4th quarter FUTA taxes and 4th quarter voluntary deductions are displayed below. Record one journal entry to account for the payment of federal unemployment taxes, and one journal entry to account for the payment of the voluntary deductions. Assume that each voluntary deduction is remitted to the respective organization on a quarterly basis, on the last day of the first month after the end of the quarter. All tax payments are made in a timely manner, on the payment due date (which, for this quarter, is not impacted by a weekend or holiday).

4th Quarter Totals			
Federal unemployment tax	$370	Charitable contribution	$700
Retirement plan	$4,240	Cafeteria plan	$5,560
Health insurance	$3,020		

PSb 6-4 Complete Form 941

Complete Form 941 for the 1st quarter of 2019 for Bouncing Babies Co. (Employer Identification #33-3333333). Assume that Bouncing Babies Co. (located at 91 Bayberry Avenue, Baton Rouge, LA 70714) chooses to complete and mail Form 941 on the due date. Based on the lookback period, Bouncing Babies Co. is a monthly depositor. Assume that all necessary deposits were made on a timely basis and that the employer made deposits equal to the total amount owed for the quarter. All 32 employees worked during each of the three months, and the company elects to allow its accountant (William Gordon, telephone #225-555-7846, PIN #83463) to discuss the form with the IRS. Additionally, William signs the form, and no employee is subject to Additional Medicare Tax during the quarter. First quarter earnings and associated taxes withheld from employee earnings are as follows:

	January Taxes	February Taxes	March Taxes	1st Quarter Earnings
FWT	$12,400.00	$12,720.00	$12,120.00	$331,200
Social Security	$7,579.50	$7,240.36	$7,990.13	$367,903
Medicare	$1,772.63	$1,693.31	$1,868.66	$367,903

PSb 6-5 Complete Form 940

Complete Form 940 for KYG Corp. (Employer Identification #55-5555555). Assume that KYG Corp. (located at 81519 Duke Lane, Dayton, OH 45377) chooses to complete and mail Form 940 on the due date. Note that KYG Corp. pays only SUTA tax in Ohio. The form is signed by the president of the company, Marcelo Coleman (telephone #937-555-8825). The company elects to delay remitting FUTA tax until it is required to do so. Total employee compensation for the year was $751,000, and total group-term life insurance contributions totaled $24,200. All earnings subject to FUTA tax are also subject to SUTA tax. KYG Corp. allows its accountant (Steve Kimmel, telephone #937-555-0040, PIN #76134) to discuss the form with the IRS. Note that nine employees of KYG Corp. earned more than $7,000 that was subject to FUTA tax (each exceeded this threshold in the 1st quarter), while a 10th employee hired during the 4th quarter earned only $5,700 that was subject to FUTA tax.

PSb 6-6 Complete Form W-2

Complete Copy A of the W-2 Form for the two employees of Gameroom Associates Corp. (Employer Identification #55-5555555). Gameroom Associates Corp. (located at 87 Rose Way, Lexington, KY 40361) utilizes control numbers, and its Kentucky State ID number is the same as its federal Employer Identification Number.

Rachel Flowers (4 Fiber Way, Lexington, KY 40361), whose Social Security number is 888-88-8888, is an employee of Gameroom Associates Corp. (Rachel's control number is #4407.) Gross earnings for federal income tax withholding, Social Security tax, and Medicare tax were $101,470 for the year, while these taxes were $9,250, $6,291.14, and $1,471.32, respectively. The annual charitable contribution was $260. Kentucky income tax withholding was $6,088.20 (based on the above gross earnings for federal income tax), with no local taxes withheld. The employer's Kentucky State ID number is the same as its federal Employer Identification Number.

Adrian Pitts (8765 Tripping Way, Lexington, KY 40361), whose Social Security number is 444-44-4444, is an employee of Gameroom Associates Corp. (Adrian's control number is #4408.) Gross earnings for federal income tax withholding were $136,960 for the year, while gross earnings for Social Security tax and Medicare tax were $141,460 for the year. The federal income tax, Social Security tax, and Medicare tax were $16,350, $8,239.80, and $1,985.92, respectively. The annual charitable contribution was $675, and the 401(k) retirement plan contribution was $4,500. Kentucky income tax withholding was $10,382.73 (based on the above gross earnings for federal income tax), with no local taxes withheld. The employer's Kentucky State ID number is the same as its federal Employer Identification Number.

PSb 6-7 Complete Form W-3

Complete the W-3 Form for Gameroom Associates Corp., based on the W-2 Forms you completed in PSb 6-6 for the two employees of the company. The form is signed by the CFO of the company, Rachel Flowers (telephone #859-555-2766), and is submitted on the due date for e-filing. The company files Form 941 during the year and selects "None apply" in the *Kind of Employer* section.

PSb 6-8 Complete Form W-3

Complete the W-3 Form for Shipbuilders of New England (Employer Identification #33-3333333). The company (located at 2 Hickory Trail, Pawtucket, RI 02860) does not use control numbers. Total employee compensation (gross pay) for the year was $1,052,400, and annual retirement plan contributions totaled $27,500. Federal income tax withholding totaled $122,300 for the year. Only three of the nine employees have earnings subject to Social Security tax less than $132,900 (these employees' earnings were $98,400, $87,200, and $53,600). Rhode Island state earnings subject to income tax withholding were the same as those subject to federal income tax withholding. State income tax withholding totaled $88,350, with no local taxes withheld. The employer's Rhode Island state ID number is the same as its federal Employer Identification Number. The form is signed by the CFO of the company, Molly Richmond (telephone #401-555-9929), and is submitted on the due date for paper filings. The company files Form 941 during the year and selects "None apply" in the *Kind of Employer* section. Note that there are no rounding differences for Social Security tax or Medicare tax between withheld amounts and those that can be calculated by using the total taxable earnings for the year, and no employee was subject to Additional Medicare Tax during the year.

Continuing Payroll Problem

The IRS forms and Excel templates needed for these assignments are included in the Student Exercise Files download for this course. If directed to do so, complete these assignments in Homework Grader.

CPP 6-1 Complete 4th Quarter and Year-End Payroll Reporting

Calculate 4th quarter taxes for TCLH Industries, a manufacturer of cleaning products. Then complete Forms 941 and 940 as of year-end. Conclude by completing Copy A of the W-2 Form for each of the four employees, as well as the associated W-3 Form. Recall from the *Form 941 Rounding Considerations* section that quarter- and year-end tax figures should not be calculated based on the total taxable earnings for the respective quarter or year. Instead, to avoid rounding discrepancies, these tax figures should be determined for each employee by adding the individual taxes across each pay period.

1. Calculate total federal income tax, Social Security tax, and Medicare tax for the 4th quarter. Assume that Zachary Fox earns the same amount for each of the final three weeks of the year (the only weeks in 2019 during which he worked) and that Calvin Bell earned the same amount during each of the 52 weeks of the year. Further assume that no changes to voluntary deductions were requested by any employee during 2019. Note that the final week of the year (beginning on December 23, 2019) is a full workweek (the 52nd workweek of 2019).

   To assist in the completion of this chapter's continuing payroll problem, the following employee earnings records display year-to-date earnings prior to the current pay period. As a result, the "4th Quarter" row excludes the final three weeks of the year. Note that the current pay period is the first pay period for Zachary Fox (SSN 121-21-2121, address: 1483 Independence Road, Durham, NC 27701); therefore, his employee earnings record is not displayed below, as it contains no previous earnings information.

Employee Earnings Record

Name	Calvin Bell	Marital Status	Single
Address	2222 Sacker Place	Fed. Withholding Allow.	2
	Durham, NC 27701	State Withholding Allow.	1
SS#	500-00-0000		

	Earnings							Deductions									
Pay Period Ending	Regular Hours Worked	Regular Pay Rate	Regular Wages	Overtime Hours Worked	Overtime Pay Rate	Overtime Wages	Gross Pay	Federal Withholding Tax	State Withholding Tax	Social Security Tax	Medicare Tax	Retirement Contribution	Life Insurance	Charitable Contribution	Additional Withholding	Check Number	Net Pay
1st Quarter	n/a	n/a	$3,796.00	n/a	n/a	$1,637.09	$5,433.09	$208.00	$255.32	$336.83	$ 78.78	$326.04	$ -	$195.00	$ 91.00		$3,942.12
2nd Quarter	n/a	n/a	$3,796.00	n/a	n/a	$1,637.09	$5,433.09	$208.00	$255.32	$336.83	$ 78.78	$326.04	$ -	$195.00	$ 91.00		$3,942.12
3rd Quarter	n/a	n/a	$3,796.00	n/a	n/a	$1,637.09	$5,433.09	$208.00	$255.32	$336.83	$ 78.78	$326.04	$ -	$195.00	$ 91.00		$3,942.12
4th Quarter	n/a	n/a	$2,920.00	n/a	n/a	$1,259.30	$4,179.30	$160.00	$196.40	$259.10	$ 60.60	$250.80	$ -	$150.00	$ 70.00		$3,032.40

Employee Earnings Record

Name	David Alexander
Address	1 Freedom Blvd.
	Durham, NC 27701
SS#	454-54-5454

Marital Status	Single
Fed. Withholding Allow.	1
State Withholding Allow.	1

	Earnings							Deductions									
Pay Period Ending	Regular Hours Worked	Regular Pay Rate	Regular Wages	Overtime Hours Worked	Overtime Pay Rate	Overtime Wages	Gross Pay	Federal Withholding Tax	State Withholding Tax	Social Security Tax	Medicare Tax	Retirement Contribution	Life Insurance	Charitable Contribution	Additional Withholding	Check Number	Net Pay
1st Quarter	n/a	n/a	$ 52,650.00	n/a	n/a	$ -	$ 52,650.00	$ 9,515.48	$ 2,316.60	$ 3,264.30	$ 763.49	$ 6,318.00	$ -	$ 260.00	$ -		$ 30,212.13
2nd Quarter	n/a	n/a	$ 52,650.00	n/a	n/a	$ -	$ 52,650.00	$ 9,515.48	$ 2,316.60	$ 3,264.30	$ 763.49	$ 6,318.00	$ -	$ 260.00	$ -		$ 30,212.13
3rd Quarter	n/a	n/a	$ 52,650.00	n/a	n/a	$ -	$ 52,650.00	$ 9,515.48	$ 2,316.60	$ 1,711.20	$ 763.49	$ 6,318.00	$ -	$ 260.00	$ -		$ 31,765.23
4th Quarter	n/a	n/a	$ 40,500.00	n/a	n/a	$ -	$ 40,500.00	$ 7,319.60	$ 1,782.00	$ -	$ 587.30	$ 4,860.00	$ -	$ 200.00	$ -		$ 25,751.10

Employee Earnings Record

Name	Michael Sierra
Address	200 Mississippi Road
	Durham, NC 27701
SS#	232-32-3232

Marital Status	Married
Fed. Withholding Allow.	4
State Withholding Allow.	3

	Earnings							Deductions									
Pay Period Ending	Regular Hours Worked	Regular Pay Rate	Regular Wages	Overtime Hours Worked	Overtime Pay Rate	Overtime Wages	Gross Pay	Federal Withholding Tax	State Withholding Tax	Social Security Tax	Medicare Tax	Retirement Contribution	Life Insurance	Charitable Contribution	Additional Withholding	Check Number	Net Pay
1st Quarter	n/a	n/a	$ 31,850.00	n/a	n/a	$ -	$ 31,850.00	$ 3,220.10	$ 1,560.00	$ 1,934.40	$ 452.40	$ -	$ 260.00	$ 65.00	$ 650.00		$ 23,708.10
2nd Quarter	n/a	n/a	$ 31,850.00	n/a	n/a	$ -	$ 31,850.00	$ 3,220.10	$ 1,560.00	$ 1,934.40	$ 452.40	$ -	$ 260.00	$ 65.00	$ 650.00		$ 23,708.10
3rd Quarter	n/a	n/a	$ 31,850.00	n/a	n/a	$ -	$ 31,850.00	$ 3,220.10	$ 1,560.00	$ 1,934.40	$ 452.40	$ -	$ 260.00	$ 65.00	$ 650.00		$ 23,708.10
4th Quarter	n/a	n/a	$ 24,500.00	n/a	n/a	$ -	$ 24,500.00	$ 2,477.00	$ 1,200.00	$ 1,488.00	$ 348.00	$ -	$ 200.00	$ 50.00	$ 500.00		$ 18,237.00

NOTE! These three images are available in an Excel file as part of the Student Exercise File download for this course. You may consider using these Excel files as a starting point for the questions listed below.

2. Complete Form 941 for the 4th quarter for TCLH Industries (Employer Identification #44-4444444), which is located at 202 Whitmore Avenue, Durham, NC 27701. Assume that all necessary deposits were made on a timely basis (new businesses in their first year of operations are automatically monthly depositors), and that the employer made deposits equal to the total amount owed for the quarter. Furthermore, note that the company had five pay periods during October and four pay periods during both November and December. The company does not have a third-party designee, nor does it use a paid preparer. All forms are signed by the CEO of the company, Michael Sierra (telephone #919-555-7485), and the form is submitted on the due date.

3. Complete Form 940 for TCLH Industries (Employer Identification #44-4444444), which is located at 202 Whitmore Avenue, Durham, NC 27701. Assume that the company does not remit FUTA tax until the latest date on which it is permitted to do so. Note that the life insurance for which employee withholdings were made is not group-term life insurance. Flexible spending accounts are reported on Form 940 as a Fringe Benefit, and all earnings subject to FUTA tax are also subject to SUTA tax. The company does not have a third-party designee, nor does it use a paid preparer. All forms are signed by the CEO of the company, Michael Sierra (telephone #919-555-7485).

4. Complete Form W-2 for each of the four employees of TCLH Industries (Employer Identification #44-4444444), which is located at 202 Whitmore Avenue, Durham, NC 27701. The company does not use control numbers, and its state identification number is the same as its federal Employer Identification Number. Note that the state withholding tax rate for regular earnings is 5%.

5. Complete Form W-3 for TCLH Industries (Employer Identification #44-4444444), which is located at 202 Whitmore Avenue, Durham, NC 27701. The company does not use establishment numbers and both signs and submits the form on its paper-filing due date. The company selects "None apply" in the *Kind of Employer* section, and all forms are signed by the CEO of the company, Michael Sierra (telephone #919-555-7485).

Critical Thinking

CT 6-1 Examine Quarterly State Payroll Forms

As you learned earlier in the chapter, Form 941 is completed by employers on a quarterly basis and submitted to the federal government. Most employers will similarly submit quarterly payroll forms to their respective states. It is important to examine the quarterly forms for your state, as the formats (and information required) are different from one state to another. In this exercise, you will use the Internet to locate and review the quarterly payroll forms for your state.

Start by searching for the state payroll forms that apply to your state. Keep in mind that although a number of states do not levy an income tax on employees, they still require that quarterly forms be submitted. One reason for this is that state unemployment tax must still be remitted in these states. Once you have located the form(s), write a paragraph of at least five sentences in which you discuss both the figures required on the form and the differences between the state forms and Form 941.

Submit your final file based on the guidelines provided by your instructor.

CT 6-2 Review the Electronic Federal Tax Payment System

The federal government strongly encourages the use of the Electronic Federal Tax Payment System (EFTPS). In comparison with the paper-based system that has traditionally been used, the EFTPS is far more efficient for the government, which is why its use is encouraged. However, the system also offers a variety of benefits to the employer. In this exercise, you will use the Internet to examine the different uses of the EFTPS and the variety of ways that it can benefit the user.

Begin by navigating to the EFTPS website (the URL was provided earlier in the chapter) to learn more about the system, and then search the Internet to discover ways in which the EFTPS proves to be beneficial to employers. Write a paragraph of at least six sentences in which you first describe the various uses of the EFTPS and then discuss how it provides benefits to the user. Be certain to focus on benefits yielded to the employer and not to the government.

Submit your final file based on the guidelines provided by your instructor.

Comprehensive Projects—
Paper-Based Versions

These comprehensive projects are designed to be completed through the use of templates available in the Student Exercise Files download for this course.

After examining the annual payroll process, it is important to practice using the skills you've learned. In this chapter, two payroll-related projects are provided. The first project focuses on Ellipses Corp. For this company you will complete all payroll-related tasks for the month of December and will then finalize all year-end reporting. The second project focuses on Ampersand, Inc. For this company you will complete all payroll-related tasks for the 4th quarter of the year, after which you will finalize all year-end payroll reporting. You will manually complete all necessary forms and schedules for these projects.

One-Month Project

NOTE! Templates needed to complete these exercises, including one containing year-to-date payroll data, are included in the Student Exercise Files download for this course.

Ellipses Corp. is a small business that operates in Herndon, VA. The company is located at 10 Period Lane, Herndon, VA 20170. Its federal Employer Identification Number is 77-7777777, and its president, who signs all tax forms, is John Parker (telephone #571-555-0073). The company does not wish to name a third-party designee on forms.

During 2019 four individuals are employed by Ellipses Corp. These employees are as follows:

Name	Address	Social Security #	Federal W/H Allowances	State W/H Allowances	Marital Status
Hunter Cranston	85 Southern Road Herndon, VA 20170	111-11-1111	2	2	Married
Allison Harrison	203A Pine Court Herndon, VA 20170	777-77-7777	4	3	Married
John Parker	212 Tradition Lane Herndon, VA 20170	444-44-4444	1	1	Single
Pierre Sternberg	41 Seward Boulevard Herndon, VA 20170	333-33-3333	2	2	Married

Note that Pierre Sternberg was hired in November, and his first day of work was Monday, November 25. Additionally, due to an economic downturn, Allison Harrison was laid off in mid-December, with her last day of work on Friday, December 13.

All employees of Ellipses Corp. work a regular 40-hour workweek (thus all hours worked over 40 in a given week are overtime hours), receive overtime pay at a rate of 1.5 times the regular wage rate, and are paid weekly on Friday for the current week (which runs from Saturday through Friday, although employees never work on weekends). The SUTA tax rate applicable to Ellipses Corp. is 3.1%, while the SUTA wage base in Virginia is $8,000.

Earnings and voluntary deduction information for each of the four employees is as follows:

Name	Regular Wage Rate	Annual Salary	Weekly 401(k) Deduction	Weekly Charitable Contribution
Hunter Cranston	$15/hour	N/A	6% of gross pay	$5
Allison Harrison	$23/hour	N/A	5% of gross pay	$5
John Parker	N/A	$203,000.20	N/A	$20
Pierre Sternberg	N/A	$112,000.20	1% of gross pay	N/A

The first 11 months of the year have passed, and all payroll-related activity has been properly accounted for as of 11/30/2019. Payroll data for each of the four employees for the first three quarters of the year, as well as for the months of October and November, is as follows:

Hunter Cranston

Period	Gross Earnings	Federal Income Tax	State Income Tax	Social Security Tax	Medicare Tax	401(k) Deduction	Charitable Cont.
1st quarter	$7,800	$221	$366.60	$483.60	$113.10	$468	$65
2nd quarter	$7,800	$221	$366.60	$483.60	$113.10	$468	$65
3rd quarter	$7,800	$221	$366.60	$483.60	$113.10	$468	$65
October	$2,400	$68	$112.80	$148.80	$34.80	$144	$20
November	$3,000	$85	$141	$186	$43.50	$180	$25

Allison Harrison

Period	Gross Earnings	Federal Income Tax	State Income Tax	Social Security Tax	Medicare Tax	401(k) Deduction	Charitable Cont.
1st quarter	$11,960	$416	$568.10	$741.52	$173.42	$598	$65
2nd quarter	$11,960	$416	$568.10	$741.52	$173.42	$598	$65
3rd quarter	$11,960	$416	$568.10	$741.52	$173.42	$598	$65
October	$3,680	$128	$174.80	$228.16	$53.36	$184	$20
November	$4,600	$160	$218.50	$285.20	$66.70	$230	$25

John Parker

Period	Gross Earnings	Federal Income Tax	State Income Tax	Social Security Tax	Medicare Tax	401(k) Deduction	Charitable Cont.
1st quarter	$50,750.05	$10,929.36	$2,537.47	$3,146.52	$735.93	$0	$260
2nd quarter	$50,750.05	$10,929.36	$2,537.47	$3,146.52	$735.93	$0	$260
3rd quarter	$50,750.05	$10,929.36	$2,537.47	$1,946.76	$735.93	$0	$260
October	$15,615.40	$3,362.88	$780.76	$0	$226.44	$0	$80
November	$19,519.25	$4,203.60	$975.95	$0	$283.05	$0	$100

Pierre Sternberg

Period	Gross Earnings	Federal Income Tax	State Income Tax	Social Security Tax	Medicare Tax	401(k) Deduction	Charitable Cont.
1st quarter	$0	$0	$0	$0	$0	$0	$0
2nd quarter	$0	$0	$0	$0	$0	$0	$0
3rd quarter	$0	$0	$0	$0	$0	$0	$0
October	$0	$0	$0	$0	$0	$0	$0
November	$2,153.85	$224.36	$106.62	$133.54	$31.23	$21.54	$0

Note that all tax payments and filings are made on the due date. Based on the data provided here, you will complete the following:

1. Establish an employee earnings record for each of the company's four employees. Complete the top portion of each record.

2. Establish and complete the payroll register for each weekly pay period during December. When calculating federal income tax withholding, use the withholding tables where possible, and refer to the percentage method only when necessary. Note that as of December 7, Hunter Cranston requests that his federal withholding allowances increase from two to three (Ellipses Corp. makes this change). Additionally, for simplicity, calculate the state income tax withholding as 5% of each employee's taxable pay (which is the same as taxable pay for FWT). Recall that state income tax withholding would ordinarily be calculated using the applicable state's withholding tables. Payroll checks are remitted to the employees in the same order (Cranston, Harrison, Parker, Sternberg) each pay period and are written from a bank account that is used solely for these payments. The first payroll check written in December is check #762.

Note that all charitable contributions are deemed to be made on the final day of each pay period. The following information will be required for the completion of these records for the two employees who are compensated via an hourly wage:

Weekly Hours Worked

Weekly Start Date	Hunter Cranston	Allison Harrison
November 30	40	37
December 7	38	41
December 14	43.5	0
December 21	40	0

WARNING! The above dates are weekly start dates. Refer to a calendar to determine the weekly end dates and associated pay dates. Keep in mind that tax liability and payment amounts are determined based on the weekly pay dates.

3. Complete the employee earnings records for December for each of the four employees. Divide the voluntary deductions from the payroll register appropriately across the associated columns within the employee earnings records. If directed to do so by your instructor, record the necessary journal entries for each pay period.

4. Complete Form 941 for the 4th quarter. Note that based on the lookback period, the company is a monthly depositor. Assume that all necessary deposits were made on a timely basis and that the employer made deposits equal to the total amount owed for the quarter. Although Virginia quarterly state payroll forms are also filed by Ellipses Corp., you will not complete these. If directed to do so by your instructor, record the necessary journal entries associated with Form 941 (including those required for any tax payments made).

> **NOTE!** Recall from the *Form 941 Rounding Considerations* section that quarter- and year-end tax figures should not be calculated based on the total taxable earnings for the respective quarter or year. Instead, to avoid rounding discrepancies, tax figures within Part 2 of Form 941 should be determined for each employee by adding the individual taxes across each pay period.

5. Complete Form 940 for Ellipses Corp. Note that FUTA payments are made only when required (i.e., if the employer is permitted to postpone the payment of these taxes, it will do so until a point in time when payment must be remitted). If directed to do so by your instructor, record the necessary journal entry associated with Form 940.

6. Calculate total SUTA tax owed by the employer. Although Ellipses Corp. will file state forms in which this figure is reported, you are required to calculate only the total amount owed for the year.

7. Complete Copy A of Form W-2 for each of the four employees. State wages were the same as federal wages subject to federal withholding tax for each of the four employees, and the state identification number for Ellipses Corp. is the same as its federal Employer Identification Number.

8. Complete Form W-3 for Ellipses Corp. Note that the company files the paper version of the form and selects "None apply" in the *Kind of Employer* section.

Three-Month Project

> **NOTE!** Templates needed to complete these exercises, including one containing year-to-date payroll data, are included in the Student Exercise Files download for this course.

Ampersand, Inc., is a small business that operates in Somerset, VT. The company is located at 732 Appalachian Way, Somerset, VT 05363. Its federal Employer Identification Number is 44-4444444, and its president, who signs all tax forms, is Stacey Jones (telephone #802-555-3917). The company does not wish to name a third-party designee on forms.

During 2019 four individuals are employed by Ampersand, Inc. These employees are as follows:

Name	Address	Social Security #	Federal W/H Allowances	State W/H Allowances	Marital Status
Maggie Hough	13 Spruce Street Somerset, VT 05363	222-22-2222	1	1	Single
William Finnegan	7 Smith Boulevard Somerset, VT 05363	999-99-9999	2	2	Married
Stacey Jones	8110 Browning Place Somerset, VT 05363	555-55-5555	2	1	Single
Francine Stewart	101 Park Court Somerset, VT 05363	888-88-8888	3	3	Married

Note that Francine Stewart was hired in September, and her first day of work was Monday, September 23. Additionally, due to an economic downturn, Maggie Hough was laid off in late November, with her last day of work on Friday, November 22.

All employees of Ampersand, Inc., work a regular 40-hour workweek (thus all hours worked over 40 in a given week are overtime hours), receive overtime pay at a rate of 1.5 times the regular wage rate, and are paid weekly on Sunday for the most recent week (which runs from Monday through Sunday, although employees never work on weekends). The SUTA tax rate applicable to Ampersand, Inc., is 2.5%, while the SUTA wage base in Vermont is $15,600.

Earnings and voluntary deduction information for each of the four employees is as follows:

Name	Regular Wage Rate	Annual Salary	Weekly 401(k) Deduction	Weekly Charitable Contribution
Maggie Hough	$14/hour	N/A	5% of gross pay	$10
William Finnegan	$18/hour	N/A	4% of gross pay	$5
Stacey Jones	N/A	$262,000.44	N/A	$15
Francine Stewart	N/A	$94,000.40	2% of gross pay	N/A

The first three quarters of the year have passed, and all payroll-related activity has been properly accounted for as of 9/30/2019. Quarterly payroll data for each of the four employees is as follows:

Maggie Hough

Quarter	Gross Earnings	Federal Income Tax	State Income Tax	Social Security Tax	Medicare Tax	401(k) Deduction	Charitable Cont.
1st quarter	$7,280	$533	$345.80	$451.36	$105.56	$364	$130
2nd quarter	$7,280	$533	$345.80	$451.36	$105.56	$364	$130
3rd quarter	$7,280	$533	$345.80	$451.36	$105.56	$364	$130

William Finnegan

Quarter	Gross Earnings	Federal Income Tax	State Income Tax	Social Security Tax	Medicare Tax	401(k) Deduction	Charitable Cont.
1st quarter	$9,360	$403	$449.28	$580.32	$135.72	$374.40	$65
2nd quarter	$9,360	$403	$449.28	$580.32	$135.72	$374.40	$65
3rd quarter	$9,360	$403	$449.28	$580.32	$135.72	$374.40	$65

Stacey Jones

Quarter	Gross Earnings	Federal Income Tax	State Income Tax	Social Security Tax	Medicare Tax	401(k) Deduction	Charitable Cont.
1st quarter	$65,500.11	$15,655.90	$3,274.96	$4,061.07	$949.78	$0	$195
2nd quarter	$65,500.11	$15,655.90	$3,274.96	$4,061.07	$949.78	$0	$195
3rd quarter	$65,500.11	$15,655.90	$3,274.96	$117.66	$949.78	$0	$195

Francine Stewart

Quarter	Gross Earnings	Federal Income Tax	State Income Tax	Social Security Tax	Medicare Tax	401(k) Deduction	Charitable Cont.
1st quarter	$0	$0	$0	$0	$0	$0	$0
2nd quarter	$0	$0	$0	$0	$0	$0	$0
3rd quarter	$1,807.70	$148.80	$88.58	$112.08	$26.21	$36.15	$0

Note that all tax payments and filings are made on the due date. Based on the data provided here, you will complete the following:

1. Establish an employee earnings record for each of the company's four employees. Complete the top portion of each record.

2. Establish and complete the payroll register for each weekly pay period in the fourth quarter. When calculating federal income tax withholding, use the withholding tables where possible, and refer to the percentage method only when necessary. Note that as of November 25, Stacey Jones requests that her federal withholding allowances decrease from two to one (Ampersand, Inc., makes this change). Additionally, for simplicity, calculate the state income tax withholding as 5% of each employee's taxable pay (which is the same as taxable pay for FWT). Recall that state income tax withholding would ordinarily be calculated using the applicable state's withholding tables. Payroll checks are remitted to the employees in the same order (Hough, Finnegan, Jones, Stewart) each pay period and are written from a bank account that is used solely for these payments. The first payroll check written in October is check #4711.

   Note that all charitable contributions are deemed to be made on the final day of each pay period. The following information will be required for the completion of these records for the two employees who are compensated via an hourly wage:

Weekly Hours Worked

Weekly Start Date	Maggie Hough	William Finnegan
September 30	40	44
October 7	42	37
October 14	38	40
October 21	40	46.5
October 28	43.5	42
November 4	40	45
November 11	39	40

Weekly Start Date	Maggie Hough	William Finnegan
November 18	41	34.5
November 25	0	40
December 2	0	41
December 9	0	43.5
December 16	0	42.5
December 23	0	40

WARNING!   The above dates are weekly start dates. Refer to a calendar to determine the weekly end dates and associated pay dates. Keep in mind that tax liability and payment amounts are determined based on the weekly pay dates.

3. Complete an employee earnings record for the 4th quarter for each of the four employees. Divide the voluntary deductions from the payroll register appropriately across the associated columns within the employee earnings records. If directed to do so by your instructor, record the necessary journal entries for each pay period.

4. Complete Form 941 for both the 3rd and 4th quarters. Assume that the employees earned the same amount during each pay period of the 3rd quarter and that there were four, four, and five pay periods during the months of July, August, and September, respectively. Note that based on the lookback period, the company is a monthly depositor. Assume that all necessary deposits were made on a timely basis and that the employer made deposits equal to the total amount owed for each quarter. Although Vermont quarterly state payroll forms are also filed by Ampersand, Inc., you will not complete these. If directed to do so by your instructor, record the necessary journal entries associated with each Form 941 (including those required for any tax payments made).

   NOTE!   Recall from the *Form 941 Rounding Considerations* section that quarter- and year-end tax figures should not be calculated based on the total taxable earnings for the respective quarter or year. Instead, to avoid rounding discrepancies, tax figures within Part 2 of Form 941 should be determined for each employee by adding the individual taxes across each pay period.

5. Complete Form 940 for Ampersand, Inc. Note that FUTA payments are made only when required (i.e., if the employer is permitted to postpone the payment of these taxes, it will do so until a point in time when payment must be remitted). If directed to do so by your instructor, record the necessary journal entry associated with Form 940.

6. Calculate total SUTA tax owed by the employer. Although Ampersand, Inc., will file state forms in which this figure is reported, you are required to calculate only the total amount owed for the year.

7. Complete Copy A of Form W-2 for each of the four employees. State wages were the same as federal wages subject to federal withholding tax for each of the four employees, and the state identification number for Ampersand, Inc., is the same as its federal Employer Identification Number.

8. Complete Form W-3 for Ampersand, Inc. Note that the company files the paper version of the form and selects "None apply" in the *Kind of Employer* section.

Comprehensive Projects— QuickBooks Versions

These comprehensive projects are designed to be completed electronically, through the use of Intuit QuickBooks. For more information about installing the QuickBooks 2019 trial software, refer to the installation guide at: lablearning.com/qbd-install

After examining the annual payroll process, it is important to practice using the skills you've learned. In this chapter, two payroll-related projects are provided. The first project focuses on Ellipses Corp. For this company you will complete all payroll-related tasks for the month of December and will then finalize all year-end reporting. The second project focuses on Ampersand, Inc. For this company you will complete all payroll-related tasks for the 4th quarter of the year, after which you will finalize all year-end payroll reporting. You will utilize QuickBooks accounting software to complete all necessary forms and schedules for these projects.

In order to complete the exercises in this chapter, you must use QuickBooks Pro 2019. To register for the five-month trial software from Intuit that will allow you to work with sample company files, see the instructions on the inside front cover of this book or go to: lablearning.com/qbd-install

One-Month Project

NOTE!   QuickBooks portable company files needed to complete these exercises are included in the Student Exercise Files download for this course. Within that download you'll also find the "Using QuickBooks for Payroll" file. Be sure to review that file and complete the instructions prior to beginning this project.

Ellipses Corp. is a small business that operates in Herndon, VA. The company is located at 10 Period Lane, Herndon, VA 20170. Its federal identification number is 77-7777777, its state identification number is 12-345678999F-012, its state unemployment number is 1234567890, and its president, who signs all tax forms, is John Parker (telephone #571-555-0073). The company does not wish to name a third-party designee on forms. Within QuickBooks the industry associated with the company is *General Service-based Business* and the business type is *Corporation*. Ellipses Corp. is on a weekly payroll schedule.

During 2019 four individuals are employed by Ellipses Corp. These employees are as follows:

Name	Address	Social Security #	Federal W/H Allowances	State W/H Allowances	Marital Status
Hunter Cranston	85 Southern Road Herndon, VA 20170	111-11-1111	2	2	Married
Allison Harrison	203A Pine Court Herndon, VA 20170	777-77-7777	4	3	Married
John Parker	212 Tradition Lane Herndon, VA 20170	444-44-4444	1	1	Single
Pierre Sternberg	41 Seward Boulevard Herndon, VA 20170	333-33-3333	2	2	Married

Note that Pierre Sternberg was hired in November, and his first day of work was Monday, November 18, 2019. Additionally, due to an economic downturn, Allison Harrison was laid off in mid-December, with her last day of work on Friday, December 20.

All employees of Ellipses Corp. work a regular 40-hour workweek (thus all hours worked over 40 in a given week are overtime hours), receive overtime pay at a rate of 1.5 times the regular wage rate, and are paid weekly on Monday for the previous week (which runs from Saturday through Friday, although employees never work on weekends). The SUTA tax rate applicable to Ellipses Corp. is 2.53%, while the SUTA wage base in Virginia is $8,000. Note that QuickBooks defaults to a Social Security wage base of $128,400 in the Ellipses Corp. company file. Although this amount differs from the 2019 wage base, please utilize this amount when completing the payroll cycle.

Earnings and voluntary deduction information for each of the four employees is as follows:

Name	Regular Wage Rate	Annual Salary	Weekly 401(k) Deduction	Weekly Charitable Contribution
Hunter Cranston	$18/hour	N/A	6% of gross pay	$5
Allison Harrison	$24/hour	N/A	5% of gross pay	$5
John Parker	N/A	$205,400	N/A	$25
Pierre Sternberg	N/A	$111,800	10% of gross pay	N/A

The first 11 months of the year have passed, and all payroll-related activity has been properly accounted for as of 11/30/2019. Note that retirement deductions are made in association with the Williams Insurance Agency. Payroll data for each of the four employees for the first three quarters of the year, as well as for the months of October and November, is as follows:

Hunter Cranston

Period	Gross Earnings	Federal Income Tax	State Income Tax	Social Security Tax	Medicare Tax	401(k) Deduction	Charitable Cont.
1st quarter	$9,360	$455	$439.92	$580.32	$135.72	$561.60	$65
2nd quarter	$9,360	$455	$439.92	$580.32	$135.72	$561.60	$65
3rd quarter	$9,360	$455	$439.92	$580.32	$135.72	$561.60	$65
October	$3,600	$175	$169.20	$223.20	$52.20	$216	$25
November	$3,123	$128	$146.78	$193.63	$45.28	$187.38	$20

Allison Harrison

Period	Gross Earnings	Federal Income Tax	State Income Tax	Social Security Tax	Medicare Tax	401(k) Deduction	Charitable Cont.
1st quarter	$12,480	$624	$592.80	$773.76	$180.96	$624	$65
2nd quarter	$12,480	$624	$592.80	$773.76	$180.96	$624	$65
3rd quarter	$12,480	$624	$592.80	$773.76	$180.96	$624	$65
October	$4,800	$240	$228	$297.60	$69.60	$240	$25
November	$4,164	$163	$197.79	$258.17	$60.38	$208.20	$20

John Parker

Period	Gross Earnings	Federal Income Tax	State Income Tax	Social Security Tax	Medicare Tax	401(k) Deduction	Charitable Cont.
1st quarter	$51,350	$12,308.57	$2,567.50	$3,183.70	$744.58	$0	$325
2nd quarter	$51,350	$12,308.57	$2,567.50	$3,183.70	$744.58	$0	$325
3rd quarter	$51,350	$12,308.57	$2,567.50	$1,519	$744.58	$0	$325
October	$19,750	$4,734.24	$987.50	$0	$286.38	$0	$125
November	$15,800	$3,787.24	$790	$0	$229.10	$0	$100

Pierre Sternberg

Period	Gross Earnings	Federal Income Tax	State Income Tax	Social Security Tax	Medicare Tax	401(k) Deduction	Charitable Cont.
1st quarter	$0	$0	$0	$0	$0	$0	$0
2nd quarter	$0	$0	$0	$0	$0	$0	$0
3rd quarter	$0	$0	$0	$0	$0	$0	$0
October	$0	$0	$0	$0	$0	$0	$0
November	$2,150	$185.53	$96.75	$133.30	$31.18	$215	$0

Note that all tax payments and filings are made on the due date and that the company is a monthly depositor. Use *Password1* as the password for the QuickBooks company file. Based on the data provided here, you will complete the following:

1. Within QuickBooks, process payroll for December for each of the four employees. When calculating federal income tax withholding, use the withholding tables where possible and refer to the percentage method only when necessary. Additionally, for simplicity, calculate the state income tax withholding as 5% of each employee's taxable pay (which is the same as taxable pay for FWT). Recall that state income tax withholding would ordinarily be calculated using the applicable state's withholding tables. Calculate and enter the Social Security and Medicare taxes, paying attention to the cumulative pay. Employees may be subject to Additional Medicare Tax, so watch cumulative pay and calculate when applicable. This is necessary because you do not have a purchased payroll subscription. Note that all charitable contributions are remitted to the organizations on the final day of each month.

   Note that as of December 7, Hunter Cranston requests that his federal withholding allowances increase from two to three. (Ellipses Corp. makes this change.) Payroll checks are remitted to the employees in the same order (Cranston, Harrison, Parker, Sternberg) each pay period and are written from a bank account that is used solely for these payments. The dates for the first pay period you enter may need to be changed. This bank account has been established within QuickBooks to reflect a balance of $500,000 as of January 1, 2019. The first payroll check written in December is check #735.

   The following information will be required for the processing of payroll for the two employees who are compensated with an hourly wage:

Weekly Hours Worked

Weekly Start Date	Hunter Cranston	Allison Harrison
November 30	40	41
December 7	39	37
December 14	38	36
December 21	24	0

WARNING! The above dates are weekly start dates. Refer to a calendar to determine the weekly end dates and associated pay dates. Dates in QuickBooks may not be correct for the first pay period you are entering. Check them and make changes accordingly. Keep in mind that tax liability and payment amounts are determined based on the weekly pay dates.

2. Within QuickBooks, create a Payroll Report that summarizes December payroll data (in the same manner that a payroll register summarizes such data). Export the report to Microsoft Excel.

3. Within QuickBooks, create a Payroll Report that summarizes 4th quarter (October–December) payroll data. Export the report to Microsoft Excel. Then complete Form 941 for the 4th quarter. Note that based on the lookback period, the company is a monthly depositor that made timely payments throughout the entire year. Although Virginia quarterly state payroll forms are also filed by Ellipses Corp., you will not complete these.

4. Within QuickBooks, create a Payroll Report that summarizes payroll data for the entire year. Export the report to Microsoft Excel. Then complete Form 940 for Ellipses Corp. Note that 401(k) deductions are taxable for FUTA and that FUTA payments are made only when required (i.e., if the employer is permitted to postpone the payment of these taxes, it will do so until a point in time when payment must be remitted).

5. Calculate total SUTA tax owed by the employer. Although Ellipses Corp. will file state forms in which this figure is reported, you are required to calculate only the total amount owed for the year and provide it to your instructor via a Microsoft Excel file.

6. Based on the QuickBooks reports previously generated, complete Copy A of Form W-2 for each of the four employees. State wages were the same as federal wages subject to federal withholding tax for each of the four employees, and the state identification number for Ellipses Corp. was given at the beginning of the project.

7. Based on the QuickBooks reports previously generated, complete Form W-3 for Ellipses Corp. Note that the company files the paper version of the form and selects "None apply" in the *Kind of Employer* section.

Three-Month Project

NOTE! QuickBooks portable company files needed to complete these exercises are included in the Student Exercise Files download for this course. Within that download you'll also find the "Using QuickBooks for Payroll" file. Be sure to review that file and complete the instructions *prior* to beginning this project.

Ampersand, Inc., is a small business that operates in Somerset, VT. The company is located at 732 Appalachian Way, Somerset, VT 05363. Its federal identification number is 12-3456789, its state identification number is WHT999999999, its state unemployment number is 222 2222, and its president, who signs all tax forms, is Stacey Jones (telephone #802-555-3917). The business does not wish to name a third-party designee on forms. Within QuickBooks the industry associated with the company is *General Service-based Business* and the business type is *Corporation*. Ampersand, Inc., is on a weekly payroll schedule.

During 2019 four individuals are employed by Ampersand, Inc. These employees are as follows:

Name	Address	Social Security #	Federal W/H Allowances	State W/H Allowances	Marital Status
William Finnegan	7 Smith Boulevard Somerset, VT 05363	999-99-9999	2	2	Married
Maggie Hough	13 Spruce Street Somerset, VT 05363	222-22-2222	1	1	Single
Stacey Jones	8110 Browning Place Somerset, VT 05363	555-55-5555	2	1	Single
Francine Stewart	101 Park Court Somerset, VT 05363	888-88-8888	3	3	Married

Note that Francine Stewart was hired in September, and her first day of work was Monday, September 16. Additionally, due to an economic downturn, Maggie Hough was laid off in late November, with her last day of work on Friday, November 15.

All employees of Ampersand, Inc., work a regular 40-hour workweek (thus all hours worked over 40 in a given week are overtime hours), receive overtime pay at a rate of 1.5 times the regular wage rate, and are paid weekly on Monday for the prior week (which runs from Monday through Sunday, although employees never work on weekends). The SUTA tax rate applicable to Ampersand, Inc., is 2.5%, while the SUTA wage base in Vermont is $15,600. Note that QuickBooks defaults to a Social Security wage base of $128,400 in the Ampersand, Inc., company file. Although this amount differs from the 2019 wage base, please utilize this amount when completing the payroll cycle.

Earnings and voluntary deduction information for each of the four employees is as follows:

Name	Regular Wage Rate	Annual Salary	Weekly 401(k) Deduction	Weekly Charitable Contribution
William Finnegan	$20/hour	N/A	4% of gross pay	$5
Maggie Hough	$15/hour	N/A	5% of gross pay	$10
Stacey Jones	N/A	$265,044	N/A	$15
Francine Stewart	N/A	$94,120	10% of gross pay	N/A

The first three quarters of the year have passed, and all payroll-related activity has been properly accounted for as of 9/30/2019. Note that retirement deductions are made in association with the Franklin Insurance Agency. Quarterly payroll data for each of the four employees is as follows:

William Finnegan

Quarter	Gross Earnings	Federal Income Tax	State Income Tax	Social Security Tax	Medicare Tax	401(k) Deduction	Charitable Cont.
1st quarter	$10,400	$507	$499.20	$644.80	$150.80	$416	$65
2nd quarter	$10,400	$507	$499.20	$644.80	$150.80	$416	$65
3rd quarter	$10,400	$507	$499.20	$644.80	$150.80	$416	$65

Maggie Hough

Quarter	Gross Earnings	Federal Income Tax	State Income Tax	Social Security Tax	Medicare Tax	401(k) Deduction	Charitable Cont.
1st quarter	$7,800	$611	$370.50	$483.60	$113.10	$390	$130
2nd quarter	$7,800	$611	$370.50	$483.60	$113.10	$390	$130
3rd quarter	$7,800	$611	$370.50	$483.60	$113.10	$390	$130

Stacey Jones

Quarter	Gross Earnings	Federal Income Tax	State Income Tax	Social Security Tax	Medicare Tax	401(k) Deduction	Charitable Cont.
1st quarter	$66,261	$16,064.62	$3,313.05	$4,108.18	$960.79	$0	$195
2nd quarter	$66,261	$16,064.62	$3,313.05	$3,778.22	$960.79	$0	$195
3rd quarter	$66,261	$16,064.62	$3,313.05	$0	$960.79	$0	$195

Francine Stewart

Quarter	Gross Earnings	Federal Income Tax	State Income Tax	Social Security Tax	Medicare Tax	401(k) Deduction	Charitable Cont.
1st quarter	$0	$0	$0	$0	$0	$0	$0
2nd quarter	$0	$0	$0	$0	$0	$0	$0
3rd quarter	$1,810	$132.79	$81.45	$112.22	$26.25	$181	$0

Note that all tax payments and filings are made on the due date and that the company is a monthly depositor. Use *Password1* as the password for the QuickBooks company file. Based on the data provided here, you will complete the following:

1. Within QuickBooks, process payroll for the 4th quarter (October through December) for each of the four employees. When calculating federal income tax withholding, use the withholding tables where possible and refer to the percentage method only when necessary. Additionally, for simplicity, calculate the state income tax withholding as 5% of each employee's taxable pay (which is the same as taxable pay for FWT). Recall that state income tax withholding would ordinarily be calculated using the applicable state's withholding tables. Calculate and enter the Social Security and Medicare taxes, paying attention to the cumulative pay. Employees may be subject to Additional Medicare Tax, so watch cumulative pay and calculate when applicable. This is necessary because you do not have a purchased payroll subscription. Note that all charitable contributions are deemed to be remitted to the charitable organizations on the final day of each month.

   Note that as of November 25, Stacey Jones requests that her federal withholding allowances decrease from two to one. (Ampersand, Inc., makes this change.) Payroll checks are remitted to the employees in the same order (Finnegan, Hough, Jones, Stewart) each pay period and are written from a bank account that is used solely for these payments. This bank account has been established within QuickBooks to reflect a balance of $152,000 at the beginning of October. The first payroll check written in October is check #4714.

   The following information will be required for the processing of payroll for the two employees who are compensated with an hourly wage:

Weekly Hours Worked

Weekly Start Date	William Finnegan	Maggie Hough
September 30	44	41
October 7	42	42
October 14	40	39
October 21	43	40
October 28	44.5	43.5
November 4	40	40
November 11	36	30

Weekly Start Date	William Finnegan	Maggie Hough
November 18	34.5	0
November 25	40	0
December 2	40	0
December 9	39	0
December 16	40	0
December 23	40	0

2. Within QuickBooks, create a Payroll Report that summarizes payroll for the 3rd quarter (July–September). Export this report to Microsoft Excel and complete Form 941 for the 3rd quarter. Assume that the employees earned the same amount during each pay period of the 3rd quarter and that there were five, four, and four pay periods during the months of July, August, and September, respectively. Note that based on the lookback period, the company is a monthly depositor that made timely payments throughout the entire year. Although Vermont quarterly state payroll forms are also filed by Ampersand, Inc., you will not complete these.

3. Within QuickBooks, create three Payroll Reports that summarize payroll data for each of the three months (October–December) of the 4th quarter (in the same manner that a payroll register summarizes such data). Export these three reports to Microsoft Excel.

4. Within QuickBooks, create a Payroll Report that summarizes payroll data for the 4th quarter (October–December). Export this report to Microsoft Excel. Then complete Form 941 for the 4th quarter. Note that based on the lookback period, the company is a monthly depositor that made timely payments throughout the entire year. Although Vermont quarterly state payroll forms are also filed by Ampersand, Inc., you will not complete these.

5. Within QuickBooks, create a Payroll Report that summarizes payroll data for the entire year. Export the report to Microsoft Excel. Then complete Form 940 for Ampersand, Inc. Note that 401(k) deductions are taxable for FUTA and that FUTA payments are made only when required (i.e., if the employer is permitted to postpone the payment of these taxes, it will do so until a point in time when payment must be remitted).

6. Calculate total SUTA tax owed by the employer. Although Ampersand, Inc., will file state forms in which this figure is reported, you are required to calculate only the total amount owed for the year and provide it to your instructor via a Microsoft Excel file.

7. Based on the QuickBooks reports previously generated, complete Copy A of Form W-2 for each of the four employees using the blank PDF form available in the Student Exercise Files download from the Learning Resource Center (labyrinthelab.com/lrc). State wages were the same as federal wages subject to federal withholding tax for each of the four employees, and the state identification number for Ampersand, Inc., was provided earlier in the project.

8. Based on the QuickBooks reports previously generated, complete Form W-3 for Ampersand, Inc. Note that the company files the paper version of the form and selects "None apply" in the *Kind of Employer* section.

2019 Federal Tax Tables

The following tables are updated annually by the IRS and are provided within Circular E. Refer to these 2019 tables when determining federal income tax withholding throughout the textbook.

Table 5. **Percentage Method—2019 Amount for One Withholding Allowance**

Payroll Period	One Withholding Allowance
Weekly	$ 80.80
Biweekly	161.50
Semimonthly	175.00
Monthly	350.00
Quarterly	1,050.00
Semiannually	2,100.00
Annually	4,200.00
Daily or miscellaneous (each day of the payroll period)	16.20

Percentage Method Tables for Income Tax Withholding

(For Wages Paid in 2019)

TABLE 1—WEEKLY Payroll Period

(a) SINGLE person (including head of household)—

If the amount of wages (after subtracting withholding allowances) is:		The amount of income tax to withhold is:	
Not over $73		$0	
Over—	But not over—		of excess over—
$73	—$260 . .	$0.00 plus 10%	—$73
$260	—$832 . .	$18.70 plus 12%	—$260
$832	—$1,692 . .	$87.34 plus 22%	—$832
$1,692	—$3,164 . .	$276.54 plus 24%	—$1,692
$3,164	—$3,998 . .	$629.82 plus 32%	—$3,164
$3,998	—$9,887 . .	$896.70 plus 35%	—$3,998
$9,887	. . . .	$2,957.85 plus 37%	—$9,887

(b) MARRIED person—

If the amount of wages (after subtracting withholding allowances) is:		The amount of income tax to withhold is:	
Not over $227		$0	
Over—	But not over—		of excess over—
$227	—$600 . .	$0.00 plus 10%	—$227
$600	—$1,745 . .	$37.30 plus 12%	—$600
$1,745	—$3,465 . .	$174.70 plus 22%	—$1,745
$3,465	—$6,409 . .	$553.10 plus 24%	—$3,465
$6,409	—$8,077 . .	$1,259.66 plus 32%	—$6,409
$8,077	—$12,003 . .	$1,793.42 plus 35%	—$8,077
$12,003	. . . .	$3,167.52 plus 37%	—$12,003

TABLE 2—BIWEEKLY Payroll Period

(a) SINGLE person (including head of household)—

If the amount of wages (after subtracting withholding allowances) is:		The amount of income tax to withhold is:	
Not over $146		$0	
Over—	But not over—		of excess over—
$146	—$519 . .	$0.00 plus 10%	—$146
$519	—$1,664 . .	$37.30 plus 12%	—$519
$1,664	—$3,385 . .	$174.70 plus 22%	—$1,664
$3,385	—$6,328 . .	$553.32 plus 24%	—$3,385
$6,328	—$7,996 . .	$1,259.64 plus 32%	—$6,328
$7,996	—$19,773 . .	$1,793.40 plus 35%	—$7,996
$19,773	. . . .	$5,915.35 plus 37%	—$19,773

(b) MARRIED person—

If the amount of wages (after subtracting withholding allowances) is:		The amount of income tax to withhold is:	
Not over $454		$0	
Over—	But not over—		of excess over—
$454	—$1,200 . .	$0.00 plus 10%	—$454
$1,200	—$3,490 . .	$74.60 plus 12%	—$1,200
$3,490	—$6,931 . .	$349.40 plus 22%	—$3,490
$6,931	—$12,817 . .	$1,106.42 plus 24%	—$6,931
$12,817	—$16,154 . .	$2,519.06 plus 32%	—$12,817
$16,154	—$24,006 . .	$3,586.90 plus 35%	—$16,154
$24,006	. . . .	$6,335.10 plus 37%	—$24,006

TABLE 3—SEMIMONTHLY Payroll Period

(a) SINGLE person (including head of household)—

If the amount of wages (after subtracting withholding allowances) is:		The amount of income tax to withhold is:	
Not over $158		$0	
Over—	But not over—		of excess over—
$158	—$563 . .	$0.00 plus 10%	—$158
$563	—$1,803 . .	$40.50 plus 12%	—$563
$1,803	—$3,667 . .	$189.30 plus 22%	—$1,803
$3,667	—$6,855 . .	$599.38 plus 24%	—$3,667
$6,855	—$8,663 . .	$1,364.50 plus 32%	—$6,855
$8,663	—$21,421 . .	$1,943.06 plus 35%	—$8,663
$21,421	. . . .	$6,408.36 plus 37%	—$21,421

(b) MARRIED person—

If the amount of wages (after subtracting withholding allowances) is:		The amount of income tax to withhold is:	
Not over $492		$0	
Over—	But not over—		of excess over—
$492	—$1,300 . .	$0.00 plus 10%	—$492
$1,300	—$3,781 . .	$80.80 plus 12%	—$1,300
$3,781	—$7,508 . .	$378.52 plus 22%	—$3,781
$7,508	—$13,885 . .	$1,198.46 plus 24%	—$7,508
$13,885	—$17,500 . .	$2,728.94 plus 32%	—$13,885
$17,500	—$26,006 . .	$3,885.74 plus 35%	—$17,500
$26,006	. . . .	$6,862.84 plus 37%	—$26,006

TABLE 4—MONTHLY Payroll Period

(a) SINGLE person (including head of household)—

If the amount of wages (after subtracting withholding allowances) is:		The amount of income tax to withhold is:	
Not over $317		$0	
Over—	But not over—		of excess over—
$317	—$1,125 . .	$0.00 plus 10%	—$317
$1,125	—$3,606 . .	$80.80 plus 12%	—$1,125
$3,606	—$7,333 . .	$378.52 plus 22%	—$3,606
$7,333	—$13,710 . .	$1,198.46 plus 24%	—$7,333
$13,710	—$17,325 . .	$2,728.94 plus 32%	—$13,710
$17,325	—$42,842 . .	$3,885.74 plus 35%	—$17,325
$42,842	. . . .	$12,816.69 plus 37%	—$42,842

(b) MARRIED person—

If the amount of wages (after subtracting withholding allowances) is:		The amount of income tax to withhold is:	
Not over $983		$0	
Over—	But not over—		of excess over—
$983	—$2,600 . .	$0.00 plus 10%	—$983
$2,600	—$7,563 . .	$161.70 plus 12%	—$2,600
$7,563	—$15,017 . .	$757.26 plus 22%	—$7,563
$15,017	—$27,771 . .	$2,397.14 plus 24%	—$15,017
$27,771	—$35,000 . .	$5,458.10 plus 32%	—$27,771
$35,000	—$52,013 . .	$7,771.38 plus 35%	—$35,000
$52,013	. . . .	$13,725.93 plus 37%	—$52,013

Percentage Method Tables for Income Tax Withholding (continued)

(For Wages Paid in 2019)

TABLE 5—QUARTERLY Payroll Period

(a) SINGLE person (including head of household)—

If the amount of wages (after subtracting withholding allowances) is: The amount of income tax to withhold is:

Not over $950 . . . . $0

Over—	But not over—		of excess over—
$950	—$3,375	$0.00 plus 10%	—$950
$3,375	—$10,819	$242.50 plus 12%	—$3,375
$10,819	—$22,000	$1,135.78 plus 22%	—$10,819
$22,000	—$41,131	$3,595.60 plus 24%	—$22,000
$41,131	—$51,975	$8,187.04 plus 32%	—$41,131
$51,975	—$128,525	$11,657.12 plus 35%	—$51,975
$128,525	. . . .	$38,449.62 plus 37%	—$128,525

(b) MARRIED person—

If the amount of wages (after subtracting withholding allowances) is: The amount of income tax to withhold is:

Not over $2,950 . . . . $0

Over—	But not over—		of excess over—
$2,950	—$7,800	$0.00 plus 10%	—$2,950
$7,800	—$22,688	$485.00 plus 12%	—$7,800
$22,688	—$45,050	$2,271.56 plus 22%	—$22,688
$45,050	—$83,313	$7,191.20 plus 24%	—$45,050
$83,313	—$105,000	$16,374.32 plus 32%	—$83,313
$105,000	—$156,038	$23,314.16 plus 35%	—$105,000
$156,038	. . . .	$41,177.46 plus 37%	—$156,038

TABLE 6—SEMIANNUAL Payroll Period

(a) SINGLE person (including head of household)—

If the amount of wages (after subtracting withholding allowances) is: The amount of income tax to withhold is:

Not over $1,900 . . . . $0

Over—	But not over—		of excess over—
$1,900	—$6,750	$0.00 plus 10%	—$1,900
$6,750	—$21,638	$485.00 plus 12%	—$6,750
$21,638	—$44,000	$2,271.56 plus 22%	—$21,638
$44,000	—$82,263	$7,191.20 plus 24%	—$44,000
$82,263	—$103,950	$16,374.32 plus 32%	—$82,263
$103,950	—$257,050	$23,314.16 plus 35%	—$103,950
$257,050	. . . .	$76,899.16 plus 37%	—$257,050

(b) MARRIED person—

If the amount of wages (after subtracting withholding allowances) is: The amount of income tax to withhold is:

Not over $5,900 . . . . $0

Over—	But not over—		of excess over—
$5,900	—$15,600	$0.00 plus 10%	—$5,900
$15,600	—$45,375	$970.00 plus 12%	—$15,600
$45,375	—$90,100	$4,543.00 plus 22%	—$45,375
$90,100	—$166,625	$14,382.50 plus 24%	—$90,100
$166,625	—$210,000	$32,748.50 plus 32%	—$166,625
$210,000	—$312,075	$46,628.50 plus 35%	—$210,000
$312,075	. . . .	$82,354.75 plus 37%	—$312,075

TABLE 7—ANNUAL Payroll Period

(a) SINGLE person (including head of household)—

If the amount of wages (after subtracting withholding allowances) is: The amount of income tax to withhold is:

Not over $3,800 . . . . $0

Over—	But not over—		of excess over—
$3,800	—$13,500	$0.00 plus 10%	—$3,800
$13,500	—$43,275	$970.00 plus 12%	—$13,500
$43,275	—$88,000	$4,543.00 plus 22%	—$43,275
$88,000	—$164,525	$14,382.50 plus 24%	—$88,000
$164,525	—$207,900	$32,748.50 plus 32%	—$164,525
$207,900	—$514,100	$46,628.50 plus 35%	—$207,900
$514,100	. . . .	$153,798.50 plus 37%	—$514,100

(b) MARRIED person—

If the amount of wages (after subtracting withholding allowances) is: The amount of income tax to withhold is:

Not over $11,800 . . . . . . $0

Over—	But not over—		of excess over—
$11,800	—$31,200	$0.00 plus 10%	—$11,800
$31,200	—$90,750	$1,940.00 plus 12%	—$31,200
$90,750	—$180,200	$9,086.00 plus 22%	—$90,750
$180,200	—$333,250	$28,765.00 plus 24%	—$180,200
$333,250	—$420,000	$65,497.00 plus 32%	—$333,250
$420,000	—$624,150	$93,257.00 plus 35%	—$420,000
$624,150	. . . .	$164,709.50 plus 37%	—$624,150

TABLE 8—DAILY or MISCELLANEOUS Payroll Period

(a) SINGLE person (including head of household)—

If the amount of wages (after subtracting withholding allowances) divided by the number of days in the payroll period is: The amount of income tax to withhold per day is:

Not over $14.60 . . . . $0

Over—	But not over—		of excess over—
$14.60	—$51.90	$0.00 plus 10%	—$14.60
$51.90	—$166.40	$3.73 plus 12%	—$51.90
$166.40	—$338.50	$17.47 plus 22%	—$166.40
$338.50	—$632.80	$55.33 plus 24%	—$338.50
$632.80	—$799.60	$125.96 plus 32%	—$632.80
$799.60	—$1,977.30	$179.34 plus 35%	—$799.60
$1,977.30	. . . .	$591.54 plus 37%	—$1,977.30

(b) MARRIED person—

If the amount of wages (after subtracting withholding allowances) divided by the number of days in the payroll period is: The amount of income tax to withhold per day is:

Not over $45.40 . . . . $0

Over—	But not over—		of excess over—
$45.40	—$120.00	$0.00 plus 10%	—$45.40
$120.00	—$349.00	$7.46 plus 12%	—$120.00
$349.00	—$693.10	$34.94 plus 22%	—$349.00
$693.10	—$1,281.70	$110.64 plus 24%	—$693.10
$1,281.70	—$1,615.40	$251.90 plus 32%	—$1,281.70
$1,615.40	—$2,400.60	$358.68 plus 35%	—$1,615.40
$2,400.60	. . . .	$633.50 plus 37%	—$2,400.60

Wage Bracket Method Tables for Income Tax Withholding

SINGLE Persons—WEEKLY Payroll Period

(For Wages Paid through December 2019)

And the wages are—		And the number of withholding allowances claimed is—										
At least	But less than	0	1	2	3	4	5	6	7	8	9	10
		The amount of income tax to be withheld is—										
$ 0	$73	$0	$0	$0	$0	$0	$0	$0	$0	$0	$0	$0
73	84	1	0	0	0	0	0	0	0	0	0	0
84	95	2	0	0	0	0	0	0	0	0	0	0
95	106	3	0	0	0	0	0	0	0	0	0	0
106	117	4	0	0	0	0	0	0	0	0	0	0
117	128	5	0	0	0	0	0	0	0	0	0	0
128	139	6	0	0	0	0	0	0	0	0	0	0
139	150	7	0	0	0	0	0	0	0	0	0	0
150	161	8	0	0	0	0	0	0	0	0	0	0
161	172	9	1	0	0	0	0	0	0	0	0	0
172	183	10	2	0	0	0	0	0	0	0	0	0
183	194	12	3	0	0	0	0	0	0	0	0	0
194	205	13	5	0	0	0	0	0	0	0	0	0
205	216	14	6	0	0	0	0	0	0	0	0	0
216	227	15	7	0	0	0	0	0	0	0	0	0
227	238	16	8	0	0	0	0	0	0	0	0	0
238	249	17	9	1	0	0	0	0	0	0	0	0
249	260	18	10	2	0	0	0	0	0	0	0	0
260	271	19	11	3	0	0	0	0	0	0	0	0
271	282	21	12	4	0	0	0	0	0	0	0	0
282	293	22	13	5	0	0	0	0	0	0	0	0
293	304	23	14	6	0	0	0	0	0	0	0	0
304	315	25	16	7	0	0	0	0	0	0	0	0
315	326	26	17	9	1	0	0	0	0	0	0	0
326	337	27	18	10	2	0	0	0	0	0	0	0
337	348	29	19	11	3	0	0	0	0	0	0	0
348	359	30	20	12	4	0	0	0	0	0	0	0
359	370	31	22	13	5	0	0	0	0	0	0	0
370	381	33	23	14	6	0	0	0	0	0	0	0
381	392	34	24	15	7	0	0	0	0	0	0	0
392	403	35	26	16	8	0	0	0	0	0	0	0
403	414	37	27	17	9	1	0	0	0	0	0	0
414	425	38	28	18	10	2	0	0	0	0	0	0
425	436	39	29	20	12	3	0	0	0	0	0	0
436	447	40	31	21	13	5	0	0	0	0	0	0
447	458	42	32	22	14	6	0	0	0	0	0	0
458	469	43	33	24	15	7	0	0	0	0	0	0
469	480	44	35	25	16	8	0	0	0	0	0	0
480	491	46	36	26	17	9	1	0	0	0	0	0
491	502	47	37	28	18	10	2	0	0	0	0	0
502	513	48	39	29	19	11	3	0	0	0	0	0
513	524	50	40	30	21	12	4	0	0	0	0	0
524	535	51	41	32	22	13	5	0	0	0	0	0
535	546	52	43	33	23	14	6	0	0	0	0	0
546	557	54	44	34	25	16	7	0	0	0	0	0
557	568	55	45	36	26	17	9	0	0	0	0	0
568	579	56	47	37	27	18	10	2	0	0	0	0
579	590	58	48	38	29	19	11	3	0	0	0	0
590	601	59	49	40	30	20	12	4	0	0	0	0
601	612	60	51	41	31	22	13	5	0	0	0	0
612	623	62	52	42	33	23	14	6	0	0	0	0
623	634	63	53	44	34	24	15	7	0	0	0	0
634	645	64	55	45	35	25	16	8	0	0	0	0
645	656	66	56	46	36	27	17	9	1	0	0	0
656	667	67	57	47	38	28	18	10	2	0	0	0
667	678	68	59	49	39	29	20	11	3	0	0	0
678	689	70	60	50	40	31	21	13	5	0	0	0
689	700	71	61	51	42	32	22	14	6	0	0	0
700	711	72	62	53	43	33	24	15	7	0	0	0
711	722	73	64	54	44	35	25	16	8	0	0	0
722	733	75	65	55	46	36	26	17	9	1	0	0
733	744	76	66	57	47	37	28	18	10	2	0	0
744	755	77	68	58	48	39	29	19	11	3	0	0
755	766	79	69	59	50	40	30	21	12	4	0	0
766	777	80	70	61	51	41	32	22	13	5	0	0
777	788	81	72	62	52	43	33	23	14	6	0	0
788	799	83	73	63	54	44	34	25	16	7	0	0
799	810	84	74	65	55	45	36	26	17	9	0	0
810	821	85	76	66	56	47	37	27	18	10	2	0
821	832	87	77	67	58	48	38	29	19	11	3	0

Publication 15 (2019)

Wage Bracket Method Tables for Income Tax Withholding

SINGLE Persons—WEEKLY Payroll Period

(For Wages Paid through December 2019)

And the wages are–		And the number of withholding allowances claimed is—										
At least	But less than	0	1	2	3	4	5	6	7	8	9	10
		The amount of income tax to be withheld is—										
832	843	89	78	69	59	49	40	30	20	12	4	0
843	854	91	80	70	60	51	41	31	21	13	5	0
854	865	93	81	71	62	52	42	32	23	14	6	0
865	876	96	82	73	63	53	43	34	24	15	7	0
876	887	98	84	74	64	55	45	35	25	16	8	0
887	898	101	85	75	66	56	46	36	27	17	9	1
898	909	103	86	77	67	57	47	38	28	18	10	2
909	920	105	88	78	68	58	49	39	29	20	11	3
920	931	108	90	79	69	60	50	40	31	21	13	4
931	942	110	93	80	71	61	51	42	32	22	14	6
942	953	113	95	82	72	62	53	43	33	24	15	7
953	964	115	97	83	73	64	54	44	35	25	16	8
964	975	118	100	84	75	65	55	46	36	26	17	9
975	986	120	102	86	76	66	57	47	37	28	18	10
986	997	122	105	87	77	68	58	48	39	29	19	11
997	1,008	125	107	89	79	69	59	50	40	30	21	12
1,008	1,019	127	109	92	80	70	61	51	41	32	22	13
1,019	1,030	130	112	94	81	72	62	52	43	33	23	14
1,030	1,041	132	114	97	83	73	63	54	44	34	25	15
1,041	1,052	135	117	99	84	74	65	55	45	36	26	17
1,052	1,063	137	119	101	85	76	66	56	47	37	27	18
1,063	1,074	139	122	104	87	77	67	58	48	38	28	19
1,074	1,085	142	124	106	88	78	69	59	49	40	30	20
1,085	1,096	144	126	109	91	80	70	60	51	41	31	21
1,096	1,107	147	129	111	93	81	71	62	52	42	32	23
1,107	1,118	149	131	113	96	82	73	63	53	43	34	24
1,118	1,129	151	134	116	98	84	74	64	54	45	35	25
1,129	1,140	154	136	118	101	85	75	65	56	46	36	27
1,140	1,151	156	139	121	103	86	76	67	57	47	38	28
1,151	1,162	159	141	123	105	88	78	68	58	49	39	29
1,162	1,173	161	143	126	108	90	79	69	60	50	40	31
1,173	1,184	164	146	128	110	92	80	71	61	51	42	32
1,184	1,195	166	148	130	113	95	82	72	62	53	43	33
1,195	1,206	168	151	133	115	97	83	73	64	54	44	35
1,206	1,217	171	153	135	118	100	84	75	65	55	46	36
1,217	1,228	173	155	138	120	102	86	76	66	57	47	37
1,228	1,239	176	158	140	122	105	87	77	68	58	48	39
1,239	1,250	178	160	143	125	107	89	79	69	59	50	40
1,250	1,261	180	163	145	127	109	92	80	70	61	51	41
1,261	1,272	183	165	147	130	112	94	81	72	62	52	43
1,272	1,283	185	168	150	132	114	96	83	73	63	54	44
1,283	1,294	188	170	152	134	117	99	84	74	65	55	45
1,294	1,305	190	172	155	137	119	101	85	76	66	56	47
1,305	1,316	193	175	157	139	122	104	87	77	67	58	48
1,316	1,327	195	177	159	142	124	106	88	78	69	59	49
1,327	1,338	197	180	162	144	126	109	91	80	70	60	50
1,338	1,349	200	182	164	147	129	111	93	81	71	61	52
1,349	1,360	202	184	167	149	131	113	96	82	73	63	53
1,360	1,371	205	187	169	151	134	116	98	84	74	64	54
1,371	1,382	207	189	172	154	136	118	100	85	75	65	56
1,382	1,393	210	192	174	156	138	121	103	86	76	67	57
1,393	1,404	212	194	176	159	141	123	105	88	78	68	58
1,404	1,415	214	197	179	161	143	126	108	90	79	69	60
1,415	1,426	217	199	181	163	146	128	110	92	80	71	61
1,426	1,437	219	201	184	166	148	130	113	95	82	72	62
1,437	1,448	222	204	186	168	151	133	115	97	83	73	64
1,448	1,459	224	206	189	171	153	135	117	100	84	75	65
1,459	1,470	226	209	191	173	155	138	120	102	86	76	66
1,470	1,481	229	211	193	176	158	140	122	105	87	77	68
1,481	1,492	231	214	196	178	160	142	125	107	89	79	69
1,492	1,503	234	216	198	180	163	145	127	109	92	80	70
1,503	1,514	236	218	201	183	165	147	130	112	94	81	72
1,514	1,525	239	221	203	185	167	150	132	114	96	83	73
1,525	1,536	241	223	205	188	170	152	134	117	99	84	74
1,536	1,547	243	226	208	190	172	155	137	119	101	85	76

1,547 and over   Use Table 1(a) for a SINGLE person on page 46. Also see the instructions on page 44.

Wage Bracket Method Tables for Income Tax Withholding

MARRIED Persons—WEEKLY Payroll Period

(For Wages Paid through December 2019)

And the wages are–		And the number of withholding allowances claimed is—										
At least	But less than	0	1	2	3	4	5	6	7	8	9	10
		The amount of income tax to be withheld is—										
$ 0	$227	$0	$0	$0	$0	$0	$0	$0	$0	$0	$0	$0
227	238	1	0	0	0	0	0	0	0	0	0	0
238	249	2	0	0	0	0	0	0	0	0	0	0
249	260	3	0	0	0	0	0	0	0	0	0	0
260	271	4	0	0	0	0	0	0	0	0	0	0
271	282	5	0	0	0	0	0	0	0	0	0	0
282	293	6	0	0	0	0	0	0	0	0	0	0
293	304	7	0	0	0	0	0	0	0	0	0	0
304	315	8	0	0	0	0	0	0	0	0	0	0
315	326	9	1	0	0	0	0	0	0	0	0	0
326	337	10	2	0	0	0	0	0	0	0	0	0
337	348	12	3	0	0	0	0	0	0	0	0	0
348	359	13	5	0	0	0	0	0	0	0	0	0
359	370	14	6	0	0	0	0	0	0	0	0	0
370	381	15	7	0	0	0	0	0	0	0	0	0
381	392	16	8	0	0	0	0	0	0	0	0	0
392	403	17	9	1	0	0	0	0	0	0	0	0
403	414	18	10	2	0	0	0	0	0	0	0	0
414	425	19	11	3	0	0	0	0	0	0	0	0
425	436	20	12	4	0	0	0	0	0	0	0	0
436	447	21	13	5	0	0	0	0	0	0	0	0
447	458	23	14	6	0	0	0	0	0	0	0	0
458	469	24	16	8	0	0	0	0	0	0	0	0
469	480	25	17	9	1	0	0	0	0	0	0	0
480	491	26	18	10	2	0	0	0	0	0	0	0
491	502	27	19	11	3	0	0	0	0	0	0	0
502	513	28	20	12	4	0	0	0	0	0	0	0
513	524	29	21	13	5	0	0	0	0	0	0	0
524	535	30	22	14	6	0	0	0	0	0	0	0
535	546	31	23	15	7	0	0	0	0	0	0	0
546	557	32	24	16	8	0	0	0	0	0	0	0
557	568	34	25	17	9	1	0	0	0	0	0	0
568	579	35	27	19	10	2	0	0	0	0	0	0
579	590	36	28	20	12	3	0	0	0	0	0	0
590	601	37	29	21	13	5	0	0	0	0	0	0
601	612	38	30	22	14	6	0	0	0	0	0	0
612	623	39	31	23	15	7	0	0	0	0	0	0
623	634	41	32	24	16	8	0	0	0	0	0	0
634	645	42	33	25	17	9	1	0	0	0	0	0
645	656	43	34	26	18	10	2	0	0	0	0	0
656	667	45	35	27	19	11	3	0	0	0	0	0
667	678	46	36	28	20	12	4	0	0	0	0	0
678	689	47	38	30	21	13	5	0	0	0	0	0
689	700	49	39	31	23	14	6	0	0	0	0	0
700	711	50	40	32	24	16	7	0	0	0	0	0
711	722	51	42	33	25	17	9	0	0	0	0	0
722	733	53	43	34	26	18	10	2	0	0	0	0
733	744	54	44	35	27	19	11	3	0	0	0	0
744	755	55	46	36	28	20	12	4	0	0	0	0
755	766	57	47	37	29	21	13	5	0	0	0	0
766	777	58	48	39	30	22	14	6	0	0	0	0
777	788	59	50	40	31	23	15	7	0	0	0	0
788	799	61	51	41	32	24	16	8	0	0	0	0
799	810	62	52	42	34	25	17	9	1	0	0	0
810	821	63	53	44	35	27	18	10	2	0	0	0
821	832	64	55	45	36	28	20	11	3	0	0	0
832	843	66	56	46	37	29	21	13	5	0	0	0
843	854	67	57	48	38	30	22	14	6	0	0	0
854	865	68	59	49	39	31	23	15	7	0	0	0
865	876	70	60	50	41	32	24	16	8	0	0	0
876	887	71	61	52	42	33	25	17	9	1	0	0
887	898	72	63	53	43	34	26	18	10	2	0	0
898	909	74	64	54	45	35	27	19	11	3	0	0
909	920	75	65	56	46	36	28	20	12	4	0	0
920	931	76	67	57	47	38	29	21	13	5	0	0
931	942	78	68	58	49	39	31	22	14	6	0	0
942	953	79	69	60	50	40	32	24	16	7	0	0
953	964	80	71	61	51	42	33	25	17	9	0	0
964	975	82	72	62	53	43	34	26	18	10	2	0
975	986	83	73	64	54	44	35	27	19	11	3	0

Wage Bracket Method Tables for Income Tax Withholding

MARRIED Persons—WEEKLY Payroll Period

(For Wages Paid through December 2019)

And the wages are—		And the number of withholding allowances claimed is—										
At least	But less than	0	1	2	3	4	5	6	7	8	9	10
		The amount of income tax to be withheld is—										
986	997	84	75	65	55	46	36	28	20	12	4	0
997	1,008	86	76	66	57	47	37	29	21	13	5	0
1,008	1,019	87	77	68	58	48	38	30	22	14	6	0
1,019	1,030	88	79	69	59	49	40	31	23	15	7	0
1,030	1,041	90	80	70	60	51	41	32	24	16	8	0
1,041	1,052	91	81	72	62	52	42	33	25	17	9	1
1,052	1,063	92	83	73	63	53	44	35	27	18	10	2
1,063	1,074	94	84	74	64	55	45	36	28	20	11	3
1,074	1,085	95	85	75	66	56	46	37	29	21	13	4
1,085	1,096	96	86	77	67	57	48	38	30	22	14	6
1,096	1,107	97	88	78	68	59	49	39	31	23	15	7
1,107	1,118	99	89	79	70	60	50	41	32	24	16	8
1,118	1,129	100	90	81	71	61	52	42	33	25	17	9
1,129	1,140	101	92	82	72	63	53	43	34	26	18	10
1,140	1,151	103	93	83	74	64	54	45	35	27	19	11
1,151	1,162	104	94	85	75	65	56	46	36	28	20	12
1,162	1,173	105	96	86	76	67	57	47	38	29	21	13
1,173	1,184	107	97	87	78	68	58	49	39	31	22	14
1,184	1,195	108	98	89	79	69	60	50	40	32	24	15
1,195	1,206	109	100	90	80	71	61	51	42	33	25	17
1,206	1,217	111	101	91	82	72	62	53	43	34	26	18
1,217	1,228	112	102	93	83	73	64	54	44	35	27	19
1,228	1,239	113	104	94	84	75	65	55	45	36	28	20
1,239	1,250	115	105	95	86	76	66	56	47	37	29	21
1,250	1,261	116	106	97	87	77	68	58	48	38	30	22
1,261	1,272	117	108	98	88	79	69	59	49	40	31	23
1,272	1,283	119	109	99	90	80	70	60	51	41	32	24
1,283	1,294	120	110	101	91	81	71	62	52	42	33	25
1,294	1,305	121	112	102	92	82	73	63	53	44	35	26
1,305	1,316	123	113	103	93	84	74	64	55	45	36	28
1,316	1,327	124	114	105	95	85	75	66	56	46	37	29
1,327	1,338	125	116	106	96	86	77	67	57	48	38	30
1,338	1,349	127	117	107	97	88	78	68	59	49	39	31
1,349	1,360	128	118	108	99	89	79	70	60	50	41	32
1,360	1,371	129	119	110	100	90	81	71	61	52	42	33
1,371	1,382	130	121	111	101	92	82	72	63	53	43	34
1,382	1,393	132	122	112	103	93	83	74	64	54	45	35
1,393	1,404	133	123	114	104	94	85	75	65	56	46	36
1,404	1,415	134	125	115	105	96	86	76	67	57	47	38
1,415	1,426	136	126	116	107	97	87	78	68	58	49	39
1,426	1,437	137	127	118	108	98	89	79	69	60	50	40
1,437	1,448	138	129	119	109	100	90	80	71	61	51	41
1,448	1,459	140	130	120	111	101	91	82	72	62	52	43
1,459	1,470	141	131	122	112	102	93	83	73	64	54	44
1,470	1,481	142	133	123	113	104	94	84	75	65	55	45
1,481	1,492	144	134	124	115	105	95	86	76	66	56	47
1,492	1,503	145	135	126	116	106	97	87	77	67	58	48
1,503	1,514	146	137	127	117	108	98	88	78	69	59	49
1,514	1,525	148	138	128	119	109	99	89	80	70	60	51
1,525	1,536	149	139	130	120	110	101	91	81	71	62	52
1,536	1,547	150	141	131	121	112	102	92	82	73	63	53
1,547	1,558	152	142	132	123	113	103	93	84	74	64	55
1,558	1,569	153	143	134	124	114	104	95	85	75	66	56
1,569	1,580	154	145	135	125	115	106	96	86	77	67	57
1,580	1,591	156	146	136	126	117	107	97	88	78	68	59
1,591	1,602	157	147	138	128	118	108	99	89	79	70	60
1,602	1,613	158	149	139	129	119	110	100	90	81	71	61
1,613	1,624	160	150	140	130	121	111	101	92	82	72	63
1,624	1,635	161	151	141	132	122	112	103	93	83	74	64
1,635	1,646	162	152	143	133	123	114	104	94	85	75	65
1,646	1,657	163	154	144	134	125	115	105	96	86	76	67
1,657	1,668	165	155	145	136	126	116	107	97	87	78	68
1,668	1,679	166	156	147	137	127	118	108	98	89	79	69
1,679	1,690	167	158	148	138	129	119	109	100	90	80	71
1,690	1,701	169	159	149	140	130	120	111	101	91	82	72
1,701	1,711	170	160	151	141	131	122	112	102	92	83	73

1,711 and over   Use Table 1(b) for a MARRIED person on page 46. Also see the instructions on page 44.

Wage Bracket Method Tables for Income Tax Withholding

SINGLE Persons—BIWEEKLY Payroll Period

(For Wages Paid through December 2019)

And the wages are—		And the number of withholding allowances claimed is—										
At least	But less than	0	1	2	3	4	5	6	7	8	9	10
		The amount of income tax to be withheld is—										
$ 0	$146	$0	$0	$0	$0	$0	$0	$0	$0	$0	$0	$0
146	157	1	0	0	0	0	0	0	0	0	0	0
157	168	2	0	0	0	0	0	0	0	0	0	0
168	179	3	0	0	0	0	0	0	0	0	0	0
179	190	4	0	0	0	0	0	0	0	0	0	0
190	201	5	0	0	0	0	0	0	0	0	0	0
201	212	6	0	0	0	0	0	0	0	0	0	0
212	223	7	0	0	0	0	0	0	0	0	0	0
223	234	8	0	0	0	0	0	0	0	0	0	0
234	245	9	0	0	0	0	0	0	0	0	0	0
245	256	10	0	0	0	0	0	0	0	0	0	0
256	267	12	0	0	0	0	0	0	0	0	0	0
267	278	13	0	0	0	0	0	0	0	0	0	0
278	289	14	0	0	0	0	0	0	0	0	0	0
289	300	15	0	0	0	0	0	0	0	0	0	0
300	311	16	0	0	0	0	0	0	0	0	0	0
311	322	17	1	0	0	0	0	0	0	0	0	0
322	333	18	2	0	0	0	0	0	0	0	0	0
333	344	19	3	0	0	0	0	0	0	0	0	0
344	355	20	4	0	0	0	0	0	0	0	0	0
355	366	21	5	0	0	0	0	0	0	0	0	0
366	377	23	6	0	0	0	0	0	0	0	0	0
377	388	24	7	0	0	0	0	0	0	0	0	0
388	399	25	9	0	0	0	0	0	0	0	0	0
399	410	26	10	0	0	0	0	0	0	0	0	0
410	421	27	11	0	0	0	0	0	0	0	0	0
421	432	28	12	0	0	0	0	0	0	0	0	0
432	443	29	13	0	0	0	0	0	0	0	0	0
443	454	30	14	0	0	0	0	0	0	0	0	0
454	465	31	15	0	0	0	0	0	0	0	0	0
465	476	32	16	0	0	0	0	0	0	0	0	0
476	487	34	17	1	0	0	0	0	0	0	0	0
487	498	35	18	2	0	0	0	0	0	0	0	0
498	509	36	20	3	0	0	0	0	0	0	0	0
509	529	37	21	5	0	0	0	0	0	0	0	0
529	549	40	23	7	0	0	0	0	0	0	0	0
549	569	42	25	9	0	0	0	0	0	0	0	0
569	589	44	27	11	0	0	0	0	0	0	0	0
589	609	47	29	13	0	0	0	0	0	0	0	0
609	629	49	31	15	0	0	0	0	0	0	0	0
629	649	52	33	17	1	0	0	0	0	0	0	0
649	669	54	35	19	3	0	0	0	0	0	0	0
669	689	56	37	21	5	0	0	0	0	0	0	0
689	709	59	39	23	7	0	0	0	0	0	0	0
709	729	61	42	25	9	0	0	0	0	0	0	0
729	749	64	44	27	11	0	0	0	0	0	0	0
749	769	66	47	29	13	0	0	0	0	0	0	0
769	789	68	49	31	15	0	0	0	0	0	0	0
789	809	71	51	33	17	1	0	0	0	0	0	0
809	829	73	54	35	19	3	0	0	0	0	0	0
829	849	76	56	37	21	5	0	0	0	0	0	0
849	869	78	59	39	23	7	0	0	0	0	0	0
869	889	80	61	42	25	9	0	0	0	0	0	0
889	909	83	63	44	27	11	0	0	0	0	0	0
909	929	85	66	47	29	13	0	0	0	0	0	0
929	949	88	68	49	31	15	0	0	0	0	0	0
949	969	90	71	51	33	17	1	0	0	0	0	0
969	989	92	73	54	35	19	3	0	0	0	0	0
989	1,009	95	75	56	37	21	5	0	0	0	0	0
1,009	1,029	97	78	59	39	23	7	0	0	0	0	0
1,029	1,049	100	80	61	42	25	9	0	0	0	0	0
1,049	1,069	102	83	63	44	27	11	0	0	0	0	0
1,069	1,089	104	85	66	46	29	13	0	0	0	0	0
1,089	1,109	107	87	68	49	31	15	0	0	0	0	0
1,109	1,129	109	90	71	51	33	17	0	0	0	0	0
1,129	1,149	112	92	73	54	35	19	2	0	0	0	0
1,149	1,169	114	95	75	56	37	21	4	0	0	0	0
1,169	1,189	116	97	78	58	39	23	6	0	0	0	0
1,189	1,209	119	99	80	61	41	25	8	0	0	0	0
1,209	1,229	121	102	83	63	44	27	10	0	0	0	0

Publication 15 (2019)

Wage Bracket Method Tables for Income Tax Withholding

SINGLE Persons—BIWEEKLY Payroll Period

(For Wages Paid through December 2019)

And the wages are—		And the number of withholding allowances claimed is—										
At least	But less than	0	1	2	3	4	5	6	7	8	9	10
		The amount of income tax to be withheld is—										
1,229	1,249	124	104	85	66	46	29	12	0	0	0	0
1,249	1,269	126	107	87	68	49	31	14	0	0	0	0
1,269	1,289	128	109	90	70	51	33	16	0	0	0	0
1,289	1,309	131	111	92	73	53	35	18	2	0	0	0
1,309	1,329	133	114	95	75	56	37	20	4	0	0	0
1,329	1,349	136	116	97	78	58	39	22	6	0	0	0
1,349	1,369	138	119	99	80	61	41	24	8	0	0	0
1,369	1,389	140	121	102	82	63	44	26	10	0	0	0
1,389	1,409	143	123	104	85	65	46	28	12	0	0	0
1,409	1,429	145	126	107	87	68	48	30	14	0	0	0
1,429	1,449	148	128	109	90	70	51	32	16	0	0	0
1,449	1,469	150	131	111	92	73	53	34	18	2	0	0
1,469	1,489	152	133	114	94	75	56	36	20	4	0	0
1,489	1,509	155	135	116	97	77	58	39	22	6	0	0
1,509	1,529	157	138	119	99	80	60	41	24	8	0	0
1,529	1,549	160	140	121	102	82	63	43	26	10	0	0
1,549	1,569	162	143	123	104	85	65	46	28	12	0	0
1,569	1,589	164	145	126	106	87	68	48	30	14	0	0
1,589	1,609	167	147	128	109	89	70	51	32	16	0	0
1,609	1,629	169	150	131	111	92	72	53	34	18	2	0
1,629	1,649	172	152	133	114	94	75	55	36	20	4	0
1,649	1,669	174	155	135	116	97	77	58	38	22	6	0
1,669	1,689	178	157	138	118	99	80	60	41	24	8	0
1,689	1,709	182	159	140	121	101	82	63	43	26	10	0
1,709	1,729	187	162	143	123	104	84	65	46	28	12	0
1,729	1,749	191	164	145	126	106	87	67	48	30	14	0
1,749	1,769	196	167	147	128	109	89	70	50	32	16	0
1,769	1,789	200	169	150	130	111	92	72	53	34	18	2
1,789	1,809	204	171	152	133	113	94	75	55	36	20	4
1,809	1,829	209	174	155	135	116	96	77	58	38	22	6
1,829	1,849	213	178	157	138	118	99	79	60	41	24	8
1,849	1,869	218	182	159	140	121	101	82	62	43	26	10
1,869	1,889	222	186	162	142	123	104	84	65	45	28	12
1,889	1,909	226	191	164	145	125	106	87	67	48	30	14
1,909	1,929	231	195	167	147	128	108	89	70	50	32	16
1,929	1,949	235	200	169	150	130	111	91	72	53	34	18
1,949	1,969	240	204	171	152	133	113	94	74	55	36	20
1,969	1,989	244	208	174	154	135	116	96	77	57	38	22
1,989	2,009	248	213	177	157	137	118	99	79	60	40	24
2,009	2,029	253	217	182	159	140	120	101	82	62	43	26
2,029	2,049	257	222	186	162	142	123	103	84	65	45	28
2,049	2,069	262	226	190	164	145	125	106	86	67	48	30
2,069	2,089	266	230	195	166	147	128	108	89	69	50	32
2,089	2,109	270	235	199	169	149	130	111	91	72	52	34
2,109	2,129	275	239	204	171	152	132	113	94	74	55	36
2,129	2,149	279	244	208	174	154	135	115	96	77	57	38
2,149	2,169	284	248	212	177	157	137	118	98	79	60	40
2,169	2,189	288	252	217	181	159	140	120	101	81	62	43
2,189	2,209	292	257	221	186	161	142	123	103	84	64	45
2,209	2,229	297	261	226	190	164	144	125	106	86	67	47
2,229	2,249	301	266	230	195	166	147	127	108	89	69	50
2,249	2,269	306	270	234	199	169	149	130	110	91	72	52
2,269	2,289	310	274	239	203	171	152	132	113	93	74	55
2,289	2,309	314	279	243	208	173	154	135	115	96	76	57
2,309	2,329	319	283	248	212	177	156	137	118	98	79	59
2,329	2,349	323	288	252	217	181	159	139	120	101	81	62
2,349	2,369	328	292	256	221	185	161	142	122	103	84	64
2,369	2,389	332	296	261	225	190	164	144	125	105	86	67
2,389	2,409	336	301	265	230	194	166	147	127	108	88	69
2,409	2,429	341	305	270	234	199	168	149	130	110	91	71
2,429	2,449	345	310	274	239	203	171	151	132	113	93	74
2,449	2,469	350	314	278	243	207	173	154	134	115	96	76
2,469	2,489	354	318	283	247	212	176	156	137	117	98	79
2,489	2,509	358	323	287	252	216	181	159	139	120	100	81
2,509	2,529	363	327	292	256	221	185	161	142	122	103	83

2,529 and over	Use Table 2(a) for a SINGLE person on page 46. Also see the instructions on page 44.

Wage Bracket Method Tables for Income Tax Withholding

MARRIED Persons—BIWEEKLY Payroll Period

(For Wages Paid through December 2019)

And the wages are—		And the number of withholding allowances claimed is—										
At least	But less than	0	1	2	3	4	5	6	7	8	9	10
		The amount of income tax to be withheld is—										
$ 0	$454	$0	$0	$0	$0	$0	$0	$0	$0	$0	$0	$0
454	464	1	0	0	0	0	0	0	0	0	0	0
464	474	2	0	0	0	0	0	0	0	0	0	0
474	484	3	0	0	0	0	0	0	0	0	0	0
484	494	4	0	0	0	0	0	0	0	0	0	0
494	504	5	0	0	0	0	0	0	0	0	0	0
504	524	6	0	0	0	0	0	0	0	0	0	0
524	544	8	0	0	0	0	0	0	0	0	0	0
544	564	10	0	0	0	0	0	0	0	0	0	0
564	584	12	0	0	0	0	0	0	0	0	0	0
584	604	14	0	0	0	0	0	0	0	0	0	0
604	624	16	0	0	0	0	0	0	0	0	0	0
624	644	18	2	0	0	0	0	0	0	0	0	0
644	664	20	4	0	0	0	0	0	0	0	0	0
664	684	22	6	0	0	0	0	0	0	0	0	0
684	704	24	8	0	0	0	0	0	0	0	0	0
704	724	26	10	0	0	0	0	0	0	0	0	0
724	744	28	12	0	0	0	0	0	0	0	0	0
744	764	30	14	0	0	0	0	0	0	0	0	0
764	784	32	16	0	0	0	0	0	0	0	0	0
784	804	34	18	2	0	0	0	0	0	0	0	0
804	824	36	20	4	0	0	0	0	0	0	0	0
824	844	38	22	6	0	0	0	0	0	0	0	0
844	864	40	24	8	0	0	0	0	0	0	0	0
864	884	42	26	10	0	0	0	0	0	0	0	0
884	904	44	28	12	0	0	0	0	0	0	0	0
904	924	46	30	14	0	0	0	0	0	0	0	0
924	944	48	32	16	0	0	0	0	0	0	0	0
944	964	50	34	18	2	0	0	0	0	0	0	0
964	984	52	36	20	4	0	0	0	0	0	0	0
984	1,004	54	38	22	6	0	0	0	0	0	0	0
1,004	1,024	56	40	24	8	0	0	0	0	0	0	0
1,024	1,044	58	42	26	10	0	0	0	0	0	0	0
1,044	1,064	60	44	28	12	0	0	0	0	0	0	0
1,064	1,084	62	46	30	14	0	0	0	0	0	0	0
1,084	1,104	64	48	32	16	0	0	0	0	0	0	0
1,104	1,124	66	50	34	18	1	0	0	0	0	0	0
1,124	1,144	68	52	36	20	3	0	0	0	0	0	0
1,144	1,164	70	54	38	22	5	0	0	0	0	0	0
1,164	1,184	72	56	40	24	7	0	0	0	0	0	0
1,184	1,204	74	58	42	26	9	0	0	0	0	0	0
1,204	1,224	76	60	44	28	11	0	0	0	0	0	0
1,224	1,244	79	62	46	30	13	0	0	0	0	0	0
1,244	1,264	81	64	48	32	15	0	0	0	0	0	0
1,264	1,284	83	66	50	34	17	1	0	0	0	0	0
1,284	1,304	86	68	52	36	19	3	0	0	0	0	0
1,304	1,324	88	70	54	38	21	5	0	0	0	0	0
1,324	1,344	91	72	56	40	23	7	0	0	0	0	0
1,344	1,364	93	74	58	42	25	9	0	0	0	0	0
1,364	1,384	95	76	60	44	27	11	0	0	0	0	0
1,384	1,404	98	79	62	46	29	13	0	0	0	0	0
1,404	1,424	100	81	64	48	31	15	0	0	0	0	0
1,424	1,444	103	83	66	50	33	17	1	0	0	0	0
1,444	1,464	105	86	68	52	35	19	3	0	0	0	0
1,464	1,484	107	88	70	54	37	21	5	0	0	0	0
1,484	1,504	110	91	72	56	39	23	7	0	0	0	0
1,504	1,524	112	93	74	58	41	25	9	0	0	0	0
1,524	1,544	115	95	76	60	43	27	11	0	0	0	0
1,544	1,564	117	98	78	62	45	29	13	0	0	0	0
1,564	1,584	119	100	81	64	47	31	15	0	0	0	0
1,584	1,604	122	103	83	66	49	33	17	1	0	0	0
1,604	1,624	124	105	86	68	51	35	19	3	0	0	0
1,624	1,644	127	107	88	70	53	37	21	5	0	0	0
1,644	1,664	129	110	90	72	55	39	23	7	0	0	0
1,664	1,684	131	112	93	74	57	41	25	9	0	0	0
1,684	1,704	134	115	95	76	59	43	27	11	0	0	0
1,704	1,724	136	117	98	78	61	45	29	13	0	0	0
1,724	1,744	139	119	100	81	63	47	31	15	0	0	0
1,744	1,764	141	122	102	83	65	49	33	17	1	0	0
1,764	1,784	143	124	105	85	67	51	35	19	3	0	0

Wage Bracket Method Tables for Income Tax Withholding

MARRIED Persons—BIWEEKLY Payroll Period

(For Wages Paid through December 2019)

And the wages are—		And the number of withholding allowances claimed is—										
At least	But less than	0	1	2	3	4	5	6	7	8	9	10
		The amount of income tax to be withheld is—										
1,784	1,804	146	127	107	88	69	53	37	21	5	0	0
1,804	1,824	148	129	110	90	71	55	39	23	7	0	0
1,824	1,844	151	131	112	93	73	57	41	25	9	0	0
1,844	1,864	153	134	114	95	76	59	43	27	11	0	0
1,864	1,884	155	136	117	97	78	61	45	29	13	0	0
1,884	1,904	158	139	119	100	80	63	47	31	15	0	0
1,904	1,924	160	141	122	102	83	65	49	33	17	1	0
1,924	1,944	163	143	124	105	85	67	51	35	19	3	0
1,944	1,964	165	146	126	107	88	69	53	37	21	5	0
1,964	1,984	167	148	129	109	90	71	55	39	23	7	0
1,984	2,004	170	151	131	112	92	73	57	41	25	9	0
2,004	2,024	172	153	134	114	95	75	59	43	27	11	0
2,024	2,044	175	155	136	117	97	78	61	45	29	13	0
2,044	2,064	177	158	138	119	100	80	63	47	31	15	0
2,064	2,084	179	160	141	121	102	83	65	49	33	17	0
2,084	2,104	182	163	143	124	104	85	67	51	35	19	2
2,104	2,124	184	165	146	126	107	87	69	53	37	21	4
2,124	2,144	187	167	148	129	109	90	71	55	39	23	6
2,144	2,164	189	170	150	131	112	92	73	57	41	25	8
2,164	2,184	191	172	153	133	114	95	75	59	43	27	10
2,184	2,204	194	175	155	136	116	97	78	61	45	29	12
2,204	2,224	196	177	158	138	119	99	80	63	47	31	14
2,224	2,244	199	179	160	141	121	102	82	65	49	33	16
2,244	2,264	201	182	162	143	124	104	85	67	51	35	18
2,264	2,284	203	184	165	145	126	107	87	69	53	37	20
2,284	2,304	206	187	167	148	128	109	90	71	55	39	22
2,304	2,324	208	189	170	150	131	111	92	73	57	41	24
2,324	2,344	211	191	172	153	133	114	94	75	59	43	26
2,344	2,364	213	194	174	155	136	116	97	77	61	45	28
2,364	2,384	215	196	177	157	138	119	99	80	63	47	30
2,384	2,404	218	199	179	160	140	121	102	82	65	49	32
2,404	2,424	220	201	182	162	143	123	104	85	67	51	34
2,424	2,444	223	203	184	165	145	126	106	87	69	53	36
2,444	2,464	225	206	186	167	148	128	109	89	71	55	38
2,464	2,484	227	208	189	169	150	131	111	92	73	57	40
2,484	2,504	230	211	191	172	152	133	114	94	75	59	42
2,504	2,524	232	213	194	174	155	135	116	97	77	61	44
2,524	2,544	235	215	196	177	157	138	118	99	80	63	46
2,544	2,564	237	218	198	179	160	140	121	101	82	65	48
2,564	2,584	239	220	201	181	162	143	123	104	84	67	50
2,584	2,604	242	223	203	184	164	145	126	106	87	69	52
2,604	2,624	244	225	206	186	167	147	128	109	89	71	54
2,624	2,644	247	227	208	189	169	150	130	111	92	73	56
2,644	2,664	249	230	210	191	172	152	133	113	94	75	58
2,664	2,684	251	232	213	193	174	155	135	116	96	77	60
2,684	2,704	254	235	215	196	176	157	138	118	99	79	62
2,704	2,724	256	237	218	198	179	159	140	121	101	82	64
2,724	2,744	259	239	220	201	181	162	142	123	104	84	66
2,744	2,764	261	242	222	203	184	164	145	125	106	87	68
2,764	2,784	263	244	225	205	186	167	147	128	108	89	70
2,784	2,804	266	247	227	208	188	169	150	130	111	91	72
2,804	2,824	268	249	230	210	191	171	152	133	113	94	74
2,824	2,844	271	251	232	213	193	174	154	135	116	96	77
2,844	2,864	273	254	234	215	196	176	157	137	118	99	79
2,864	2,884	275	256	237	217	198	179	159	140	120	101	82
2,884	2,904	278	259	239	220	200	181	162	142	123	103	84
2,904	2,924	280	261	242	222	203	183	164	145	125	106	86
2,924	2,944	283	263	244	225	205	186	166	147	128	108	89
2,944	2,964	285	266	246	227	208	188	169	149	130	111	91
2,964	2,984	287	268	249	229	210	191	171	152	132	113	94
2,984	3,004	290	271	251	232	212	193	174	154	135	115	96
3,004	3,024	292	273	254	234	215	195	176	157	137	118	98
3,024	3,044	295	275	256	237	217	198	178	159	140	120	101
3,044	3,064	297	278	258	239	220	200	181	161	142	123	103
3,064	3,084	299	280	261	241	222	203	183	164	144	125	106
3,084	3,104	302	283	263	244	224	205	186	166	147	127	108

3,104 and over	Use Table 2(b) for a MARRIED person on page 46. Also see the instructions on page 44.

Wage Bracket Method Tables for Income Tax Withholding

SINGLE Persons—SEMIMONTHLY Payroll Period

(For Wages Paid through December 2019)

And the wages are—		And the number of withholding allowances claimed is—										
At least	But less than	0	1	2	3	4	5	6	7	8	9	10
		The amount of income tax to be withheld is—										
$ 0	$158	$0	$0	$0	$0	$0	$0	$0	$0	$0	$0	$0
158	169	1	0	0	0	0	0	0	0	0	0	0
169	180	2	0	0	0	0	0	0	0	0	0	0
180	191	3	0	0	0	0	0	0	0	0	0	0
191	202	4	0	0	0	0	0	0	0	0	0	0
202	213	5	0	0	0	0	0	0	0	0	0	0
213	224	6	0	0	0	0	0	0	0	0	0	0
224	235	7	0	0	0	0	0	0	0	0	0	0
235	246	8	0	0	0	0	0	0	0	0	0	0
246	257	9	0	0	0	0	0	0	0	0	0	0
257	268	10	0	0	0	0	0	0	0	0	0	0
268	279	12	0	0	0	0	0	0	0	0	0	0
279	290	13	0	0	0	0	0	0	0	0	0	0
290	301	14	0	0	0	0	0	0	0	0	0	0
301	312	15	0	0	0	0	0	0	0	0	0	0
312	323	16	0	0	0	0	0	0	0	0	0	0
323	334	17	0	0	0	0	0	0	0	0	0	0
334	345	18	1	0	0	0	0	0	0	0	0	0
345	356	19	2	0	0	0	0	0	0	0	0	0
356	367	20	3	0	0	0	0	0	0	0	0	0
367	378	21	4	0	0	0	0	0	0	0	0	0
378	389	23	5	0	0	0	0	0	0	0	0	0
389	400	24	6	0	0	0	0	0	0	0	0	0
400	411	25	7	0	0	0	0	0	0	0	0	0
411	422	26	8	0	0	0	0	0	0	0	0	0
422	433	27	9	0	0	0	0	0	0	0	0	0
433	444	28	11	0	0	0	0	0	0	0	0	0
444	455	29	12	0	0	0	0	0	0	0	0	0
455	466	30	13	0	0	0	0	0	0	0	0	0
466	477	31	14	0	0	0	0	0	0	0	0	0
477	488	32	15	0	0	0	0	0	0	0	0	0
488	499	34	16	0	0	0	0	0	0	0	0	0
499	510	35	17	0	0	0	0	0	0	0	0	0
510	530	36	19	1	0	0	0	0	0	0	0	0
530	550	38	21	3	0	0	0	0	0	0	0	0
550	570	40	23	5	0	0	0	0	0	0	0	0
570	590	43	25	7	0	0	0	0	0	0	0	0
590	610	45	27	9	0	0	0	0	0	0	0	0
610	630	47	29	11	0	0	0	0	0	0	0	0
630	650	50	31	13	0	0	0	0	0	0	0	0
650	670	52	33	15	0	0	0	0	0	0	0	0
670	690	55	35	17	0	0	0	0	0	0	0	0
690	710	57	37	19	2	0	0	0	0	0	0	0
710	730	59	39	21	4	0	0	0	0	0	0	0
730	750	62	41	23	6	0	0	0	0	0	0	0
750	770	64	43	25	8	0	0	0	0	0	0	0
770	790	67	46	27	10	0	0	0	0	0	0	0
790	810	69	48	29	12	0	0	0	0	0	0	0
810	830	71	50	31	14	0	0	0	0	0	0	0
830	850	74	53	33	16	0	0	0	0	0	0	0
850	870	76	55	35	18	0	0	0	0	0	0	0
870	890	79	58	37	20	2	0	0	0	0	0	0
890	910	81	60	39	22	4	0	0	0	0	0	0
910	930	83	62	41	24	6	0	0	0	0	0	0
930	950	86	65	44	26	8	0	0	0	0	0	0
950	970	88	67	46	28	10	0	0	0	0	0	0
970	990	91	70	49	30	12	0	0	0	0	0	0
990	1,010	93	72	51	32	14	0	0	0	0	0	0
1,010	1,030	95	74	53	34	16	0	0	0	0	0	0
1,030	1,050	98	77	56	36	18	1	0	0	0	0	0
1,050	1,070	100	79	58	38	20	3	0	0	0	0	0
1,070	1,090	103	82	61	40	22	5	0	0	0	0	0
1,090	1,110	105	84	63	42	24	7	0	0	0	0	0
1,110	1,130	107	86	65	44	26	9	0	0	0	0	0
1,130	1,150	110	89	68	47	28	11	0	0	0	0	0
1,150	1,170	112	91	70	49	30	13	0	0	0	0	0
1,170	1,190	115	94	73	52	32	15	0	0	0	0	0
1,190	1,210	117	96	75	54	34	17	0	0	0	0	0
1,210	1,230	119	98	77	56	36	19	1	0	0	0	0
1,230	1,250	122	101	80	59	38	21	3	0	0	0	0

Publication 15 (2019)

Wage Bracket Method Tables for Income Tax Withholding

SINGLE Persons—SEMIMONTHLY Payroll Period

(For Wages Paid through December 2019)

And the wages are—		And the number of withholding allowances claimed is—										
At least	But less than	0	1	2	3	4	5	6	7	8	9	10
		The amount of income tax to be withheld is—										
1,250	1,270	124	103	82	61	40	23	5	0	0	0	0
1,270	1,290	127	106	85	64	43	25	7	0	0	0	0
1,290	1,310	129	108	87	66	45	27	9	0	0	0	0
1,310	1,330	131	110	89	68	47	29	11	0	0	0	0
1,330	1,350	134	113	92	71	50	31	13	0	0	0	0
1,350	1,370	136	115	94	73	52	33	15	0	0	0	0
1,370	1,390	139	118	97	76	55	35	17	0	0	0	0
1,390	1,410	141	120	99	78	57	37	19	2	0	0	0
1,410	1,430	143	122	101	80	59	39	21	4	0	0	0
1,430	1,450	146	125	104	83	62	41	23	6	0	0	0
1,450	1,470	148	127	106	85	64	43	25	8	0	0	0
1,470	1,490	151	130	109	88	67	46	27	10	0	0	0
1,490	1,510	153	132	111	90	69	48	29	12	0	0	0
1,510	1,530	155	134	113	92	71	50	31	14	0	0	0
1,530	1,550	158	137	116	95	74	53	33	16	0	0	0
1,550	1,570	160	139	118	97	76	55	35	18	0	0	0
1,570	1,590	163	142	121	100	79	58	37	20	2	0	0
1,590	1,610	165	144	123	102	81	60	39	22	4	0	0
1,610	1,630	167	146	125	104	83	62	41	24	6	0	0
1,630	1,650	170	149	128	107	86	65	44	26	8	0	0
1,650	1,670	172	151	130	109	88	67	46	28	10	0	0
1,670	1,690	175	154	133	112	91	70	49	30	12	0	0
1,690	1,710	177	156	135	114	93	72	51	32	14	0	0
1,710	1,730	179	158	137	116	95	74	53	34	16	0	0
1,730	1,750	182	161	140	119	98	77	56	36	18	1	0
1,750	1,770	184	163	142	121	100	79	58	38	20	3	0
1,770	1,790	187	166	145	124	103	82	61	40	22	5	0
1,790	1,810	189	168	147	126	105	84	63	42	24	7	0
1,810	1,830	193	170	149	128	107	86	65	44	26	9	0
1,830	1,850	197	173	152	131	110	89	68	47	28	11	0
1,850	1,870	202	175	154	133	112	91	70	49	30	13	0
1,870	1,890	206	178	157	136	115	94	73	52	32	15	0
1,890	1,910	211	180	159	138	117	96	75	54	34	17	0
1,910	1,930	215	182	161	140	119	98	77	56	36	19	1
1,930	1,950	219	185	164	143	122	101	80	59	38	21	3
1,950	1,970	224	187	166	145	124	103	82	61	40	23	5
1,970	1,990	228	190	169	148	127	106	85	64	43	25	7
1,990	2,010	233	194	171	150	129	108	87	66	45	27	9
2,010	2,030	237	199	173	152	131	110	89	68	47	29	11
2,030	2,050	241	203	176	155	134	113	92	71	50	31	13
2,050	2,070	246	207	178	157	136	115	94	73	52	33	15
2,070	2,090	250	212	181	160	139	118	97	76	55	35	17
2,090	2,110	255	216	183	162	141	120	99	78	57	37	19
2,110	2,130	259	221	185	164	143	122	101	80	59	39	21
2,130	2,150	263	225	188	167	146	125	104	83	62	41	23
2,150	2,170	268	229	191	169	148	127	106	85	64	43	25
2,170	2,190	272	234	195	172	151	130	109	88	67	46	27
2,190	2,210	277	238	200	174	153	132	111	90	69	48	29
2,210	2,230	281	243	204	176	155	134	113	92	71	50	31
2,230	2,250	285	247	208	179	158	137	116	95	74	53	33
2,250	2,270	290	251	213	181	160	139	118	97	76	55	35
2,270	2,290	294	256	217	184	163	142	121	100	79	58	37
2,290	2,310	299	260	222	186	165	144	123	102	81	60	39
2,310	2,330	303	265	226	188	167	146	125	104	83	62	41
2,330	2,350	307	269	230	192	170	149	128	107	86	65	44
2,350	2,370	312	273	235	196	172	151	130	109	88	67	46
2,370	2,390	316	278	239	201	175	154	133	112	91	70	49
2,390	2,410	321	282	244	205	177	156	135	114	93	72	51
2,410	2,430	325	287	248	210	179	158	137	116	95	74	53
2,430	2,450	329	291	252	214	182	161	140	119	98	77	56
2,450	2,470	334	295	257	218	184	163	142	121	100	79	58
2,470	2,490	338	300	261	223	187	166	145	124	103	82	61
2,490	2,510	343	304	266	227	189	168	147	126	105	84	63
2,510	2,530	347	309	270	232	193	170	149	128	107	86	65
2,530	2,550	351	313	274	236	197	173	152	131	110	89	68

2,550 and over	Use Table 3(a) for a SINGLE person on page 46. Also see the instructions on page 44.

Wage Bracket Method Tables for Income Tax Withholding

MARRIED Persons—SEMIMONTHLY Payroll Period

(For Wages Paid through December 2019)

And the wages are—		And the number of withholding allowances claimed is—										
At least	But less than	0	1	2	3	4	5	6	7	8	9	10
		The amount of income tax to be withheld is—										
$ 0	$492	$0	$0	$0	$0	$0	$0	$0	$0	$0	$0	$0
492	502	1	0	0	0	0	0	0	0	0	0	0
502	512	2	0	0	0	0	0	0	0	0	0	0
512	522	3	0	0	0	0	0	0	0	0	0	0
522	532	4	0	0	0	0	0	0	0	0	0	0
532	542	5	0	0	0	0	0	0	0	0	0	0
542	552	6	0	0	0	0	0	0	0	0	0	0
552	562	7	0	0	0	0	0	0	0	0	0	0
562	572	8	0	0	0	0	0	0	0	0	0	0
572	582	9	0	0	0	0	0	0	0	0	0	0
582	592	10	0	0	0	0	0	0	0	0	0	0
592	602	11	0	0	0	0	0	0	0	0	0	0
602	612	12	0	0	0	0	0	0	0	0	0	0
612	622	13	0	0	0	0	0	0	0	0	0	0
622	632	14	0	0	0	0	0	0	0	0	0	0
632	642	15	0	0	0	0	0	0	0	0	0	0
642	652	16	0	0	0	0	0	0	0	0	0	0
652	662	17	0	0	0	0	0	0	0	0	0	0
662	672	18	0	0	0	0	0	0	0	0	0	0
672	682	19	1	0	0	0	0	0	0	0	0	0
682	692	20	2	0	0	0	0	0	0	0	0	0
692	702	21	3	0	0	0	0	0	0	0	0	0
702	712	22	4	0	0	0	0	0	0	0	0	0
712	722	23	5	0	0	0	0	0	0	0	0	0
722	732	24	6	0	0	0	0	0	0	0	0	0
732	742	25	7	0	0	0	0	0	0	0	0	0
742	752	26	8	0	0	0	0	0	0	0	0	0
752	762	27	9	0	0	0	0	0	0	0	0	0
762	772	28	10	0	0	0	0	0	0	0	0	0
772	782	29	11	0	0	0	0	0	0	0	0	0
782	792	30	12	0	0	0	0	0	0	0	0	0
792	802	31	13	0	0	0	0	0	0	0	0	0
802	812	32	14	0	0	0	0	0	0	0	0	0
812	822	33	15	0	0	0	0	0	0	0	0	0
822	832	34	16	0	0	0	0	0	0	0	0	0
832	842	35	17	0	0	0	0	0	0	0	0	0
842	852	36	18	1	0	0	0	0	0	0	0	0
852	862	37	19	2	0	0	0	0	0	0	0	0
862	872	38	20	3	0	0	0	0	0	0	0	0
872	882	39	21	4	0	0	0	0	0	0	0	0
882	892	40	22	5	0	0	0	0	0	0	0	0
892	902	41	23	6	0	0	0	0	0	0	0	0
902	912	42	24	7	0	0	0	0	0	0	0	0
912	922	43	25	8	0	0	0	0	0	0	0	0
922	932	44	26	9	0	0	0	0	0	0	0	0
932	942	45	27	10	0	0	0	0	0	0	0	0
942	952	46	28	11	0	0	0	0	0	0	0	0
952	962	47	29	12	0	0	0	0	0	0	0	0
962	972	48	30	13	0	0	0	0	0	0	0	0
972	982	49	31	14	0	0	0	0	0	0	0	0
982	992	50	32	15	0	0	0	0	0	0	0	0
992	1,002	51	33	16	0	0	0	0	0	0	0	0
1,002	1,022	52	35	17	0	0	0	0	0	0	0	0
1,022	1,042	54	37	19	2	0	0	0	0	0	0	0
1,042	1,062	56	39	21	4	0	0	0	0	0	0	0
1,062	1,082	58	41	23	6	0	0	0	0	0	0	0
1,082	1,102	60	43	25	8	0	0	0	0	0	0	0
1,102	1,122	62	45	27	10	0	0	0	0	0	0	0
1,122	1,142	64	47	29	12	0	0	0	0	0	0	0
1,142	1,162	66	49	31	14	0	0	0	0	0	0	0
1,162	1,182	68	51	33	16	0	0	0	0	0	0	0
1,182	1,202	70	53	35	18	0	0	0	0	0	0	0
1,202	1,222	72	55	37	20	2	0	0	0	0	0	0
1,222	1,242	74	57	39	22	4	0	0	0	0	0	0
1,242	1,262	76	59	41	24	6	0	0	0	0	0	0
1,262	1,282	78	61	43	26	8	0	0	0	0	0	0
1,282	1,302	80	63	45	28	10	0	0	0	0	0	0
1,302	1,322	82	65	47	30	12	0	0	0	0	0	0
1,322	1,342	85	67	49	32	14	0	0	0	0	0	0
1,342	1,362	87	69	51	34	16	0	0	0	0	0	0

Wage Bracket Method Tables for Income Tax Withholding

MARRIED Persons—SEMIMONTHLY Payroll Period

(For Wages Paid through December 2019)

And the wages are—		And the number of withholding allowances claimed is—										
At least	But less than	0	1	2	3	4	5	6	7	8	9	10
		The amount of income tax to be withheld is—										
1,362	1,382	89	71	53	36	18	1	0	0	0	0	0
1,382	1,402	92	73	55	38	20	3	0	0	0	0	0
1,402	1,422	94	75	57	40	22	5	0	0	0	0	0
1,422	1,442	97	77	59	42	24	7	0	0	0	0	0
1,442	1,462	99	79	61	44	26	9	0	0	0	0	0
1,462	1,482	101	81	63	46	28	11	0	0	0	0	0
1,482	1,502	104	83	65	48	30	13	0	0	0	0	0
1,502	1,522	106	85	67	50	32	15	0	0	0	0	0
1,522	1,542	109	88	69	52	34	17	0	0	0	0	0
1,542	1,562	111	90	71	54	36	19	1	0	0	0	0
1,562	1,582	113	92	73	56	38	21	3	0	0	0	0
1,582	1,602	116	95	75	58	40	23	5	0	0	0	0
1,602	1,622	118	97	77	60	42	25	7	0	0	0	0
1,622	1,642	121	100	79	62	44	27	9	0	0	0	0
1,642	1,662	123	102	81	64	46	29	11	0	0	0	0
1,662	1,682	125	104	83	66	48	31	13	0	0	0	0
1,682	1,702	128	107	86	68	50	33	15	0	0	0	0
1,702	1,722	130	109	88	70	52	35	17	0	0	0	0
1,722	1,742	133	112	91	72	54	37	19	2	0	0	0
1,742	1,762	135	114	93	74	56	39	21	4	0	0	0
1,762	1,782	137	116	95	76	58	41	23	6	0	0	0
1,782	1,802	140	119	98	78	60	43	25	8	0	0	0
1,802	1,822	142	121	100	80	62	45	27	10	0	0	0
1,822	1,842	145	124	103	82	64	47	29	12	0	0	0
1,842	1,862	147	126	105	84	66	49	31	14	0	0	0
1,862	1,882	149	128	107	86	68	51	33	16	0	0	0
1,882	1,902	152	131	110	89	70	53	35	18	0	0	0
1,902	1,922	154	133	112	91	72	55	37	20	2	0	0
1,922	1,942	157	136	115	94	74	57	39	22	4	0	0
1,942	1,962	159	138	117	96	76	59	41	24	6	0	0
1,962	1,982	161	140	119	98	78	61	43	26	8	0	0
1,982	2,002	164	143	122	101	80	63	45	28	10	0	0
2,002	2,022	166	145	124	103	82	65	47	30	12	0	0
2,022	2,042	169	148	127	106	85	67	49	32	14	0	0
2,042	2,062	171	150	129	108	87	69	51	34	16	0	0
2,062	2,082	173	152	131	110	89	71	53	36	18	1	0
2,082	2,102	176	155	134	113	92	73	55	38	20	3	0
2,102	2,122	178	157	136	115	94	75	57	40	22	5	0
2,122	2,142	181	160	139	118	97	77	59	42	24	7	0
2,142	2,162	183	162	141	120	99	79	61	44	26	9	0
2,162	2,182	185	164	143	122	101	81	63	46	28	11	0
2,182	2,202	188	167	146	125	104	83	65	48	30	13	0
2,202	2,222	190	169	148	127	106	85	67	50	32	15	0
2,222	2,242	193	172	151	130	109	88	69	52	34	17	0
2,242	2,262	195	174	153	132	111	90	71	54	36	19	1
2,262	2,282	197	176	155	134	113	92	73	56	38	21	3
2,282	2,302	200	179	158	137	116	95	75	58	40	23	5
2,302	2,322	202	181	160	139	118	97	77	60	42	25	7
2,322	2,342	205	184	163	142	121	100	79	62	44	27	9
2,342	2,362	207	186	165	144	123	102	81	64	46	29	11
2,362	2,382	209	188	167	146	125	104	83	66	48	31	13
2,382	2,402	212	191	170	149	128	107	86	68	50	33	15
2,402	2,422	214	193	172	151	130	109	88	70	52	35	17
2,422	2,442	217	196	175	154	133	112	91	72	54	37	19
2,442	2,462	219	198	177	156	135	114	93	74	56	39	21
2,462	2,482	221	200	179	158	137	116	95	76	58	41	23
2,482	2,502	224	203	182	161	140	119	98	78	60	43	25
2,502	2,522	226	205	184	163	142	121	100	80	62	45	27
2,522	2,542	229	208	187	166	145	124	103	82	64	47	29
2,542	2,562	231	210	189	168	147	126	105	84	66	49	31
2,562	2,582	233	212	191	170	149	128	107	86	68	51	33
2,582	2,602	236	215	194	173	152	131	110	89	70	53	35
2,602	2,622	238	217	196	175	154	133	112	91	72	55	37
2,622	2,642	241	220	199	178	157	136	115	94	74	57	39
2,642	2,662	243	222	201	180	159	138	117	96	76	59	41
2,662	2,682	245	224	203	182	161	140	119	98	78	61	43

2,682 and over Use Table 3(b) for a MARRIED person on page 46. Also see the instructions on page 44.

Wage Bracket Method Tables for Income Tax Withholding

SINGLE Persons—MONTHLY Payroll Period

(For Wages Paid through December 2019)

And the wages are—		And the number of withholding allowances claimed is—										
At least	But less than	0	1	2	3	4	5	6	7	8	9	10
		The amount of income tax to be withheld is—										
$ 0	$317	$0	$0	$0	$0	$0	$0	$0	$0	$0	$0	$0
317	327	1	0	0	0	0	0	0	0	0	0	0
327	337	2	0	0	0	0	0	0	0	0	0	0
337	347	3	0	0	0	0	0	0	0	0	0	0
347	357	4	0	0	0	0	0	0	0	0	0	0
357	367	5	0	0	0	0	0	0	0	0	0	0
367	377	6	0	0	0	0	0	0	0	0	0	0
377	387	7	0	0	0	0	0	0	0	0	0	0
387	397	8	0	0	0	0	0	0	0	0	0	0
397	407	9	0	0	0	0	0	0	0	0	0	0
407	417	10	0	0	0	0	0	0	0	0	0	0
417	427	11	0	0	0	0	0	0	0	0	0	0
427	437	12	0	0	0	0	0	0	0	0	0	0
437	447	13	0	0	0	0	0	0	0	0	0	0
447	457	14	0	0	0	0	0	0	0	0	0	0
457	467	15	0	0	0	0	0	0	0	0	0	0
467	477	16	0	0	0	0	0	0	0	0	0	0
477	487	17	0	0	0	0	0	0	0	0	0	0
487	497	18	0	0	0	0	0	0	0	0	0	0
497	507	19	0	0	0	0	0	0	0	0	0	0
507	517	20	0	0	0	0	0	0	0	0	0	0
517	527	21	0	0	0	0	0	0	0	0	0	0
527	537	22	0	0	0	0	0	0	0	0	0	0
537	547	23	0	0	0	0	0	0	0	0	0	0
547	557	24	0	0	0	0	0	0	0	0	0	0
557	567	25	0	0	0	0	0	0	0	0	0	0
567	577	26	0	0	0	0	0	0	0	0	0	0
577	587	27	0	0	0	0	0	0	0	0	0	0
587	597	28	0	0	0	0	0	0	0	0	0	0
597	607	29	0	0	0	0	0	0	0	0	0	0
607	617	30	0	0	0	0	0	0	0	0	0	0
617	627	31	0	0	0	0	0	0	0	0	0	0
627	637	32	0	0	0	0	0	0	0	0	0	0
637	647	33	0	0	0	0	0	0	0	0	0	0
647	657	34	0	0	0	0	0	0	0	0	0	0
657	667	35	0	0	0	0	0	0	0	0	0	0
667	677	36	1	0	0	0	0	0	0	0	0	0
677	687	37	2	0	0	0	0	0	0	0	0	0
687	697	38	3	0	0	0	0	0	0	0	0	0
697	707	39	4	0	0	0	0	0	0	0	0	0
707	717	40	5	0	0	0	0	0	0	0	0	0
717	727	41	6	0	0	0	0	0	0	0	0	0
727	737	42	7	0	0	0	0	0	0	0	0	0
737	747	43	8	0	0	0	0	0	0	0	0	0
747	757	44	9	0	0	0	0	0	0	0	0	0
757	767	45	10	0	0	0	0	0	0	0	0	0
767	777	46	11	0	0	0	0	0	0	0	0	0
777	787	47	12	0	0	0	0	0	0	0	0	0
787	797	48	13	0	0	0	0	0	0	0	0	0
797	807	49	14	0	0	0	0	0	0	0	0	0
807	817	50	15	0	0	0	0	0	0	0	0	0
817	827	51	16	0	0	0	0	0	0	0	0	0
827	837	52	17	0	0	0	0	0	0	0	0	0
837	847	53	18	0	0	0	0	0	0	0	0	0
847	857	54	19	0	0	0	0	0	0	0	0	0
857	867	55	20	0	0	0	0	0	0	0	0	0
867	877	56	21	0	0	0	0	0	0	0	0	0
877	887	57	22	0	0	0	0	0	0	0	0	0
887	897	58	23	0	0	0	0	0	0	0	0	0
897	907	59	24	0	0	0	0	0	0	0	0	0
907	917	60	25	0	0	0	0	0	0	0	0	0
917	927	61	26	0	0	0	0	0	0	0	0	0
927	937	62	27	0	0	0	0	0	0	0	0	0
937	947	63	28	0	0	0	0	0	0	0	0	0
947	957	64	29	0	0	0	0	0	0	0	0	0
957	967	65	30	0	0	0	0	0	0	0	0	0
967	977	66	31	0	0	0	0	0	0	0	0	0
977	987	67	32	0	0	0	0	0	0	0	0	0
987	997	68	33	0	0	0	0	0	0	0	0	0
997	1,007	69	34	0	0	0	0	0	0	0	0	0

Wage Bracket Method Tables for Income Tax Withholding

SINGLE Persons—MONTHLY Payroll Period

(For Wages Paid through December 2019)

And the wages are–		And the number of withholding allowances claimed is—										
At least	But less than	0	1	2	3	4	5	6	7	8	9	10
		The amount of income tax to be withheld is—										
1,007	1,027	70	35	0	0	0	0	0	0	0	0	0
1,027	1,047	72	37	2	0	0	0	0	0	0	0	0
1,047	1,067	74	39	4	0	0	0	0	0	0	0	0
1,067	1,087	76	41	6	0	0	0	0	0	0	0	0
1,087	1,107	78	43	8	0	0	0	0	0	0	0	0
1,107	1,127	80	45	10	0	0	0	0	0	0	0	0
1,127	1,147	82	47	12	0	0	0	0	0	0	0	0
1,147	1,167	85	49	14	0	0	0	0	0	0	0	0
1,167	1,187	87	51	16	0	0	0	0	0	0	0	0
1,187	1,207	89	53	18	0	0	0	0	0	0	0	0
1,207	1,227	92	55	20	0	0	0	0	0	0	0	0
1,227	1,247	94	57	22	0	0	0	0	0	0	0	0
1,247	1,267	97	59	24	0	0	0	0	0	0	0	0
1,267	1,287	99	61	26	0	0	0	0	0	0	0	0
1,287	1,307	101	63	28	0	0	0	0	0	0	0	0
1,307	1,327	104	65	30	0	0	0	0	0	0	0	0
1,327	1,347	106	67	32	0	0	0	0	0	0	0	0
1,347	1,367	109	69	34	0	0	0	0	0	0	0	0
1,367	1,387	111	71	36	1	0	0	0	0	0	0	0
1,387	1,407	113	73	38	3	0	0	0	0	0	0	0
1,407	1,427	116	75	40	5	0	0	0	0	0	0	0
1,427	1,447	118	77	42	7	0	0	0	0	0	0	0
1,447	1,467	121	79	44	9	0	0	0	0	0	0	0
1,467	1,487	123	81	46	11	0	0	0	0	0	0	0
1,487	1,507	125	83	48	13	0	0	0	0	0	0	0
1,507	1,527	128	86	50	15	0	0	0	0	0	0	0
1,527	1,547	130	88	52	17	0	0	0	0	0	0	0
1,547	1,567	133	91	54	19	0	0	0	0	0	0	0
1,567	1,587	135	93	56	21	0	0	0	0	0	0	0
1,587	1,607	137	95	58	23	0	0	0	0	0	0	0
1,607	1,627	140	98	60	25	0	0	0	0	0	0	0
1,627	1,647	142	100	62	27	0	0	0	0	0	0	0
1,647	1,667	145	103	64	29	0	0	0	0	0	0	0
1,667	1,687	147	105	66	31	0	0	0	0	0	0	0
1,687	1,707	149	107	68	33	0	0	0	0	0	0	0
1,707	1,727	152	110	70	35	0	0	0	0	0	0	0
1,727	1,747	154	112	72	37	2	0	0	0	0	0	0
1,747	1,767	157	115	74	39	4	0	0	0	0	0	0
1,767	1,787	159	117	76	41	6	0	0	0	0	0	0
1,787	1,807	161	119	78	43	8	0	0	0	0	0	0
1,807	1,827	164	122	80	45	10	0	0	0	0	0	0
1,827	1,847	166	124	82	47	12	0	0	0	0	0	0
1,847	1,867	169	127	85	49	14	0	0	0	0	0	0
1,867	1,887	171	129	87	51	16	0	0	0	0	0	0
1,887	1,907	173	131	89	53	18	0	0	0	0	0	0
1,907	1,927	176	134	92	55	20	0	0	0	0	0	0
1,927	1,947	178	136	94	57	22	0	0	0	0	0	0
1,947	1,967	181	139	97	59	24	0	0	0	0	0	0
1,967	1,987	183	141	99	61	26	0	0	0	0	0	0
1,987	2,007	185	143	101	63	28	0	0	0	0	0	0
2,007	2,047	189	147	105	66	31	0	0	0	0	0	0
2,047	2,087	194	152	110	70	35	0	0	0	0	0	0
2,087	2,127	199	157	115	74	39	4	0	0	0	0	0
2,127	2,167	203	161	119	78	43	8	0	0	0	0	0
2,167	2,207	208	166	124	82	47	12	0	0	0	0	0
2,207	2,247	213	171	129	87	51	16	0	0	0	0	0
2,247	2,287	218	176	134	92	55	20	0	0	0	0	0
2,287	2,327	223	181	139	97	59	24	0	0	0	0	0
2,327	2,367	227	185	143	101	63	28	0	0	0	0	0
2,367	2,407	232	190	148	106	67	32	0	0	0	0	0
2,407	2,447	237	195	153	111	71	36	1	0	0	0	0
2,447	2,487	242	200	158	116	75	40	5	0	0	0	0
2,487	2,527	247	205	163	121	79	44	9	0	0	0	0
2,527	2,567	251	209	167	125	83	48	13	0	0	0	0
2,567	2,607	256	214	172	130	88	52	17	0	0	0	0
2,607	2,647	261	219	177	135	93	56	21	0	0	0	0

2,647 and over   Use Table 4(a) for a SINGLE person on page 46. Also see the instructions on page 44.

Wage Bracket Method Tables for Income Tax Withholding

MARRIED Persons—MONTHLY Payroll Period

(For Wages Paid through December 2019)

And the wages are—		And the number of withholding allowances claimed is—										
At least	But less than	0	1	2	3	4	5	6	7	8	9	10
		The amount of income tax to be withheld is—										
$ 0	$983	$0	$0	$0	$0	$0	$0	$0	$0	$0	$0	$0
983	994	1	0	0	0	0	0	0	0	0	0	0
994	1,005	2	0	0	0	0	0	0	0	0	0	0
1,005	1,016	3	0	0	0	0	0	0	0	0	0	0
1,016	1,027	4	0	0	0	0	0	0	0	0	0	0
1,027	1,038	5	0	0	0	0	0	0	0	0	0	0
1,038	1,049	6	0	0	0	0	0	0	0	0	0	0
1,049	1,060	7	0	0	0	0	0	0	0	0	0	0
1,060	1,071	8	0	0	0	0	0	0	0	0	0	0
1,071	1,082	9	0	0	0	0	0	0	0	0	0	0
1,082	1,093	10	0	0	0	0	0	0	0	0	0	0
1,093	1,104	12	0	0	0	0	0	0	0	0	0	0
1,104	1,115	13	0	0	0	0	0	0	0	0	0	0
1,115	1,126	14	0	0	0	0	0	0	0	0	0	0
1,126	1,137	15	0	0	0	0	0	0	0	0	0	0
1,137	1,148	16	0	0	0	0	0	0	0	0	0	0
1,148	1,159	17	0	0	0	0	0	0	0	0	0	0
1,159	1,170	18	0	0	0	0	0	0	0	0	0	0
1,170	1,181	19	0	0	0	0	0	0	0	0	0	0
1,181	1,192	20	0	0	0	0	0	0	0	0	0	0
1,192	1,203	21	0	0	0	0	0	0	0	0	0	0
1,203	1,214	23	0	0	0	0	0	0	0	0	0	0
1,214	1,225	24	0	0	0	0	0	0	0	0	0	0
1,225	1,236	25	0	0	0	0	0	0	0	0	0	0
1,236	1,247	26	0	0	0	0	0	0	0	0	0	0
1,247	1,258	27	0	0	0	0	0	0	0	0	0	0
1,258	1,269	28	0	0	0	0	0	0	0	0	0	0
1,269	1,280	29	0	0	0	0	0	0	0	0	0	0
1,280	1,291	30	0	0	0	0	0	0	0	0	0	0
1,291	1,302	31	0	0	0	0	0	0	0	0	0	0
1,302	1,313	32	0	0	0	0	0	0	0	0	0	0
1,313	1,324	34	0	0	0	0	0	0	0	0	0	0
1,324	1,335	35	0	0	0	0	0	0	0	0	0	0
1,335	1,346	36	1	0	0	0	0	0	0	0	0	0
1,346	1,357	37	2	0	0	0	0	0	0	0	0	0
1,357	1,368	38	3	0	0	0	0	0	0	0	0	0
1,368	1,379	39	4	0	0	0	0	0	0	0	0	0
1,379	1,390	40	5	0	0	0	0	0	0	0	0	0
1,390	1,401	41	6	0	0	0	0	0	0	0	0	0
1,401	1,412	42	7	0	0	0	0	0	0	0	0	0
1,412	1,423	43	8	0	0	0	0	0	0	0	0	0
1,423	1,434	45	10	0	0	0	0	0	0	0	0	0
1,434	1,445	46	11	0	0	0	0	0	0	0	0	0
1,445	1,456	47	12	0	0	0	0	0	0	0	0	0
1,456	1,467	48	13	0	0	0	0	0	0	0	0	0
1,467	1,478	49	14	0	0	0	0	0	0	0	0	0
1,478	1,489	50	15	0	0	0	0	0	0	0	0	0
1,489	1,500	51	16	0	0	0	0	0	0	0	0	0
1,500	1,511	52	17	0	0	0	0	0	0	0	0	0
1,511	1,522	53	18	0	0	0	0	0	0	0	0	0
1,522	1,533	54	19	0	0	0	0	0	0	0	0	0
1,533	1,544	56	21	0	0	0	0	0	0	0	0	0
1,544	1,555	57	22	0	0	0	0	0	0	0	0	0
1,555	1,566	58	23	0	0	0	0	0	0	0	0	0
1,566	1,577	59	24	0	0	0	0	0	0	0	0	0
1,577	1,588	60	25	0	0	0	0	0	0	0	0	0
1,588	1,599	61	26	0	0	0	0	0	0	0	0	0
1,599	1,610	62	27	0	0	0	0	0	0	0	0	0
1,610	1,621	63	28	0	0	0	0	0	0	0	0	0
1,621	1,632	64	29	0	0	0	0	0	0	0	0	0
1,632	1,643	65	30	0	0	0	0	0	0	0	0	0
1,643	1,654	67	32	0	0	0	0	0	0	0	0	0
1,654	1,665	68	33	0	0	0	0	0	0	0	0	0
1,665	1,676	69	34	0	0	0	0	0	0	0	0	0
1,676	1,687	70	35	0	0	0	0	0	0	0	0	0
1,687	1,698	71	36	1	0	0	0	0	0	0	0	0
1,698	1,709	72	37	2	0	0	0	0	0	0	0	0
1,709	1,720	73	38	3	0	0	0	0	0	0	0	0
1,720	1,731	74	39	4	0	0	0	0	0	0	0	0
1,731	1,742	75	40	5	0	0	0	0	0	0	0	0

Wage Bracket Method Tables for Income Tax Withholding

MARRIED Persons—MONTHLY Payroll Period

(For Wages Paid through December 2019)

And the wages are–		And the number of withholding allowances claimed is—										
At least	But less than	0	1	2	3	4	5	6	7	8	9	10
		The amount of income tax to be withheld is—										
1,742	1,753	76	41	6	0	0	0	0	0	0	0	0
1,753	1,773	78	43	8	0	0	0	0	0	0	0	0
1,773	1,793	80	45	10	0	0	0	0	0	0	0	0
1,793	1,813	82	47	12	0	0	0	0	0	0	0	0
1,813	1,833	84	49	14	0	0	0	0	0	0	0	0
1,833	1,853	86	51	16	0	0	0	0	0	0	0	0
1,853	1,873	88	53	18	0	0	0	0	0	0	0	0
1,873	1,893	90	55	20	0	0	0	0	0	0	0	0
1,893	1,913	92	57	22	0	0	0	0	0	0	0	0
1,913	1,933	94	59	24	0	0	0	0	0	0	0	0
1,933	1,953	96	61	26	0	0	0	0	0	0	0	0
1,953	1,973	98	63	28	0	0	0	0	0	0	0	0
1,973	1,993	100	65	30	0	0	0	0	0	0	0	0
1,993	2,013	102	67	32	0	0	0	0	0	0	0	0
2,013	2,033	104	69	34	0	0	0	0	0	0	0	0
2,033	2,053	106	71	36	1	0	0	0	0	0	0	0
2,053	2,073	108	73	38	3	0	0	0	0	0	0	0
2,073	2,093	110	75	40	5	0	0	0	0	0	0	0
2,093	2,113	112	77	42	7	0	0	0	0	0	0	0
2,113	2,133	114	79	44	9	0	0	0	0	0	0	0
2,133	2,153	116	81	46	11	0	0	0	0	0	0	0
2,153	2,173	118	83	48	13	0	0	0	0	0	0	0
2,173	2,193	120	85	50	15	0	0	0	0	0	0	0
2,193	2,213	122	87	52	17	0	0	0	0	0	0	0
2,213	2,233	124	89	54	19	0	0	0	0	0	0	0
2,233	2,253	126	91	56	21	0	0	0	0	0	0	0
2,253	2,273	128	93	58	23	0	0	0	0	0	0	0
2,273	2,293	130	95	60	25	0	0	0	0	0	0	0
2,293	2,313	132	97	62	27	0	0	0	0	0	0	0
2,313	2,333	134	99	64	29	0	0	0	0	0	0	0
2,333	2,353	136	101	66	31	0	0	0	0	0	0	0
2,353	2,373	138	103	68	33	0	0	0	0	0	0	0
2,373	2,393	140	105	70	35	0	0	0	0	0	0	0
2,393	2,413	142	107	72	37	2	0	0	0	0	0	0
2,413	2,433	144	109	74	39	4	0	0	0	0	0	0
2,433	2,453	146	111	76	41	6	0	0	0	0	0	0
2,453	2,473	148	113	78	43	8	0	0	0	0	0	0
2,473	2,493	150	115	80	45	10	0	0	0	0	0	0
2,493	2,513	152	117	82	47	12	0	0	0	0	0	0
2,513	2,553	155	120	85	50	15	0	0	0	0	0	0
2,553	2,593	159	124	89	54	19	0	0	0	0	0	0
2,593	2,633	163	128	93	58	23	0	0	0	0	0	0
2,633	2,673	168	132	97	62	27	0	0	0	0	0	0
2,673	2,713	173	136	101	66	31	0	0	0	0	0	0
2,713	2,753	178	140	105	70	35	0	0	0	0	0	0
2,753	2,793	182	144	109	74	39	4	0	0	0	0	0
2,793	2,833	187	148	113	78	43	8	0	0	0	0	0
2,833	2,873	192	152	117	82	47	12	0	0	0	0	0
2,873	2,913	197	156	121	86	51	16	0	0	0	0	0
2,913	2,953	202	160	125	90	55	20	0	0	0	0	0
2,953	2,993	206	164	129	94	59	24	0	0	0	0	0
2,993	3,033	211	169	133	98	63	28	0	0	0	0	0
3,033	3,073	216	174	137	102	67	32	0	0	0	0	0
3,073	3,113	221	179	141	106	71	36	1	0	0	0	0
3,113	3,153	226	184	145	110	75	40	5	0	0	0	0
3,153	3,193	230	188	149	114	79	44	9	0	0	0	0
3,193	3,233	235	193	153	118	83	48	13	0	0	0	0
3,233	3,273	240	198	157	122	87	52	17	0	0	0	0
3,273	3,313	245	203	161	126	91	56	21	0	0	0	0
3,313	3,353	250	208	166	130	95	60	25	0	0	0	0
3,353	3,393	254	212	170	134	99	64	29	0	0	0	0
3,393	3,433	259	217	175	138	103	68	33	0	0	0	0
3,433	3,473	264	222	180	142	107	72	37	2	0	0	0
3,473	3,513	269	227	185	146	111	76	41	6	0	0	0
3,513	3,553	274	232	190	150	115	80	45	10	0	0	0
3,553	3,593	278	236	194	154	119	84	49	14	0	0	0

3,593 and over   Use Table 4(b) for a MARRIED person on page 46. Also see the instructions on page 44.

Wage Bracket Method Tables for Income Tax Withholding

SINGLE Persons—DAILY Payroll Period

(For Wages Paid through December 2019)

And the wages are—		And the number of withholding allowances claimed is—										
At least	But less than	0	1	2	3	4	5	6	7	8	9	10
		The amount of income tax to be withheld is—										
$ 0	$15	$0	$0	$0	$0	$0	$0	$0	$0	$0	$0	$0
15	25	1	0	0	0	0	0	0	0	0	0	0
25	35	2	0	0	0	0	0	0	0	0	0	0
35	45	3	1	0	0	0	0	0	0	0	0	0
45	55	4	2	0	0	0	0	0	0	0	0	0
55	65	5	3	1	0	0	0	0	0	0	0	0
65	75	6	4	2	1	0	0	0	0	0	0	0
75	85	7	5	3	2	0	0	0	0	0	0	0
85	95	8	6	4	3	1	0	0	0	0	0	0
95	105	10	8	6	4	2	0	0	0	0	0	0
105	115	11	9	7	5	3	1	0	0	0	0	0
115	125	12	10	8	6	4	2	1	0	0	0	0
125	135	13	11	9	7	5	3	2	0	0	0	0
135	145	14	12	10	8	7	5	3	1	0	0	0
145	155	16	14	12	10	8	6	4	2	1	0	0
155	165	17	15	13	11	9	7	5	3	2	0	0
165	175	18	16	14	12	10	8	6	4	3	1	0
175	185	20	17	15	13	11	9	7	6	4	2	0
185	195	23	19	16	14	13	11	9	7	5	3	1
195	205	25	21	18	16	14	12	10	8	6	4	2
205	215	27	24	20	17	15	13	11	9	7	5	3
215	225	29	26	22	19	16	14	12	10	8	6	5
225	235	31	28	24	21	17	15	13	12	10	8	6
235	245	34	30	27	23	19	17	15	13	11	9	7
245	255	36	32	29	25	22	18	16	14	12	10	8
255	265	38	35	31	27	24	20	17	15	13	11	9
265	275	40	37	33	30	26	22	19	16	14	12	11
275	285	42	39	35	32	28	25	21	18	16	14	12
285	295	45	41	38	34	30	27	23	20	17	15	13
295	305	47	43	40	36	33	29	26	22	18	16	14
305	315	49	46	42	38	35	31	28	24	21	17	15
315	325	51	48	44	41	37	33	30	26	23	19	17
325	335	53	50	46	43	39	36	32	29	25	21	18
335	345	56	52	49	45	41	38	34	31	27	24	20
345	360	59	55	51	48	44	41	37	34	30	26	23
360	375	62	58	55	51	47	44	40	37	33	30	26
375	390	66	62	58	54	51	47	44	40	37	33	29
390	405	69	66	62	58	54	51	47	43	40	36	33
405	420	73	69	65	61	58	54	50	47	43	40	36
420	435	77	73	69	65	61	57	54	50	46	43	39
435	450	80	76	73	69	65	61	57	53	50	46	43
450	465	84	80	76	72	68	65	61	57	53	50	46
465	480	87	84	80	76	72	68	64	60	56	53	49
480	495	91	87	83	79	76	72	68	64	60	56	53
495	510	95	91	87	83	79	75	71	68	64	60	56
510	525	98	94	91	87	83	79	75	71	67	63	60
525	540	102	98	94	90	86	83	79	75	71	67	63
540	555	105	102	98	94	90	86	82	78	74	71	67
555	570	109	105	101	97	94	90	86	82	78	74	70
570	585	113	109	105	101	97	93	89	86	82	78	74
585	600	116	112	109	105	101	97	93	89	85	81	78
600	615	120	116	112	108	104	101	97	93	89	85	81
615	630	123	120	116	112	108	104	100	96	92	89	85
630	645	127	123	119	115	112	108	104	100	96	92	88
645	660	132	127	123	119	115	111	107	104	100	96	92
660	675	137	132	127	123	119	115	111	107	103	99	96
675	690	142	137	132	126	122	119	115	111	107	103	99
690	705	147	141	136	131	126	122	118	114	110	107	103
705	720	151	146	141	136	131	126	122	118	114	110	106
720	735	156	151	146	141	136	130	125	122	118	114	110
735	750	161	156	151	146	140	135	130	125	121	117	114
750	765	166	161	156	150	145	140	135	130	125	121	117
765	780	171	165	160	155	150	145	140	134	129	125	121
780	795	175	170	165	160	155	150	144	139	134	129	124
795	810	180	175	170	165	160	154	149	144	139	134	129
810	825	186	180	175	170	164	159	154	149	144	139	133
825	840	191	185	180	174	169	164	159	154	149	143	138
840	855	196	190	185	179	174	169	164	158	153	148	143
855	870	201	196	190	184	179	174	168	163	158	153	148
870	885	207	201	195	190	184	178	173	168	163	158	153

Wage Bracket Method Tables for Income Tax Withholding

SINGLE Persons—DAILY Payroll Period

(For Wages Paid through December 2019)

And the wages are–		And the number of withholding allowances claimed is—										
At least	But less than	0	1	2	3	4	5	6	7	8	9	10
		The amount of income tax to be withheld is—										
885	900	212	206	201	195	189	184	178	173	168	163	157
900	915	217	211	206	200	194	189	183	178	173	167	162
915	930	222	217	211	205	200	194	188	183	177	172	167
930	945	228	222	216	211	205	199	194	188	182	177	172
945	960	233	227	222	216	210	205	199	193	188	182	177
960	975	238	232	227	221	215	210	204	199	193	187	182
975	990	243	238	232	226	221	215	209	204	198	192	187
990	1,005	249	243	237	232	226	220	215	209	203	198	192
1,005	1,020	254	248	243	237	231	226	220	214	209	203	197
1,020	1,035	259	253	248	242	236	231	225	220	214	208	203
1,035	1,050	264	259	253	247	242	236	230	225	219	213	208
1,050	1,065	270	264	258	253	247	241	236	230	224	219	213
1,065	1,080	275	269	264	258	252	247	241	235	230	224	218
1,080	1,095	280	274	269	263	257	252	246	241	235	229	224
1,095	1,110	285	280	274	268	263	257	251	246	240	234	229
1,110	1,125	291	285	279	274	268	262	257	251	245	240	234
1,125	1,140	296	290	285	279	273	268	262	256	251	245	239
1,140	1,155	301	295	290	284	278	273	267	262	256	250	245
1,155	1,170	306	301	295	289	284	278	272	267	261	255	250
1,170	1,185	312	306	300	295	289	283	278	272	266	261	255
1,185	1,200	317	311	306	300	294	289	283	277	272	266	260
1,200	1,215	322	316	311	305	299	294	288	283	277	271	266
1,215	1,230	327	322	316	310	305	299	293	288	282	276	271
1,230	1,245	333	327	321	316	310	304	299	293	287	282	276
1,245	1,260	338	332	327	321	315	310	304	298	293	287	281
1,260	1,275	343	337	332	326	320	315	309	304	298	292	287
1,275	1,290	348	343	337	331	326	320	314	309	303	297	292
1,290	1,305	354	348	342	337	331	325	320	314	308	303	297
1,305	1,320	359	353	348	342	336	331	325	319	314	308	302
1,320	1,335	364	358	353	347	341	336	330	325	319	313	308
1,335	1,350	369	364	358	352	347	341	335	330	324	318	313
1,350	1,365	375	369	363	358	352	346	341	335	329	324	318
1,365	1,380	380	374	369	363	357	352	346	340	335	329	323
1,380	1,395	385	379	374	368	362	357	351	346	340	334	329
1,395	1,410	390	385	379	373	368	362	356	351	345	339	334
1,410	1,425	396	390	384	379	373	367	362	356	350	345	339
1,425	1,440	401	395	390	384	378	373	367	361	356	350	344
1,440	1,455	406	400	395	389	383	378	372	367	361	355	350
1,455	1,470	411	406	400	394	389	383	377	372	366	360	355
1,470	1,485	417	411	405	400	394	388	383	377	371	366	360
1,485	1,500	422	416	411	405	399	394	388	382	377	371	365
1,500	1,515	427	421	416	410	404	399	393	388	382	376	371
1,515	1,530	432	427	421	415	410	404	398	393	387	381	376
1,530	1,545	438	432	426	421	415	409	404	398	392	387	381
1,545	1,560	443	437	432	426	420	415	409	403	398	392	386
1,560	1,575	448	442	437	431	425	420	414	409	403	397	392
1,575	1,590	453	448	442	436	431	425	419	414	408	402	397
1,590	1,605	459	453	447	442	436	430	425	419	413	408	402
1,605	1,620	464	458	453	447	441	436	430	424	419	413	407
1,620	1,635	469	463	458	452	446	441	435	430	424	418	413
1,635	1,650	474	469	463	457	452	446	440	435	429	423	418
1,650	1,665	480	474	468	463	457	451	446	440	434	429	423
1,665	1,680	485	479	474	468	462	457	451	445	440	434	428
1,680	1,695	490	484	479	473	467	462	456	451	445	439	434
1,695	1,710	495	490	484	478	473	467	461	456	450	444	439
1,710	1,725	501	495	489	484	478	472	467	461	455	450	444
1,725	1,740	506	500	495	489	483	478	472	466	461	455	449
1,740	1,755	511	505	500	494	488	483	477	472	466	460	455
1,755	1,770	516	511	505	499	494	488	482	477	471	465	460
1,770	1,785	522	516	510	505	499	493	488	482	476	471	465
1,785	1,800	527	521	516	510	504	499	493	487	482	476	470
1,800	1,815	532	526	521	515	509	504	498	493	487	481	476
1,815	1,830	537	532	526	520	515	509	503	498	492	486	481
1,830	1,845	543	537	531	526	520	514	509	503	497	492	486
1,845	1,860	548	542	537	531	525	520	514	508	503	497	491
1,860	1,862	551	545	540	534	528	523	517	511	506	500	494

1,862 and over	Use Table 8(a) for a SINGLE person on page 47. Also see the instructions on page 44.

Wage Bracket Method Tables for Income Tax Withholding

MARRIED Persons—DAILY Payroll Period

(For Wages Paid through December 2019)

And the wages are–		And the number of withholding allowances claimed is—										
At least	But less than	0	1	2	3	4	5	6	7	8	9	10
		The amount of income tax to be withheld is—										
$ 0	$46	$0	$0	$0	$0	$0	$0	$0	$0	$0	$0	$0
46	56	1	0	0	0	0	0	0	0	0	0	0
56	66	2	0	0	0	0	0	0	0	0	0	0
66	76	3	1	0	0	0	0	0	0	0	0	0
76	86	4	2	0	0	0	0	0	0	0	0	0
86	96	5	3	1	0	0	0	0	0	0	0	0
96	106	6	4	2	1	0	0	0	0	0	0	0
108	116	7	5	3	2	0	0	0	0	0	0	0
116	126	8	6	4	3	1	0	0	0	0	0	0
126	136	9	7	5	4	2	0	0	0	0	0	0
136	146	10	8	6	5	3	1	0	0	0	0	0
146	156	11	9	7	6	4	2	1	0	0	0	0
156	166	12	10	9	7	5	3	2	0	0	0	0
166	176	14	12	10	8	6	4	3	1	0	0	0
176	186	15	13	11	9	7	5	4	2	1	0	0
186	196	16	14	12	10	8	6	5	3	2	0	0
196	206	17	15	13	11	9	7	6	4	3	1	0
206	216	18	16	15	13	11	9	7	5	4	2	0
216	226	20	18	16	14	12	10	8	6	5	3	1
226	236	21	19	17	15	13	11	9	7	6	4	2
236	246	22	20	18	16	14	12	10	8	7	5	3
246	256	23	21	19	17	15	13	12	10	8	6	4
256	266	24	22	21	19	17	15	13	11	9	7	5
266	276	26	24	22	20	18	16	14	12	10	8	6
276	286	27	25	23	21	19	17	15	13	11	9	7
286	296	28	26	24	22	20	18	16	14	12	11	9
296	306	29	27	25	23	21	19	18	16	14	12	10
306	316	30	28	27	25	23	21	19	17	15	13	11
316	326	32	30	28	26	24	22	20	18	16	14	12
326	336	33	31	29	27	25	23	21	19	17	15	13
336	346	34	32	30	28	26	24	22	20	18	17	15
346	361	36	34	32	30	28	26	24	22	20	18	16
361	376	39	36	33	31	30	28	26	24	22	20	18
376	391	43	39	35	33	31	29	27	26	24	22	20
391	406	46	42	39	35	33	31	29	27	25	23	21
406	421	49	46	42	38	35	33	31	29	27	25	23
421	436	52	49	45	42	38	35	33	31	29	27	25
436	451	56	52	49	45	42	38	35	33	31	29	27
451	466	59	55	52	48	45	41	38	35	33	31	29
466	481	62	59	55	52	48	45	41	37	34	32	30
481	496	66	62	59	55	51	48	44	41	37	34	32
496	511	69	65	62	58	55	51	48	44	40	37	34
511	526	72	69	65	62	58	54	51	47	44	40	37
526	541	76	72	68	65	61	58	54	51	47	44	40
541	556	79	75	72	68	65	61	58	54	50	47	43
556	571	82	79	75	71	68	64	61	57	54	50	47
571	586	85	82	78	75	71	68	64	61	57	53	50
586	601	89	85	82	78	75	71	67	64	60	57	53
601	616	92	88	85	81	78	74	71	67	64	60	56
616	631	95	92	88	85	81	78	74	70	67	63	60
631	646	99	95	92	88	84	81	77	74	70	67	63
646	661	102	98	95	91	88	84	81	77	73	70	66
661	676	105	102	98	95	91	87	84	80	77	73	70
676	691	109	105	101	98	94	91	87	84	80	77	73
691	706	112	108	105	101	98	94	91	87	83	80	76
706	721	116	112	108	104	101	97	94	90	87	83	80
721	736	119	115	111	108	104	101	97	94	90	86	83
736	751	123	119	115	111	108	104	100	97	93	90	86
751	766	126	122	119	115	111	107	104	100	97	93	89
766	781	130	126	122	118	114	111	107	103	100	96	93
781	796	134	130	126	122	118	114	110	107	103	100	96
796	811	137	133	129	126	122	118	114	110	106	103	99
811	826	141	137	133	129	125	121	117	114	110	106	103
826	841	144	140	137	133	129	125	121	117	113	110	106
841	856	148	144	140	136	132	129	125	121	117	113	109
856	871	152	148	144	140	136	132	128	124	121	117	113
871	886	155	151	147	144	140	136	132	128	124	120	116
886	901	159	155	151	147	143	139	135	132	128	124	120
901	916	162	158	155	151	147	143	139	135	131	127	124
916	931	166	162	158	154	150	147	143	139	135	131	127

Publication 15 (2019)

Wage Bracket Method Tables for Income Tax Withholding

MARRIED Persons—DAILY Payroll Period

(For Wages Paid through December 2019)

And the wages are–		And the number of withholding allowances claimed is—										
At least	But less than	0	1	2	3	4	5	6	7	8	9	10
		The amount of income tax to be withheld is—										
931	946	170	166	162	158	154	150	146	142	139	135	131
946	961	173	169	165	162	158	154	150	146	142	138	134
961	976	177	173	169	165	161	157	153	150	146	142	138
976	991	180	176	173	169	165	161	157	153	149	145	142
991	1,006	184	180	176	172	168	165	161	157	153	149	145
1,006	1,021	188	184	180	176	172	168	164	160	157	153	149
1,021	1,036	191	187	183	180	176	172	168	164	160	156	152
1,036	1,051	195	191	187	183	179	175	171	168	164	160	156
1,051	1,066	198	194	191	187	183	179	175	171	167	163	160
1,066	1,081	202	198	194	190	186	183	179	175	171	167	163
1,081	1,096	206	202	198	194	190	186	182	178	175	171	167
1,096	1,111	209	205	201	198	194	190	186	182	178	174	170
1,111	1,126	213	209	205	201	197	193	189	186	182	178	174
1,126	1,141	216	212	209	205	201	197	193	189	185	181	178
1,141	1,156	220	216	212	208	204	201	197	193	189	185	181
1,156	1,171	224	220	216	212	208	204	200	196	193	189	185
1,171	1,186	227	223	219	216	212	208	204	200	196	192	188
1,186	1,201	231	227	223	219	215	211	207	204	200	196	192
1,201	1,216	234	230	227	223	219	215	211	207	203	199	196
1,216	1,231	238	234	230	226	222	219	215	211	207	203	199
1,231	1,246	242	238	234	230	226	222	218	214	211	207	203
1,246	1,261	245	241	237	234	230	226	222	218	214	210	206
1,261	1,276	249	245	241	237	233	229	225	222	218	214	210
1,276	1,291	252	248	245	241	237	233	229	225	221	217	214
1,291	1,306	257	252	248	244	240	237	233	229	225	221	217
1,306	1,321	262	257	252	248	244	240	236	232	229	225	221
1,321	1,336	267	262	257	252	248	244	240	236	232	228	224
1,336	1,351	272	267	261	256	251	247	243	240	236	232	228
1,351	1,366	276	271	266	261	256	251	247	243	239	235	232
1,366	1,381	281	276	271	266	261	255	251	247	243	239	235
1,381	1,396	286	281	276	271	265	260	255	250	247	243	239
1,396	1,411	291	286	281	275	270	265	260	255	250	246	242
1,411	1,426	296	291	285	280	275	270	265	259	254	250	246
1,426	1,441	300	295	290	285	280	275	269	264	259	254	250
1,441	1,456	305	300	295	290	285	279	274	269	264	259	254
1,456	1,471	310	305	300	295	289	284	279	274	269	264	258
1,471	1,486	315	310	305	299	294	289	284	279	274	268	263
1,486	1,501	320	315	309	304	299	294	289	283	278	273	268
1,501	1,516	324	319	314	309	304	299	293	288	283	278	273
1,516	1,531	329	324	319	314	309	303	298	293	288	283	278
1,531	1,546	334	329	324	319	313	308	303	298	293	288	282
1,546	1,561	339	334	329	323	318	313	308	303	298	292	287
1,561	1,576	344	339	333	328	323	318	313	307	302	297	292
1,576	1,591	348	343	338	333	328	323	317	312	307	302	297
1,591	1,606	353	348	343	338	333	327	322	317	312	307	302
1,606	1,621	358	353	348	343	337	332	327	322	317	312	306
1,621	1,636	363	358	353	347	342	337	332	327	322	316	311
1,636	1,651	369	363	357	352	347	342	337	331	326	321	316
1,651	1,666	374	368	362	357	352	347	341	336	331	326	321
1,666	1,681	379	373	368	362	357	351	346	341	336	331	326
1,681	1,696	384	379	373	367	362	356	351	346	341	336	330
1,696	1,711	390	384	378	373	367	361	356	351	346	340	335
1,711	1,726	395	389	383	378	372	367	361	355	350	345	340
1,726	1,741	400	394	389	383	377	372	366	360	355	350	345
1,741	1,756	405	400	394	388	383	377	371	366	360	355	350
1,756	1,771	411	405	399	394	388	382	377	371	365	360	354
1,771	1,786	416	410	404	399	393	388	382	376	371	365	359
1,786	1,801	421	415	410	404	398	393	387	381	376	370	364
1,801	1,816	426	421	415	409	404	398	392	387	381	375	370
1,816	1,831	432	426	420	415	409	403	398	392	386	381	375
1,831	1,846	437	431	425	420	414	409	403	397	392	386	380
1,846	1,861	442	436	431	425	419	414	408	402	397	391	385
1,861	1,876	447	442	436	430	425	419	413	408	402	396	391
1,876	1,891	453	447	441	436	430	424	419	413	407	402	396
1,891	1,906	458	452	446	441	435	430	424	418	413	407	401
1,906	1,908	461	455	449	444	438	432	427	421	416	410	404

1,908 and over	Use Table 8(b) for a MARRIED person on page 47. Also see the instructions on page 44.

Annual Federal Payroll Tax Calendar

The following calendar displays payroll-related due dates that affect the majority of employers.

January

01/15	Monthly depositor payment of December federal income tax, Social Security tax, and Medicare tax
01/31	Form 941—4th quarter of prior year (additional 10 days to file if timely deposits in full payment of quarterly taxes were made)
01/31	Form 940 (additional 10 days to file if all FUTA tax was deposited when due)
01/31	Deposit FUTA tax—may be included with Form 940 (filed on 1/31) if undeposited FUTA tax does not exceed $500
01/31	W-2 Forms must be provided to all employees
01/31	1099-MISC Forms must be provided to all independent contractors

February

02/15	Monthly depositor payment of January federal income tax, Social Security tax, and Medicare tax

March

03/01	If paper copies are being remitted, W-2 and W-3 forms are due to be sent to the Social Security Administration
03/01	Forms 1096 and 1099-MISC are due to be sent to the IRS
03/15	Forms 1120 and 1120S corporate tax returns
03/15	Monthly depositor payment of February federal income tax, Social Security tax, and Medicare tax
03/31	If e-filing, W-2 and W-3 Forms are due to be sent to the Social Security Administration

April

04/15	Form 1040 individual tax return
04/15	Monthly depositor payment of March federal income tax, Social Security tax, and Medicare tax
04/30	Form 941—1st quarter (additional 10 days to file if timely deposits in full payment of quarterly taxes were made)
04/30	Deposit FUTA tax—only if undeposited FUTA tax exceeds $500

May

05/15	Monthly depositor payment of April federal income tax, Social Security tax, and Medicare tax

June

06/15	Monthly depositor payment of May federal income tax, Social Security tax, and Medicare tax

July

07/15	Monthly depositor payment of June federal income tax, Social Security tax, and Medicare tax
07/31	Form 941—2nd quarter (additional 10 days to file if timely deposits in full payment of quarterly taxes were made)
07/31	Deposit FUTA tax—only if undeposited FUTA tax exceeds $500

August

08/15	Monthly depositor payment of July federal income tax, Social Security tax, and Medicare tax

September

09/15	Monthly depositor payment of August federal income tax, Social Security tax, and Medicare tax

October

10/15	Monthly depositor payment of September federal income tax, Social Security tax, and Medicare tax
10/31	Form 941—3rd quarter (additional 10 days to file if timely deposits in full payment of quarterly taxes were made)
10/31	Deposit FUTA tax—only if undeposited FUTA tax exceeds $500

November

11/15	Monthly depositor payment of October federal income tax, Social Security tax, and Medicare tax

December

12/15	Monthly depositor payment of November federal income tax, Social Security tax, and Medicare tax

When considering the above due dates, keep in mind the following:

- Any due dates falling on a weekend or legal holiday are extended to the next business day.
- Semiweekly depositors must make payments either by the subsequent Wednesday (for Wednesday through Friday paydays) or the subsequent Friday (for Saturday through Tuesday paydays).
- Federal tax payment must be made on the following business day if the liability exceeds $100,000 (next-day deposit rule).

State Tax Department Websites

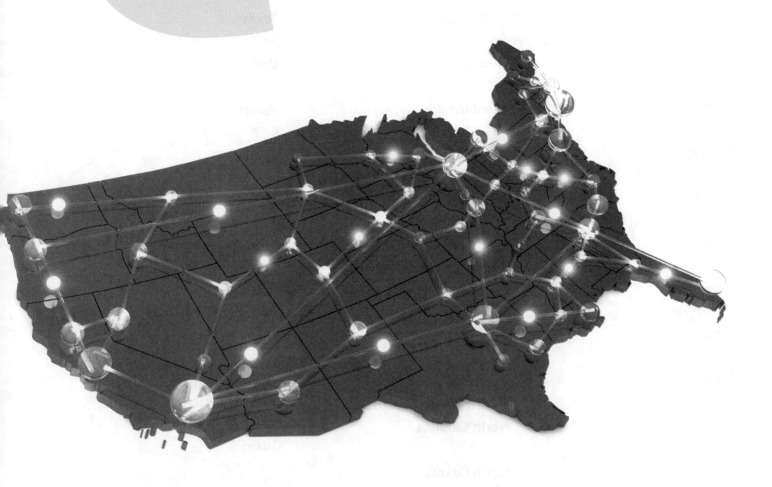

It's important to understand not only the federal payroll tax considerations discussed throughout this book but also the state payroll tax requirements that apply to you. The following websites will enable you to further research these requirements.

Alabama
revenue.alabama.gov

Alaska
tax.alaska.gov

Arizona
azdor.gov

Arkansas
dfa.arkansas.gov

California
taxes.ca.gov

Colorado
colorado.gov/revenue

Connecticut
ct.gov/drs

Delaware
revenue.delaware.gov

Florida
dor.myflorida.com/dor

Georgia
dor.georgia.gov/taxes

Hawaii
tax.hawaii.gov

Idaho
tax.idaho.gov

Illinois
www.revenue.state.il.us

Indiana
in.gov/dor

Iowa
iowa.gov/tax

Kansas
ksrevenue.org

Kentucky
revenue.ky.gov

Louisiana
revenue.louisiana.gov

Maine
maine.gov/revenue

Maryland
dat.state.md.us

Massachusetts
mass.gov/dor

Michigan
michigan.gov/treasury

Minnesota
revenue.state.mn.us

Mississippi
dor.ms.gov

Missouri
dor.mo.gov

Montana
revenue.mt.gov

Nebraska
revenue.nebraska.gov

Nevada
tax.nv.gov

New Hampshire
revenue.nh.gov

New Jersey
state.nj.us/treasury/taxation

New Mexico
tax.newmexico.gov

New York
tax.ny.gov

North Carolina
ncdor.gov

North Dakota
nd.gov/tax

Ohio
tax.ohio.gov

Oklahoma
ok.gov/tax

Oregon
oregon.gov/DOR

Pennsylvania
revenue.pa.gov

Rhode Island
dor.ri.gov

South Carolina
dor.sc.gov

South Dakota
dor.sd.gov

Tennessee
tn.gov/revenue

Texas
comptroller.texas.gov

Utah
tax.utah.gov

Vermont
tax.vermont.gov

Virginia
tax.virginia.gov

Washington
dor.wa.gov

West Virginia
tax.wv.gov

Wisconsin
revenue.wi.gov

Wyoming
revenue.wyo.gov

American Samoa
americansamoa.gov
/department-of-treasury-1

Guam
guamtax.com

Northern Mariana Islands
cnmidof.net

Puerto Rico
hacienda.gobierno.pr

U.S. Virgin Islands
ltg.gov.vi

Washington D.C.
dgs.dc.gov

State Tax/Revenue Department Addresses

When examining state payroll tax issues, you may find it necessary to contact your state tax department. Each state's respective tax and/or revenue department address is listed here for your convenience.

Alabama
Alabama Department of Revenue
50 North Ripley Street
Montgomery, AL 36104

Alaska
Department of Revenue
PO Box 110420
Juneau, AK 99811-0420

Arizona
Arizona Revenue Department
1600 West Monroe Street
Phoenix, AZ 85007-2650

Arkansas
Arkansas Department of Revenue
1509 West 7th Street
Little Rock, AR 72201

California
Employment Development
Department
PO Box 826880
Sacramento, CA 94280-0001

Colorado
Revenue Department
1375 Sherman Street
Denver, CO 80261

Connecticut
Department of Revenue Services
450 Columbus Blvd., Suite 1
Hartford, CT 06103

Delaware
Division of Revenue
820 North French Street
Wilmington, DE 19801

Florida
Florida Department of Revenue
5050 West Tennessee Street
Tallahassee, FL 32399-0100

Georgia
Department of Revenue
1800 Century Boulevard
Atlanta, GA 30345

Hawaii
Taxation Department
75 Aupuni Street, #101
Hilo, HI 96720-4245

Idaho
Idaho State Tax Commission
PO Box 36
Boise, ID 83722-0410

Illinois
Revenue Department
101 West Jefferson Street
Springfield, IL 62702

Indiana
Revenue Department
100 North Senate Avenue
Indianapolis, IN 46204

Iowa
Department of Revenue
Hoover State Office Building – 4th Floor
1305 East Walnut
Des Moines, IA 50319

Kansas
Kansas Department of Revenue
120 SE 10th Avenue
Topeka, KS 66612-1103

Kentucky
Kentucky Department of Revenue
501 High Street
Frankfort, KY 40601-2103

Louisiana
Louisiana Department of Revenue
Baton Rouge Headquarters
617 North Third Street
Baton Rouge, LA 70802

Maine
Maine Revenue Services
51 Commerce Drive
Augusta, ME 04330

Maryland
Department of Assessments
and Taxation
301 West Preston Street
Baltimore, MD 21201-2395

Massachusetts
Revenue Department
100 Cambridge Street
Boston, MA 02114

Michigan
Michigan Department of Treasury
3060 West Grand Boulevard
Detroit, MI 48202-6060

Minnesota
Minnesota Department of Revenue
600 North Robert Street
St. Paul, MN 55146

Mississippi
Mississippi Department of Revenue
500 Clinton Center Drive
Clinton, MS 39056

Missouri
Missouri Department of Revenue
301 West High Street
Jefferson City, MO 65101

Montana
Department of Revenue
Sam W. Mitchell Building
125 North Roberts, 3rd Floor
Helena, MT 59601

Nebraska
Nebraska Department of Revenue
301 Centennial Mall South
Lincoln, NE 68508

Nevada
Nevada Department of Taxation
1550 College Parkway, Suite 115
Carson City, NV 89706

New Hampshire
New Hampshire Department of
Revenue Administration
109 Pleasant Street
Concord, NH 03301

New Jersey
New Jersey Division of Taxation
50 Barrack Street
Trenton, NJ 08695

New Mexico
New Mexico Taxation and Revenue
Department
1100 South St. Francis Drive
Santa Fe, NM 87504

New York

New York State Department of
Taxation and Finance
WA Harriman State Campus
Albany, NY 12227

North Carolina

North Carolina Department of
Revenue
501 North Wilmington Street
Raleigh, NC 27604

North Dakota

Office of State Tax Commissioner
600 East Boulevard Avenue
Bismarck, ND 58505-0599

Ohio

Ohio Department of Taxation
4485 Northland Ridge Boulevard
Columbus, OH 43229

Oklahoma

Oklahoma Tax Commission
2501 North Lincoln Boulevard
Oklahoma City, OK 73194

Oregon

Oregon Department of Revenue
955 Center Street Northeast
Salem, OR 97301-2555

Pennsylvania

Pennsylvania Department of Revenue
110 N. 8th Street
Philadelphia, PA 19107-2412

Rhode Island

One Capitol Hill
Providence, RI 02908

South Carolina

South Carolina Department of
Revenue
300A Outlet Pointe Boulevard
Columbia, SC 29210

South Dakota

South Dakota Department of Revenue
445 East Capitol Avenue
Pierre, SD 57501

Tennessee

Department of Revenue
500 Deaderick Street
Nashville, TN 37242

Texas

Texas Comptroller of Public Accounts
111 East 17th Street
Austin, TX 78774

Utah

Utah State Tax Commission
210 North 1950 West
Salt Lake City, UT 84134

Vermont

Vermont Department of Taxes
133 State Street
Montpelier, VT 05633

Virginia

Virginia Department of Taxation
1957 Westmoreland Street
Richmond, VA 23230

Washington

Washington State Department of
Revenue
PO Box 47450
Olympia, WA 98504-7450

West Virginia

West Virginia Department of Revenue
Taxpayer Services
1124 Smith Street
Charleston, WV 25301

Wisconsin

Wisconsin Department of Revenue
2135 Rimrock Road
Madison, WI 53713

Wyoming

Wyoming Department of Revenue
122 West 25th Street, 3rd Floor East
Cheyenne, WY 82002-0110

American Samoa

Executive Office Building
Pago Pago
American Samoa, 96799

Guam

Guam Department of Revenue and
Taxation
1240 Army Drive
Barrigada, Guam 96913

Northern Mariana Islands

Division of Revenue and Taxation
PO Box 5234 CHRB
Saipan, MP 96950

Puerto Rico

Department of Treasury
Intendente Ramirez Building
10 Paseo Covadonga
San Juan, PR 00901

U.S. Virgin Islands

5049 Kongens Gade
St. Thomas, VI 00802

Washington D.C.

Office of Tax and Revenue
1101 4th Street, Southwest
Suite 270 West
Washington, DC 20024

Self-Assessment Answer Keys

Chapter 1: Processing a New Employee

	Answer	Page Number
1	False	Page 4
2	True	Page 5
3	False	Page 5
4	False	Page 8
5	True	Page 9
6	True	Page 14
7	True	Page 14
8	False	Page 20
9	True	Page 24
10	False	Page 27
11	B	Page 3
12	C	Page 6
13	C	Pages 5–6
14	D	Page 7
15	A	Page 14
16	C	Pages 15–16
17	C	Page 19
18	B	Page 20
19	A	Page 27
20	B	Page 28

Chapter 2: Calculating Employee Pay

	Answer	Page Number
1	False	Page 42
2	True	Page 42
3	False	Page 44
4	False	Page 45
5	True	Page 48
6	True	Page 48
7	True	Page 55
8	False	Page 56
9	False	Page 59
10	True	Page 63
11	D	Page 41
12	A	Page 44
13	B	Page 45
14	B	Page 48
15	C	Page 49
16	A	Page 52
17	C	Page 56
18	D	Page 59
19	D	Page 60
20	B	Page 61

Chapter 3: Federal and State Income Tax Withholding

	Answer	Page Number
1	False	Page 85
2	True	Page 85
3	True	Page 87
4	True	Page 89
5	False	Page 89
6	False	Page 92
7	True	Page 93
8	False	Page 97
9	True	Page 97
10	False	Page 99
11	B	Page 85
12	D	Page 89
13	D	Page 91
14	C	Page 91
15	D	Page 91
16	B	Page 91
17	C	Page 92
18	A	Page 95
19	C	Page 97
20	A	Page 97

Chapter 4: FICA Taxes

	Answer	Page Number
1	False	Page 117
2	True	Page 117
3	False	Page 118
4	True	Page 118
5	False	Page 121
6	False	Page 123
7	True	Page 124
8	False	Page 125
9	True	Page 125
10	False	Page 128
11	A	Page 117
12	A	Page 118
13	B	Page 118
14	C	Page 121
15	D	Page 121
16	D	Page 125
17	B	Page 125
18	B	Page 123
19	A	Page 125
20	D	Page 128

Chapter 5: Federal and State Unemployment Taxes

	Answer	Page Number
1	True	Page 147
2	False	Page 147
3	True	Page 147
4	True	Page 151
5	False	Page 151
6	True	Page 151
7	True	Page 151
8	True	Page 153
9	False	Page 157
10	True	Page 164
11	A	Page 147
12	C	Page 147
13	A	Pages 147–148
14	D	Page 151
15	C	Page 151
16	A	Page 151
17	C	Page 153
18	B	Page 153
19	A	Page 164
20	C	Page 164

Chapter 6: Periodic and Year-End Payroll Reporting

	Answer	Page Number
1	True	Page 179
2	False	Page 180
3	True	Page 182
4	False	Page 183
5	False	Page 183
6	False	Page 194
7	True	Page 194
8	True	Page 202
9	False	Page 208
10	True	Page 208
11	C	Page 179
12	C	Page 180
13	D	Page 182
14	B	Page 182
15	D	Page 194
16	B	Page 194
17	A	Page 202
18	C	Page 202
19	D	Page 202
20	B	Page 210

Glossary

401(k) plan   A defined-contribution retirement plan in which a set amount of tax-deferred funds may be withheld from gross earnings each pay period.

403(b) plan   A retirement savings plan, similar to a 401(k), that is available only to certain employees of specific types of institutions; also referred to as a *tax-sheltered annuity (TSA) plan*.

bonuses   Additional employee earnings that may be either planned or unplanned.

cafeteria plans   Plans in which tax-free funds may be contributed (through voluntary withholdings from earnings) in order to provide a range of benefits to the employee.

Circular E   An employer's tax guide (also referred to as *Publication 15*), distributed by the IRS, which provides guidance on a variety of payroll-related topics.

commissions   Employee earnings calculated as a percentage of sales.

Current Tax Payment Act of 1943   An act that modified the federal income tax system, directing that payments could no longer be made in the subsequent year but instead must be paid during the year in which the associated income is earned. This act resulted in employers withholding taxes from employees' pay.

deductions   Amounts withheld from employee pay that are therefore not included in employees' paychecks.

dependent care benefits   Benefits used to care for a qualifying individual that may be exempt from FWT, Social Security tax, and Medicare tax.

discretionary bonus   An unplanned bonus that is not contingent on an employee reaching specific goals.

Electronic Federal Tax Payment System (EFTPS)   A telephone- and Internet-based system that provides employers with the most convenient method for remitting federal tax payments.

employee earnings record   A record maintained by the employer for each employee displaying key employee information and payroll figures for a given year.

Employee Retirement Income Security Act of 1974   An act, passed in 1974, setting forth regulations that must be followed by employers who offer retirement plans to their employees. Often referred to as *ERISA*.

Employer Identification Number (EIN)   A unique number that an employer must obtain from the IRS prior to submitting payroll-related forms.

Equal Pay Act of 1963 (EPA)   An amendment, passed in 1963, to the Fair Labor Standards Act dictating that no employer may discriminate against any employee by paying a lower wage than that paid to someone of the opposite gender for a similar job.

experience rating   A calculation that differs from state to state and that is used to determine an employer's SUTA tax rate.

Fair Labor Standards Act (FLSA)   An act, passed into law in 1938, dictating labor conditions and regulations that must be followed by the majority of employers.

federal income tax withholding   Tax withheld from employee earnings used to fund a range of government agencies and services. Also called *federal income tax*.

federal minimum wage   The lowest wage that may be paid to employees for whom an exception (or a higher state minimum wage) does not apply.

federal unemployment tax (FUTA)   A tax levied on employers based on the taxable earnings of their employees. These taxes are used by the federal government to provide unemployment compensation to individuals who are out of work.

flexible spending account   A type of cafeteria plan in which employees may be reimbursed for qualified benefits, such as dependent care expenses and medical expenses.

gross pay   Total employee earnings prior to subtracting taxes and other withholding amounts.

gross wages   See *gross pay*.

Immigration Reform and Control Act of 1986 (IRCA)   An act, passed in 1986, that strengthened U.S. immigration law and that led to the requirement that employers maintain I-9 Forms for all employees.

incentive plans   Plans that tie increased employee earnings to increases in productivity.

independent contractors   Individuals who perform services for an employer without qualifying as employees.

local income tax withholding   Tax withheld from employee earnings (by certain local municipalities), used to fund local operations. Also called *local income tax*.

lookback period   A time period used by employers to determine the applicable payment increment for federal income tax, Social Security tax, and Medicare tax; it encompasses the previous July 1 through June 30 for a given year.

mandatory deductions   Amounts that are required, by either federal or state government, to be withheld from employee earnings.

medical plans   Plans in which funds are set aside (through voluntary withholdings from employee earnings) to cover medical costs.

Medicare tax (HI)   Tax withheld from employee earnings, used to operate the Medicare federal health insurance program covering individuals 65 years of age or older, as well as certain disabled individuals. Also known as *hospital insurance tax*.

monthly depositor   An employer who must remit payment of federal income tax, Social Security tax, and Medicare tax on a monthly basis.

net pay   The amount paid to an employee within the paycheck.

net self-employment income   The income of a self-employed individual after certain business expenses have been subtracted.

next-day deposit rule   A rule dictating that an employer must remit all owed taxes on the next business day if the total accumulated amount owed exceeds $100,000 at the end of any day.

nondiscretionary bonus   A planned bonus paid by an employer as a result of a specific metric being met.

pay period   A specific period during which employees earn their pay; common types include weekly, biweekly, semimonthly, and monthly.

pay-as-you-go   A type of system in which income tax must be paid as the associated income is earned.

paycheck   A typical form of payment provided to employees.

payroll deduction IRA   A simple retirement plan option often used by self-employed individuals.

payroll register   A record maintained by an employer in which all employee earnings for a single period are displayed.

payroll service   An outside company that handles a variety of payroll-related tasks for an employer.

paystub   A paycheck attachment displaying the breakdown of an employee's earnings.

percentage method   A method for determining an employee's federal income tax withholding in which a three-step process that includes referencing the percentage method tables is used.

Personal Responsibility and Work Opportunity Reconciliation Act of 1996 (PRWORA)   An act that significantly strengthened the child support program throughout the United States and that led to the mandatory reporting of new employees.

piecework system   An employee compensation system in which earnings are determined based on the number of units produced.

premium rate   The additional pay over the regular hourly rate to which a piecework employee is entitled for overtime hours worked.

retirement plans Plans providing funds to employees after retirement, which may be funded through voluntary withholdings from employee earnings.

salary An annual pay amount, typically agreed upon by the employer and employee.

Self-Employment Contributions Act of 1954 An act establishing that self-employed individuals must pay self-employment taxes.

self-employment income The earnings of individuals who work for themselves, on which taxes must be paid.

semiweekly depositor An employer who must remit payment of federal income tax, Social Security tax, and Medicare tax within a few days of the pay date and up to twice per week.

SIMPLE IRA A retirement savings plan designed for employees of small businesses.

Social Security tax (OASDI) Tax withheld from employee earnings, used to fund the Social Security system, which pays benefits to retired or disabled workers and their dependents or survivors. Also known as *old age, survivors, and disability insurance tax*.

state disability insurance tax Tax withheld from employee earnings (by a small number of states/territories), used to provide benefits to temporarily disabled employees who are unable to work for a period of time.

state income tax withholding Tax withheld from employee earnings (by the majority of states), used to fund state operations. Also called *state income tax*.

state unemployment tax (SUTA) A tax levied on employers, based on the taxable earnings of their employees. Along with federal unemployment taxes, these taxes are used to operate unemployment programs.

statutory employees Those individuals who would otherwise be considered independent contractors but who meet certain requirements that dictate that they be categorized as employees.

statutory nonemployees Workers who are considered to be self-employed by virtue of their professions. These include direct sellers, real-estate agents, and companion sitters.

time card A document that tracks the hours worked by an employee.

tip pool An acceptable method under the Fair Labor Standards Act for dividing tips, in which all tips are added together and then divided among tipped employees.

Title XII advances Loans from the federal government to individual states that provide unemployment benefits to all eligible individuals in the state.

union dues Dues paid by unionized employees that may be voluntarily withheld from employee earnings.

voluntary deductions Amounts that an employee may elect to have withheld from his/her earnings.

wage A compensation amount paid to employees, typically on an hourly basis.

wage-bracket method A method for determining an employee's federal income tax withholding in which federal income tax withholding tables are used.

wage garnishment The withholding of a portion of an employee's earnings, in compliance with a court order or other legal proceeding.

workers' compensation A form of insurance that provides financial assistance to employees injured during the course of their employment.

workweek Any seven-day period, designated by the employer, that begins and ends consistently each week.

Index

NOTES

NOTES

NOTES

NOTES

NOTES